# THE EXPANDING SPACES OF LAW

# THE EXPANDING
# SPACES OF LAW

*A Timely Legal Geography*

---

EDITED BY IRUS BRAVERMAN,

NICHOLAS BLOMLEY, DAVID DELANEY,

AND ALEXANDRE (SANDY) KEDAR

STANFORD LAW BOOKS

*An Imprint of Stanford University Press*
*Stanford, California*

Stanford University Press
Stanford, California

Printed in the United States of America on acid-free, archival-quality paper

Library of Congress Cataloging-in-Publication Data

The expanding spaces of law : a timely legal geography / edited by Irus
Braverman, Nicholas Blomley, David Delaney, and Alexandre (Sandy) Kedar.
    pages cm
  Includes bibliographical references and index.
  ISBN 978-0-8047-8718-5 (cloth : alk. paper)
  ISBN 978-0-8047-9728-3 (pbk. : alk. paper)
    1. Law and geography.   2. Sociological jurisprudence.   I. Braverman,
Irus, editor of compilation.   II. Blomley, Nicholas, editor of compilation.
III. Delaney, David, editor of compilation.   IV. Kedar, Alexandre, editor of
compilation.
  K487.G45E97 2014
  340'.115—dc23

                                                                2014002233

ISBN 978-0-8047-9187-8 (electronic)

Typeset by Newgen in 10/13.5 Minion

*In memory of Franz von Benda-Beckmann*

# CONTENTS

# ACKNOWLEDGMENTS

This project has been two years in the making, and there are many people who we would like to thank for their contributions. First, we are grateful to the Baldy Center for Law and Social Policy, and its director Errol Meidinger in particular, for the financial and institutional support that enabled us to convene the workshop that initially brought the contributors of this collection together. After two days of intense discussions, it was clear to most of us that we wanted to translate our discussions, debates, and realizations into a book format. One of the liveliest voices in the workshop was that of Franz von Benda-Beckmann, whose rich and invaluable cultural experiences provided a rare foundation for the workshop and an inspiration for this book. We were all distraught to find out that Franz passed away unexpectedly in January 2013, and we unanimously decided to commemorate his thoughtful influence on this book by dedicating it to his memory.

Our gratitude also extends to Michelle Lipinski of Stanford University Press for her patience and support of this project from the start, as well as the much-appreciated administrative support by Mary Voglmayr at SUNY Buffalo Law School.

# CONTRIBUTORS

**Antonio Azuela** is professor of sociology at the Universidad Nacional Autónoma de México (UNAM). Since the late 1970s, he has been engaged in research and teaching on urban and environmental law from a sociolegal perspective. His most recent book, *Visionarios y pragmáticos: Una aproximación sociológica al derecho ambiental* (Fontamara, 2006) is a sociological reconstruction of his experience as attorney general for the environment in Mexico's federal government. He is a member of the Social Research Institute (Instituto de Investigaciones Sociales) at UNAM.

**Franz von Benda-Beckmann** was, until his untimely death in 2013, professor emeritus and head of the Legal Pluralism Project Group at the Max Planck Institute for Social Anthropology in Halle, Germany. He was also honorary professor at the Universities of Leipzig and Halle. He authored numerous articles and book chapters on issues of property rights, social (in)security and legal pluralism in developing countries, and legal anthropological theory. Together with Keebet von Benda-Beckmann, he authored *Political and Legal Transformations of an Indonesian Polity* (Cambridge University Press 2013).

**Keebet von Benda-Beckmann** is associate of the Max Planck Institute for Social Anthropology in Halle, Germany. She is also honorary professor at the Universities of Leipzig and Halle. She authored numerous articles and book chapters on disputing, social (in)security, decentralization, and legal pluralism. Together with Franz von Benda-Beckmann, she authored *Political and Legal Transformations of an Indonesian Polity* (Cambridge University Press 2013).

**Melinda Harm Benson** is an assistant professor in the Department of Geography and Environmental Studies at the University of New Mexico. She is the author of "Regional Initiatives: Scaling the Climate Response and Responding to Conceptions of Scale," published in 2010 by *Annals of the Association of American Geographers*, and "Mining Sacred Space: Law's Enactment of Competing Ontologies in the American West," published in 2012 by *Environment and Planning A*. Prior to her academic life, she worked as an attorney representing environmental organizations in the intermountain West.

**Nicholas Blomley** is professor of geography at Simon Fraser University. He has a long-standing interest in legal geography (particularly in relation to property). He is the author of *Law, Space and the Geographies of Power* (Guilford 1994), *Unsettling the City* (Routledge 2004), and *Rights of Passage: Sidewalks and the Regulation of Public Flow* (Routledge 2012). He also coedited *The Legal Geographies Reader* (Blackwell 2001).

**Irus Braverman** is professor of law and adjunct professor of geography at the State University of New York (SUNY) Buffalo. Her main interests lie in the interdisciplinary study of law, geography, and anthropology. She is author of *House Demolitions in East Jerusalem: "Illegality" and Resistance* (2004), *Planted Flags: Trees, Land, and Law in Israel/Palestine* (Cambridge University Press 2009), and *Zooland: The Institution of Captivity* (Stanford University Press 2012).

**David Delaney** teaches in the Department of Law, Jurisprudence and Social Thought at Amherst College. He is the author of *Race, Place and the Law* (University of Texas Press 1998), *Law and Nature* (Cambridge University Press 2003), *Territory: A Short Introduction* (Blackwell 2005), and *The Spatial, the Legal and the Pragmatics of World-Making: Nomospheric Investigations* (Routledge/GlassHouse 2010), as well as numerous articles on the theme of legal geography. He also coedited *The Legal Geographies Reader* (Blackwell 2001).

**Alexandre (Sandy) Kedar** is senior lecturer at University of Haifa's law school. His principal research focus is on legal geography, legal history, law and society, and land regimes in settler societies and in Israel. He is coeditor of *The History of Law in a Multi-Cultural Society: Israel 1917–1967* (2002), as well as numerous articles in English and Hebrew.

**Rodrigo Meneses-Reyes** is professor researcher in the Department of Legal Studies of the Center for Research and Teaching in Economics (CIDE) in Mexico City. He is the author of *Public Legalities: Law, Street Vendors and the Historical Downtown in Mexico City (1930–2010)* (CIDE and Universidad Nacional Autónoma de México 2012).

**Lisa R. Pruitt** is professor of law at the University of California, Davis, School of Law. She has written extensively about law and rural livelihoods, studying how rural spatiality inflects dimensions of gender, race, and ethnicity. Her publications include "Toward a Feminist Theory of the Rural," in *Utah Law Review* (2007);

"Rural Rhetoric," in *Connecticut Law Review* (2006); and "Justice Deserts: Spatial Inequality and Local Funding of Indigent Defense," in *Arizona Law Review* (2010).

**Michael D. Smith** is a PhD candidate at the University of British Columbia in Vancouver. He has published articles and reviews in *Urban Geography, Social and Legal Studies* (coauthored with Joel Bakan), *Political Geography,* and *Dialogues in Human Geography.* His research interests span legal, political, and economic geography, and his PhD research focuses on the legal geographies and political economy of the Canadian state. He has been a practicing lawyer since 1998, working primarily as criminal appellate counsel providing legal services to low-income people.

**Mariana Valverde** is professor of criminology at the Centre for Criminology and Sociolegal Studies at the University of Toronto. She has published six sole-authored books (two of them popular), six coedited anthologies, and more than forty-five refereed scholarly articles. Her most recent book, *Everyday Law on the Street,* received the Law and Society Association's Herbert Jacobs Prize for best book of 2012 in sociolegal studies, which was also awarded to her 1998 book *Diseases of the Will: Alcohol and the Dilemmas of Freedom.*

THE EXPANDING SPACES OF LAW

*[handwritten: Society is the where and how of law]*

# INTRODUCTION *[handwritten: legal geography as an Intellectual project]*

## Expanding the Spaces of Law

*Irus Braverman, Nicholas Blomley, David Delaney,*

*and Alexandre (Sandy) Kedar*

### LEGAL GEOGRAPHY: A DYNAMIC DEFINITION

Legal geography is a stream of scholarship that makes the interconnections between law and spatiality, and especially their reciprocal construction, into core objects of inquiry. Legal geographers contend that in the world of lived social relations and experience, aspects of the social that are analytically identified as either legal or spatial are conjoined and co-constituted. Legal geographers note that nearly every aspect of law is located, takes place, is in motion, or has some spatial frame of reference. In other words, law is always "worlded" in some way. Likewise, social spaces, lived places, and landscapes are inscribed with legal significance. Distinctively legal forms of meaning are projected onto every segment of the physical world. These meanings are open to interpretation and may become caught up in a range of legal practices. Such fragments of a socially segmented world—the *where* of law—are not simply the inert sites of law but are inextricably implicated in *how* law happens. *[handwritten: Def]*

Legal geography is not a subdiscipline of human geography, nor does it name an area of specialized legal scholarship. Rather, it refers to a truly interdisciplinary intellectual project. It is less a "field" than braided lines of inquiry that have emerged out of the confluence of various intellectual interests. The now scores of articles, books, collections, special issues, workshops, conference papers, and courses that constitute this project evince a fairly wide range of topics and theoretical approaches. Some practitioners, such as the editors of this volume, may identify themselves as legal geographers, but the majority are more casual or itinerant participants whose primary intellectual concerns are elsewhere. We therefore identify the lines of inquiry that constitute legal geography more with the content of the work produced than with the self-declared identity of the scholar.

Legal geography shares important conceptual similarities with other interdisciplinary and subdisciplinary endeavors, such as historical geography, law and society, legal anthropology, and legal history. Whereas in law and society scholarship, interactions between the "legal" and the "social" are foregrounded, and in legal history time serves as the major organizing concept, in legal geography space is foregrounded and serves as an organizing principle. Unlike either of these traditions, however, legal geography occupies little institutional presence: it has no specialized journals, graduate programs, or professional associations, and it is rarely taught in law schools or geography departments. This is the result, in part, of the relative novelty of this project as well as the inertia in processes of academic institutionalization.

Our introduction identifies and elaborates on three modes of legal geography research. The first mode of legal geography includes disciplinary work in law or in geography that is modeled on the conventional image of import and export. The second is an interdisciplinary pursuit in which scholars in law and geography draw on the work of one another and seek to contribute to the development of a common project. The third mode moves beyond the interdisciplinary to transdisciplinary, or perhaps even postdisciplinary, modes of scholarship. Although these three modes exist concurrently, the general trajectory over time has been from disciplinary to interdisciplinary and, finally, to postdisciplinary orientations. This triadic classification helps organize the rich yet eclectic legal geography scholarship that has evolved over the past thirty years or so. It is, however, also limited for two reasons. First, explorations of the relationship between law and space occurred even before the starting point of our review in the 1980s. Second, the linear depiction of these modes as progressing in time—namely, of subsequent modes that supersede what preceded them—is not fully accurate. As discussed here, antecedents of postdisciplinary work were discernible already in the 1980s, and much excellent and necessary discipline-specific work continues to be done today.

While this volume contains elements of each mode, it also urges interested scholars to move legal geography beyond the disciplinary boundaries into the horizons of a post–legal geography. Ironically, then, the ultimate success of legal geography will be in its ability to transcend the bidisciplinary focus that has characterized so much of its scholarship up to this point. The following account, while intended to provide a rich flavor of the legal geography enterprise, is by no means exhaustive.

## The First Mode of Legal Geography: Cross-Disciplinary Encounters

In the 1980s and early 1990s, scholars such as Gerald Neuman, John Calmore, and Gerald Frug found space without having found geography, in a disciplinary sense. For example, Neuman (1987) attended to social space in the form of territoriality. This attention explicated dimensions of discrimination—and so, instances of violations of equal protection rights—that had previously escaped notice. Likewise, Calmore (1995) undertook a sophisticated and sustained legal analysis of the spatial underpinnings of anti-black racism. Finally, the work of Gerald Frug (1996) and Richard Briffault (1990a, 1990b) on the spatial dimensions of community, the ideologies of localism and regionalism, and the effects of the city-suburb distinction enriched the appreciation of the placedness of law. However, these legal scholars were rarely interested in a full engagement with the problematic, complex, and fluid nature of social space; nor were they usually interested in the range of unconventional intellectual resources for thinking through the spatialities that critical human geographers were developing at the same time.

One prominent exception to this generalization in sociolegal studies was Boaventura Santos's 1987 article "Law: A Map of Misreading—Toward a Postmodern Conception of Law." In the midst of the disciplinary mode of pre–legal geography, this article portended a postdisciplinary ethos. Specifically, Santos opened up unconventional ways of understanding spatialities in the service of initiating "a new [postmodern] legal common sense" (279). The article brought the work of theoretical cartographers such as Marc Monmonier to bear on questions of representation and truth in law. "There are," Santos wrote, "many unresolved problems in the sociological study of the law that may be solved by comparing law with other ways of imagining the real. Maps are one such way" (286). Santos deployed cartographic notions of scale, projection, and symbolization to look at legal phenomena in new and startling ways. Especially prescient was his conception of interlegality, which sought to capture the ways in which "different legal spaces [are] superimposed, interpenetrated and mixed in our minds as much as in our actions, in occasions of qualitative leaps or sweeping crises in our life trajectories as well as in the dull routine of eventless everyday life" (297). "Interlegality," wrote Santos, "is a highly dynamic process because the different legal spaces are non-synchronic and thus result in uneven and unstable mixings of legal codes" (298). This exploration exploded conventional conceptions about the "where" of law and, in so doing, questioned the definition of law itself.

Alongside the inquiries into space by legal scholars, the first mode of legal geography may also be characterized by human geographers' independent concern with legal themes. Many of these human geographers have been informed by neo-Marxist and, increasingly, poststructuralist epistemological commitments, and are therefore concerned with unraveling how space is produced rather than merely assuming its existence. This line of scholarship has come to have a pronounced effect on how legal geographers formulate questions about law. Studies of redistricting in political geography and, more generally, studies of metropolitan governance are examples of geography scholarship that concerns itself with law. Generally, however, these scholars understood law as a given and were not concerned with debates about law within legal scholarship.

More notable, in hindsight, is the neglect of spatial concerns by the established interdisciplinary field of sociolegal studies associated with the law and society movement, which was established in 1964 and gained momentum in the 1970s and 1980s. This vibrant international and interdisciplinary research community was founded on the premise that social science can contribute much to the understanding of law and that legal scholarship is crucial to the investigation of social processes and outcomes. The roots of this interaction can be tied back to the legal realist movement of the 1920s and 1930s and to the antecedent sociological jurisprudence of Roscoe Pound in the early twentieth century. Initially, the law and society community included sociologists, anthropologists, historians, political scientists, and even psychologists—but it did not include geographers. A local aspect of this story is conveyed by Hari Osofsky (2007), who argues that the US perception of academic geography as an intellectual backwater that emerged in the 1950s and 1960s has resulted in the dismantling of geography departments in many of the most elite universities in the country. This perception, Osofsky continues, has also precluded law scholars at Yale University, and presumably elsewhere, from availing themselves of geography's potentially useful resources, despite their concern with space.

## The Second Mode of Legal Geography: Interdisciplinary Engagements

If the initial expressions of legal geography have been characterized by relatively narrow disciplinary concerns and a relative lack of cross-disciplinary engagement, the second mode of legal geography has been characterized by a strong and explicit commitment to interdisciplinary research and programmatic bridge building. This shift was triggered by the rise of the critical legal studies (CLS) movement in the 1980s and 1990s. The CLS movement challenged the functionalist social scientism of legal scholarship, dramatically expanded the range of resources available for asking questions about law, and took radical positions on questions of power. The CLS movement had a strong impact on legal geography: working within neo-Marxist and poststructuralist literatures, legal scholars and human geographers were suddenly reading the same theorists, asking similar questions, and taking account of one another's scholarship (Blomley and Bakan 1992).

The work of economic geographer Gordon Clark is central to the second mode of legal geography. In addition to his position as a geographer, Clark was also affiliated with Harvard University when Harvard Law School was at the center of the CLS movement. Clark focused on models of local autonomy, bringing to the geography literature a novel perspective on why attending to law and new modes of legal theory would deliver important benefits to geographers, especially to those geographers who had critical political and ethical commitments. In various articles (1982, 1984, 1986a, 1986b) and in his book *Judges and the Cities* (1985), Clark demonstrated a familiarity and fluency with sophisticated legal philosophical resources. Among the more lasting contributions of this work is its sustained and nuanced attention to problems of interpretation and to jurisprudential strategies that wish those problems away.

During this period, critical geographer Nicholas Blomley also published a number of agenda-setting pieces. Blomley's 1994 book *Law, Space, and Geographies of Power* is arguably the founding treatise of the second mode of legal geography. This book was published both when the "interpretive turn" (namely, the heightened attention to the problematics of discourse or representation) was having an enormous impact in human geography and as CLS reached its high-water mark in law schools. This book and Blomley's subsequent scholarship over the following two decades are notable for their reflective allegiance to distinctively critical modes of scholarly practice, their sustained suspicion of power, and their normative commitment to a radical vision of social justice. Much of Blomley's work has sought to think through the geographies of property in land through empirically grounded studies of particular conflicts, such as inner-city gentrification, and has attempted to reveal (and critique) the presence of distinctively liberal spatialities.

In the 1990s, American geographer Don Mitchell began a long career that has brought a strong commitment to neo-Marxist political analysis to topics as diverse as labor law, public space, and public housing. Much of Mitchell's work takes seriously the legal dimensions of struggles over public space in American cities, particularly in relation to the plight of marginalized people, such as the homeless. In an influential article from 1997, Mitchell traced the growing reach of local legislation that targeted homeless people, arguing that its effect was to brutally "annihilate space by law" (303). In that article, Mitchell argued that the spatial logics of globalization and the desire to construct particular landscapes of accumulation are crucial causal mechanisms in the creation of a purified public space. In subsequent work, Mitchell (2003) argued for a spatialized right to the city.

Another contribution from the 1990s, David Delaney's (1998) *Race, Place, and the Law: 1836–1948* sought to bring a balance of critical legal, sociospatial, and historical interpretation to the understanding of anti-black racism and racializations in the United States. Finally, Steve Herbert's (1997) ethnographic studies of the territorial strategies of policing and Benjamin Forest's (2001, 2004) work on race and redistricting were also significant in broadening the reach of geographic analysis into legal questions.

Alongside the deep engagement by geography scholars with social and legal literature, legal scholars also began engaging with space. British legal scholar Davina Cooper's (1998) *Governing out of Order: Space, Law, and the Politics of Belonging* was notable for its spatiolegal sensitivity. Cooper focused on institutional excess and political transgression, as manifested in, and disciplined through, legal and spatial arrangements. Trained in law and anthropology, Eve Darian-Smith's (1999) *Bridging Divides: The Channel Tunnel and English Legal Identity in the New Europe* offered a related reading of the anxieties occasioned by the building of the Tunnel, which was caught up in particular representations of legal geography and identity. An emphasis on representations of place and law is evident in much of Darian-Smith's continued scholarship.

Still during legal geography's bridge-building era, Richard Ford (1994, 1999) published two significant law review articles that pointed to the crucial organizing work of jurisdiction in producing racialized spatial differences, work that enabled racial segregation to persist absent overtly racist law. This racist legal geography has escaped scrutiny, Ford argued, because of a widespread assumption that political boundaries are either neutral or prepolitical.

In 1996, a special issue of *Stanford Law Review*, "Surveying Law and Borders," provided a sustained critical engagement with space and spatiality. It featured articles by prominent legal scholars such as Gerald Frug, Keith Aoki, Gerald Neuman, and Rosemary Coombe. While their work was deeply situated within legal scholarship, these authors also drew heavily on the work of critical geographers. This issue included an afterword by the prominent critical geographer Edward Soja.

One notable feature of the trajectory of the legal geography work produced by scholars trained as geographers and by CLS-oriented legal scholars is that its orientation was, from the start, explicitly and normatively critical. This designation refers not only to avowed leftist or radical political commitments but also to a broad skepticism toward the state and the pieties of many rule-of-law claims, as well as a broad disinterest in reformist policy discussions. The radical normative commitment of many legal geographers has become a distinctive characteristic of this tradition in the bridge-building era. Hari Osofsky (2012) has pushed back against the tendency to yoke the terms *critical* and *theory* together, arguing for the value of "applied" scholarship. Similarly, British geographer Rachel Pain (2006) argues for the merits of applied research, contesting the stereotype of the policy researcher as an acquiescent tool of power. There are, however, undeniable challenges in such applied work, particularly in the legal context. Some worry, for example, that arguments for "policy-relevant" research fail to acknowledge the ways in which ethical perspectives may become blunted or discredited (see, e.g., Beaumont, Loopmans, and Uitermark 2005).

Following the initial bridge-building period, the twenty-first century saw an escalation and stabilization of the legal geography tradition, manifested in numerous collaborations. In 2001, Nicholas Blomley, David Delaney, and Richard Ford edited *The Legal Geographies Reader*, and in 2002, the collection *Law and Geography*, edited by Jane Holder and Carolyn Harrison, was released. This was followed by Austin Sarat, Lawrence Douglas, and Martha Umphrey's (2003) *The Place of Law*. These collections brought together contributions by geographers, legal scholars, and others from Europe, North America, and Israel. The volumes signified a turn in legal geography scholarship: it had by then become a recognized project. The increased interest in legal geography also saw the publication of a number of special issues of journals, notably *Historical Geography: Geography, Law, and Legal Geographies* (2000); *Political and Legal Anthropology Review: Putting Law in Its Place in Native North America* (2002); *Society and Space: Displacements* (2004); *Law/Text/Culture: Legal Spaces* (2005); *Haifa Law Review: Law and Geography* (2005); *American Quarterly: Legal Borderlands* (2006); *International Journal of Legal Semiotics: The Spaces and Places of Law* (2006); *Santa Clara Journal of International Law* (2007); *Griffith Law Review* (2008); *Law, Culture, and the Humanities* (2010); and *Hagar, Studies in Culture, Polity and Identities: A Spatial Age: The Turn to Space in Law, the Social Sciences and the Humanities* (2010).

The impact of this now-sustained and still-expanding "spatial turn" in legal thought has been notable also in applied legal research. In international law, for example, scholars such as Jean Connolly Carmalt (2007), Bruce D'Arcus (2014), Carl Landauer (2010–11), Tayyab Mahmud (2010), Zoe Pearson (2008), and Kal Raustiala (2004–5) have shown the value of looking more closely at the spatial presuppositions that underpin the dominant narratives of international law and its doctrines. They have also revealed the ways in which these continue to inform both the scholarship of international law and humanitarian policies. In the words of Zoe Pearson (2008, 495–96), "These critiques provide us with an opportunity to see that spaces within the terrain of international law are not static, linear and ordered, but rather, complex, fluid and uncertain, evolving continuously along with the interactions of the different actors present, and emphasizing varying sites of legal and non-legal regulation." These international law scholars have emphasized that a contingent way of imagining space is foundational for international law as a discourse and that reimagining and investigating the difference that space makes may severely problematize the practices carried out under the auspices of the conventionally imagined "international community."

Another elaboration of legal spatiality in international law is Kal Raustiala's (2004–5) "The Geography of Justice," which attends to the territorial conditions of rights and the presence or absence of their protections. This work emphasizes the role that spatial assumptions play in rendering some forms of violence legitimate while withholding that honorific from other forms. Raustiala argues that inherited legal spatialities are superseded by the proliferation of extraterritorial legal operations, signaling a significant, but unheralded, respatialization of legal power. In his words, "The evolution of American law has been a process in which formalistic categories based on spatial location and geographic borders were rejected in favor of more supple, contextual concepts such as 'effects' and 'minimum contacts'" (2548).

The legal geography perspective has also contributed to other doctrinal investigations in law. In American constitutional law, Allan Erbsen (2011), Reginald Oh (2003–4), and Timothy Zick (2009b) have offered spatially informed rereadings of the US Constitution, its doctrines, and its case law to disclose otherwise obscure but highly significant contingencies and imaginative structures that, again, have important consequences. For example, in a series of articles, Zick (2006, 2009a, 2010) documents and critiques the ways in which political speech is increasingly circumscribed and suppressed through spatialized legal restrictions that go beyond traditional forms of state regulation. The danger, Zick (2006, 585) fears, is the creation of a "perfect geometry of control over just the sort of speech the First Amendment ought to protect." Such spatial tactics have withstood judicial scrutiny, he argues, because of an implicit view of space as inert and passive, as merely a background for speech rather than, as Zick insists, itself constitutive of expression. The work of legal scholar Lisa Pruitt also presents a sustained and subtle use of geographic scholarship. In a series of articles such as "Gender, Geography, and Rural Justice" (2008), "Geography of the Class Culture Wars" (2011), and "Justice Deserts: Spatial Inequality and Local Funding of Indigent Defense" (Pruitt and Colgan 2010), Pruitt has systematically exposed the unacknowledged "metronormative" urban bias not only in legal and geographical scholarship but also in the actual workings of the law in a wide range of contexts. She continues this project with her contribution to the present volume. Legal scholars have also drawn on and contributed to the legal geography project to uncover the workings of the legal with respect to race (Boddie 2010–11; Ford 1994), settler and colonial societies (Kedar 2003), and microspaces such as restrooms, courtrooms, and zoos (Braverman 2009a, 2012; Kogan 2009; Mulcahy 2010). Although some of these legal scholars have become thoroughly versed in the work of human geographers and social studies, most others continue to explore space, place, and landscape without the full benefit of the array of resources developed by geographers and others.

Increasingly, legal geography has become influential outside of North America. It has been especially vibrant in Israel and Australia, where its convergence with local conditions and scholarship has produced much powerful analysis. In Israel, legal geography has been useful for explicating and questioning "facts on the ground." For example, Israeli legal scholar Alexandre (Sandy) Kedar (1998, 2001, 2003), both alone and in collaboration with Oren Yiftachel, Geremy Forman, and others (Forman and Kedar 2003, 2004; Kedar and Yiftachel 2006; Yiftachel, Kedar, and Amara 2012), has produced a sustained legal geographic genealogy of land dispossession and occupation. Yiftachel (2005, 2006, 2009a, 2009b) has published several important works making critical use of legal geography insights, as has Forman (2006, 2009, 2011). Also, sociology scholar Ronen Shamir (1996) has analyzed Israel's attempts to control Bedouins and nomadic culture, and Irus Braverman (2009b, 2013a) has explored how political wars are legitimized through what are seen as natural materialities such as olive and pine landscapes and zoo animals. Other Israeli scholars who have been highly committed to legal geography explorations in this region include Yishai Blank and Issi Rosen-Zvi (Blank 2005; Blank and Rosen-Zvi 2010; Rosen-Zvi 2004).

Legal geography is also becoming increasingly visible in Australia (e.g., Chris Butler, Robyn Bartel, Kurt Iveson, Nicole Graham), where the Legal Geography Study Group of the Institute of Australian Geographers was recently formed; in the United Kingdom (e.g., Anne Griffiths, Davina Cooper, Sarah Blandy, Phil Hubbard, Antonia Layard, Jane Holder, Sarah Whatmore, Andreas Philippopoulos-Mihalopoulos); and in Europe (e.g., Franz von Benda-Beckmann, Keebet von Benda-Beckmann, Andrea Mubi Brighenti, Ken Olwig, Mats Widgren). Of special note is the 2009 volume *Géographie du droit: Épistémologie, développement et perspectives*, edited by Patrick Forest, which brought the work of Anglo-American, European, and Quebecois legal geographers to a Francophone audience. While this is encouraging, it is nonetheless important to recognize that, unfortunately, legal geography is still quite limited in its geographic range. As the editors of this collection, we believe that the legal geography project would be enriched by studies situated out of the usual ambit of the largely urban, Global Northwest. We also think that legal geography will prove a useful tool in marginalized contexts. Looking forward to what legal geography might still become, we hope that this gap will be addressed soon.

## The Third Mode of Legal Geography: Postdisciplinary Scholarship

Beyond its significance for disciplinary projects and for bidisciplinary interactions, legal geography is also important for elucidating third-discipline interests.

Anthropologists, political scientists, sociologists, historians, and others have all engaged with and contributed to the legal geography project to advance their particular disciplinary concerns about interests as diverse as land tenure, democracy, identity, labor relations, or the structuration of organizations. Indeed, the critical investigation of social space in its relationship with law has never been the monopoly of professional geographers and legal scholars.

The "third field" with the strongest engagement with legal geography is cultural anthropology. Anthropology has long been concerned with the themes of territory, boundaries, place, and landscape as these bear on questions of culture and, in this sense, it is inherently geographical. Law has been present in cultural anthropology since its founding (Benda-Beckmann and Strijbosch 1986; Darian-Smith 2007; Donovan 2008; S. F. Moore 2005). There has, then, been a consistent stream of autochthonous engagement with legal geography at the heart of the anthropological project, although it has rarely been identified as such. Interest has increased in recent years as anthropologists have taken up topics such as globalization, mobility, and displacement, and as they have expanded their scrutiny to include "insider" and "para" ethnographies of Western cultures (see Chapter 5 in this volume).

Still within the legal anthropology tradition (and increasingly encompassing other sociolegal scholarship), a rich and vibrant literature on legal pluralism has emerged out of a dissatisfaction with the assumption that law is inherently a project of the state. Legal pluralism scholars have come to realize that how the spatiality of law operates in the West has much relevance to non-Western, nonstate, and especially colonial contexts. Prominent scholars in this endeavor are the legal anthropologists Franz von Benda-Beckmann and Keebet von Benda-Beckmann, whose rich theoretical and empirical studies of non-Western spaces since the 1970s have demonstrated an acute sensitivity to the complexities of social space in a variety of geographical and cultural contexts. The 2009 volume *Spatializing Law: An Anthropological Geography of Law in Society* (coedited with Anne Griffiths) is only a recent contribution. This collection includes empirical studies from Peru, Indonesia, Bhutan, Scotland, Sierra Leone, and other locations that significantly expand the horizons of legal geography scholarship.

In addition to the integration of third-field concerns into the traditionally bidisciplinary focus of law and geography, the third mode of legal geography consists of studies that move beyond legal geography in a way that both draws on and contributes to broader social and humanities studies. We refer to this mode as the postdisciplinary scholarship within legal geography. Among the works that signal a distinctively postdisciplinary orientation to legal geography thought is David Delaney's (2010) *The Spatial, the Legal, and the Pragmatics of World-Making:*

*Nomospheric Investigations.* This book identifies impediments to advancing the legal geography project, such as the tacit alignment of the legal with discursivity and of spatiality with materiality, the generally disjointed or "archipelagic" nature of legal geography, and the lack of distinctive theoretical frameworks that can be deployed across a range of contexts. To remedy this, Delaney offers a set of neologisms, most important of which are the *nomosphere*, the *nomic setting*, and the *nomoscape*.

The nomosphere refers to "the cultural-material environs that are constituted by the reciprocal materializations of 'the legal,' the legal signification of the 'socio-spatial,' and the practical, performative engagements through which such constitutive moments happen and unfold" (Delaney 2010, 25). Delaney assumes that the discursive, the material, the embodied-performative, and the temporal aspects of our objects of attention—say, "law" and "space"—do not exist autonomously in separate realms or dimensions but are always already fused. Delaney defines nomic settings accordingly as such "determinable segments of the material world that are socially fabricated by way of inscription or assignment of traces of legal meanings. They are invested with significance and they, in turn, signify. They *confer* significance *onto* actions, events, relationships, and situations. They are *lived*" (59).

At the same time, Delaney clarifies that nomic settings (e.g., homes, public spaces, borders, prisons, workplaces) are not isolated from one another. Rather, they are constellated into ensembles or assemblages that form wider, recognizable worlds. "These nomic worlds," according to Delaney, "are the contingent products of pervasive cultural processes and forces associated with ideological projects" (100). He refers to such ensembles as *nomoscapes*. One may discern numerous nomoscapes that are mutually entangled with one another, such as (neo)liberal nomoscapes and nomoscapes of race, gender, labor, death, justice, and so forth. The utility of this novel framework is demonstrated with illustrations from a wide variety of historical, cultural, political, and experiential contexts that draw as deeply from history, sociology, anthropology, political theory, and cultural studies as they do from the disciplines of law and geography, narrowly construed.

The work of Irus Braverman is also exemplary of this third mode of legal geography. Grounded in both contemporary social and cultural theory and in legal geography studies, Braverman's mostly ethnographic work seeks to illuminate the significance of spatiolegal operations for understanding dimensions of the social life of power generally, and in relation to nature and nonhumans in particular. From initial investigations of the spatiolegalities of trees and checkpoints in Israel/Palestine (2009b, 2011a), Braverman has extended the reach of legal geography to the sanitary and mundane surveillance of restrooms (2009a), visuality and technology (2011b, 2013b), and animality and zoos (2012, 2013a). Arguing for the expansion of legal geography to nonhuman legalities, Braverman poses the following questions. First, she asks, what happens when nonhuman animals are forced to fit into humanistic regulatory frameworks (e.g., those of legal rights) that seek to define them as liberal subjects? Second, what might a "posthumanist" framework, which does not attempt to make liberal subjects of nonhuman animals, look like? And finally, what does it mean to "care better" for the animal— and how might this form of care translate into law? "It is time to think about the possibility of *more-than-human legalities*," stresses Braverman (forthcoming).

Additionally, a number of legal scholars—for example, Russell Hogg (2002), Desmond Manderson (2005), and Richard Mohr (2003)—have directed legal readership toward the rich conceptualizations of the difference that space and human geography can make to critical legal analyses. Space figures here less in terms of traditional conceptions of place, landscape, and scale, for example, than as a way of approaching alterity, diversity, and multiplicity. Some sense of the orientation of this work can be glimpsed in Stramignoni's (2004, 181) claim that "if it will hardly be doubted that law is (seen to be) everywhere in space . . . it is also clearly the case that conversely, 'space' is each time everywhere in law. . . . But exactly how and where is the space that is everywhere in law? And how might the container, so to speak, be contained by its contents?" Less interested in responding to disciplinary questions from law and geography, these scholars are offering innovative understandings of space in relation to law.

More recent philosophically inflected work by Andreas Philippopoulos-Mihalopoulos (2011) and Andrea Mubi Brighenti (2010) has also taken the spatial dimension of the legal to novel places. For example, in his conceptualization of a genuine "spatial justice"—and in contrast with conventional *aspatial* notions of spatial justice—Philippopoulos-Mihalopoulos (2010, 207) enlists the Deleuzian idea of folds to identify "*manifold* space [that] keeps on spreading by folding itself like a boundless origami. In its gurgling, it makes any multitude explode, splayed out. In that sense, space is not different to body, thought, individual, collectivity, animal, human; it is instead the curling surrounding that is folded within, ingesting the outside inside and simultaneously unfolding what is inside on a plane." Philippopoulos-Mihalopoulos also claims that "law is spacing itself away from space—it turns against its own turning, brutally returning to the banality of the locality, the incantation of the particular and the hasty concealment of a certain fear of space and its manifold, uncontrollable, unpredictable folding" (207–8).

## EXPANDING THE SPACES OF LAW

As we have shown, legal geography is a lively and creative line of scholarship. But it could be livelier, and even more creative. Its full potential, we would argue, has yet to be fully realized. This section offers a few ideas about how we might expand our explorations of the spaces of law. In part, some of the issues we point to are already nascent in recent legal geography scholarship. In that sense, we see these suggestions as further nudges rather than as an attempt to map out an entirely new scholarly agenda.

## Expanding on Power and Time

It is conventional for critical legal geographers to underscore the presence of power in law's spaces. But legal geography scholars still need to think carefully about the particularities of power. Power, the geographer John Allen (2003) argues, is never power in general but always power of a specific kind, expressed as domination, authority, coercion, seduction, and—we might add—solidarity, responsibility, altruism, protection, and even care and love. While much legal geography scholarship is open to such diversity, a more explicit recognition of the specificities of power would be useful. If we are to understand a legal world that includes ideology, routinized practice, enrollment, myth, narrative, things, nonhuman animals, nature, brutality, redemption, courtroom layout, and the construction of difference, for example, we will clearly need a more flexible and nuanced analysis of power. Viewed more closely, law can entail both power over others and associational power: power with others. Pragmatism also invites us to think of power less as a "power over" and more in terms of a contingent and relational effect, experienced as the power to act (see Chapter 3). These complex explorations of power are very much in line with Foucauldian conceptions of governmentality, biopower, and pastoral power (see, e.g., Foucault 1977, 1980, 2007), which recognize the considerable diversity of forms that power takes and the complex ways in which power "makes up" subjects, arguments that have been taken up by a number of legal geographers (e.g., Blomley 2012; Braverman 2012; Valverde 2011). Following Sally Engle Merry (2001) and Mariana Valverde (2010), it is about time that legal geographers also engage more seriously with Foucault's (2007) insights into neoliberal apparatuses.

While we begin disaggregating law's power and recognizing its variability, we must also attend carefully to how the diversities of space—organized into networks, landscapes, places, scales, flows, alterities, relations, and topologies—affect the reach and effects of law. Although we welcome Allen's (2003, 205) claim that space be recognized as an integral, rather than an additional, part of any analysis of power, we still need to ask: what difference does space (or space-time) make to law? We need, as Allen puts it, "to be a little more curious about power's spatial constitution" (4). Even twenty years in, the legal geography project could still do better at specifying the real difference that thinking legally about space-time, and thinking temporally and geographically about law, makes.

Moreover, although legal geography has long recognized the dynamic nature of legal spaces and has emphasized their enacted, sustained qualities, it is nonetheless guilty of privileging space over time. Interestingly, with a few exceptions (Blomley 2007; Delaney 2001; Yiftachel, Kedar, and Amara 2012), deep engagements with history or historiography are relatively infrequent in contemporary legal geography. As a number of contributors to the present volume argue, greater inquisitiveness not only about the past but also about multiple aspects of temporality, alongside a more sophisticated conception of space-time, is necessary for the further development of legal geography.

Foregrounding the relationship between time and space, as we have tried to do in this collection, lends all the more urgency to the need to be more careful in our understandings of the temporality of *legal* spaces. Performativity theory, particularly as developed in conversation with science studies and economic sociology, might offer a productive set of tools with which to explore these notions. Eschewing an open-ended form of social constructionism, the emphasis of the performativity scholarship is on the iterative and citational nature of performances, which enrolls things and bodies, subjectivity and practice, in complex assemblages that stabilize particular social arrangements. Although legal geographies are fully a social product, they are no less real as such (Blomley 2013a). An emphasis on performativity also highlights the crucial legal work performed by (and with) things (Braverman 2008, 2009a, 2011a; Brown 2001; Delaney 2010). Such things can be material objects, such as roads (Kernaghan 2012), but they can also be nature (Blomley 2007; Braverman 2014). In so doing, we are invited to begin to move away from legal geography's traditional focus on humans as its subjects of study. David Delaney's (2003) *Law and Nature* helps initiate this conversation with a series of provocative questions: "First, what does law say about nature? . . . Second, what does what law says about nature tell us about the legal construction and figurations of the human? What are we that nature is not? What are we that is not 'natural'?" (5; see also Otomo and Mussawir 2013). Irus Braverman takes on some of these questions in her studies of treescaping practices as "lawfare" (2009b) and of contemporary zoos as metropolitan sites for the human production of animality (2012, 2013a, 2014). Legal geography would benefit from deepening its connections with scholarship on posthumanism (e.g., Wolfe 2013) and animal geographies (e.g., Buller forthcoming), and from explorations of the vibrancy of matter (Bennett 2010) as well as its science and entanglements (Barad 2007). Such explorations will ground legal geography in corporal matters, moving it away from abstract and anthropocentric notions of space into posthuman, or "more-than-human" (Whatmore 2006) legal geographies (Braverman forthcoming).

## Expanding on Law and Space

Beyond the reevaluation of power and time in our scholarship, it might be helpful to draw from nascent theoretical resources, many of which were unavailable or disregarded in the previous explorations of legal geography. Although legal geographers are already actively engaged with postcolonial theory, science studies, poststructuralism, thing theory, performativity, and many other fields, we ought to be engaging with still more fields, such as the humanities and posthumanities, physical geography, economics, psychology and psychoanalysis, material culture, architecture, organizational studies, and visual culture. Furthermore, the raw materials with which we work—the core categories and definitions of law and space and their material becomings—require even more careful attention than we have previously afforded them.

Most significant, perhaps, is how we think about the term *law*. In the 1990s, critical legal geographers came to understand law as a cultural artifact, one that should be thought of with reference to meaning and its contestation; law was perceived as social, both in its effects and in its constitution. Many legal geographers thus concerned themselves with the constitutive effects of law and its effects upon consciousness. In line with other sociolegal scholarship, and CLS in particular, legal geographers, too, wrenched law from Law—namely, they treated law as a social and cultural manifestation. The law they were concerned with and which they critiqued was, essentially, Anglo-American common law. To socialize this law, they excavated its profound connections to Western liberalism.

However, in at least three senses, this rethinking of law by the earlier modes of legal geography scholarship was partial and limited. First, the drive to socialize law may have come at some cost. The danger of thinking about law as a manifestation of the broader social context is that one loses sight of the particular ways in which legal actors (however defined) think and act. Law is obviously social and political; but it is not society and politics. Several scholars have foregrounded the forms of knowledge specific to law. For Annelise Riles (2011, 89), "legal knowledge is not a flourish or a detour; it is a very serious thing. The legal techniques at work in doing state work are real. They are consequential. And thinking of the state as the practice and effects of knowledge work does not trivialize it, but specify it." Mariana Valverde (2011) has directed considerable energy toward uncovering such legal knowledges through paying careful attention to the particular work they perform. Urban law, she notes, has a specific form, governing through framings such as police powers and related practices such as licensing and land use. Nicholas Blomley (2011) has also explored the legal regulation of public space, arguing that dominant scholarly accounts overlook a deeply ingrained set of legal and bureaucratic knowledges and practices that operate, in many senses, in a distinctive register.

The earlier socialization of law was also incomplete in a second sense: it narrowly focused on a critique of Western law, on what certain postcolonial scholars would refer to as "provincialized" Western law. Rather than representing a universal law, laws are now understood as plural products of particular local cultural formations. The common law, the mainstay of legal geography research, is therefore only one of many other legalities, including forms of indigenous law apparently subsumed by settler law, that nevertheless retain a remarkable vital spatiality (Braverman 2009b; Borrows 2010a, 2010b; Robertson forthcoming).

Third and finally, earlier modes of legal geography scholarship have confined themselves to the investigation of specific jurisdictions, mostly within the confines of the nation-state or, on occasion, at the level of international law. So far, however, hardly any legal geographical comparative work has been published. While mainstream contemporary comparative law is conspicuously nongeographic and does not sufficiently engage with local socio-spatial conditions, some of its main scholarly projects have to do with the classification and mapping of legal systems across the globe and the tracing of the movement and transplantation of law across jurisdictions—issues that could become the subject of legal geography investigations. Indeed, new voices among comparative law scholars signal the readiness for a dialogue between these fields (see, e.g., Legrand and Munday 2003; Twining 2009; Chapter 4 in this volume).

Alongside the shifting understanding of law, the other important category at play in legal geography scholarship—space—has also begun to mean something other than it did two decades ago. Judging by some of the earlier scholarship (e.g., Blomley and Clark 1990), space was most often understood through the lens of interpretation and the complications of emplaced meaning. As such, one tendency was to note the tension between law's claim to universality and determinacy and the evident spatial diversity of legal meanings, as constituted in the localized places of social life. Similarly, legal geographer Wes Pue (1990, 572, 577–79) perceived law as necessarily "anti-geography," arguing that "any geographical approach to law is fundamentally insurrectionist," since geography is the antithesis of abstraction. Evident here is a tendency to imagine space as a material surface upon which phenomena such as law are distributed. Despite numerous attempts to reveal space as socially produced (and, in turn, as socially constitutive), there has been a tendency to think of space in quite limited ways: space has been imagined as distinct and as an object in and of itself, over and above the material objects that are distributed "in" space. It has thus been very tempting to think topographically, imagining territories, scales, and spaces as having an object-quality to them and as more or less anchored in the world. The task was framed as one of inserting law onto these material surfaces.

However, an alternative view of space, and one that has played a powerful role in reshaping much geographic scholarship, invites us to think of space in relational terms (Murdoch 2006). Relational thinking eschews essentialism by insisting that all social entities are to be understood and explained according to their interactions, avoiding a view of internally stable concepts and entities. According to this view, "relations are dynamic, unfolding processes, rather than static ties between inert substances" (Sunley 2008, 5). Space, in this view, cannot be an object in itself; rather, "objects *are* space, space *is* objects, and moreover objects can be understood only in relation to other objects, with all this being a perpetual becoming of heterogeneous networks and events that connect internal spatiotemporal relations" (Jones 2009, 491). Spaces such as cities or regions are not territorial units but dynamic compositions. Seen in this way, "cities and regions come with no promise of territorial or systemic integrity, since they are made through the spatiality of flow, juxtaposition, porosity and relational connectivity" (Amin 2002, 34).

Such an invitation to think of space relationally may be a promising one for legal geography. For example, to the extent that it counters the view of space or law as objects in themselves, it provides a useful place from which to try and think relationally and "nomospherically" about legal spaces. Such a shift would allow us to begin to transform our analysis from legally consequential spaces such as the state border, to more creative explorations of the process of bordering, where borders are understood not as inert, fixed sites, but as fluid, nonlinear, and experiential practices produced through law. Undocumented workers in the United States, for example, may also experience the border deep inside state territory (Coleman 2009).

Moreover, considering space from a relational perspective may offer analytical tools by which we can think against some of the powerful topographic architectures of law, such as jurisdiction. Cultural anthropologists James Ferguson and Akhil Gupta (2005) point to two related metaphors at work in our conceptions of the state (and, even more so, perhaps, of law): "verticality" entails a view of the state as an institution above civil society; "encompassment" conceives the state as located within an ever-widening set of circles that begin with family and end with the system of states. "This is a profoundly consequential understanding of scale," they argue, "one in which the locality is encompassed by the region, the region by the nation-state, and the nation-state by the international community" (Ferguson and Gupta 2005, 106). The two metaphors, they conclude, "work together to produce a taken-for-granted spatial and scalar image of a state that both sits above and contains its localities, regions and communities" (106). At work here is an areal view of space as a series of categorical and nested containers.

Yet it is hard to escape such scalar framings. American geographer Adam Moore (2008, 208–9) notes, along these lines, that even scholars who emphasize the socially constructed character of scale still implicitly adhere to a view of scales as "actually existing entities that constitute the spatial context within and among which social action takes place." Others have argued against such a scalar framing, even going so far as to argue that we must abandon scale entirely in pursuit of "flat ontologies" (Marston, Jones, and Woodward 2005). Yet while there may be merits to such abandonment, there are also dangers. We may question a modernist, nonrelational view of space, but it continues to operate with powerful performative force, organizing legal geographies in the world. Such a scalar logic, Nicholas Blomley (2013b) notes, has striking ethical and analytical effects on the ways in which we think about categories such as jurisdiction. Mariana Valverde (2009, 141) states similarly that jurisdiction operates such that "legal powers and legal knowledges appear to us as always already distinguished by scale." More generally, borrowing from scholarship on the "state-effect" (Mitchell 1991), scalar framings work to produce the effect of law as a disembedded presence that circulates at the level of the nation-state. Rather than treating space as a thing in the world, then, our task should be to uncover the ways in which scale solidifies and is made real, thereby making sense of the work that such solidifications do (Moore 2008). Law's territories will then begin to appear less as objects in the world than as complicated effects (Painter 2010). Such alternatives, in combination with attempts to rethink law, power, and time, offer exciting tools for enriching and perhaps remaking legal geography.

## CHAPTER OVERVIEW

Chapter 1, "Places That Come and Go: A Legal Anthropological Perspective on the Temporalities of Space in Plural Legal Orders"—by Franz von Benda-Beckmann and Keebet von Benda-Beckmann, sets the investigatory tone of this collection and expresses our interest in exploring space in time. The authors contend that the anthropology of law—and legal pluralism in particular—is gravely absent from the conceptual framework of critical legal geography. They argue that attentiveness to plural legal constellations, especially to nonstate legal formations and to contradictory and coexisting notions of space, will force legal geographers to adopt a more nuanced perspective on the law-space-power nexus. The authors call attention to the temporality of legal space and place making, arguing that legal spaces and places "come and go," fade in and out, but do so at different paces, depending, among other things, on the particular legal system that constitutes the space. In addition, the authors point to the paradoxical results of the intensification and complexity of modern regulation: attempts to create consistent and enduring spatiolegal regimes necessitate frequent alterations, in turn generating unintended ambiguous and temporary legal spaces. This chapter also introduces the theme of comparative law, which is echoed throughout the collection. The authors set the stage for understanding comparative law not so much in its doctrinal meaning but rather in the different ways that the law-space nexus manifests in various cultures and temporalities.

In Chapter 2, "'Time Thickens, Takes on Flesh': Spatiotemporal Dynamics in Law," Mariana Valverde continues the exploration of the complex entanglements of space, time, and law. The chapter begins by arguing that the success of the law and geography literature has produced the unintended effect of reviving an old metaphysical fallacy, namely, treating space and time as abstract and separate entities. According to Valverde, Kant's critique of the objectivist metaphysics of space and time can therefore be usefully revived today as an antidote for the tendency to objectify and isolate space that is inherent—though not inevitably so—in law and geography as a field of inquiry. Legal geography's first theoretical risk, in other words, is the unwitting reification of space and the black boxing of the very processes that radical studies open up and problematize. A second and closely related problem for legal geography, according to Valverde, is its analytic marginalization of temporality. Although many law and space studies pay attention to history, Valverde argues that the historicizing of legal spaces that is often included in legal geographical studies (and in critical legal studies generally) captures only one aspect of temporality's many flows and dynamics. By way of experimenting with ways to think about spatiotemporalization processes in a pluralistic and dynamic manner, the chapter concludes with a reflection on the possible adaptation, for legal analysis purposes, of Mikhail Bakhtin's oft-mentioned but rarely used notion of chronotopes.

Chapter 3, "Learning from Larry: Pragmatism and the Habits of Legal Space," by Nicholas Blomley, draws from another conceptual tradition: American pragmatism. In particular, this chapter sketches the work of John Dewey in an attempt to think more carefully about the ways in which people take up and practice everyday legal geographies, such as those materialized at a property boundary. The chapter contemplates Dewey's analysis of habit, suggesting that the concept may be useful for legal geographers especially because of its refusal of dualistic thinking, its emphasis on transaction and event, and its resistance to the idea of "law" and "space" as independent categories, as well as the degrees to which these are "taken up" by actors. An emphasis on habit, conversely, points us to practices and actions, thus opening the door to more processual and temporal legal geographies. Blomley suggests that while one can thus begin to imagine legal-spatial habits of territory, jurisdiction, and property, pragmatism cautions against metaphysical thinking in relation to such terms. Pragmatism problematizes the idea that a fence, for example, is a manifestation of the larger phenomenon of property that operates at a grander and more abstract scale. Thinking through habit finally directs us to questions of power. Dewey's analysis, Blomley suggests, recognizes that habits can be a site for experimentation and change, yet also alerts us to habits' resistance to change.

In Chapter 4, "Expanding Legal Geographies: A Call for a Critical Comparative Approach," Alexandre (Sandy) Kedar argues for the initiation of a comparative project informed by both comparative law and legal geography, integrating them into a critical comparative legal geographical investigation. Such a critical comparative perspective, Kedar argues, is conspicuously absent from current scholarship. Particularly promising for legal geographers is the work of critical and postcolonial comparatists and their concept of legal transplants in particular, which provides insights into the movement, adoption, and transformation of legal doctrines, illuminating how structures and ideas manifest over space and time. Kedar demonstrates the potential of such an approach by exploring instances of displacement and dispossession. He presents a case study that investigates a legal geography triangle set within the British "legal family," showing how ideas and legal concepts embodied in British war legislation were transplanted to, and transformed in, postpartition India/Pakistan as well as in Israel/Palestine in the form of legislation that facilitated the taking of refugee property. Kedar calls for a dialogue between critical comparatists and critical legal geographers, and suggests initiating collaborative comparative research projects among scholars from different disciplines and regions.

In Chapter 5, "Who's Afraid of Methodology? Advocating a Methodological Turn in Legal Geography," Irus Braverman suggests that alongside the push to expand legal geography into new spaces and temporalities "out there," legal geography might benefit from an *inward* expansion: a reflection on how we come to write what we write rather than where, when, and why we do so. Such greater awareness to the craftsmanship of our scholarship will pay off in a range of ways, Braverman argues and, most important, by increasing the methodological diversity and interdisciplinarity of legal geography scholarship. The chapter reflects on the pitfalls and virtues of the author's zoo ethnography as a way to invite legal geographers to become acutely attentive to how they craft their own research. Because of the unique training of many legal geographers, Braverman argues finally, this tradition is well equipped to explore the working of particular administrative structures, which deserve heightened attention in our tradition. For this to happen, Braverman claims, we need to engage in discussions about the art of craftsmanship.

Chapter 6, "States That Come and Go: Mapping the Geolegalities of the Afghanistan Intervention," by Michael D. Smith, moves beyond the legal geographies of the nation-state and investigates the production and use of legal violence in international, transnational, and multinational arenas. Smith explores the relationship between the martial and the legal in the context of contemporary Western interventionism, in particular the war in Afghanistan, as a way to open up a number of avenues of inquiry for a renewed project of critical legal geography. Multinational incursions reveal a complex interplay of "states that come and go" in which law plays an important ordering role. Smith claims that we should pay attention to the ongoing rescaling of the state, to the transformations of state sovereignty, and to the hybrid—and often violent—legal geographies associated with political and economic globalization. The chapter introduces two concepts. First, "geolegality" reorients critical legal geography toward the role of the spatiolegal in geopolitics and geoeconomics. Then, "martial law" extends previous work on the relations between law and violence and offers a new terminology for addressing the theoretical and empirical aspects of late-modern war's geolegalities. Smith suggests that the spatiotemporalities of law are essential to grasping the hybrid political and economic formations associated with Western interventionism: the fusing of military and civil functions; the recasting of sovereignty as contingent and occupation as transformative; and the emergence of so-called operational law, a  hybrid body of law shaped by the exigencies of military missions. Smith concludes by examining Western intervention in terms of four different but overlapping moments—invasion, occupation, pacification, and autonomization—allowing us to begin to discern how the spatiotemporalities of law are crucial to the oscillating sovereignties and violent passages of "states that come and go."

In Chapter 7, "The Everyday Formation of the Urban Space: Law and Poverty in Mexico City," Antonio Azuela and Rodrigo Meneses-Reyes add voices and perspectives that have not been sufficiently represented in legal geography scholarship. Attentive to the temporalities of the social, spatial, and legal phenomena, the authors investigate the interactions between legal practices and urban formation in Mexico City. The chapter analyzes how two developments in the nomospheric transformation of Mexico City—the creation of a workplace for the urban poor and the regulation of land as a means for housing the poor—were shaped and resisted in legal disputes in the wider context of the formation of the postrevolutionary state in Mexico City (1930–50), a transitional period in the Mexican capital and its legal system. Azuela and Meneses-Reyes unravel the important role of the Mexican courts in providing a site in which the urban environment was imagined, contested, and reproduced. The chapter locates its findings within the wider setting of the (trans)formation of the state, inviting law and geography scholars to investigate the processes of state formation as products of myriad localized social, legal, and spatial interactions.

Chapter 8, "The Rural Lawscape: Space Tames Law Tames Space," by Lisa R. Pruitt, illuminates another hitherto-neglected zone of legal geography scholarship. Pruitt argues that law and rural space are at odds with each other because the presence of law as a force of the state is in tension with the socio-spatial construction of rurality. Law seeks to tame or control rural spatiality, but the material characteristics (e.g., low population density, dominance of nature over the built environment) and associated social characteristics of rural and remote places effectively resist those efforts. Rural spatiality's features tend to impede the efforts of law's agents and processes, thus making for a thinner, less robust legal presence. Pruitt argues that critical legal geographers have largely ignored the rural end of the rural-urban continuum, reflecting a rarely acknowledged urban normativity, not to mention urban hubris. The chapter begins the work of recovering the rural, bringing it into scholarly view to broaden our understanding of the diffuse and localized operation of law in rural places. The chapter is thus a step toward theorizing the significance and force of rural spatiality in relation to law and legal processes. The investigation into the rural lawscape reveals something not only about rural difference, Pruitt argues, but also about the otherwise obscure nature of law as variegated and variable. Finally, Pruitt contends that looking to the rural margins reveals something about the center because the process by which law differentiates the rural also depicts, at least implicitly, the default urban norm.

In Chapter 9, "Rules of Engagement: The Spatiality of Judicial Review," Melinda Harm Benson posits that litigation is itself a space that has, to date, been underexamined by legal geographers. She highlights the privileged position of judges as actors holding an inordinate amount of power to construct and police the spaces they occupy. Benson argues that legal geography would greatly benefit from an investigation of what she refers to as "rules of engagement" in litigation. She conceives the operational tenets of litigation as creating a legal arena in which various legal actors perform their roles according to highly formalized scripts. Often described as "procedural" as opposed to "substantive" aspects of the law, these legal requirements operate under a veil of neutrality. In reality, however, rules of engagement, which range from jurisdictional limitations to burdens of proof, reflect cultural assumptions about boundaries, privileges, power, and control. The chapter focuses on the norms governing the ability to challenge government conduct in environmental litigation. In this particular field of law, rules of engagement include not only statutory requirements but also constitutional and judge-made rules that prescribe conditions and prudential limitations, such as ripeness, mootness, and the political question doctrine. These rules determine not only when the government can be legally challenged but also the level of scrutiny on state conduct. Of particular interest to Benson is the requirement that a prospective plaintiff prove that he or she has standing before bringing a citizen suit enforcement action against the state. The chapter charts the manners in which rules of engagement produce legal spaces, how they control who may access these distinctive territories, and their policing of movement within their confines. Benson concludes that without gaining entry into legal spaces, the capacity to protect other spaces, such as endangered species habitats and public lands, is greatly hampered.

Finally, in Chapter 10, "At Work in the Nomosphere: The Spatio-Legal Production of Emotions at Work," David Delaney initiates an exploration of possible new scholarly connections, new questions, and underutilized resources so as to better understand some of the "so what?" of legal geography. Specifically, Delaney draws on the literature associated with law and the emotions, psychoanalysis and law, geography of emotions, psychoanalytic geography, and critical organization studies to formulate undeveloped lines of inquiry focused on the spatiolegal (or nomospheric) production of social suffering. This chapter's initial investigation focuses on the dynamics associated with the nomic setting of "the workplace" and the distinctive nomospheric situations that arise there. Among the larger project's guiding questions are the following: How does power in the workplace operate through the governing of, with, or through emotions? What are the distinctive spatialities that condition social relationality in ways that engender or ameliorate the felt sense of anxiety, forms of precariousness, and modes of social suffering? In contexts that are organized around relations of domination and submission, is it useful to posit the workings of a "legal unconscious" that fosters the prevalence of certain psychological dynamics and so facilitates the social production of certain kinds of legal subjects?

## REFERENCES

Allen, John. 2003. *Lost Geographies of Power*. Malden, MA: Blackwell.

Amin, Ash. 2002. "Spatialities of Globalization." *Environment and Planning A: Society and Space* 34: 385–99.

Aoki, Keith. 1996. "(Intellectual) Property and Sovereignty: Notes Toward a Cultural Geography of Authorship." *Stanford Law Review* 48: 1293–1356.

———. 2000. "Space Invaders: Critical Geography, the 'Third World' in International Law and Critical Race Theory." *Villanova Law Review* 45: 913–57.

Barad, Karen. 2007. *Meeting the Universe Halfway: Quantum Physics and the Entanglement of Matter and Meaning.* Durham, NC: Duke University Press.

Beaumont, J., M. Loopmans, and J. Uitermark. 2005. "Politicization of Research and the Relevance of Geography: Some Experiences and Reflections for an Ongoing Debate." *Area* 37: 118–26.

Benda-Beckmann, Franz von, Keebet von Benda-Beckmann, and Anne Griffiths, eds. 2009. *Spatializing Law: An Anthropological Geography of Law in Society.* Farnham, UK: Ashgate.

Benda-Beckmann, Keebet von, and Fons Strijbosch, eds. 1986. *Anthropology of Law in the Netherlands: Essays on Legal Pluralism.* Dordrecht, Netherlands: Foris Publications.

Bennett, Jane. 2010. *Vibrant Matter: A Political Ecology of Things.* Durham, NC: Duke University Press.

Blank, Yishai. 2005. "Community, Space, Subject: Theses on Law and Space Following Issi Rosen-Zvi Book." *Haifa Law Review* 2: 19–60.

Blank, Yishai, and Issi Rosen-Zvi. 2010. "The Spatial Turn in Legal Theory." *HAGAR: Studies in Culture, Polity and Identities* 10: 39–62.

Blomley, Nicholas. 1994. *Law, Space, and the Geographies of Power.* New York: Guilford Press.

———. 2007. "Making Private Property: Enclosure, Common Right and the Work of Hedges." *Rural History* 18: 1–21.

———. 2011. *Rights of Passage: Sidewalks and the Regulation of Public Flow.* New York: Routledge.

———. 2012. "Colored Rabbits, Dangerous Trees, and Public Sitting: Sidewalks, Police, and the City." *Urban Geography* 33 (7): 917–35.

———. 2013a. "Performing Property, Making the World." *Canadian Journal of Law and Jurisprudence* 26: 23–48.

———. 2013b. "What Sort of Legal Space Is a City?" In *Interstices: The Aesthetics and Politics of Urban In-Betweens*, edited by Andrea Mubi Brighenti, 1–20. Farnham, UK: Ashgate.

Blomley, Nicholas, and Joel Bakan. 1992. "Spacing Out: Towards a Critical Geography of Law." *Osgoode Hall Law Journal* 30: 661–90.

Blomley, Nicholas, and Gordon Clark. 1990. "Law, Theory and Geography." *Urban Geography* 11: 433–46.

Blomley, Nicholas, David Delaney, and Richard Ford, eds. 2001. *The Legal Geographies Reader.* Oxford, UK: Blackwell.

Boddie, Elise. 2010–11. "Racial Territoriality." *UCLA Law Review* 58: 401–63.

Borrows, John. 2010a. *Canada's Indigenous Constitution.* Toronto: University of Toronto Press.

———. 2010b. *Drawing Out Law: A Spirit's Guide.* Toronto: University of Toronto Press.

Braverman, Irus. 2008. "Governing Certain Things: The Regulation of Street Trees in Four North American Cities." *Tulane Environmental Law Journal* 22 (1): 35–60.

———. 2009a. "Loo Law: The Public Washroom as a Hyper-Regulated Space." *Hastings Women's Law Journal* 20: 45–71.

———. 2009b. *Planted Flags: Trees, Land, and Law in Israel/Palestine.* Cambridge: Cambridge University Press.

———. 2011a. "Civilized Borders: A Study of Israel's New Crossing Administration." *Antipode* 43: 264–95.

———. 2011b. "Hidden in Plain View: Legal Geography from a Visual Perspective." *Journal of Law, Culture, and the Humanities* 7 (2): 173–86.

————. 2012. *Zooland: The Institution of Captivity.* Stanford, CA: Stanford University Press.

————. 2013a. "Animal Frontiers: A Tale of Three Zoos in Israel/Palestine." *Cultural Critique* 85: 122–62.

————. 2013b. "Passing the Sniff Test: Police Dogs as Biotechnology." *Buffalo Law Review* 61: 81–168.

————. 2014. "Conservation Without Nature: The Trouble with *In Situ* Versus *Ex Situ* Conservation." *Geoforum* 51: 47–57.

————. Forthcoming. "Nonhuman Legalities." In *The Wiley Handbook of Law and Society*, edited by Patricia Ewick and Austin Sarat. New York: Wiley.

Briffault, Richard. 1990a. "Our Localism: Part I—The Structure of Local Government Law." *Columbia Law Review* 90: 1–115.

————. 1990b. "Our Localism: Part II—The Structure of Local Government Law." *Columbia Law Review* 90: 346–454.

Brighenti, Andrea Mubi. 2010. "Lines, Barred Lines, Movement, Territory and the Law." *International Journal of Law in Context* 6: 217–27.

Brown, Bill. 2001. "Thing Theory." *Critical Inquiry* 28: 1–22.

Buller, Henry. Forthcoming. "Animal Geographies I." *Progress in Human Geography.*

Calmore, John. 1995. "Racialized Space and the Culture of Segregation: Hewing a Stone of Hope from a Mountain of Despair." *University of Pennsylvania Law Review* 143: 1233–74.

Carmalt, Jean Connolly. 2007. "Rights and Place: Using Geography in Human Rights Work." *Human Rights Quarterly* 29: 68–85.

Clark, Gordon. 1982. "Rights, Property, and Community." *Economic Geography* 58: 120–38.

————. 1984. "A Theory of Local Autonomy." *Annals of the Association of American Geographers* 74: 195–208.

————. 1985. *Judges and the Cities: Interpreting Local Autonomy.* Chicago: University of Chicago Press.

————. 1986a. "Adjudicating Jurisdictional Disputes in Chicago and Toronto: Legal Formalism and Urban Structure." *Urban Geography* 7: 63–80.

————. 1986b. "Making Moral Landscapes: John Rawls' Original Position." *Political Geography Quarterly* 5: S147–62.

Coleman, Mathew. 2009. "What Counts as the Politics and Practice of Security, and Where? Devolution and Immigrant Insecurity after 9/11." *Annals of the Association of American Geographers* 99: 904–13.

Coombe, Rosemary. 1996. "Authorial Cartographies: Mapping Proprietary Borders in a Less-Than-Brave New World." *Stanford Law Review* 48: 1357–66.

Cooper, Davina. 1998. *Governing out of Order: Space, Law and the Politics of Belonging.* London: Rivers Oram Press.

D'Arcus, Bruce. 2014. "Extraordinary Rendition, Law and the Spatial Architecture of Rights." *ACME: An International E-Journal for Critical Geographies* 13: 79–99.

Darian-Smith, Eve. 1999. *Bridging Divides: The Channel Tunnel and English Legal Identity in the New Europe.* Berkeley: University of California Press.

————. 2007. *Ethnography and Law.* Burlington, VT: Ashgate.

Delaney, David. 1998. *Race, Place, and the Law: 1836–1948.* Austin: University of Texas Press.

————. 2001. "Running with the Land: Legal-Historical Imagination and the Spaces of Modernity." *Journal of Historical Geography* 27: 493–506.

————. 2003. *Law and Nature.* New York: Cambridge University Press.

————. 2010. *The Spatial, the Legal, and the Pragmatics of World-Making: Nomospheric Investigations.* London: GlassHouse Books.

Donovan, James M. 2008. *Legal Anthropology: An Introduction.* Lanham, MD: Altamira Press.

Erbsen, Allen. 2011. "Constitutional Spaces." *Minnesota Law Review* 95: 1168–1267.

Ferguson, J., and Gupta, A. 2005. "Spatializing States: Toward an Ethnography of Neoliberal Governmentality." In *Anthropologies of Modernity: Foucault, Governmentality, and Life Politics,* edited by J. X. Inda, 105–31. Malden, MA: Blackwell.

Ford, Richard. 1994. "The Boundaries of Race: Political Geography in Legal Analysis." *Harvard Law Review* 107: 1841–1921.

————. 1999. "Law's Territory (A History of Jurisdiction)." *Michigan Law Review* 97: 843–930.

Forest, Benjamin. 2001. "Mapping Democracy, Racial Identity, and the Quandary of Political Representation." *Annals of the Association of American Geographers* 91: 143–66.

————. 2004. "The Legal (De)Construction of Geography: Race and Political Community in Supreme Court Redistricting Decisions." *Social and Cultural Geography* 5: 55–73.

Forest, Patrick, ed. 2009. *Géographie du droit: Épistémologie, développement et perspectives.* Montreal: Presses de l'Universite Laval.

Forman, Geremy. 2006. "Law and the Historical Geography of the Galilee: Israel's Litigatory Advantages during the Special Operation of Land Settlement." *Journal of Historical Geography* 32: 796–817.

————. 2009. "A Tale of Two Regions: Diffusion of the Israeli '50 Percent Rule' from the Galilee to the Occupied West Bank." *Law and Social Inquiry* 34: 671–711.

————. 2011. "Israeli Supreme Court Doctrine and the Battle over Arab Land in Galilee: A Vertical Assessment." *Journal of Palestine Studies* 40: 24–44.

Forman, Geremy, and Alexandre Kedar. 2003. "Colonialism, Colonization, and Land Law in Mandate Palestine: The Zor al-Zarqa/Barrat Qisarya Land Disputes in Historical Perspective." *Theoretical Perspectives in Law* 4: 491–539.

————. 2004. "From Arab Land to Israel Lands: The Legal Dispossession of the Palestinians Displaced by Israel in the Wake of 1948." *Environment and Planning D: Society and Space* 22: 809–30.

Foucault, Michel. 1977. *Discipline and Punish: The Birth of the Prison.* New York: Vintage.

————. 2007. *Security, Territory, Population: Lectures at the Collège de France 1977–78.* Edited by Michel Senellart. Translated by Graham Burchell. New York: Picador/Palgrave.

————. 1980. *The History of Sexuality, Volume I.* Translated by R. Hurley. New York: Vintage.

Frug, Gerald. 1996. "The Geography of Community." *Stanford Law Review* 48: 1047–1108.

Herbert, Steve. 1997. *Policing Space: Territoriality and the Los Angeles Police Department.* Minneapolis: University of Minnesota Press.

Hogg, Russell. 2002. "Law's Other Spaces." *Law/Text/Culture* 6: 29–40.

Holder, Jane, and Carolyn Harrison, eds. 2002. *Law and Geography.* Vol. 5 of *Current Legal Issues.* Oxford: Oxford University Press.

Jones, Martin. 2009. "Phase Space: Geography, Relational Thinking, and Beyond." *Progress in Human Geography* 33: 487–506.

Kedar, Alexandre. 1998. "Majority Time, Minority Time: Land, Nation and the Law of Adverse Possession in Israel." *Tel-Aviv University Law Review* 21: 655–746 (Hebrew).

————. 2001. "The Legal Transformation of Ethnic Geography: Israeli Law and the Palestinian Landholder, 1948–1967." *New York University Journal of International Law and Politics* 33: 923–1000.

————. 2003. "On the Legal Geography of Ethnocratic Settler States: Notes towards a Research Agenda." *Current Legal Issues* 5: 401–41.

Kedar, Alexandre, and Oren Yiftachel. 2006. "Land Regimes and Social Relations in Israel." In *Realizing Property Rights: Swiss Human Rights Book*, edited by Hernando de Soto and Francis Cheneval, 1:129–46. N.p.: n.p.

Kernaghan, Richard. 2012. "Furrows and Walls, or the Legal Topography of a Frontier Road in Peru." *Mobilities* 7: 501–20.

Kogan, Terry. 2009. "Transsexuals in Public Restrooms: Law, Cultural Geography and *Etsitty v. Utah Transit Authority*." *Temple Political and Civil Rights Law Review* 18: 673–97.

Landauer, Carl. 2010–11. "Regionalism, Geography, and the International Legal Imagination." *Chicago Journal of International Law* 11: 557–95.

Legrand, Pierre, and Roderick Munday, eds. 2003. *Comparative Legal Studies: Traditions and Transitions*. Cambridge: Cambridge University Press.

Mahmud, Tayyab. 2010. "Law of Geography and the Geography of Law: A Post-Colonial Mapping." *Washington University Jurisprudence Review* 3: 64–106.

Manderson, Desmond. 2005. "Interstices: New Works on Legal Spaces." *Law/Text/Culture* 9: 1–10.

Marston, Sallie, John Paul Jones, and Keith Woodward. 2005. "Human Geography without Scale." *Transactions of the Institute of British Geographers* 30: 416–32.

Merry, Sally Engle. 2001. "Spatial Governmentality and the New Urban Social Order: Controlling Gender Violence Through Law." *American Anthropologist* 103 (1): 16–29.

Mitchell, Don. 1997. "The Annihilation of Space by Law: The Roots and Implications of Anti-Homeless Laws in the United States." *Antipode* 29: 303–35.

————. 2003. *The Right to the City: Social Justice and the Fight for Public Space*. New York: Guilford.

Mitchell, Timothy. 1991. "The Limits of the State: Beyond Statist Approaches and Their Critics." *American Political Science Review* 85: 77–96.

Mohr, Richard. 2003. "Law and Identity in Spatial Contexts." *National Identities* 5: 53–66.

Moore, Adam. 2008. "Rethinking Scale as a Geographic Category: From Analysis to Practice." *Progress in Human Geography* 32: 203–25.

Moore, Sally Falk, ed. 2005. *Law and Anthropology: A Reader*. Malden, MA: Blackwell.

Mulcahy, Linda. 2010. *Legal Architecture: Justice, Due Process, and the Place of Law*. Abingdon, UK: Routledge.

Murdoch, Jonathan. 2006. *Post-Structuralist Geography: A Guide to Relational Space*. London: Sage Publications.

Neuman, Gerald. 1987. "Territorial Discrimination, Equal Protection, and Self-Determination." *University of Pennsylvania Law Review* 135: 261–382.

Oh, Reginald. 2003–4. "Re-Mapping Equal Protection Jurisprudence: A Legal Geography of Race and Affirmative Action." *American University Law Review* 53: 1305–60.

Osofsky, Hari. 2007. "A Law and Geography Perspective on the New Haven School." *Yale Journal of International Law* 32: 421–53.

————. 2012. "Towards a Holistic Vision of Law and Geography? Possibilities for Bridging the Gap between Critical and Non-Critical Scholarship." Presentation at the workshop

"Where Now? Moving beyond Traditional Legal Geographies," Baldy Center for Law and Social Policy, Buffalo, NY, April 19–20.

Otomo, Yoriko, and Edward Mussawir, eds. 2013. *Law and the Question of the Animal: A Critical Jurisprudence*. New York: Routledge.

Pain, Rachel. 2006. "Social Geography: Seven Deadly Myths in Policy Research." *Progress in Human Geography* 30: 250–59.

Painter, Joe. 2010. "Rethinking Territory." *Antipode* 45: 1090–1118.

Pearson, Zoe. 2008. "Spaces of International Law." *Griffith Law Review* 17: 489–514.

Philippopoulos-Mihalopoulos, Andreas. 2010. "Spatial Justice: Law and the Geography of Withdrawal." *International Journal of Law in Context* 6: 201–16.

———. 2011. "Law's Spatial Turn: Geography, Justice and a Certain Fear of Space." *Law, Culture and the Humanities* 7: 187–202.

Pruitt, Lisa. 2008. "Gender, Geography, and Rural Justice." *Berkeley Journal of Gender, Law and Justice* 23: 338–89.

———. 2011. "The Geography of the Class Culture Wars." *Seattle University Law Review* 34: 767–814.

Pruitt, Lisa, and Beth Colgan. 2010. "Justice Deserts: Spatial Inequality and Local Funding of Indigent Defense." *Arizona Law Review* 52: 219–316.

Pue, Wesley. 1990. "Wrestling with Law: (Geographical) Specificity vs. (Legal) Abstraction." *Urban Geography* 11: 566–95.

Raustiala, Kal. 2004–5. "The Geography of Justice." *Fordham Law Review* 73: 2501–60.

———. 2006. "The Evolution of Territoriality: International Relations and American Law." In *Territoriality and Conflict in an Age of Globalization*, edited by Miles Kahler and Barbara Walter, 219–50. Cambridge: Cambridge University Press.

Riles, Annelise. 2011. *Collateral Knowledge: Legal Reasoning in the Global Financial Markets*. Chicago: University of Chicago Press.

Robertson, Sean. Forthcoming. "Extinction Is the Dream of Modern Powers: Bearing Witness to the Return of Life of the Sinixt Peoples?" *Antipode*.

Rosen-Zvi, Issi. 2004. *Taking Space Seriously: Law, Space, and Society in Contemporary Israel* Aldershot, UK: Ashgate.

Santos, Boaventura. 1987. "Law: A Map of Misreading—Toward a Postmodern Conception of Law." *Journal of Law and Society* 14: 279–302.

Sarat, Austin, Lawrence Douglas, and Martha Umphrey, eds. 2003. *The Place of Law*. Ann Arbor: University of Michigan Press.

Shamir, Ronen. 1996. "Suspended in Space: Bedouins under the Law of Israel." *Law and Society Review* 30: 231–58.

Stramignoni, Igor. 2004. "Francesco's Devilish Venus: Notations on the Matter of Legal Space." *California Western Law Review* 41: 147–240.

Sunley, Peter. 2008. "Relational Economic Geography: A Partial Understanding or a New Paradigm." *Economic Geography* 84: 1–26.

Twining, William 2009. *General Jurisprudence: Understanding Law from a Global Perspective*. Cambridge: Cambridge University Press.

Valverde, Mariana. 2009. "Jurisdiction and Scale: Legal 'Technicalities' as Resources for Theory." *Social and Legal Studies* 18: 139–57.

———. 2010. "Specters of Foucault in Law and Society Scholarship." *Annual Review of Law and Social Science* 6: 45–59.

———. 2011. "Seeing Like a City: The Dialectic of Premodern and Modern Knowledge Formats in Urban Governance." *Law and Society Review* 45: 247–312.

Whatmore, Sarah. 2006. "Materialist Returns: Practising Cultural Geography in and for a More-Than-Human World." *Cultural Geographies* 13 (4): 600–609.

Wolfe, Cary. 2013. *Before the Law: Humans and Other Animals in a Biopolitical Frame.* Chicago: University of Chicago Press.

Yiftachel, Oren. 2005. "A Geographer in Legal Space: Teaching 'Legal Geography' as Navigation on the Academic Frontier." *Haifa Law Review* 2: 211–19.

———. 2006. *Ethnocracy: Land and Identity Politics in Israel/Palestine.* Philadelphia: University of Pennsylvania Press.

———. 2009a. "Critical Theory and 'Gray Space': Mobilization of the Colonized." *City* 13: 240–56.

———. 2009b. "Theoretical Notes on 'Gray Cities': The Coming of Urban Apartheid?" *Planning Theory* 8: 88–100.

Yiftachel, Oren, Alexandre (Sandy) Kedar, and Ahmad Amara. 2012. "Re-Examining the 'Dead Negev Doctrine': Property Rights in Arab Bedouin Regions." *Law and Government* 14: 7–147 (Hebrew).

Zick, Timothy. 2006. "Speech and Spatial Tactics." *Texas Law Review* 84: 581–651.

———. 2009a. "Constitutional Displacement." *Washington University Law Review* 86: 515–608.

———. 2009b. *Speech out of Doors: Preserving First Amendment Liberties in Public Places.* Cambridge: Cambridge University Press.

———. 2010. "Territoriality and the First Amendment: Free Speech at—and beyond—Our Borders." *Notre Dame Law Review* 85: 1543–1628.

# 1 PLACES THAT COME AND GO

## A Legal Anthropological Perspective on the Temporalities of Space in Plural Legal Orders

*Franz von Benda-Beckmann and Keebet von Benda-Beckmann*

The anthropology of law, and in particular the study of space and time in plural legal orders, is still an underrated node in the field of law and geography, despite the expanding network of scholars approaching the field from a variety of disciplines (see also Valverde, in this volume). Adding to the growing scholarship in the law and geography field so meticulously described and analyzed by the editors in the introduction to this volume, the anthropology of law offers a social science perspective on law and space that is of interest for two reasons.[1] Anthropological studies, with their methodological emphasis on participant observation and discursive techniques for capturing emic perspectives, have generated knowledge of a great variety of "folk geographies." This term refers to local understandings and constructions of space that entail specific normative connotations, representations, and power relations, which serve as orientations in social interaction. Folk geographies could enrich the law and geography studies that thus far have been based mainly on "northern" and urban examples. In addition, the anthropology of law draws attention to plural legal constellations in which unalike and often-contradictory notions of space and boundaries come to coexist in mutual interdependence within the same physical or sociopolitical space.[2] Multiple legal constructions of space open up diverse arenas for the exercise of political authority and the localization of rights and obligations. Showing nonstate (e.g., religious, traditional) legal constructions of space, and analyzing them in the Global North as well as in the Global South, offers a more complex perspective on the law-space-power nexus. To be sure, spaces are not necessarily multilegal, and the degree to which this might be the case varies a great deal. However, we suggest that a full-fledged legal geography should incorporate the *possibility* of coexisting legal spaces systematically into its theoretical and methodological framework. This offers insight into the different ways in which people perceive these spaces and operate and navigate among the spaces' various authority positions.

In the first part of our chapter we briefly elaborate on our view of legal pluralism with respect to space and place, and how we locate it in the wider sociopolitical organization. We then focus on the dynamics of concretizing legal spaces as places in plural legal orders, that is, on the temporality of legal space and place making. Following the earlier work of Harvey (1996) and others that emphasizes that space cannot exist without time, we see places as (relative) "permanences" of people, relationships, and objects located and bounded in space (Harvey 1996, 261). Places are relative in time and vary in permanence. They are "contingent on the processes that create, sustain and dissolve them" (Harvey 1996, 261; see also pp. 264 and 294). We argue not only that legal spaces and places are perpetually perishing, as Harvey pointed out, but also that they "come and go"; that is, they move and alternate with other spaces, but they do so at different paces, depending, among other things, on the kind of legal system that constitutes the space, for each legal (sub)system has characteristic ways in which spaces are being "timed." A central question we explore concerns what happens within the period in which spaces are emerging and disappearing but are not yet or no longer officially in place. In a last section we discuss how processes of time-space compression (Giddens 1996) and acceleration (Rosa 2006; Rosa and Scheuerman 2009) lead to complex and changing constellations of overlapping spaces. Delaney (2010, 138) has argued that the result of this is hyperterritoriality, a steep increase of overlapping legal spaces for which ever more "regimes of continuity" are created, to solve socio-economic problems once and for all. Taking this argument a step further, we argue that since every newly created space has its own regulation, hyperterritoriality implies hyperregulation, that is, a steep increase of overlapping regulations that requires ever more complex legal coordination. We suggest that this poses a paradox, for the very need for coordination that is required every time such a regime is established is inhibitive for the long duration that is pursued with the regime of continuity. Instead of providing a sense of certainty, these legal spaces often generate deep feelings of uncertainty among the addressees of the regulations, because they are constantly confronted with coordinative adjustments. And if no adjustment is made, they have to cope with the changing and contradictory regulations of the overlapping legal spaces. Including the analysis of legal plurality and a pronounced time perspective may provide the geography of law with a deeper understanding of the volatile, contradictory, and fractured nature of legal space making, and of the uncertainties with which addressees of spatial regulation have to live.

## WEAVING SPACE INTO LAW AND LEGAL PLURALISM

### Law and Space

Space and time are important aspects of any empirical research or social theory. They form constituent elements of social life and organization that help to individuate people, social interactions, and relationships (Giddens 1984, 1985; Goldschmidt 1966; Harvey 1996, 53, 210, 264; Lash and Urry 1994, 223). Space and time are analytical concepts that point to the multidimensional nature of the physical world. Infinite space and "stellar time" (Leach 1961) are formal social constructions that allow for comparison of a broad array of more substantive constructions, such as social, religious, political, ecological, and "hydrological" spaces (spaces defined by a common hydrological system; see also Werlen 1988), ranging in scope from a living room to the "global," or even the position of the earth in the universe, and from measured minutes, individual lifetimes, the time of families, and states to the evolution of the earth. Such formal concepts also allow for comparison of very different modalities of time (e.g., lineal, cyclical, iterative) (see Engel 1987; French 2001, 691; Geertz 1973; Greenhouse 1989, 1996; Khan 2009, 56; Leach 1961).[3]

All notions of space and time are social constructions, whether defined by social, economic, or political relations and units or by reference to physical (e.g., ecological, hydrological) characteristics.[4] There is no unique, theoretically superior substantive definition. Any primacy given to a particular type of time and space reflects the pragmatic political or theoretical and methodological purposes for which they are selected (Harvey 1996, 266). The choice of a certain spatiotemporality is not innocent with respect to the social relations that are thereby highlighted or rendered invisible (e.g., the spatiotemporality of many women's lives, colonized subjects, and the like). Natural and physical scientists tend to define space in terms of physical criteria whereby, for example, territorial, property, or administrative spaces and scales become secondary, subject to definition of space in terms of physical characteristics. For social scientists, social, political, or administrative demarcations of space tend to be the point of departure.

There is a rather taxing discussion of whether space is structural, normatively constructed, relational, or individual. We think this discussion is misconceived (also see the introduction to this volume). To be sure, notions of space are experienced and held individually, "via the experience of the subject's own body through the conscious self in movement" (Werlen 1988, 161). These experiences and the ideas of space vary considerably between different segments of the population, per age, gender, class, social status, in combination with idiosyncratic features. But each individual human being is born into social structures and organizations that are already full with social constructions of space within which that person is socialized.[5] In most contemporary societies there exists a broad array of coexisting social, religious, economic, and political constructions of space and places, which sometimes differ from one another and sometimes reinforce one another. Spaces and places often have moral or religious values attached to them. Inevitably,

individual notions of space are affected by these more general cultural and legal notions of space. This holds especially for those in which legally constructed
spaces create and legitimate social, economic, and political resources. These tend
to become resources in social interaction and power struggles (Harvey 1996, 44,
266). Space, in other words, is structural, normatively constructed, relational, and
individual at the same time.

Notions of space are inscribed into law, and thus acquire particular social,
political, and economic relevance. We call such abstract constructions categorical.[6] Such legal-institutional notions of space to some extent share the normative
and justificatory character of more general cultural-ideological notions of space,
but they tend to be more specific. The chronotopes that Valverde discusses in her
chapter in this volume are cases in point. Categorical legal constructions define
normatively the spaces for which law claims validity; they construct specific legal spaces and their legal relevance at different scales, using physical, economic,
social, and administrative criteria. Legal rules ascribe specific functions to such
spaces and localize rights and obligations of persons in them. With legal means,
territories—however vaguely or clearly they may be demarcated—are plotted on,
above, or below the terrestrial and marine surface of the earth. They range from
political territories, such as states, to internal administrative divisions of political territories, economic zones on the surface of land and water, and small plots
of property demarcated in cadastral registration systems. Legal rules also localize
people's rights and obligations in space, whether this is for purposes of acquiring state citizenship, organizing tax obligations, or establishing residence rights
and duties for married spouses. The internal differentiation and complexity of
modern legal systems has led to myriad overlapping and nested spaces, created
by legal regulations that pertain to specific domains of social and economic life
(Tickamyer 2000, 806). Each of these spaces is systemically linked to other spaces
and regulations at different scale, some more densely, others only loosely. Despite
all attempts of lawyers to create an image of a consistent body of law, regulations
within each legal system are often contradictory.

Legal constructions of space are, as it were, projected onto the geographical
space for which they claim validity—on "maps" of different scale, as Santos (1987)
has suggested in his "cartography of law." But the mere existence of such maps
does not mean that law actually exists within that space. Unless there is further
empirical evidence, legal constructions of space are in the books, on the maps,
on paper, and in the minds of people only as "imagined spaces" (Anderson 1991).
Postulating the "existence" of such legal constructions independent of further empirical evidence is inherent in the normativity of general legal rules that claim
validity here and there, now and in the future. Only when concretized can we

ascertain whether and in which form law actually exists in space, in the sense of becoming a point of orientation for social practices and relationships grounded in space. Concretized law gives actual meaning and acquires significance in the relations between person and organizations and the physical environment.[7]

## Space and Legal Pluralism

The notion of legal pluralism is a sensitizing concept that draws attention to the possibility that law of various kinds, with different foundations of legitimacy, validity, power, and authority, and with different degrees of institutionalization and formalization, can coexist within the same social space, often at different scales. Traditional ethnic laws usually claim validity and exist at an infrastate scale, although some transcend national boundaries. Human rights law is cosmopolitan in its claims. Transnational laws also transcend national boundaries. Religious laws usually claim universal validity for all believers.[8] Increasingly international organizations generate their own regulated spaces, whether catchment areas for water management or nature reserves, often crosscutting other important social, economic, administrative, or even national boundaries. Smith (in this volume) analyzes particularly disturbing examples in which international organizations and coalitions of national governments create new legal spaces defined by security and development.

Such plurality of cognitive and normative schemes of meaning and procedures provides actors with a range of options to structure interactions, transactions, and relationships. Plural legal orders produce more complex webs of overlapping spaces (Warren 2007). Multiple legal constructions of space open up multiple arenas for the exercise of political authority and for the localization of rights and obligations. In these arenas clashes occur in which diverging notions of political and legal space, loaded with economic and moral values, are mobilized against each other in strategic interactions over contested forms of political authority in the (sometimes violent) fight for control over resources. An early instance of contrasting economic moralities is the colonial legal treatment of natural resource environments. In the moral categories of expanding capitalist agriculture in the nineteenth-century colonies, land that was not cultivated in an efficient economic sense was deemed "waste." By contrast, according to many local legal systems, such land and forest represent the moral value of taking care of future generations of the community that owns the land. Other kinds of common property were subject to similar competing moral evaluations. For example, resources held as inalienable lineage property according to local law in West Sumatra served the moral good of perpetuating the lineage and, according to the moral values of the colonial state, were "not yet" accessible for "the market" and therefore "backward" (see F. von Benda-Beckmann and K. von Benda-Beckmann 2006b, 195). The colonial governments used their moral evaluation as an argument to disregard local property law and to claim authority to pass over rights to plantation owners to make the land economically productive, thereby expropriating the land from the indigenous population. But indigenous property law was not annihilated. After the fall of the Suharto regime in Indonesia, for example, land that was expropriated decades earlier was successfully reclaimed on the basis of the indigenous people's customary law when the political climate allowed for the reassertion of that law that had once seemed to have become obsolete (F. von Benda-Beckmann and K. von Benda-Beckmann 2013).

In such clashes divergent notions of political and legal space are pitted against each other (see Orlove 1991). In the pursuit of their economic and political objectives, actors may use different constructions of legally relevant spaces and project these onto or inscribe them into the same physical space and the associated political and administrative powers, such as villages, communities, private or state property on land, nature parks, game reserves, and so on.[9] Their strategy may be informed by the differences in lines of authority, the foundations for legitimation, or the differences in the basic categories by which spaces are defined. Their strategy may also be based on the systemic characteristics of those categories and on the social embeddedness of property and authority relationships.

Although the opposition between state law and local customary or indigenous law is the best-known form of legal pluralism, there may be other relevant constellations. Religious law may have conceptions of sacred places and what is allowed there that may contradict the law of the state, and possibly also traditional laws or other religious laws. Even within the same religion, different interpretations of the normative regime of spaces may be a source of deep conflict (Turner 2013). The plurality of categorical cognitive and normative schemes of meaning also widens the range for inscribing categorical notions into social spatial relationships. In our own work on resource management in the Moluccas, we showed how different spatial regimes, based on different versions of Ambonese traditional law called *adat*, have led to parallel and competing authority over spaces that has dominated village politics for centuries (see F. von Benda-Beckmann 1999; F. von Benda-Beckmann and K. von Benda-Beckmann 2009). Legal pluralism often has implications for who and what is considered an insider or an outsider. For example, when migrants from other regions of Indonesia settle in a village, they become citizens and residents with full political and economic rights and obligations according to governments' law, whereas according to the traditional law of the dominant population groups, they remain strangers with limited rights (see

F. von Benda-Beckmann and K. von Benda-Beckmann 2007, 2009; F. von Benda-Beckmann and Taale 1992). In other words, spatial relations are often "multinormative" and contextual, and what the "true" nature is depends on the perspective of the groups and persons that have authority in that context.

Multinormative spaces are complex phenomena; they are particularly problematic if regarded from a dynamic stance. The processes that create, sustain, and dissolve places all have their own specific temporality that is shaped by a complex interplay of physical, social, and legal factors. In the following sections we look more closely at some manifestations of that temporality and discuss the problems this poses under conditions of legal pluralism. We shall see that legal systems respond quite differently to what we call moving and alternating places. However, emerging and disappearing spaces not only may be multinormative; the incremental emergence and disappearance are a source of legal pluralism.

## MOVING PLACES

Legal places may literally move in space. This happens, for example, where rivers change their course. For example, as a result of the geophysical constitution of the Himalaya mountains, every rainy season in Nepal changes the riverbeds, so that agricultural fields and intakes of irrigation systems may disappear under tons of sediment. The owners of the submerged fields then negotiate how the land that has emerged because of the river's change of course is to be distributed and where the new intake is to be built. The space is considered the same, but the individual property places and irrigation intakes and canals have moved to new locations. The places of cultivation disappear—and reappear elsewhere—in repetition, thereby effectively moving (K. von Benda-Beckmann, Spiertz, and F. von Benda-Beckmann 1997; see also Blomley 2008). Local legal systems have a flexible way of dealing with this, but the sudden movement due to monsoon rains creates problems within the state property regimes that, as Blomley (2008, 1827) has pointed out, are predicated on "processes of legal simplification ... [that] ... relies upon a categorical logic" that does not adequately capture the moving nature of boundaries. Poor peasants who have no other place to cultivate than on the land immediately bordering on the river have only weak effective rights to their land when it comes to defending those in the context of the state legal system.

Legal places may also move as the result of the physical characteristics of vegetation. A striking example is that of sago gardens in the Moluccas. Sago starch from the trunk of the sago palm is the major food crop for Ambonese villagers. Cultivated palm trees are owned by the cultivator and as inherited family property (*pusaka*) by his male and female descendants. The starch has to be harvested before the palm enters into the flowering stage, because when the palm flowers, the accumulated starch is used for inflorescence and seeds. The palm reaches the flowering stage when it is between ten and twenty years of age. Sago palms have two reproductive strategies, by means of seeds or, more important vegetatively, through root systems called stools that produce suckers that form new palms, known as the "children" of the sago palm. By preventing sago palm trees from flowering and by allowing a few suckers to develop into new trunks, a stand of sago palms may be exploited for centuries in continuity. In the course of time the place of the sago stand travels. The roots (or stools) of the palm grow several meters sideward before they form suckers that develop into new palm trees, and the original palm tree dies after flowering or after having been harvested. After one or two palm generations, a stool may invade the area of another stand of sago palms that grew out of a different stool with a different owner. The new palms that grow out of a stool have the same legal status (usually family property) as the mother palm. If a sago owner has cleared a space in the forest and planted several sago stands, this does not create a problem because one sago owner will own the whole stand. However, sago is often planted to fill gaps between other vegetation in an existing garden. This may create a problem because it enhances the probability of sago palms growing in all directions, and this may interfere with rights that others may have to the other vegetation, including sago palms planted by others. Moreover, palm stools and stands are inherited by the descendants of the original acquirer, so that after a few generations the stand is owned by a complex set of right holders.[10] Thus, sago palms of different kind and different legal status may grow within the same space that is often part of a garden that has yet a different owner. The space of one particular sago stand thus keeps moving, encroaching into spaces of other sago stands and other types of vegetation, creating complex and overlapping legal places.

Moving legal places are often a result of moving people. This may occur when persons or groups are displaced by colonizers or "ethnocratic settler states" (Kedar 2006, 401), as a result of war, or because a population is evicted from a place that is redefined as nature reserve. Often the displaced groups consider the new location a temporary place, a diaspora, that exists as long as the conditions do not allow them to return to the original space. Here, they often intend to live as much as possible according to the laws of the place of origin, but over time those laws diverge more and more from those of the place of origin as they are adjusted to the social and legal context of the diaspora (on Moluccans in the Netherlands, see K. von Benda-Beckmann 2007). And if, as in the case of the Curonian Spit in Lithuania a new population, that was displaced elsewhere, settles in the place of origin, a similar change in the local laws occurs and the reminiscence that the people who have emigrated from there have of that place diverges more and more from the actual situation (Peleikis 2006).

Places may also move as a result of the way the people-space-power nexus is legally defined. While Western legal systems tend to define legal spaces and places primarily by reference to bounded territory, other legal systems have different approaches and may define places primarily by reference to persons. If those persons move, then their social and property spaces move with them. Bohannan (1967, 55) showed that the Tiv people of West Africa "see geography in the same image as they see social organization. The idiom of descent and genealogy provides not only the basis for lineage grouping, but also of territorial grouping and agricultural farm sites." The connections between kin groups and their physical surrounding were always temporary and moved on as cultivation and farm tenure moved on, and only vague reminiscences of the previous places remained in the collective memory of the group.

In short, places may move because physical characteristics of land or vegetation generate movement, as a result of forceful displacement, or because persons move and places are defined by reference to the persons occupying them. The way in which the multiplicity of legal regulation works out in such moving spaces can be fully grasped only when one looks closely at the temporalities of the movement.

## ALTERNATING LEGAL PLACES

Sometimes, the same space may be subject to different legal regulations, which are activated at different times. Who has access to the space and which kind of behavior is permitted there depends on the status that happens to be valid at a particular time. For example, the kind of physical injuries that are permitted on a sports field during a game are not allowed on the same place outside the sports context. Another example is the Jewish *eruv*, a religiously defined space that effectively exists only during the Shabbat. According to Orthodox rules, entering public spaces is prohibited on the Shabbat. Certain spaces, that during the rest of the week and for the non-Jewish population are public spaces, are redefined as a—temporary—religious space, which allows believers to go from their homes to the synagogue without offending religious laws (Siemiatycki 2005). The character of the space is defined by Jewish law, whereas state legal systems may be indifferent to this but condone or accept it as an internal regulation of the Jewish community. The conviction that such a construction is really necessary and prescriptive may not be shared by all members of the community of believers, but the marking assures those who wish to live according to those rules that they can do so.

Markets are yet another example of alternating legal places. As Turner (2005) has shown, on market days, a legal regime operates in the marketplace in the Sous in Morocco that differs substantially from the legal regime that applies on non-market days. Although it is quite common for men to carry weapons, and the use of weapons to carry out a conflict is not unusual, and to a certain degree is accepted or even encouraged, during market hours the market is viewed as an occasion to negotiate and settle disputes by peaceful means rather than violence. Carrying weapons on the market space and during market hours is strictly prohibited, and infringements of the prohibition are heavily sanctioned. The market has also become a place of legal contestation among the majority of the local population, with its market rules, and Salafists who try to impose their moral and legal rules. Thus, during market hours the marketplace becomes a different place from what it is in the periods between markets, and market time has become a time with competing legal regulations.

The transformation of places that occurs as a result of the alternating temporality of regulation is predicated on the fact that a physical space acquires specific social-economic or religious meanings.

## LEGAL SPACES THAT "FADE IN"

Although legal orders define the temporal existence and validity of spaces in their own terms, spaces do not necessarily begin or end according to prevailing normative definitions. They may start exerting an influence long before the law defines the beginning of a legal space. This is most markedly the case in countries that have entered or are in the process of entering the European Union (on rural Lithuania, see, e.g., Harboe Knudsen 2012). The EU space throws its legal shadow ahead, and persons in new member states began to behave as if they were under EU rule long before they were formally part of the EU space or before their country even obtained the status of aspirant member. The period of anticipation has its own temporal dynamics. It starts out haltingly by a few courageous persons who adjust agricultural production patterns to EU requirements, but as more people get involved over time, anticipation picks up speed and becomes more broadly shared. During this period people are faced with legal pluralism, for the anticipated new legal regime coexists—and sometimes collides—with the existing official legal order that is gradually fading out before being officially abolished (Harboe Knudsen 2012).

A remarkable example of such "fading in" spaces could be observed in Indonesia after the fall of the Suharto regime in 1998. Indonesian citizens began to effectively press human rights claims against the state long before the relevant conventions had been signed that would make the legal instruments formally applicable within Indonesia. People started anticipating becoming part of the legal space of political and civil human rights. By so doing, they took considerable risks, as it was unclear whether Indonesia would actually adopt the conventions. In some areas, such as West Sumatra, some courts and the police acted as if this were already the case and no longer applied the Indonesian laws that prohibited publicly criticizing the regime.[11]

Smith (in this volume) offers a particularly striking example of emerging spaces of international intervention, as, for example, in Afghanistan. Not only does the space-to-be-created begin to deeply affect the lives of the population before it is fully established, but also the projects are so complex that they have to operate under conditions of incremental regulation. The local population is expected to adjust to a regulatory regime that over a long period is only partially in place. In such periods of "fading in," it is entirely unclear for the majority of the population which laws are applicable and how rights and obligations are being implemented within their lived-in spaces. Anticipating a new, more tolerant legal regime in this context is a risky business that takes considerable courage.

Phases in which new spaces are fading in are typically characterized by the coexistence of the old legal order and an emerging new regulatory regime. The anticipation of a dimly understood economic EU regime, a constitutional reform as in Indonesia, or a regulatory regime that cannot be known because it exists only in rudimentary form as in the case of interventions that may or may not materialize in an uncertain future requires making investments and putting oneself temporarily at a disadvantage vis-à-vis local competitors, as well as taking high political risk. Such phases in which a territory is in the process of becoming part of a new legal space that is slowly fading in are therefore often characterized by a certain liminality.

## DISAPPEARING LEGAL SPACES

Legal spaces may disappear but continue to exist as social or physical spaces, and vice versa, and a space that has been abolished in terms of one legal system may continue to exist in terms of an alternative legal system. Legal spaces may disappear in a number of ways. If the legal construction is directly linked to physical characteristics, legal spaces may disappear when they physically cease to exist. The sea carves away the coast; a tsunami wipes out the coastal occupied zone; the wind displaces dunes covering villages that are rebuilt elsewhere, as happens on the Curonian Spit (Peleikis 2006). In cases of war, villages may be wiped out, or the population may be evicted and the buildings demolished so that only the vaguest traces are left of the space that once constituted the village.

Legal space may also physically disappear in a more regulated manner. Land may be intentionally inundated, as, for example, land adjacent to the rivers Rheine, Meuse, Mulde, and Elbe that serves as a reserve basin in case of high water, to avoid flooding in populated areas. Other examples are artificial lakes created for hydroelectric power, or the lakes made in exhausted lignite surface mines, that already had made the previous agricultural and village spaces disappear. Here the physical appearance of spaces changes because of the implementation of state regulations. Putting up fences may make property spaces that lie beyond the fence factually, if not legally or emotionally, disappear, as the fence between the German Democratic Republic (GDR) and Federal Republic of Germany, or the fences put up by Israel show (Blandy and Sibley 2010, 276; Braverman 2009). In these examples the disappearance of places is more or less enduring, if not altogether permanent.

Legal-political spaces may disappear because borderlines are redrawn so that they become part of a new political, social, economic, or administrative entity, as happened with the former GDR or the former Soviet Union. These disappearances are a result of political negotiations and legal regulation at different scales. They involve changes in authority and power relationships, and often new regulations or even a new legal regime. Such disappearing spaces also entail in one way or another exclusion, expropriation, and loss of rights for some and the establishment of new rights for others.

## LINGERING SPACES, LINGERING LAW

Once formally abolished, legal spaces do not necessarily disappear but may be maintained in practice or memory. There are many reasons spaces may linger on after having been officially abolished (F. von Benda-Beckmann and K. von Benda-Beckmann 2006a). One reason may be that the change in law is so contested that people cling to the old law, disregarding what the new law stipulates. It may also be technically impossible to undo all the regulations at once. Ideally, transition periods between an old and a new regulation last only a short period of time, but in practice they may last longer. This is especially the case where large-scale regulatory regimes are to be established, in which the process of lawmaking is complicated and time consuming. Just as emerging law generates a certain degree of legal pluralism, so does lingering law. It leaves some actors operating within that space in a somewhat liminal stage while it opens up opportunities for others. Such phases of overlapping regulation often turn out to be the period in which differences in power and wealth are forged that would be unlikely to happen under the old or the new legal regime.

Often the old spaces linger on in the terms of the very legal order by which they were abandoned. The most prominent example is the dismantling of the GDR and the disappearance of its territory. Despite the official abolition, the former space of the GDR is still legally and socially highly relevant, defining differences in salaries, old-age pensions, and social aid, and in many other ways (Thelen 2006). Peleikis (2006, 216–23) showed for the Curonian Spit in Lithuania how various laws of previous eras (e.g., pre–World War II, socialism) have lingered on, each with specific ways of defining spaces. For example, in a conflict among Protestants and Catholics about property rights to the village church that had been expropriated under Soviet rule, and after Lithuania's independence was to be returned to the religious community, each side based its claim on laws that had been abolished long ago but that had been valid in different periods of history. The majority of the population that now lives in the village is Catholic. They had been expelled from other regions within the Soviet Union and had immigrated into the village after World War II. They claimed rights to the building because they formed the vast majority of the current population and had used the church before it was expropriated. The very small Protestant community claimed property rights on the basis that the Protestant community had built the church long before World War II and that it had been their parish church until they had to flee. They were backed by emigrant descendants of people who had fled from the village toward the end of World War II and had since lived in Germany. When Lithuania allowed them entrance again, many had visited their village regularly and regarded themselves as its citizens. The initial skepticism among the local population that these returning emigrants might reclaim their houses soon faded, because the majority made it clear that they were not interested in doing so. But as members of the village community these emigrants felt entitled to actively support a property claim to the village church that the Protestant community was pursuing. This claim referred to the time when the village had been part of a different political space. In the end, the Protestants won, and the church was officially handed over to their community. However, a new Catholic Church building was erected for the Catholic majority in a prominent place, right in the village center, to acknowledge the fact that the majority of the population is of Catholic faith. Thus, different layers of place making at different temporal scales linger on and affect current claims to property spaces. The large-scale dislocation movements at the end of World War II, the abolishment of the Lithuanian state and its law, and the inclusion in the Soviet Union with its socialist law repeatedly changed the place that the village and its church had been. Withdrawal from the Soviet Union, independence, and entrance into the European Union—with its legal implications—once again re-made the village space and that of the church. The result is what Roquas (2002), in her analysis of conflicts over land and property in Honduras, has called "stacked law," an accumulation of layers of law of various temporal depth that have not disappeared with formal repeal but continue to exert their influence within concrete spaces, thereby creating a complex situation of legal pluralism within the state legal system.[12]

Sometimes, legal spaces linger on when law is captured and transformed into another type of law. Thus, much of what today is regarded as customary law in Latin America in fact used to be the law of the (colonial) state, as Nuijten and Lorenzo (2009) have demonstrated for Peru. A hacienda was once an institution defined by colonial law. Within the space of the hacienda a set of rules existed that regulated rights to the land and labor. Territorial strategies allowed hacienda owners to control labor far beyond the confines of the hacienda space itself. These laws have long been abolished by the state, but the local population, in particular its elites, have captured them and made them into their own local law. Rights to hacienda land and inheritance of such plots follow these rules. The regulations have moved from the realm of state law to that of local law. A hacienda is no longer a valid legal space under state law, but it continues to be so under what has become local law that coexists with a state regime that defines the space in a different way.

The lingering and capturing that we have discussed here is not confined to state law. The colonial experience of Indonesia, for example, reveals that local laws, called *adat*, have been captured by the state, for example, in regions of indirect rule, by which the spaces ruled by *adat* changed in a fundamental way. Before colonial rule, overlapping and nested spaces of authority were primarily defined by reference to persons who were ruled by a sultan or king. The sultan or king was the highest authority, but his power was limited, and he yielded no absolute power over lower authorities. Under colonial rule these authority spaces became fixed, with clearly defined boundaries. The authority of the rulers that was attached to these spaces expanded, while the lines of authority with lower rulers became more hierarchical. Thus, the colonial government captured the spaces of authority and reformulated them according to their views. This was in part a result of a clear strategy to control a heterogeneous population through simple lines of authority. In part it was a result of misunderstanding and misrepresentation of the indigenous authority spaces. However, in many parts of Indonesia these *adat* notions of authority have continued to live on, to some limited extent, as lived practice, but more often only in memory and as a dream for the future. In the post-Suharto era, some descendants of these former rulers have recaptured the state's interpretation of their *adat* and now claim authority over these spaces as territorially defined by the colonial government (a point we revisit later). The issue is politically highly contentious, and it remains to be seen how much authority they will manage to realize, but the *adat* authorities and the spaces they claim are today part of a widely shared imagination. The legal pluralism that for decades was of limited practical significance, if not dormant, has recently gained more currency than anyone had expected (see Klinken 2007; F. von Benda-Beckmann and K. von Benda-Beckmann 2013).

## ACCELERATING LEGAL SPACES

The study of globalization has sparked discussions about the temporalities of change. Concepts such as acceleration (Rosa 2006; Rosa and Scheuerman 2009), time-space compression (Giddens 1985), hyperglobalization (Giddens 1996), and hyperterritoriality (Delaney 2010, 138) all refer to the various social implications of accelerated change that is considered characteristic of modern society. Giddens has pointed to the messy and contradictory processes captured under the term globalization that entail both fragmentation and new forms of unity and solidarity.[13] Hirst and Thompson (2002, 2009) argue that globalization was stronger in the late nineteenth century. Although Held and colleagues (1999) acknowledge that certain sectors of social life are indeed subject to acceleration, they also point out that globalization is taking place at very different paces, depending on the place and position one has within global networks. In some sectors and in some places, globalization is hardly occurring. Yet despite these qualifiers, there is general agreement that acceleration and globalization, if not omnipresent, are nevertheless crucial features of current life. Globalization is accompanied by an ever-increasing stream of regulations. Enduring regulation is generally considered indispensable for predictable government and for orderly and reliable social and economic relations. Many regulations are therefore meant to establish a new legal regime that regulates once and for all the issue at stake, whether rights to land and natural resources, protection of the environment, migration, trade relations, or the financial world. These regimes create their own spaces in which certain actions are allowed or prescribed and others are discouraged or prohibited, including some persons and excluding others. Such regimes are often very complex, involving regulations at very different scale, including international treaties, national laws, and implementation regulations at subnational levels. However, the very regulations that are meant to establish certainty have a paradoxical effect. The paradox is that the more of such spatial regimes that are created and the more complex those are, the more they may come into conflict with other spaces that operate for other purposes, with their own regulations. The result is an incessant need for adjustment at different scales of regulation to create and maintain a minimum of coherence, but this undermines the very idea of durability. Instead of establishing new "regimes of continuity" (Delaney 2010, 138), these new regimes have to be so frequently adjusted that the spaces they create are everything but enduring.

The question is whether conditions of legal pluralism sharpen these effects or have an ameliorating effect. Local laws or religious law may not subject spaces to the same hectic change as the laws of a state administration, but such spaces of longer duration often come to overlap with spaces subject to rapid sequences of regulations. People operating under such conditions have to adjust their relationships and position within a space every time the regulations of that space are changed by one of the relevant legal systems. These paradoxical features can be clearly discerned in the struggles over village land in West Sumatra, where decentralization policies allow for increasing authority to lower-level legal actors to issue regulations (F. von Benda-Beckmann and K. von Benda-Beckmann 2013). The Indonesian example shows that such situations of legal pluralism, operating under conditions of decentralization and heightened international involvement, have left deep and complex imprints on the legal landscape, with new administrative spaces, new rules of inclusion and exclusion based on images of traditional social stratification, and new opportunities for local officials and the local population. Drawing on both international law and *adat* law, local communities claimed control over natural resource spaces that had been expropriated under colonial rule or by the Suharto regime. However, what the local communities were, what the status of their territory was, and who was to manage and control the territory was subject to intense disagreement. *Adat* authorities in the village claimed ultimate control because they represented the *adat* community that was the owner of the territory according to *adat* and made regulations about the use and exploitation of village commons. But unexpectedly, descendants of former kings and sultans claimed control over supravillage spaces on the basis of their interpretation of *adat*, which often deviated from local understandings of *adat*. Village governments claimed authority as the democratically elected representatives of the village community and issued their own regulations, thereby often restating *adat* property law. The district also claimed control as guardians of natural resources. Positioning themselves as independent levels of decentralized government, they made regulations without consulting higher levels of state administration. In a very long process of lawmaking at the national and provincial level, the province issued a regulation on village property that contradicted the existing national legislation, which in turn contradicted the new constitution. In addition to this, several international and bilateral donor agencies intervened and tried to introduce regulations about village property based on mistaken ideas of what local *adat* law entailed. In some cases legislators anticipated the potential changes expected to occur at different levels, but within districts and villages, rule makers often simply ignored any higher legislation. Decentralization generated much anxiety and fear, and in some cases it immobilized local government, which was completely at a loss as to what official regulations were applicable or might be applicable in the near future. Only a few years after the first decentralization operation had begun and revisions of the laws on local government were initiated, the initial enthusiasm had made place for disillusionment. The reforms, meant to streamline local government, were already taking back some of the authority that local governments had just began to use within their village. The village once again became a different space with a different power and authority structure (F. von Benda-Beckmann and K. von Benda-Beckmann 2009). The time frame of each of the processes of legislation was different and inconsistent with that of others, so that at any point in time actors involved in the management and use of village property were at a loss as to what the precise legal status of their village property was. For the village population the village was a legally multivalent but totally uncertain place in which they experienced continuous and haphazard legal change at different scales of administrative law, formal legislation, and *adat* law.

## CONCLUSIONS

We have sketched some vital implications of conceptualizing space and place with particular attention to their normative and legally pluralist dimensions. Looking at the legal regulation of space through a temporal lens reveals that law is not simply there; it begins and ends, comes and goes, is anticipated and lingers on. With it, spaces, as abstract categories, and places, as the concretized nexus between persons, relationships, and objects, come and go. We have shown that the geography of space and the pace with which a space's legal regimes change differ between legal systems and within legal systems. Arguably, with globalization these various and overlapping legal orders have become increasingly intertwined, so that what happens within one legal order tends to affect the others as well. Thus, even if the pace of change within religious law or within customary law is not as fast as in the laws of national states, the effect is that people have to operate in ever-changing constellations of overlapping spaces created by different legal orders. With the intensification of regulation that has become increasingly complex and the sensitive negotiations entailed in international and transboundary regulation that is often incrementally generated, the fading in and out of legal spaces becomes a more pronounced part of the process. The relative time in which old legal regimes linger on or new ones emerge increases in relation to the total duration of a regulatory regime. The paradox of this is that attempts to create regulatory regimes intended to endure in effect need so much and such frequent adaptation that they generate all but the unambiguous and enduring legal spaces that they intended to create. Instead, spaces are increasingly subject to multiple legal regulation with different legal requirements, positions of authority, and procedures in which actors try to navigate without the necessary information. The result is that many people are uncertain about the place they are living in and what it allows or requires them to do. This chapter has sketched some of the most important temporal dimensions of spaces. The examples discussed suggest that the fading in and out and the entailed multiple legality of spaces are the least understood aspects of the temporality of space. Yet they are critical for the power relations within multinormative spaces and for the degree of legal uncertainty that persons living in those spaces are facing. There is an urgent need for the geography of law to look more systematically into the temporalities of space and thereby pay more attention to the dynamics of legal pluralism.

## NOTES

1. Stanford Law Review (vol. 48, no. 5) published a special issue on law and geography in 1996. Blomley, Delaney, and Ford (2001) published a reader on the geographies of law, and Holder and Harrison (2006) published a large volume on law and geography (see also Blomley 1994, 2006; Delaney 2006, 2010; Kedar 2006; Massey 2005; Taylor 2006). On the spatial turn in social science, see Appadurai (1990); Giddens (1979, 1984, 1985); Harvey (1996); Lash and Urry (1994). On the significance of the spatial and the temporal for ethnography, see Marcus (1992). On spatializing in the global context, see Appadurai (1990, 2003); Featherstone and Lash (1995); Low and Lawrence-Zúñiga (2003); Perry and Maurer (2003); Robertson (1990); Tsing (2005); F. von Benda-Beckmann, K. von Benda-Beckmann, and Griffiths (2005, 2009). On governance and scale, see Valverde (2008).

2. For legal pluralism and the relationship between law and space, see F. von Benda-Beckmann (1999, 2001); F. von Benda-Beckmann and K. von Benda-Beckmann (1991); F. von Benda-Beckmann, K. von Benda-Beckmann, and Griffiths (2009).

3. Within the anthropology of law we find many spatial metaphors. "Semi-autonomous social fields" (Moore 1973), "rooms" and "landscapes" (Galanter 1981, 1983), "structural places" (Santos 1985), and the "external-internal" (Kidder 1979) usually refer to social spaces and boundaries and are unsuitable for an analysis of the interdependence of social, legal, and physical spaces. See F. von Benda-Beckmann and K. von Benda-Beckmann (1991); F. von Benda-Beckmann, K. von Benda-Beckmann, and Griffiths (2009).

4. The "social constructivist" character of space must be acknowledged, but whatever social constructions of space there may be, the physical environment is there to be constructed while having an existence independent from whatever social construction that may be given to them.

5. See Giddens (1985); Harvey (1996). Blomley, in this volume, refers to the same idea with his notion of habit and custom.

6. See F. von Benda-Beckmann and K. von Benda-Beckmann (1994, 1999); F. von Benda-Beckmann, K. von Benda-Beckmann, and Wiber (2006); F. von Benda-Beckmann, K. von Benda-Beckmann, and Griffiths (2009).

7. The barbed fences would be such an example of what Blomley (2006, 23–24) calls the material force of law.

8. Delaney (2010) is one of the few who explicitly deals with other normative orders than state law. "Nomic traces" serve to capture the totality of norms that constitute and are constituted by space, including rules of etiquette, customs, religion, and written statutory law or court decisions. The term *law* remains reserved for a state legal system. According to this view, norms obtain a fundamentally different character once they have been captured by the law of the state. Authors working on legal pluralism have tried to escape this kind of statism.

9. For Costa Rica, see Brooijmans (1997); for the United States, see Geisler and Bedford (1996); for East Kalimantan, see Bakker (2009).

10. See Brouwer (1996); Ellen (1978); Volker (1925); F. von Benda-Beckmann (1990); Taale (1990).

11. See F. von Benda-Beckmann and K. von Benda-Beckmann (2013).

12. Santos (2006, 47) uses the metaphor of palimpsest.

13. For a critique on hyperglobalization and its skeptics, see Giddens (1996).


## REFERENCES

Anderson, Ben. 1991. *Imagined Communities*. London: Verso.

Appadurai, Arjun. 1990. "Disjuncture and Difference in the Global Cultural Economy." *Theory, Culture, and Society* 7 (2): 295–310.

———. 2003. "Sovereignty without Territoriality: Notes for a Post-national Geography." In *The Anthropology of Space: Locating Culture*, edited by Setha M. Low and David Lawrence-Zúñiga, 337–49. Oxford, UK: Blackwell.

Bakker, Laurens. 2009. "The Sultan's Map: Arguing One's Land in Pasir." In *Spatializing Law: An Anthropological Geography of Law in Society*, edited by Franz von Benda-Beckmann, Keebet von Benda-Beckmann, and Anne Griffiths, 95–113. Farnham, UK: Ashgate.

Benda-Beckmann, Franz von. 1990. "Sago, Law and Food Security on Ambon: Food Security versus Economic Development." In *The World Food Crisis: Food Security in Comparative Perspective*, edited by J. I. Hans Bakker, 157–99. Toronto: Canadian Scholars' Press.

———. 1999. "Multiple Legal Constructions of Socio-Economic Spaces: Resource Management and Conflict in the Central Moluccas." In *Frontiers and Borderlands: Anthropological Perspectives*, edited by Michael Rösler and Tobias Wendl, 131–58. Frankfurt: Lang.

———. 2001. "On the Reproduction of Law: Micro and Macro in the Time-Space Geography of Law." In *Begegnung und Konflikt. Eine kulturanthropologische Bestandsaufnahme*, edited by Wolfgang Fikentscher, 119–31. Munich: C. H. Beck Verlag.

Benda-Beckmann, Franz von, and Keebet von Benda-Beckmann. 1991. "Law in Society: From Blindman's-Bluff to Multilocal Law." *Recht der Werkelijkheid* 1: 119–39.

———. 1994. "Coping with Insecurity." In *Focaal* 22–23: 7–31.

———. 1999. "A Functional Analysis of Property Rights, with Special Reference to Indonesia." In *Property Rights and Economic Development: Land and Natural Resources in*

*Southeast Asia and Oceania*, edited by Toon van Meijl and Franz von Benda-Beckmann, 15–56. London: Kegan Paul.

———, eds. 2006a. "Dynamics of Plural Legal Orders." *Journal of Legal Pluralism and Unofficial Law* 53–54: 1–270.

———. 2006b. "How Communal Is Communal and Whose Communal Is It? Lessons from Minangkabau." In *Changing Properties of Property*, edited by Franz von Benda-Beckmann, Keebet von Benda-Beckmann, and Melanie G. Wiber, 194–217. New York: Berghahn Books.

———. 2007. *Social Security between Past and Future: Ambonese Networks of Care and Support*. Münster: LIT Verlag.

———. 2009. "Contested Spaces of Authority in Indonesia." In *Spatializing Law: An Anthropological Geography of Law in Society*, edited by Franz von Benda-Beckmann, Keebet von Benda-Beckmann, and Anne Griffiths, 115–35. Farnham, UK: Ashgate.

———. 2013. *Political and Legal Transformations of an Indonesian Polity: The Nagari from Colonisation to Decentralisation*. Cambridge: Cambridge University Press.

Benda-Beckmann, Franz von, Keebet von Benda-Beckmann, and Anne Griffiths. 2005. "Mobile People, Mobile Law: An Introduction." In *Mobile People, Mobile Law: Expanding Legal Relations in a Contracting World*, edited by Franz von Benda-Beckmann, Keebet von Benda-Beckmann, and Anne Griffiths, 1–25. Aldershot, UK: Ashgate.

———, eds. 2009. *Spatializing Law: An Anthropological Geography of Law in Society*. Farnham, UK: Ashgate.

Benda-Beckmann, Franz von, Keebet von Benda-Beckmann, and Melanie G. Wiber, eds. 2006. *Changing Properties of Property*. New York: Berghahn Books.

Benda-Beckmann, Franz von, and Tanja Taale. 1992. "The Changing Laws of Hospitality: Guest Labourers in the Political Economy of Rural Legal Pluralism." In *Law as a Resource in Agrarian Struggles*, edited by Franz von Benda-Beckmann and Menno van der Velde, 33:61–87. Wageningen, The Netherlands: Pudoc.

Benda-Beckmann, Keebet von. 2007. "Developing Families: Moluccan Women and Changing Patterns of Social Security in the Netherlands." In *Social Security between Past and Future: Ambonese Networks of Care and Support*, edited Franz von Benda-Beckmann and Keebet von Benda-Beckmann, 257–79. Berlin: LIT Verlag.

Benda-Beckmann, Keebet von, Joep Spiertz, and Franz von Benda-Beckmann. 1997. "Disputing Water Rights: Scarcity of Water in Nepal Hill Irrigation." In *The Scarcity of Water: Emerging Legal and Policy Responses*, edited by Edward H. P. Brans, Esther J. de Haan, André Nollkaemper, and Jan Ritzema, 224–42. London: Kluwer International.

Blandy, Sarah, and David Sibley. 2010. "Law, Boundaries and the Production of Space." *Social and Legal Studies* 19: 275–84.

Blomley, Nicholas K. 1994. *Law, Space, and the Geographies of Power*. New York: Guilford.

———. 2006. "From 'What?' to 'So What?' Law and Geography in Retrospect." In *Law and Geography*, edited by Jane Holder and Carolyn Harrison, 17–34. Oxford: Oxford University Press.

———. 2008. "Simplification Is Complicated: Property, Nature, and the Rivers of Law." *Environment and Planning* 40 (8): 1825–40.

Blomley, Nicholas K., David Delaney, and Richard T. Ford, eds. 2001. *The Legal Geographies Reader: Law, Power, and Space*. Oxford, UK: Blackwell.

Bohannan, Paul. 1967. "Africa's Land." In *Tribal and Peasant Economies*, edited by George Dalton, 51–60. Austin: University of Texas Press.

Braverman, Irus. 2009. "Uprooting Identities: The Regulation of Olive Trees in the Occupied West Bank." *PoLAR* 32: 237–64.

Brooijmans, Willemien. 1997. "The Plains of Tortuguero: Tropical Paradise or Paradise Lost? Natural Resources, Environment and Legal Pluralism." In *Law and Anthropology* 9: 258–301.

Brouwer, Arie R. 1996. "Natural Resources, Sustainability and Social Security: Simplifying Discourses and the Complexity of Actual Resource Management in a Central Moluccan Village." In *Remaking Maluku: Social Transformation in Eastern Indonesia*, edited by David Mearns and Chris Healey, 64–79. Darwin, Australia: Northern Territory University, Centre for Southeast Asian Studies.

Delaney, David. 2006. "Beyond the Word: Law as a Thing of This World." In *Law and Geography*, edited by Jane Holder and Carolyn Harrison, 67–84. Oxford: Oxford University Press.

———. 2010. *The Spatial, the Legal and the Pragmatics of World-Making: Nomospheric Investigations*. Abingdon, UK: Routledge.

Ellen, Roy F. 1978. *Nuaulu Settlement and Ecology: An Approach to the Environmental Relations of an Eastern Indonesian Community*. Verhandelingen van het Koninklijk Instituut voor 'Taal-', Land- en Volkenkunde 83. The Hague: Martinus Nijhoff.

Engel, David. 1987. "Law, Time and Community." *Law and Society Review* 21: 605–38.

Featherstone, Mike, and Scott Lash. 1995. "Globalization, Modernity and the Spatialization of Social Theory." In *Global Modernities*, edited by Mike Featherstone, Scott Lash, and Roland Robertson, 1–24. London: Sage.

French, Rebecca. 2001. "Time in Law." *University of Colorado Law Review* 72: 663–748.

Galanter, Marc. 1981. "Justice in Many Rooms; Courts, Private Ordering and Indigenous Law." *Journal of Legal Pluralism* 19: 1–47.

———. 1983. *Reading the Landscape of Disputes: What We Know and Don't Know (and Think We Know) about Our Allegedly Litigious Society*. Madison: University of Wisconsin Law School.

Geertz, Clifford. 1973. *The Interpretation of Cultures: Selected Essays*. New York: Basic Books.

Geisler, Charles, and Barbara L. Bedford. 1996. *Who Owns the Ecosystem?* Madison: Land Tenure Center, University of Wisconsin–Madison.

Giddens, Anthony. 1979. *Central Problems in Social Theory: Action, Structure and Contradiction in Social Analysis*. London: Macmillan Press.

———. 1984. "Agency, Institution, and Time-Space Analysis." In *Advances in Social Theory and Methodology: Toward an Integration of Micro- and Macro-Sociologies*, edited by Karin Knorr-Cetina and Aaron V. Cicourel, 161–74. Boston: Routledge and Kegan Paul.

———. 1985. "Time, Space and Regionalisation." In *Social Relations and Spatial Structures*, edited by Derek Gregory and James Urry, 265–95. Basingstoke, UK: Macmillan.

———. 1996. "Essential Matter: Globalization Excerpts from a Keynote Address at the UNRISD Conference on Globalization and Citizenship." UN Research Institute for Social Development. http://www.unrisd.org/unrisd/website/newsview.nsf/%28http News%29/3F2A5BF8EF7300D480256B750053C7EC?OpenDocument.

Goldschmidt, Walter. 1966. *Comparative Functionalism*. Berkeley: University of California Press.

Greenhouse, Carol J. 1989. "Just in Time: Temporality and the Cultural Legitimation of Law." *Yale Law Review* 98: 1631–51.

———. 1996. *A Moment's Notice: Time Politics across Cultures*. Ithaca, NY: Cornell University Press.

Harboe Knudsen, Ida. 2012. *New Lithuania in Old Hands: Effects and Outcomes of Europeanization in Rural Lithuania*. London: Anthem Press.

Harvey, David. 1996. *Justice, Nature and the Geography of Difference*. Oxford, UK: Blackwell.

Held, David, Andrew McGrew, David Goldblatt, and Jonathan Perraton. 1999. *Global Transformations: Politics, Economics and Culture*. Cambridge, UK: Polity Press.

Hirst, Paul Q., and Grahame Thompson. 2002. "The Future of Globalization." *Cooperation and Conflict: Journal of the Nordic International Studies Association* 37: 247–65.

———. 2009. *Globalization in Question: The International Economy and the Possibilities of Governance*. Cambridge, UK: Polity Press.

Holder, Jane, and Carolyn Harrison, eds. 2006. *Law and Geography*. Current Legal Issues 5. Oxford: Oxford University Press.

Kedar, Alexandre S. 2006. "On the Legal Geography of Ethnocratic Settler States: Notes towards a Research Agenda." In *Law and Geography*, edited by Jane Holder and Carolyn Harrison, 401–41. Oxford: Oxford University Press.

Khan, Liaquat Ali. 2009. "Temporality of Law." *McGeorge Law Review* 40: 55–106.

Kidder, Robert L. 1979. "Towards an Integrated Theory of Imposed Law." In *The Imposition of Law*, edited by Sandra B. Burman and Barbara E. H. Bond, 289–306. New York: Academic Press.

Klinken, Gerry van. 2007. "Return of the Sultans: The Communitarian Turn in Local Politics." In *The Revival of Tradition in Indonesian Politics: The Deployment of Adat from Colonialism to Indigenism*, edited by Jamie S. Davidson and David Henley, 149–69. London: Routledge.

Lash, Scott, and John Urry. 1994. *Economies of Signs and Space*. London: Sage.

Leach, Edmund R. 1961. *Rethinking Anthropology*. London: Athlone Press.

Low, Setha M., and David Lawrence-Zúñiga, eds. 2003. *The Anthropology of Space and Place: Locating Culture*. Oxford, UK: Blackwell and Carlton.

Marcus, George. 1992. "Past, Present and Emergent Identities: Requirements for Ethnographies of Late Twentieth-Century Modernity Worldwide." In *Modernity and Identity*, edited by Scott Lash and Jonathan Friedman, 309–30. Oxford, UK: Blackwell.

Massey, Doreen. 2005. *For Space*. London: Sage Publications.

Moore, Sally F. 1973. "Law and Social Change: The Semi-Autonomous Social Field as an Appropriate Subject of Study." *Law and Society Review* 7 (4): 719–46.

Nuijten, Monique, and David Lorenzo. 2009. "Peasant Community and Territorial Strategies in the Andean Highlands of Peru." In *Spatializing Law: An Anthropological Geography of Law in Society*, edited by Franz von Benda-Beckmann, Keebet von Benda-Beckmann, and Anne Griffiths, 31–55. Farnham, UK: Ashgate.

Orlove, Benjamin S. 1991. "Mapping Reeds and Reading Maps: The Politics of Representation in Lake Titicaca." *American Ethnologist* 18: 3–38.

Peleikis, Anja. 2006. "Whose Heritage? Legal Pluralism and the Politics of the Past: A Case Study from the Curonian Spit (Lithuania)." *Journal of Legal Pluralism and Unofficial Law* 53–54: 209–37.

Perry, Richard W., and Bill Maurer, eds. 2003. *Globalisation under Construction: Governmentality, Law and Identity*. Minneapolis: University of Minnesota Press.

Robertson, Roland. 1990. "Mapping the Global Condition: Globalization as the Central Concept." In *Global Culture: Nationalism, Globalization and Modernity*, edited by Mike Featherstone, 15–30. London: Sage Publications.

Roquas, Esther. 2002. *Stacked Law: Land, Property and Conflict in Honduras*. Thela Latin America Series. Amsterdam: Rozenberg Publishers.

Rosa, Hartmut. 2006. *Beschleunigung: Die Veränderung der Zeitstrukturen in der Moderne.* Frankfurt: Suhrkamp.

Rosa, Hartmut, and William Scheuerman, eds. 2009. *High-Speed Society: Social Acceleration, Power, and Modernity.* University Park: Pennsylvania State University Press.

Santos, Boaventura de Sousa. 1985. "On Modes of Production of Law and Social Power." *International Journal of the Sociology of Law* 13: 299–336.

———. 1987. "Law: A Map of Misreading—Toward a Post-Modern Conception of Law." *Journal of Law and Society* 14: 279–302.

———. 2006. "The Heterogeneous State and Legal Pluralism in Mozambique." *Law and Society Review* 40: 39–75.

Siemiatycki, Myer. 2005. "Contesting Sacred Urban Space: The Case of the *Eruv.*" *Journal of International Migration and Integration* 6: 255–70.

Taale, Tanja. 1990. "Looking for a Livelihood in Hila: Continuity and Change in Land Use and Its Implications for Social Security in an Ambonese Village." Unpublished master's thesis, Wageningen University, Wageningen, The Netherlands.

Taylor, William, ed. 2006. *The Geography of Law: Landscape, Identity and Regulation.* Oxford, UK: Hart Publishing.

Thelen, Tatjana. 2006. "Law and Mutual Assistance in Families: A Comparison of Socialist Legacies in Hungary and Eastern Germany." In *Dynamics of Plural Legal Orders* 53–54: 177–207.

Tickamyer, Ann R. 2000. "Space Matters! Spatial Inequality in Future Sociology." *Contemporary Sociology* 29: 805–13.

Tsing, Anna L. 2005. *Friction: An Ethnography of Global Connection.* Princeton, NJ: Princeton University Press.

Turner, Bertram. 2005. "Transnational Legal Standards and the Local Market as Legal Focus in the Moroccan Countryside: Readjusting Legal Action in Time and Space." Paper presented at the international conference "Developing Anthropology of Law in a Transnational World: Territoriality and Time." Edinburgh University, June 9–11.

———. 2013. "Religious Subtleties in Disputing: Spatiotemporal Inscriptions of Faith in the Nomosphere in Rural Morocco." In *Religion in Disputes,* edited by Franz von Benda-Beckmann, Keebet von Benda-Beckmann, and Martin Ramsted, 55–71. Basingstoke, UK: Palgrave Macmillan.

Valverde, Mariana. 2008. "Analyzing the Governance of Security: Jurisdiction and Scale." *Behemoth: A Journal on Civilisation* 1: 3–15.

Volker, T. 1925. "Het Recht van Sasi in de Molukken." *Adatrechtbundel* 24: 296–313.

Warren, Carol. 2007. "*Adat* in Balinese Discourse and Practice: Locating Citizenship and the Commonweal." In *The Revival of Tradition in Indonesian Politics: The Deployment of Adat from Colonialism to Indigenism,* edited by Jamie S. Davidson and David Henley, 170–202. London: Routledge.

Werlen, Benno. 1988. *Society, Action and Space: An Alternative Human Geography.* London: Routledge.

# "TIME THICKENS, TAKES ON FLESH"

## Spatiotemporal Dynamics in Law

*Mariana Valverde*

This chapter begins by showing that the success of the law and geography literature has had the unintended effect of reviving an old metaphysical fallacy, namely, treating space and time as abstract and separate entities. Kant's critique of the objectivist metaphysics of space and time can therefore be usefully revived today as an antidote for the tendency to objectify and isolate space that I argue is inherent—though not inevitable—in law and geography as a field of inquiry. If legal geography's first theoretical risk is the unwitting reification of space and the black boxing of the very processes that many studies open up and problematize, a second and closely related problem is the analytic marginalization of temporality. Many law and geography studies do pay attention to history; but the historicizing of legal spaces that is often included within legal geographical studies (and in critical legal studies generally) captures only one aspect of temporality's many flows and dynamics. How recent work exploring some of the nonhistorical temporalities of law might converse with studies of legal space so as to bring together temporal and spatial dimensions of sociolegal processes is not yet clear. But by way of experimenting with ways to think about spatiotemporalization processes in a pluralistic and dynamic manner, the chapter concludes with a reflection on the possible adaptation, for legal analysis purposes, of Mikhail Bakhtin's oft-mentioned but rarely used notion of chronotopes.

## THE INTELLECTUAL CONTEXT: PRIVILEGING SPACE AS THEORETICALLY INTERESTING WHILE REDUCING TEMPORALITY TO EMPIRICAL HISTORY

Since its inception, the law and society movement has defined its distinction in terms of object studied: the mutual constitution of legal and social relations. In regard to both methods and theory, as distinct from subject matter, sociolegal scholarship has borrowed tools from various schools of critical social science, from Marxist structuralist theories of world capitalism to anthropological tools that shed light on the legal consciousness of ordinary people at more local and human scales. Some sociolegal scholars are also remembering, rather belatedly, that legal thought and legal practice can themselves contribute something by way of both theory and method to the interdisciplinary project, rather than act merely as objects of study (Benson, in this volume; Riles 2005; Valverde 2009). But even when law's "technicalities" are highlighted, this move is mainly an antidote to sociological determinism. Paying attention to law's technicalities is certainly not a call to "Durkheimize" legal studies by declaring that the field (sociolegal studies in general or legal geography in particular) is characterized by a single and unique set of methods and/or theories.

The epistemological pluralism that is produced as a result of the fact that law and society scholars share an object of study but do not attempt to generate a unique set of research methods is conducive to pleasant, nonconfrontational professional relationships; and the Law and Society Association is indeed known for friendliness and a marked absence of heated theoretical controversies. But this pluralism has its own risks, because respect for others' perspectives can easily turn into slapdash eclecticism. Furthermore, the desire to be open to new perspectives and learn something from every encounter can unwittingly act as a brake on the collective and individual reflexivity that all scholarly pursuits need to cultivate (see Braverman, in this volume).

In keeping with the tradition of borrowing various theories to study legal processes, sociolegal studies has witnessed much enthusiasm, in recent years, for theoretical explorations of space and spatial governance; but we have had few collective reflections on the reasons for and the implications of this trend. The fact that sessions on legal geography draw large numbers of people at Law and Society Association meetings, whereas legal history is not seen as fashionable or theoretical (even though law schools, institutionally resistant to change, generally employ legal historians but not legal geographers), appears to be a trend whose driving forces are mysterious or simply invisible to the very people caught up in it. Why legal history should appear as antiquated and empiricist while legal geography appears as youthful, theoretical, and trendy is not a question that our current academic arrangements encourage us to ask.

But whatever the reasons, there is no doubt that the abstract category of "space" has acquired a strongly theoretical patina in recent years. Doreen Massey, unusual among theoretical geographers for engaging in a sustained reflexive critique of the dangers of privileging space as a category, helpfully strings together some quotes, drawn from texts already sanctioned as major theoretical contributions in geography, that demonstrate the pitfalls of the collective rush to wave the banner of "space": "'Space' is very much on the agenda these days. . . . 'It is *space, not time,* that hides consequences from us' (Berger) . . . 'that new spatiality implicit in the postmodern' (Jameson); 'it is *space rather than time* which is the distinctively significant dimension of contemporary capitalism' (Urry)" (Massey 1994, 249, emphasis added; see also Massey 2005). On his part, David Harvey (who, to give him credit, includes history as a dimension of analysis in some of his work) features Kant in a prominent position in his book on cosmopolitanism—but instead of engaging with the critique of objectivist notions of time and space developed in the transcendental aesthetic, Harvey takes it for granted that if Kant is to have any interest today, it is as a theorist of "space" and, indeed, even as a geographer. He thus takes a few trite comments made by Kant about exotic countries and climates and recuperates them as protogeographical insights: "it is possible to reconstruct some of Kant's putative principles of geographical knowledge from the general corpus of his writings" (Harvey 2009, 31). In the same book Harvey berates assorted other thinkers, from Newton to Heidegger to Martha Nussbaum, for being unaware of "geographical realities" (116), a comment that simply assumes that spatial analyses promoted by geographers ought to be hegemonic throughout the human sciences.

The simultaneous black boxing and privileging of geography that is effected in Harvey's text is not necessarily typical of either geography or spatially oriented social theory; the introduction to this volume, for example, makes no claims about geography as the queen of the sciences. However, as Doreen Massey notes, all manner of influential theorists counterpose "space" as such to "time" as such, whether in grand ontological claims or in methodological assumptions embedded in research programs (Ed Soja being one of Massey's bêtes noires). Historians have not been rushing to defend "time" as such as a category of analysis, perhaps because few of them are theoretically inclined, and those who are inclined are more likely to read philosophy or anthropology than geography. But however one-sided the battle between advocates of "space" and those of "time" may be, Massey is certainly diagnosing an important problem that haunts not only geography but also sociolegal studies of spatial governance.

Sociolegal discussions of space often import the binary and reified construction of "time versus space" critiqued by Massey into research questions. One common move facilitated by the time-space binary is that while temporal dimensions are by no means neglected in legal geography, time is reduced to history—to the neglect not only of lived temporality but also of the ahistorical temporalities of the common law, and of the aboriginal and spiritual temporalities that ground many non-Western legalities (Appadurai 1996; Chakrabarty 2000). To put it differently, the way in which legal spaces are constituted historically is an important, and indeed central, element in many studies by legal geographers;[1] but the temporal dimension of human experience is all too often reduced to a rather atheoretical notion of history. By contrast, "space" appears as a privileged object of philosophical inquiry, as is seen, for example, in the influential anthology *Thinking Space* (Crang and Thrift 2000) and in discussions among theoretical geographers about "scale"—discussions that presuppose that only spatial scale is theoretically interesting, not temporal scales (e.g., Herod and Wright 2002).[2]

Thus, the spatial turn in sociolegal studies contains and effects a process that is not mentioned in either social theorists' discussions of "the end of temporality" (Jameson 2003) or in sociolegal arguments in favor of spatial analysis: the privileging of space as somehow more theoretically interesting than time, a move that goes hand in hand with the reduction of time to history. This dual move has allowed some promoters of the new spatial analyses to slide from the very plausible remark that the nineteenth century's historicist arguments are inadequate for today to what amounts to a metaphysical claim that temporality as such is old fashioned and perhaps irrelevant, at least theoretically irrelevant.

It is worth emphasizing that the conceptual moves just described are by no means indigenous to legal geography, because, in keeping with the usual sociolegal habit of borrowing theories, studies of law and geography generally defer to theorists working not on law specifically but at a more abstract scale. Frederic Jameson is one such theorist whose work is read across many disciplines. In relation to the issue of reifying time and space, Jameson's grandiloquent phrase "the end of temporality" serves as the title of an article in which he identifies the twentieth century's modernist aesthetic and theoretical sensibilities with time as such and postmodern sensibilities in turn with spatialization. (Space, incidentally, is somehow always already global, for Jameson as well as for many theoretical geographers). Admittedly, Jameson's text is not a polemical statement against time or history. Instead, it wavers between describing the current intellectual phenomenon of privileging and reifying space, on the one hand, and embracing it, on the other hand. But whether describing or prescribing, Jameson's text repeatedly performs a crucial slippage between the defects of old-fashioned historicism and the demise of temporality as such. Jameson's observation that postmodern sensibilities (not just postmodern theory) neglect both historicity and personal memory is quietly ratcheted up to become a general diagnosis of the aesthetics of late capitalism in the urban West (which for Jameson is the material basis of what he calls, in a highly reified term, "postmodern*ism*").[3] Whether the postmodern sensibilities that Jameson constructs as particularly spatial are to be embraced or simply taken as fact remains unclear; but what is clear is that for Jameson, as for David Harvey, there is a strong link between the socioeconomic structure of the consumer societies of the late-capitalist West, on the one hand, and "the end of temporality," on the other hand. To compound the conceptual problem, Jameson does not always distinguish between temporality as an objective dimension of life and temporality as a vector of analysis. One gets the impression that it is the latter, not the former, that concerns him; but at times it seems that he is claiming that space really is more important in today's social relations, a claim that, as mentioned earlier, not only is wholly unverifiable but also has the effect of making the reified abstraction "space" seem more real than the struggles and relationships that concepts in social theory should help to illuminate.

By contrast with theorists like Jameson, sociolegal scholars rarely engage in the kind of global-scale grand theorizing that privileges the most abstract formulations that one can possibly generate out of existing problematics (a genre in which for some reason male Marxist geographers excel). But the temptation to ratchet up one's analysis in the direction of higher levels of abstraction is always present. This can be discerned in recent work by David Delaney, one of the founders of the law and geography literature and author of the well-regarded 2010 book *The Spatial, the Legal, and the Pragmatics of World-Making: Nomospheric Investigations.*

Delaney's book offers many concrete vignettes, but its main purpose is to offer a few philosophical neologisms. The key term *nomosphere* is defined as the combination or the joint action of space with the norms and rules that form the subject of sociolegal studies: "the nomic includes, for example, the rules of politeness . . . and the social rules or norms governing gender, sexuality, or race" (Delaney 2010, 26–27). The observation that power, both legal and informal, is exercised through spatial governance (meaning both the governance of space and the governance of people and problems through space) is certainly a useful insight, and Delaney's work has given many scholars inspiration for their own work, as seen in several chapters in this book. But to engage in concrete analyses of spatialized power relations, do we need a neologism that takes the grammatical form of a noun (*nomosphere*), and thus constantly risks reifying sociolegal relations?[4] Why is it not sufficient to simply highlight the spatial dimensions of all governance, legal and extralegal, formal and informal? Does the production of terms such as *nomosphere* have the effect of positing the existence, even as a concept, of space in general? Delaney is far too sophisticated to make or support metaphysical claims; despite the analogy with *stratosphere* and *atmosphere*, he does not claim that the nomosphere exists objectively somewhere. And yet terms such as *nomicity* and *nomosphere* have the effect—or can have the effect, at any rate—of reifying the spatial and privileging, a priori, spatial over temporal analyses.

The same effects flow from other neologisms used by other legal geographers—for example, Michael Smith's *geolegality* (Smith, in this volume). Although no doubt useful in intellectually sparring for position with proponents of geopolitics,

*geolegality* is a term that if taken ontologically (rather than as a tactical intervention in a debate about disciplinary issues and the prestige of different fields) runs
the risk of privileging and isolating space as such. In my view, Smith's novel insights into state practices should get all of the reader's attention instead of being
read as examples or forms of something as abstract as "geolegality."[5]

But let us return to Delaney's book, not out of any polemical motive but precisely because it is both influential and sophisticated. The book avoids grandiose
claims about "the end of temporality"; but nevertheless, the spatial dimensions are
treated more carefully and thoroughly than the temporal dimensions, which in
my view is an effect of the more widespread tendency to treat space as more philosophically interesting than time. A typical passage reads: "Particular spaces . . . and
constellations of spaces can therefore be investigated in terms of their performative characteristics and effects. . . . [M]ore extensive landscapes are organized into
fields of power" (Delaney 2010, 5). Inspiring as these statements can be for legal
scholars previously insensitive to the spatial and material location of legal power,
given the larger intellectual context described earlier by Doreen Massey, the accumulation of statements along these lines has the eventual result of constructing a
framework for sociolegal analysis that marginalizes the temporal. This dimension
of human experience ends up being treated as empirically important but theoretically uninteresting. In keeping with the demotion of time to the realm of the
empirical, Delaney includes historical factors in his analyses of concrete situations;
like other American critical scholars, he is keenly aware of how the history of an-
tiblack racism, for example, has shaped current American spatial-legal practices.
But while history is included in concrete analyses, temporality is not given the
same billing as spatialization.

The claim here is not that every study of a legal process needs to account for
every dimension, including the various nonhistorical temporalities that might be
present. Studies that focus on a single factor, whether it be substantive (e.g., racialization) or methodological (e.g., spatial governance), are not invalid by virtue
of being selective. The law and society literature can certainly pursue analyses of
what Sally Merry (2001), in an influential article, called "spatial governmentality,"
without implying or assuming that the temporal (including historical) dimensions of governance either are not as important as they used to be or are somehow
mired in old-fashioned modernist logics. However, given the fact that in social
theory circles there is a tendency to privilege space and isolate it from time and
to reduce time to empirical history, those interested in practicing legal geography
will need to be alert to the intellectual risks that flow from the development and
current configuration of spatial theory, risks that can easily and perhaps unwittingly be imported into legal geography.

## REMEMBERING KANT'S CRITIQUE

To think about undertaking sociolegal research that is not skewed in favor of spatial analyses to the detriment of temporalities (especially the kind of nonhistorical temporalities found, for example, in common law reasoning [Parker 2011]), it is useful to begin at the beginning—the beginning of modern philosophy in the radical critique of classical Newtonian notions of time and space carried out by Immanuel Kant.

David Harvey's book on cosmopolitan geography praises Kant for being a protogeographer, but then goes on to a lengthy critique of Kant's supposedly modernist notion of space and time. Acknowledging that Kant did not endorse Newton's assertions about time and space as ontologically solid entities whose existence is independent of human perception, Harvey (2009, 31, 32) claims that Kant nevertheless fell into objectivism and absolutism, and that "in the Kantian view, as we have seen, space is empty, pristine, and waiting to be divided" (166). (This description, not coincidentally, bears many similarities to James Scott's [1998] hugely influential description of the "high modernism" that begins with the Enlightenment's gaze). Harvey then claims that Kant separates time from space and history from geography. However, contrary to Harvey's claim, in an early section of the *Critique of Pure Reason* Kant carefully demolishes the old metaphysical habit of imagining that space and time exist objectively.

In the "Transcendental Aesthetic" section of the *Critique of Pure Reason*, Kant famously argues, probably for the first time in Western philosophy, that we cannot know anything about space or time, since they cannot themselves be observed or theorized because they are the most fundamental preconditions for any experience and any thought. Whatever space and time might be for actual or hypothetical divinities, Kant argues, for humans, space and time are the most basic of all the filters through which we see, think, and categorize. One can study planets, but not space as such, or historical events, but not time as such. While the old-style metaphysicians thought that philosophy's task was to concoct theories of space and time (along with theories of, for example, freedom or beauty), Kant argues that philosophy's key task is to map the limits of all possible human knowledge, thus encouraging better empirical and theoretical work outside of philosophy by putting a stop to metaphysical speculation about entities that cannot ever be known, at least by humans (e.g., time, space, things in themselves).

The rather ironic fact that Kant, often taken as the prophet of old-fashioned humanism and modernism, actually developed a skeptical and somewhat subjectivist analysis of space and time has not escaped the notice of all theorists of postmodern spatialization. Indeed, while at the outset of the essay cited earlier

Jameson states that as a matter of fact there is indeed a shift from modernist time to postmodernist space ("I don't see how we can avoid identifying an epochal change here" [Jameson 2003, 696]), on the next page he cites Kant as an authority as he warns against asking such meaningless questions as whether time in general is more important than space: "Indeed, why separate the two at all? Did not Kant teach us that space and time are both a priori conditions of our experience or perception, neither one to be gazed at with the naked eye and quite inseparable from each other?" (And, by happy coincidence anticipating my own discussion of Bakhtin in the fourth section of this chapter, Jameson adds: "And did not Bakhtin wisely recombine them in his notion of the chronotope, recommending a historical account of each specific space-time continuum as it jelled or chrystallized?" [Jameson 2003, 697]). Be that as it may, Jameson continues: "But it is not so easy to be moderate or sensible in the force field of modernism, where Time and Space are at war in Homeric combat" (698).

Since Jameson only gestures toward Kant's transcendental aesthetic, and since in sociolegal studies Kant is rarely read or mentioned, it may be useful to briefly recap Kant's analysis of time and space here. As is well known, Kant developed his own post-metaphysical take on time and space by rejecting both of the then-prevailing views. One was that time and space exist objectively, and absolutely (Newton's view). The other theory was that time and space are properties of conceptual and material objects, and therefore exist objectively but only as properties, not as entities. By contrast with both of these views, which in different ways reify time and space, Kant argued that it is wrong to even ask whether time and space are objective entities or rather properties of entities, because the human mind cannot either observe or theorize time and space. On its part, space is a condition of perception rather than something that can itself be perceived with either the mind or the eye. "Space is not an empirical concept which has been derived from outer experience. . . . Space is nothing but the form of all appearances of the outer senses. It is the subjective condition of sensibility [i.e., sensation, experience]" (Kant [1781] 1965, 70–71). And if all perceptions are necessarily spatial, since we cannot imagine an object that is not spatialized, so too all concepts as well as perceptions are temporal: "Time is not an empirical concept that has been derived from any experience" (74); "Time is, therefore, given a priori" (75); "Time is not something which exists of itself, or which inheres in things as an objective determination. . . . Time is the formal a priori condition of all appearances whatsoever" (77).

How is Kant's critique of the reification of space and time relevant for sociolegal scholarship? One implication is that it may be best to avoid making space and time into the grammatical subjects of sentences, since such language works to sideline all potential debate about whether space and time do actually exist objectively or whether they are only, as Kant showed, necessary conditions of all possible human experience. Focusing on historical and social specificity (as most of the chapters in this book do) certainly helps to remind us that if space exists, it is not available to us to describe or theorize, and all that we can do is document various practices of governance that work on people and problems by governing, arranging, or changing spaces. On the whole, law and society scholars have focused on specific practices rather than theorizing time or space; but—and this is where the siren song of metaphysics becomes audible, and Kant's critique becomes highly relevant—we have as a group experienced great trouble analyzing temporal and spatial dimensions of governance *at the same time.* And geographers who see spatial scale as the only scale are hardly unique in this. Let us thus turn to the two main fields within sociolegal studies that focus on temporality—legal anthropology, first, and then legal history—before proceeding to the more experimental and final part of the article, in which Bakhtin's notion of chronotope is adapted for sociolegal use.

## LEGAL TEMPORALITIES: SOME CONCEPTUAL TOOLS FROM ANTHROPOLOGY

One of the most important works in the legal anthropology of temporality is Carol Greenhouse's 1996 book *At a Moment's Notice*, which examines the way in which particular temporalizations shaped large-scale legal systems, including Western law. The book contains a critical analysis of the hegemony of "linear time," which she argues was first elaborated in European Christian narratives of creation, sin, and redemption and then given scientific and bureaucratic twists throughout the Western legal and political apparatus: "Since the Middle Ages, linear time has been the time of the nation-state, although its modes of rationalization (as technology and social control) vary with time and place" (Greenhouse 1996, 179).

That linear forms of temporality (including historicism, but by no means limited to that) have played a constitutive role in the development of Western law is an insight that could deepen legal geographers' understanding of the temporal logics that, even if they are not analyzed in depth, need to be understood and kept in mind so as not to unwittingly privilege space over time. Aboriginal legal scholars and legal anthropologists working on aboriginal law have made this point repeatedly, although often only in the context of the evidentiary difficulties faced by aboriginal collectives attempting to legally prove possession of a territory, or more generally what the Canadian constitution marks out as "aboriginal rights" (Borrows 2010; Valverde 2012a).

That clashes between legal traditions with different epistemologies often involve fundamental differences about the relation between law and temporality is by now well known, at least among sociolegal scholars with some knowledge of aboriginal and other non-Western perspectives (see Benda-Beckmann and Benda-Beckmann, in this volume). But what is perhaps less well known, or appreciated, is that one and the same "culture" can easily contain conflicting temporal and spatial logics, and that those conflicts are not necessarily zero-sum games in which a "dominant" spatiotemporality automatically drives out older or less prestigious ones (Valverde 2011). In relation to temporalization, there are anthropologists of modernity who have highlighted the temporal pluralism of Western life to great effect: a good example is Arjun Appadurai's (1996) influential exploration of the differences between history and genealogy, and between duration and history. But this kind of fine-grained analysis of modernity's temporal pluralism has not been much used by sociolegal scholars. While social theorists of space have written volumes on multiscalar governance and multiscalar analysis (e.g., Herod and Wright 2002), the coexistence, in the same place at the same time, of different and sometimes incommensurable temporalities has not attracted much attention, with some exceptions.

One study that illustrates that the legal anthropological study of plural temporalities can be a resource for sociolegal scholars wishing to include temporalization in their studies of spatial regulation is Justin Richland's (2008) careful analysis of the implications, for legal and social purposes, of two quite distinct and indeed contradictory temporalities—temporalities that become visible in the words used by Hopi people in the course of legal proceedings. Richland shows that close textual analysis of Hopi courtroom speech reveals two kinds of time. The first is a "sovereign time" that is closely linked to, and indeed reproduced by, particular actions and words, with aboriginal sovereign claims being thus directly, albeit implicitly, enacted in courtroom speech. But, second, Richland notes that the courtroom speech of the Hopi also employs a temporalization that is more experiential and situated.

In Richland's article sovereign time is acknowledged to have a spatial dimension as well (and indeed, like Jameson, Richland [2008, 10] appeals, very briefly, to Bakhtin's notion of the chronotope, which he describes as concrete "space-time envelopes"). However, the spatial aspect is not explored, a fact that reinforces the dualism of space versus time that this chapter seeks to deconstruct. It may be that Richland neglects spatialization because it is obvious that the "tradition" that grounds claims of aboriginal jurisdiction involves making spatial claims (at least in contexts in which Western notions of sovereignty and territory prevail), whereas the temporal aspects of indigenous sovereignty are far less apparent. In general, jurisdiction and sovereignty tend to be experienced as spatial more than as temporal, at least since the time when territorial jurisdictions (especially those based on states) came to prevail over less spatial forms of jurisdiction, such as the spiritual jurisdiction that the pope had over much of Europe in the Middle Ages (Elden 2013, 135–89). But whatever the reasons, it is unfortunate that, as does Greenhouse, Richland isolates the temporal dimension of legal processes and does not explore how various legal temporalities are connected to modes of spatialization.

Legal anthropologists have shown how property, kinship, and so on, are temporalized for legal purposes, and they are able to compare this to how life is experienced and described by another group or by the same group when engaged in a different legal context. However, the empirical study of how conflicting temporalities operate in legal contexts does not necessarily disrupt the disciplinary habits that have over many years now separated anthropology from both geography (or more generally studies of space) and history. A brief discussion of a recent trend in legal historiography that seeks to decenter historicity itself in a highly reflexive manner is thus in order here. Turning to some of these studies will help to broaden the discussion of legal studies of temporality. In so doing, the next section lays the groundwork for the concluding discussion of possible avenues open to sociolegal scholars who are uncomfortable with the fragmentation of critical studies into legal geography, legal anthropology, and legal history.

## THE POVERTY OF HISTORICISM: LEGAL HISTORIANS OPEN UP THE QUESTION OF TEMPORALITY

Kunal Parker's (2011) recent book on the contradictory temporal logics and assumptions evident in nineteenth-century American common-law thinking ends by pointing out that critical legal scholars (and not only historians) tend to take it for granted that historicization is a key, if not *the* key, maneuver that distinguishes the critical from the conservative. Critical sociolegal scholars have repeatedly shown that legal doctrines and notions that present themselves as timeless or inevitable can be denaturalized, and thus debunked, by means of historical research (Parker 2011, 280–82). While not denying the continuing relevance and usefulness, for critical purposes, of this "historicizing" move (which as mentioned earlier is also made by many legal geographers), Parker shows that the by now routine invocation of historical specificity serves to conceal from view all manner of other complex relations between modes of power/knowledge and modes of temporalization.

A point made by Parker in his analysis of common-law thought in nineteenth-century America is particularly pertinent here, namely, that the various temporalities that circulated through legal texts did not necessarily have a fixed political direction. For instance, while the common law's ideology of insensible and largely unwilled change, which relies on and constructs a very special temporality, certainly appealed to Burkean conservatives afraid of rapid statutory change effected by democratic legislatures, democrats too had frequent recourse to the temporality of the common law. In particular, pro-legislation democrats were just as likely as Burkean conservatives to rely on the classic common law trope of a multigenerational, implicit consent discerned and made explicit by judges; they did not limit themselves to Thomas Paine–style invocations of explicit, single-generation, politically articulated consent, as one might have thought. The present- and future-oriented temporality of US revolutionary thought, therefore, turns out to not have excluded the past-oriented temporality of mainstream common-law discourse.

Parker thus demonstrates that multiple and conflicting temporalizations of law clearly coexisted throughout nineteenth-century legal thought, even within the narrow sphere of US-based, white, respectable, nonradical writing on the common law. And furthermore, each temporalization of law, far from being hardwired to a particular politic, exhibited remarkable flexibility and fluidity.

In her recent work, Renisa Mawani also questions the identification of the temporality of law with historicity made in critical legal studies as well as by mainstream historians; but, unlike Parker, who does not engage with the literature on law and geography, she specifically links her critique of the narrowness of historicism to an equally critical view of the privileging of space as the theoretically interesting dimension of legal power that was identified in the first two sections of this chapter. She makes the point that although questions of race and law have in recent years often been read through the lens of space, with racialization processes linked to colonial practices of segregation and boundary management, temporalization is also a key dimension of legally enacted racialization (Mawani forthcoming). A point of particular interest to studies of colonialism and space is that she points out that temporal divisions sometimes create new ethnic and/or racial identities, giving as an example how Indian (from India, that is) British subjects emigrating to South Africa claimed a civilizing identity in respect to the native African population, with this identity being available only to those that migrated (Mawani forthcoming; see also Mawani 2012).

Postcolonial studies of both historical and spatial dynamics have generally relied on the same identification of the temporality of law with history that Parker critiques. Exploring legal temporalities beyond those of historicism, Mawani (2012) makes very good use of the peculiar nonhistorical temporality of the spectral (in Derrida's sense) when discussing a fascinating situation in which representations of Canadian aboriginality were deployed to deny entry into Canada to "real" Indians (from India, that is). While not fully developed, the experiment with using Derrida's spectrality—a dynamic that interacts with but is certainly not contained by conventional history—may open up new possibilities for the temporal analysis of legal practices, in colonial settings and elsewhere.

Derrida's specters of justice owe a great deal to Derrida's close reading of Walter Benjamin's nonhistorical, messianic notion of justice. And not coincidentally, Benjamin's notions of mythic violence and nonlegal justice also play a key role in noted legal historian Chris Tomlins's recent work. In "The Threepenny Constitution," Tomlins (2007–8) combines Walter Benjamin, Bertolt Brecht, and mainstream US legal texts in a novel interpretation that, among other things, sheds light on the ways in which legal processes and legal logics—not just in colonial settings or in the periphery of empire, but at the heart of "the West"— escape the kind of historicist analysis generally produced by critical legal studies. Benjamin's critique of evolutionist notions of progress and justice, together with his admittedly sketchy ideas about justice as facing the future and the past simultaneously, help Tomlins to uncover nonhistorical and ahistorical logics in US legal history that have hitherto remained invisible. Indeed, Tomlins (2010, 563) goes so far as to read the Civil War as an event transcending historicist logics altogether, and he makes the somewhat mysterious but clearly Benjaminian, nonhistoricist claim that "American history is an eternal succession of beginnings—each a primal enactment of foundation in a moment of purity and human invention that fills the void beyond civility with legality" (543).

We thus see that even without exploring the vast resources of aboriginal legal and temporal traditions, some legal historians have begun to go beyond the identification of "historical" with "critical" that is found in critical sociolegal studies generally (in legal geography as well as legal history). Whether attentive to the constant return of the temporally unstable "specters" that Western positive law represses, or mining the common law's own, internal legal-temporal pluralism, or even daring to follow Benjamin in his half-Marxist, half-messianic contemplation of radical breaks in human time, legal historians oriented toward contemporary philosophically are radically questioning the taken-for-granted identification of time as such with "history"—the intellectual move that grounds the common assumption that outlining the historical context of law amounts to and suffices for critical legal studies.

This recent historiographical work has not been taken up in any serious way by sociolegal scholars primarily interested in spatial logics, probably because of the institutional boundaries that continue to separate legal geography from legal history (and legal anthropology), even as individual scholars are increasingly free to roam across fields. But critical legal studies is mature, if not elderly, whereas legal geography, though younger, has also become a developed field. It may thus be time to pay closer attention to the ways in which taken-for-granted notions (e.g., the reduction of time as such to history) have thus far prevented us from even trying to synthesize temporal and spatial considerations as we try to analyze the internal pluralism of all legal systems and legal contexts.

## LEGAL CHRONOTOPES

In the first section of this chapter a critical discussion of the rise of the law and geography literature led to a reflection on the relevance of Kant's critique of the reification of space and time. We then went on to consider work in legal anthropology and legal historiography that in different ways demonstrates not only that temporalization is as complex and theoretically interesting as spatialization but also that reducing the temporal dimension of law to a section on historical background or historical critique by no means captures the richness of law's temporal dynamics.

In this final section we return to the Bakhtinian term *chronotope*—mentioned in both Jameson's and Richland's articles discussed earlier. I am by no means arguing that Bakhtin gives us the one and only solution to the vexed problems of how to consider time and space at the same time and how to appreciate the internal spatiotemporal pluralism of legal processes and legal thought. Many other intellectual resources—Henri Bergson, Gilles Deleuze, Walter Benjamin, and the work of aboriginal legal scholars—have been used to good effect by some scholars. The reason for choosing Bakhtin as the focus of this last section is simply that, unlike most of the legal geographers, anthropologists, and historians whose work is widely read in sociolegal circles, Bakhtin devised a notion—the chronotope—for the precise purpose of surmounting the traditional practice of separating temporal from spatial dimensions of life and governance.[6] How exactly the term could be used for sociolegal studies requires translation, however, because Bakhtin's main goal was to understand the specificity of literary genres, not sociolegal mechanisms or logics.

The essay "Forms of Time and Chronotope in the Novel" develops not just a new interpretation of how the modern novel differs from earlier literary forms but, a much loftier objective, a novel method for understanding differences between genres, the "distinctions" that make each genre what it is. In addressing the age-old literary theory question of genre specificity, Bakhtin chooses to focus precisely on space and time, but with these two dimensions of human life and human perception taken together rather than (as is generally the case in legal geography, legal anthropology, and legal history) separately. The chronotope, Bakhtin (1981,

84) states, is "the intrinsic connectedness of spatial and temporal relationships that are artistically expressed in literature. . . . *Time, as it were, thickens, takes on flesh, becomes artistically visible; likewise, space becomes charged and responsive to the movements of time, plot, and history*" (emphasis added).

Time and space are thus taken not as separate dimensions to be considered one after the other (as is done in sociolegal case studies that provide historical context in one section and an analysis of spatial governance in another section). The specificity of a particular literary genre—a particular, collectively produced, and culturally established way of telling stories and capturing human relations—lies precisely in the way in which, in each genre, time "thickens" and becomes spatialized in distinct ways, whereas "space becomes charged and responsive to the movements of time, plot, and history," with the particular shape of this process being specific to each of the genres that are available within the same culture or across historical and geographical boundaries.

An interesting point, given our earlier discussion of Kant's transcendental aesthetic, is that Bakhtin references the same passage of the *Critique of Pure Reason* as a source, in the paragraph following the one cited; but Bakhtin (1981, 86) notes that he is transposing Kant's transcendental aesthetic into a phenomenal key, since for him—Bakhtin—time and space are "forms of the most immediate reality" and not simply transcendental a priori conditions for the possibility of perception.

For Bakhtin, the specificity of each literary genre lies primarily in its typical chronotope (with *chronotope*, a term loosely borrowed from early twentieth-century developments in physics, referring to the ways in which time and space interact and shape each other, most familiarly in Einstein's theory of relativity). Analyzing the progression of Western protonovelistic genres since the Greek romance, Bakhtin shows not only that each genre constructs time and space in characteristic ways (an insight that legal historians and legal anthropologists could easily produce without reading Bakhtin) but also, more profoundly, that particular spatiotemporal modes constitute the "essence" of each genre, each major mode of cultural expression. When a genre routinely uses fate to move the plot along, for instance, a certain spatiotemporality is at work, one that contrasts with the modern novel's emphasis on the autonomous Western subject's penchant for rationally acting upon the world. The logic of fate is not merely temporal—it is spatiotemporal, as Bakhtin shows with examples of the peculiarly static and rather featureless geographic settings of premodern romances.

Bakhtin's interest lies in showing how certain literary techniques presuppose and reproduce particular spatiotemporalities. For example, he notes that the final reunion of the star-crossed lovers characteristic of Greek romance (and Shakespearean comedies, one might add) erases time twice, since the lovers do not visibly age despite the lengthy and arduous adventures they undergo, and because the world to which they return also turns out to have remained static while they were undergoing trials and mishaps. But there are in Bakhtin glimpses of extra-literary applications of the term *chronotope* that point, however tentatively, toward a sociolegal interpretation or appropriation of the term. The main relevant passage is his brief discussion of the Greek locus of political and economic action, the agora. As what he calls a "real-life chronotope," Bakhtin (1981, 131) notes in passing, the agora's spatiotemporality was essential to the Greek sense of a free self engaged in becoming wise and thus learning to practice freedom, since what we would call personality, character, or for that matter freedom acquired meaning and reality, in ancient Greece, only as it was made visible and seen by others in the space-time that was the agora. Now, Bakhtin does not explain why he thinks the agora is a chronotope rather than merely a space; but perhaps he was thinking about the fact that the political speeches, criminal trials, and market transactions that formed the substance of "the agora" were as limited by temporal markers as by the perhaps more apparent spatial markers still visible in Greek town ruins across the Mediterranean. An encomium speech, for instance, would not function as an encomium if delivered in the middle of the night or at the wrong time (as Derrida [1997, 2006] notes, from a very different perspective, in his discussions of embodied practices of friendship and their relation to justice).

The agora, like other places of economic and social exchange, then and now, was defined by time constraints as well as by legal spatializations. The spatiotemporal market regulations that have constituted public socioeconomic spaces since the agora (e.g., the complex medieval rules about which markets could be held in which churchyards on which feast days) have not been immortalized in high culture like their rhetorical counterparts (e.g., the biographical encomium, the call to military sacrifice); but they continue to shape what is meant by valid transactions. Contemporary techniques that constitute markets temporally, for example, include the stock market's crucial performative, namely the opening bell, and the techniques used by electronic financial systems for stopping trade on some stocks or bonds in the wake of temporally unusual trading patterns. Therefore, if we build on Bakhtin's passing comment about the agora as a "real-life" chronotope, we can see that it is very productive to understand the venue that was the agora as the chronotope that simultaneously enabled the earliest formulations of Western-style citizenship, Western-style market transactions, and Western-style narratives of honor and civic virtue, with *simultaneous* being the most important term for purposes of our analysis. And the agora is not the only nonfictional space-time mentioned in Bakhtin's (1981) essay; the Roman patrician household is another example (137). It is noteworthy for sociolegal research purposes that both the agora and the Roman family household, Bakhtin's main nonliterary examples of a chronotope, are hugely important sites in and for the history of Western legality.

How can Bakhtin's chronotopes help us to understand modern legal processes, since today's legal processes are often spatially and temporally more separate from other aspects of life than was the case in the case of the Greek agora or the Roman household? I here give two examples illustrating how our understanding of modern legal entities or venues can benefit from borrowing Bakhtin's term.

The first example of a legally important venue that can be understood as a "chronotope" is the courtroom. The spatial differentiation of courts and courtrooms has, of course, been discussed by many sociolegal scholars and legal historians, mainly with a view to showing how certain notions of the majesty of law are given architectural form. But temporality is integral to the law's majesty as well. Working courtrooms are temporally specific, not only because, like other state institutions, they effect and perform state power only during certain times, but also, more specific to law, because the space becomes a courtroom only at a highly particular time that is not the same as clock time. The court's time begins only when the judge enters the room and the clerk says, "All rise" (or "the court is now in session"). The courtroom might well be physically open at 9 a.m., and legally relevant people (e.g., lawyers talking with one another, the accused being brought in) might well populate the space and engage in some legal work; but if the judge's official entrance is delayed until 10:15 a.m., then 10:15 becomes time zero, not the time at which the door was opened or the time at which whispered conversations began among lawyers.[7] The way in which a specific temporality (the judge-centric temporality of official court time) shapes and helps define the space of the courtroom perfectly exemplifies Bakhtin's point about how time "thickens" space. In turn, the interior design of the courtroom as a space is constitutive of judicial time, official legal time, because if lawyers talk with the judge in chambers, or in the hallway, the spatial location of the speech interactions has the effect of excluding those bits of time from the official written record of the progress of the trial through time.

Seeing the courtroom as a chronotope, therefore, amounts to more than adding an analysis of the temporal logic of trials to existing analyses of court design and architecture. The term *chronotope* encourages us to instead explore how different legal times create or shape legal spaces, and how the spatial location and spatial dynamics of legal processes in turn shape law's times—how spatial dynamics "thicken" time, to use Bakhtin's evocative phrase. It is also possible that paying attention to the way in which time and space interact to constitute "the courtroom" helps to shed light on the dynamics of what is called justice. Just as the chronotope of the agora is constitutive of Greek-style citizenship, Greek-style commerce, and

Greek-style justice, at the same time and through the same processes, so too the spatiotemporality of the courtroom (or better, the spatiotemporality that *is* the courtroom) may be constitutive of what is called justice—although to prove this claim, one would need to undertake close studies of courtroom activities, their spatiotemporal dynamics, and their effects.

The second example of a legal chronotope is drawn from the legal field in which I have done most of my empirical work in recent years, namely local urban law. Studying how North American cities use their legal tools, historically (Valverde 2011) and in the present (Valverde 2012b), it has become clear to me that one of the key chronotopes of local law—and one that is not found at other scales or in more exalted jurisdictions—is that privileged bearer of urban citizenship: the home-owning nuclear family. The exclusion of homeless people from citizenship in all its dimensions has received much attention among sociolegal scholars. But what has received less attention is that while homelessness certainly acts to create political and not just social exclusion, having a private place to eat and sleep does not guarantee citizenship and belonging. Renters, young single people living with their parents or with roommates, low-income seniors living in rooming houses or retirement "homes," families who are temporarily sharing a dwelling with another family for economic reasons, boarders and lodgers, those who illegally occupy residences or build shacks on land they do not own—there are numerous groups, and not only in third-world cities, whose exclusion from legal as well as symbolic citizenship at the local level is effected in large part by the privileging of a particular form of domestic life.

Legal tools of diverse provenance help to constitute this paradigmatic domestic life form, as critical urban geographers well know. However, what is less well known is that the same tools can also undermine it—a reminder that law's control over life is never total, not only because of what is called "resistance" but also because of law's contradictory internal dynamics. Zoning ordinances, for instance, clearly prop up the ideologically privileged home-owning nuclear family, in that single-family detached is the top, least restricted land use in every North American zoning scheme (as anthropologist Constance Perin [1979] noted, before legal geography had developed). However, the "fit" between the socioeconomic-cultural-sexual unit that is the nuclear family and the land use that is single-family detached is by no means perfect, and this Perin did not pursue, since one has to look beyond local planning rules to discern this contradiction. For example, the family with children does not stop being a family for family law purposes if the parents split up and move to different homes, a common situation that creates a disjuncture between one legal system (family law) and another (planning law). The lack of fit between family law and planning law could be analyzed from a Bakhtinian perspective as a matter of conflicting spatiotemporalities; the rules about child support, for example, are based on a spatiotemporality that is generational and future oriented, in contrast to the more static and localized spatiotemporality of zoning definitions.

The lack of perfect fit between legal containers and the social-sexual-emotional-financial content that is normatively assumed to naturally occupy the containers is suppressed (or repressed, perhaps) through the sociological narrative by which people, rigidly divided by stage of the life course, sort themselves into different forms of housing in an orderly and predictable manner. Any feminist attentive to the normative effects of temporal divisions could easily debunk the ideology of *the* life course; but a Bakhtinian lens would help to bring into focus the intertwining of spatial and temporal norms that is visible in *the* life course norm enshrined in planning law and in real estate discourse. Rental apartments are seen as "naturally" occupied by those who are young and single (with this being classified as an early, preparatory stage); single-family detached homes appear as the proper spatial domain of the spatiotemporal entity known as "married with children," and so on. In turn, the in-between life-course categories of the just married and the empty nesters are supposed to be spatially contained in transitional real estate categories, such as condominiums.

The cultural narrative by which types of building and types of property relations are associated with stages in the life course is supported by municipal legal rules, as critical planning scholars have documented; but it is also undermined, at least on occasion, by the same rules, insofar as law (because of its own internal pluralism) can never actually reserve family-oriented suburbs for actual families, or for that matter exclude all nonfamily domestic arrangements from them. The wholly arbitrary local rules about how many unrelated people can legally live in a "single-family" home, for example, highlight the persistent contradictions between the spatiotemporal logic of one legal process—say, zoning—and the logics of other legal complexes, mainly, in this case, state and federal equal rights and privacy laws.

The complex entity that is the home-owning nuclear family, constituted in part through financial instruments (e.g., federally guaranteed mortgages), in part by real estate practices, in part by bricks and mortar, and in part by law, is thus usefully considered a highly moralized spatiotemporality that has close connections with legal rules (e.g., the lists of numbers that make up zoning regulations) but is never completely coterminous with any one legal complex. The quiet process that brings together "home" (already a hybrid of a building, some highly temporalized financial arrangements, and myriad cultural tropes) and "family" (another hybrid of people, objects, norms, and myths), and then wraps that superhybrid assemblage in layers of architectural, financial, aesthetic, and legal rules, relies largely on spatiotemporalizations that are not unique, taken individually, but form a distinct chronotope when taken together.

Spatial normalization has long been critiqued by progressive planners and feminist urban geographers. But in keeping with the general tendency to not examine temporality other than by way of historical "background," few have noted that the archetypal home-owning family is constituted not only spatially but also temporally, through daily, weekly, and seasonal rhythms that anthropologists study but that are largely invisible in planning law—the normalized temporalities of breadwinners going to work, children returning home from school, weekend family outings, and of course yearly holiday celebrations. The overall spatiotemporality of life-course ideology contains many micro-spatiotemporalities, each of which would be worth studying in detail.

These examples cannot be developed here; but they may help to show that Bakhtin's chronotope can shed light on relationships and effects that are not captured by most critical legal geography scholarship. Critical legal geographers and critical planners have written many volumes describing the normative effects of suburban design and classic, family-oriented domestic architecture; but to understand the relationship between domestic life and law it is not sufficient to focus on spatial relations. Domestic or residential living is also constituted by temporalizations that have legal dimensions and that are not independent of space.[8] That the temporality of the hegemonic, standardized life course helps to constitute the hierarchical list of residential zoning categories (and eventually, once zoning categories have become naturalized, vice versa) is just one example of a dynamic and culturally specific relationship that comes into view if we follow Bakhtin's example and document how specific temporalities constitute specific spaces, and vice versa.

In conclusion, the examples given here suggest that entities that have been generally studied as spaces by critical legal scholars (e.g., courtrooms, single-family homes) could be usefully studied as chronotopes in work that highlights the way in which, as is the case for particle physics, temporality cannot be measured or analyzed as if it were independent of spatial considerations, and vice versa.

## CONCLUSION

It is by no means novel to observe that legal processes and legal knowledges are fundamentally spatialized and temporalized; but sociolegal scholars, like social theorists generally, have tended to treat questions of space separately from those of time. Separating temporality from spatialization tends to reify both of these terms, turning them either into things or concepts, and/or turning one into the other (as when researchers speak of time as a "fourth dimension").

The reification process is particularly evident in theoretical work on space used by legal geographers and others. Legal anthropologists, in turn, have tended to isolate time from space, whereas legal historians (in keeping with critical legal studies generally) do not theorize abstract time in the way that theoretical geographers theorize space, but they have tended to reduce time as such to history, thus occluding various temporal dynamics that are not conventionally historical ones.

Fighting against the tendency of academic work to fragment along disciplinary lines (the tendency that has divided legal geography's analyses of space from legal anthropology's and legal history's explorations of temporalities) is thus necessary if we are going to avoid the objectivist reifications of space that circulate today among some social theorists. Eschewing reified concepts is necessary if we want to undertake concrete analyses of legal and sociolegal assemblages that illuminate particularity (including novel or submerged spatiotemporalities) instead of simply classifying what one studies under this or that inherited abstract concept.

While acknowledging that a rich array of theoretical and other resources exist that could help to take us beyond the confines of legal geography, legal anthropology, and legal history respectively, I select one particular resource—namely, Bakhtin's chronotope. This chapter ends with a consideration of two assemblages—the courtroom and the single-family detached, homeowner-occupied home—that are generally analyzed from a purely spatial point of view, but which I argue are usefully seen as chronotopes whose dynamics are always in an uneasy relationship with the legal rules that both constitute them and (sometimes) also undermine them.

This chapter does not claim that Bakhtin's chronotope is the magic theoretical bullet, however, and offers the chronotope merely as an experiment in trying to think time and space simultaneously and dynamically. That time can "thicken" space and space in turn can shape time is the key insight to be gained from Bakhtin. Combined with the critical legal studies' traditional interest in revealing internal conflicts within law and governance, tools derived from other sources could also help to produce studies that undertake concrete analyses in an open-ended manner, remembering that our first commitment is understanding the world we live in, not the prestige or theoretical rigor of the disciplines or fields.

## NOTES

1. See, for example, Braverman (2009), Nicholas Blomley's (2003) work, and Richard Ford's (1999) influential discussion of the history of jurisdiction.

2. By contrast, Saskia Sassen's (2006) massive history of jurisdiction and rights synthesizes analyses of spatial and territorial dimensions of political power with temporal scales and temporal dynamics.

3. Falling into the metaphysical black hole that is time as such, Jameson only occasionally distinguishes between the temporality of modernist literature, on the one hand, and the historicism of many modernist philosophical approaches: the reified abstraction *modernism* encompasses them both and erases their notable differences. Deconstructing the modernism-postmodernism binary of reified abstractions is outside the scope of this chapter; but in can be noted that a useful, Nietzschean tip for avoiding abstract reified thinking is to use adjectives (e.g., *modern* architecture, *modernist* literary fiction) rather than nouns (e.g., *postmodernity*). Similarly, terms such as *temporal* and *spatial*, or *temporalization* and *spatialization* are much more useful for sociolegal analysis than are *space* and *time*.

4. I am here relying on Nietzsche's analysis of the way in which languages that privilege nouns used as grammatical subjects create the impression that all activity has to have an actor, that all doing has to have a "doer." For more on how Nietzsche's critique of the metaphysical effects of the subject-predicate form is relevant to sociolegal studies, see Valverde (2005).

5. My argument here is part of a more general attack on concepts as the currency of theory that is developed more fully elsewhere, as in my critique of the way in which Foucault's analyses of penitentiary and medical techniques of power have been reduced to nothing but examples of the concept of discipline (Valverde 2010).

6. Interestingly, there is a chapter on Bakhtin in the influential anthology *Thinking Space* (Crang and Thrift 2000), but in keeping with the geographical bias of the work, the contribution illuminates how Bakhtin's dialogical imagination could be used to understand space, with the chronotope receiving only passing mention (Holloway and Knealey 2000).

7. I owe this insight to Karrie Sandford's not-yet-published ethnography of high-volume courts in Toronto.

8. A very important multiyear temporalization of family life is that imposed by banking practices regarding the length of home mortgages. The fact that critical legal geography is very aware of the cultural prejudices of zoning and other rules established by public law, but has generally neglected private law and semiprivate regulation by banks and government mortgage regulators, underlines the dangers of focusing on the regulation of space to the detriment of other temporalization.

## REFERENCES

Appadurai, Arjun, 1996. *Modernity at Large: Cultural Dimensions of Globalization.* Minneapolis, MN: University of Minnesota Press.

Bakhtin, Mikhail M. 1981. *The Dialogic Imagination: Four Essays.* Translated by C. Emerson and M. Holquist. Austin: University of Texas Press.

Blomley, Nicholas. 2003. *Unsettling the City: Urban Land and the Politics of Property.* New York: Routledge.

Borrows, John. 2010. *Canada's Indigenous Constitution.* Toronto, ON: University of Toronto Press.

Braverman, Irus. 2009. *Planted Flags: Trees, Land, and Law in Israel/Palestine.* Cambridge: Cambridge University Press.

Chakrabarty, Dipesh. 2000. *Provincializing Europe: Postcolonial Thought and Historical Difference.* Princeton, NJ: Princeton University Press.

Crang, Mike, and Nigel Thrift, eds. 2000. *Thinking Space.* New York: Routledge.

Delaney, David. 2010. *The Spatial, the Legal, and the Pragmatics of World-Making: Nomospheric Investigations.* London: Glasshouse/Routledge.

Derrida, Jacques. 1997. *Politics of Friendship.* London: Verso.

————. 2006. *Spectres of Marx: The State of the Debt, the Work of Mourning, and the New International.* New York: Routledge.

Elden, Stuart. 2013. *The Birth of Territory.* Chicago: University of Chicago Press.

Ford, Richard. 1999. "Law's Territory: A History of Jurisdiction." *Michigan Law Review* 97 (4): 843–930.

Greenhouse, Carol. 1996. *A Moment's Notice: Time Politics across Cultures.* Ithaca, NY: Cornell University Press.

Harvey, David. 2009. *Cosmopolitanism and the Geographies of Freedom.* New York: Columbia University Press.

Herod, Andrew, and Melissa Wright, eds. 2002. *Geographies of Power: Placing Scale.* Oxford, UK: Blackwell.

Holloway, Julian, and James Knealey. 2000. "Mikhail Bakhtin: Dialogics of Space." In *Thinking Space*, edited by Mike Crang and Nigel Thrift, 71–84. New York: Routledge.

Jameson, Frederic. 2003. "The End of Temporality," *Critical Inquiry* 29 (4): 695–718.

Kant, Immanuel. (1781) 1965. *Critique of Pure Reason.* Translated by N. K. Smith. New York: St. Martin's Press.

Massey, Doreen. 1994. *Space, Place, and Gender.* Minneapolis: University of Minnesota Press.

————. 2005. *For Space.* London: Sage.

Mawani, Renisa. 2012. "Specters of Indigeneity in British-Indian Migration, 1914." *Law and Society Review* 46 (2): 369–403.

————. Forthcoming. "Law as Temporality: Colonial Politics and Indian Settlers." *Irvine Law Review.*

Merry, Sally. 2001. "Spatial Governmentality and the New Urban Social Order: Controlling Gender Violence Through Law." *American Anthropologist* 103 (1): 16–29.

Parker, Kunal. 2011. *Common Law, History, and Democracy in America, 1790–1900.* Cambridge: Cambridge University Press.

Perin, Constance. 1979. *Everything in Its Place: Social Order and Land Use in America.* Princeton, NJ: Princeton University Press.

Richland, Justin. 2008. "Sovereign Time, Storied Moments: The Temporalities of Law, Tradition and Ethnography in Hopi Tribal Court." *Political and Legal Anthropology Review* 31 (1): 8–27.

Riles, Annelise. 2005. "A New Agenda for the Cultural Study of Law: Taking on the Technicalities." *Buffalo Law Review* 53: 973–1025.

Sassen, Saskia. 2006. *Territory, Authority, Rights: From Medieval to Global Assemblages.* Princeton, NJ: Princeton University Press.

Scott, James. 1998. *Seeing Like a State: How Certain Schemes to Improve the Human Condition Have Failed.* New Haven, CT: Yale University Press.

Tomlins, Christopher. 2007–8. "The Threepenny Constitution." *Alabama Law Review* 58: 979–1008.

Tomlins, Christopher. 2010. *Freedom Bound: Law, Labor and Civic Identity in Colonizing English America, 1580–1865.* Cambridge: Cambridge University Press.

Valverde, Mariana .2005. "Pain, Memory and the Creation of the Liberal Subject: Nietzsche and the Criminal Law." In *Nietzsche and Legal Theory: Half-Written Laws,* edited by P. Goodrich and M. Valverde, 85–101. New York: Routledge.

———. 2009. "Jurisdiction and Scale: Using Legal Technicalities as Resources for Theory." *Social and Legal Studies* 18 (2): 139–58.

———. 2010. "Specters of Foucault in Law and Society Scholarship." *Annual Review of Law and Social Science* 6 (1): 45–59.

———. 2011. "Seeing Like a City: The Dialectic of Premodern and Modern Ways of Seeing in Urban Governance." *Law and Society Review* 45 (2): 277–313.

———. 2012a. "The Crown in a Multicultural Age: The Changing Epistemology of (Post) colonial Sovereignty." *Social and Legal Studies* 21 (1): 3–21.

———. 2012b. *Everyday Law on the Street: City Governance in an Age of Diversity.* Chicago: University of Chicago Press.

# 3 LEARNING FROM LARRY

## Pragmatism and the Habits of Legal Space

*Nicholas Blomley*

My wife is an enthusiastic and accomplished gardener who loves planting large shrubs and trees. As our neighbor's house to the east is close to the property line, she has planted so as to visually screen out the neighbor's house as much as possible. As her plants grew, some of the branches occasionally crossed over the property line. With our former neighbor, this did not seem to be an issue. However, when Larry moved in, a retiree who had lived on a larger property elsewhere in town, he took a more aggressive approach to these botanical incursions. Rather than asking us to snip them back, he would surreptitiously do so himself. We politely questioned him on this, asking him to let us do it for him. Larry agreed, although grumbled about "his space" and "his rights." However, he continued with his sneaky prunings, often throwing the offending clippings back on our side of the fence. He even cut back beyond the property line, noting (when challenged) that the plants grew so quickly that it was necessary for him to be proactive. Despite our eco-friendly sign on our front lawn, announcing to the world our resistance to chemical herbicides, he went so far as to spray weed killer on various shrubs and plants on our side of the fence. My wife, who loves her garden dearly, finds Larry's behavior bizarre and worries about the well-being of her plants. She imagines him sitting at home, brooding obsessively about floral encroachments. Recently she has started tying small red flags on his illegitimate prunings, to signal that she is aware of his covert actions.

Of course, while being entirely sympathetic to my wife's concerns, and annoyed at my neighbor, it's impossible for me not to also come at this through a legal geographic lens. Some years ago, I conducted a research project in inner-city Vancouver in an attempt to understand how gardeners enact property and make space as they garden, whether through the construction of neighborly boundaries or in the interface between public and private space (e.g., Blomley 2004, 2005a, 2005b). Much legal geography scholarship similarly argues that law is made present in a variety of geographic configurations (indeed, without such geographies, law would be an empty command) and that such geographies constitute action, behavior, and belief in consequential ways, helping to shape belief and practice (Delaney et al. 2001; Delaney 2010). Geographer Robert Sack's (1986) treatment of territoriality is significant here: he argues that territorialization provides a particularly efficient means by which power relations can be communicated. The boundary, like our garden fence, is said to be a succinct statement, serving as a symbolic form that "combines a statement about direction in space and a statement about possession and exclusion" (Sack 1986, 21). Legal geographers similarly argue the following:

> Boundaries *mean*. They signify, they differentiate, they unify the insides of the spaces that they mark. . . . And the form that this meaning often takes—the meaning that social actors confer on lines and spaces—is *legal* meaning. How they mean is through the authoritative inscription of legal categories. . . . The trespasser and the undocumented alien, no less than the owner and the citizen, are figures who are located within circuits of legally defined power by reference to physical location vis-à-vis bounded spaces. (Delaney et al. 2001, xviii)

On this account, our relations with Larry are structured according to a set of legal beliefs and practices, expressed in and constituted by a set of spatial arrangements. What motivates Larry is not something I have access to. He appears to be the embodiment of the "separative self," noted by critical property theory, wherein autonomy can be secured only through the creation and maintenance of sharp boundaries between the self and others (Nedelsky 1990).

However, we don't yet have a good sense of how such legal geographies work, particularly in relation to action, behavior, and belief. At least two questions seem to present themselves. First, how do the subjects of law "take up" legal meaning? This is not entirely clear. If we follow critical legal studies or the legal consciousness literature, it would seem that law shapes beliefs and thoughts (Engel 1998). This, then, provides a basis for action. But how? And what difference does the spatiality of law make in the constitution of legal identity and practice? Second, where does law reside in my neighborly encounter? Although we would point to its constitutive effects, we may also be tempted to think of it as something "larger," outside or beyond us, that we draw upon or take up. Wherever it lives, what are its effects? Is it a resource that we draw upon, or is law itself produced through our engagements? Is it purely a set of ideas or representations or something also constituted through action? What of the complexities and departures from what we might think of as "official" forms of law?

## HABIT

Legal geography lacks a tool kit for thinking systematically about many of these important questions. Here, I attempt to answer them by borrowing from pragmatism—and in particular, from John Dewey's notion of habit, which is concerned with the embodied experience of acting within the world. Legal scholars and geographers, separately, have engaged with pragmatism, yet not in thinking about legal spatiality in particular. A review of the history and scope of pragmatism is beyond the range of this chapter. Dewey's work (1859–1952) can be considered part of the first wave of pragmatism, which included thinkers such as Charles Sanders Peirce, William James, and Oliver Wendell Holmes (Menand 2001). While there are important differences among these thinkers, common ground can be found in relation to their core commitment to antifoundationalism. Pragmatism rejected the "Platonic urge"—the desire "to escape . . . to something atemporal, which lies in the background" (Bernstein 1983, 199). It declared war on abstractions and the belief in pure ideas that claim to represent the essence of the world. Pragmatists rejected the possibility of humans acquiring a God's-eye view of the world and that of a "correspondence theory of truth" such that a description of the world is true if it corresponds to this essential reality (what Dewey termed the "Kodak fixation" [Westbrook 2005, 5]). Ideas are simply tools that accomplish particular tasks. To the extent that they allow those truths to be realized, they could be deemed true. For James (1907, 30), "the true is the name of whatever proves itself to be good in the way of belief." Truth, in this sense, is always provisional, grounded in experience rather than in the nature of things. Thus, "truth happens to an idea. It *becomes* true, it is *made* true by events" (201).

John Dewey's prodigious scholarship covered a remarkable and wide-ranging terrain. However, it is his attention to habit that I wish to focus on here. I do so, in true pragmatist style, experimentally. Although he does not engage extensively with law, and has very little to say about space, Dewey's reading of habit, I wish to suggest, offers us some useful ways of thinking through the quite particular question of how everyday legal geographies are practiced by people such as my neighbor, Larry. Moreover, as I hope to argue, the antifoundationalism upon which his argument rests offers some valuable ways of countering some pervasive and problematic tendencies to treat law and power as abstract concepts, rather than as contingent and particular effects. His account, moreover, is not simply descriptive, but normative. As such, I argue, Dewey offers some useful resources for critical legal geography, especially in his attention to the nature and limits of social change.

Dewey's understanding of habit draws from pragmatism's primary emphasis on experience. Experience is understood not in the Lockean sense of the reception of the mind to external events but in a more interactive form. For Dewey, experience is "a process situated in a natural environment, mediated by a socially shared symbolic system, actively exploring and responding to the ambiguities of the world by seeking to render the most problematic of them determinate" (Alexander 1987, xiii). It is to be understood, then, as present in the ecological transactions between a living being and its multiple, shifting social and physical environments.[1] As Hildreth (2009, 788) notes, "Experience always includes both the act of experiencing and the object experienced, the 'how' and the 'what' of experience. Subject and object become functional elements that emerge from within the very process of experience." Dewey (1925, 18) stresses, borrowing from William James, that experience is "a double-barrelled word" that "recognizes no division between act and material, subject and object, but contains both in an unanalyzed totality." We experience the world, and experiment within it, through a process of acting in the world and responding to the outcomes of such actions. Experience, for Dewey, is bodily experience. The body must be understood not as a stimulus-response mechanism but rather as "a center of life activity, as a developer of experience, an explorer of the world" (Alexander 1987, xviii).

Bodily experience is structured by what Dewey terms *habit*.[2] Habit is often thought about as something external to us, a disposition that we acquire and can shake off (a "bad habit," for example), distinct from some internalized, pure self, or from mere routine or rote ("it is my habit to have tea in the morning"). Dewey, however, uses the term in a holistic way that eschews a view of subjectivity as either transcendental or lodged in some inner self. For Dewey, our habits both constitute our knowledge of the world and provide us with ways to interact with it on the basis of a view of the self and the environment as mutually constitutive. Habits serve as "mechanisms of action, physiologically engrained, which [operate] spontaneously, automatically, whenever the cue is given" (Dewey 1922, 50). Habits organize activity in an instrumental fashion: they "have a projectile power. . . . All habits are demands for certain kinds of activity" (25). They direct us to certain forms of engagement and thought. Habits allow us to mediate and respond to situations, serving as "energetic and dominating ways of acting" (25).

But while habit is embodied, it is also evident in the ways we think, reason, represent, and appraise. Writing an academic paper and preparing a legal judgment are as much "mechanisms of action," therefore, as are walking on a sidewalk and pruning a tree. Dewey rejects the distinction between habit and thought, and a view of the latter as conservative and the former as active. Thinking, for Dewey (1922, 50), is a particular habit: the so-called separation of theory and practice "means in fact the separation of two kinds of practice, one taking place in the outdoor world, the other in the study."[3]

Habits are not inherent capacities that we bring to encounters with the world. There is no "immaculate conception of meanings or purposes" (Dewey 1922, 30–31). Rather, "habits predispose use actively, they determine what we see, what we focus upon, and how we may respond" (Alexander 1987, 146). They make the world legible for us in quite particular yet powerful ways;

> [Habits] integrate and unify situations, they tend to project a context, to structure a situation around any immediate object, both temporally and spatially. We see a wheel as part of the car rather than as part of the ground, and we see space itself as having depth and direction because of habit. We also see things temporally as processes: we see the car's movement as part of one process, the growth of a child as another. (Alexander 1987, 147)

Although we may think of habits as something we take up or discard, our habits are intrinsic to who we are (which is not the same as saying that our habits are to be treated in individualistic terms, as some manifestation of an autonomous self, a point to which I return later). For Dewey, the agency of the self—its will—is realized through habit, not in opposition to it: "We are our habits; they are our very structure as corporeal, bodily selves; thus there is no thinking of who we are apart from the habits that we embody" (Sullivan 2000, 26). Habit, then, is not something that overlies and shapes a prior self; it is rather that which constitutes the self. However, there is not one "ready-made self behind activities. There are complex, unstable, opposing attitudes, habits, impulses which gradually come to terms with one another, and assume a certain consistency of configuration" (Dewey 1922, 96).

Will is not prior to habit, nor is habit a means for which the will is the end. Our will is constituted through forms of action. To acquire a new habit, therefore, is to acquire a new relationship to the world, thus opening up new forms of meaning through action in "an adventure in discovery of a self which is possible but as yet unrealized, an experiment in creating a self which shall be more inclusive than the one which exists" (Dewey 1922, 97).

Dewey (1922, 15) insists that habits enroll the world as well as the body, entailing "the cooperation of organism and environment."[4] Thus, "walking implicates the ground as well as the legs" (14). Habit, then, is embodied, lived, and practiced. I know how to bicycle only when I have bodily knowledge of it, not when I am required to make mental calculations about how I am to move my weight or my legs. I cannot think how to ride a bike until my body knows how to do so. Yet habit is not action *on* the world; rather, "habits are ways of using and incorporating the environment in which the latter has its say as surely as the former" (15). We act *with* the world, in other words. Nails and boards are not means of a box, he notes, they "are means only when they enter into organization with things which independently accomplish definite results. These organizations are habits" (22).

As each situation is always different, so the same acts are never repeated. Our habits are adaptable and diverse: "The essence of habit is an acquired predisposition to *ways* or modes of response, not to particular acts except as, under special conditions, these express a way of behaving" (Dewey 1922, 32). Habits, therefore "are arts. They involve skill of sensory and motor organs, cunning and craft, and objective materials" (15). They are sites of expression, intelligence, and experimentation. Ideally, they can be a site of learning. Dewey characterizes the experience of the child learning to walk as a "romantic adventuring into the unknown; and every gained power is a delightful discovery of one's own powers and of the wonders of the world" (50), and encourages adults to retain the "zest of intelligence" (50–51). He resists viewing bodily repetition as opposed to life and creativity. We may think that the art of the musician is acquired through mechanical repetition in which skill, not thought, is the aim until, magically, imagination takes over. However, even in routine practice, he notes, skill is at work: a flexible, sensitive habit grows more varied by practice and use (51).

## LAW AND HABIT

How might we begin to think of law through this lens? If we follow Dewey, we would need to begin with the realm of experience, rather than with a priori abstractions of law as "structure" or "essence." Dewey consistently resists abstraction, arguing that we should not think of human social life as "one thing which may be called society" (Dewey 1925–27, 278–79). His account, refreshingly, does not seem particularly architectural (invoking larger, more important structures, containing smaller agents) but is more horizontal or topological, echoing a non-metaphysical view of law as made up only of what it is constituted by (Pottage 2012). Rather than a logic of hierarchy, this is one predicated on assemblage and affordance. If there is a difference between the components of law, it is simply a function of their relative scope and longevity. That which we deem a "structure," he argues, is not something "intrinsic and *per se*" (Dewey 1925, 64):

> A house has a structure; in comparison with the disintegration and collapse that would occur without its presence, this structure is fixed. Yet it is not something external to which the changes involved in building and using the house have to submit. It is rather an arrangement of changing events such that properties which change slowly, limit and direct a series of quick changes and give them an order which they do not otherwise possess. . . . Structure is what makes

construction possible and cannot be discovered or defined except in some realized construction, construction being, of course, an evident order of changes. (Dewey 1925, 64–65)

To isolate "structure" from these changes is to engage in a form of meaningless metaphysics, constituting it as a kind of "ghostly queerness" (Dewey 1925, 65). Similarly, if "individual habits are links in forming the endless chain of humanity" (Dewey 1922, 19), that which we call law is made present in the world through particular habits, understood as a form of human activity "which is influenced by prior activity and is in that sense acquired; which contains within itself a certain ordering or systematization of minor elements of action; which is projective, dynamic in nature, ready for overt manifestation; and which is operative in some subdued subordinate form even when not obviously dominating activity" (Dewey 1922, 31).[5]

Order, therefore, is not something "outside" habit but is produced through it. This is a useful suggestion, directing us away from a view of law as an external power that acts upon subjects. At work here is a conception of power as a capacity to act. We thus move away from a view of power as a force to be reckoned with, as something held over others, to a view of power as something that makes things happen in the world. Rather than viewing power as some force external to ourselves or as a set of structural constraints, pragmatism invites a consideration of the capacities of human actors. The effect is to resituate law's power, now "registered in antagonistic settings through our active experience of what confronts us and how we respond to that engagement" (Allen 2008, 1618).

Viewed as such, we might think of legal habits of judging or policing. We might also think of habits present in more quotidian settings. Gardening, for example, is replete with spatial choices relating to particular actions, many of which seem to relate to what we might consider to be legal concerns, such as property law. For example, if my neighbor's tree grows over my fence, may I prune it back? If so, under which circumstances? How am I to respond if my neighbor elects to unilaterally and aggressively prune my plants? There are no formal "rules" upon which people can be expected to draw (or if there are, they are likely hidden in the case law). However, there do appear to be certain patterned responses common to many gardeners.

Rather than subsuming the actions of my neighbor within an a priori category of the law, it becomes useful to think about gardening as a set of habits, some of which might usefully be bundled into what we can designate as law. Decisions about the placement of vegetables or the pruning of fence-crossing plants, therefore, entail the application of habit. They are essentially instrumental encounters with an environment (although one in which the mind and body are at work, alongside dirt, tools, sun, and so on). To garden is, of course, innately embodied, yet it is also reflexive. I do not bring my will to the gardening habit; rather, it is constituted through it. Though often repetitive, habit is skilled and creative, and potentially experimental. At the same time, it is not open ended. I think of the garden through forms of habit that close down or diminish certain possibilities.

How, then, might Dewey's account of habit start to help us think about law's *geographies* in different ways?[6] Space, it would seem, is central to the working of habit. The way we visualize the world and act spatially within it is a form of habit; we *in*habit space. Territories, put another way, like those that divide my neighbor and myself, are not an a priori space but a form of learned geographic disposition and action. We learn territory, we take it up, we do it, Dewey would suggest.[7] Territorial habits direct us to act in particular ways that are both thoughtful and unreflexive. Such territorial habits entail complicated composites of thought and action, through which will and selfhood emerge.[8] However, there is no such thing as a generalized habit of territory: as every situation differs, so the habits of territory will necessarily change. Territory depends on its context. But we cannot talk of the fence line as a "social construction," as if it were simply a product of detached representations. It has, Dewey would note, a facticity. Branches grow. Leaves drop here, not there. It is also not my fence alone—there is another person, Larry, with his own habits, against whom my habits bump up.

Yet where do such facticities come from? How is it, put another way, that my fence line is more than a combination of wood and nails, that it is also imbued with concepts of mine and his? Where did my neighbor acquire his assertive spatio-legal habits? It is tempting to point to larger structures of power (such as Property-in-General) that generate habits and then aggregate them up to a larger nexus of power. Yet, as noted, Dewey would direct us to a more contingent, practiced sense of law's geographic "power." Most immediately, as geographer John Allen (2008, 1618) notes, an emphasis on experience would suggest that power is "unlikely to be grasped as an intended effect of some 'far-off' power, but rather through a shared understanding of what is experienced subjectively." We might also follow Dewey's antifoundationalism in arguing that there are no predetermined outcomes that can be derived from law's geographies, such as our fence line.[9] Rather, such geographies should be thought of as experimental and contingent: "what matters in this pragmatic line of reasoning is how . . . resources are *used* to produce the tenuous effect that we call power. More to the point, what works best in any given situation cannot be known in advance, only *in practice*" (Allen 2008, 1616). Additionally, as many geographers will be quick to note, practice is inherently contextual. As such, as Allen puts it, it "comes without guarantees" (1623).

This is more than to say that because contexts vary, they make law different in diverse places. Rather, it is to insist that contexts, such as places, cannot be severed from law. There is no intrinsic form to property: "It is the contextual grain of places, the interplay of their social, economic and cultural dynamics, which give forces their shape, not the other way around. On this view, because nothing is pre-contextual, there is no question of lifting things out of place" (1619).[10]

When we garden, most of us do not plant vegetables up front. Habitual legal geographies are not open ended and idiosyncratic. We usually do not tear down our fences and create a garden commons with our neighbor. We understand my neighbor's aggressive pruning as a manifestation (albeit rather assertive) of certain types of expected behavior relating to ownership. We attempt to maintain a tidy face to the world, ensuring that we keep our gardens neat, the grass mowed, and the weeds removed. My habits are clearly not simply a function of my idiosyncratic engagement with the world: we do not garden alone. My habits are not my invention: they come to me shaped by a dense social environment. Certain habits become more collectively engrained or congealed in what Dewey terms *custom*. Customs exist, he notes, because individuals face the same situation and react in like fashion. More importantly, customs persist because individuals form their habits under conditions set by prior custom: "The stuff of belief and proposition is not originated by us. It comes to us from others, by education, tradition, and the suggestion of the environment. Our intelligence is bound up, so far as its materials are concerned, with the community life of which we are a part. We know what it communicates to us, and know according to the habits it forms in us" (Dewey 1922, 216).

The question then becomes how "more or less deeply grooved systems of interaction . . . modify the activities of individuals who perforce are caught up in them, and how the activities of component individuals remake and redirect previously established customs" (Dewey 1922, 44). For Dewey, refreshingly, there is no characterization of "society in general"; nor is he concerned with the exact nature of the relationship between society and the individual (the pursuit of which he dubs "nonsensical metaphysics" [Dewey 1922, 44]). Similarly, he resists metaphysical characterizations of concepts such as law, or the state: "The moment we utter the words 'The State' a score of intellectual ghosts rise to obscure our vision. . . . The notion of 'The State' draws us imperceptibly into a consideration of the logical relationship of various ideas to one another, and away from facts of human activity" (Dewey 1927, 8–9). Rather, his claim for the power of custom rests on the simple observation of a preexisting association of human beings prior to every person born into the world. Habit, put simply, operates individually and in relation to larger numbers of humans. Customs create "active demands for certain ways of acting" (Dewey 1927, 54). However, they do so in complicated, nonreductive ways that close up certain possibilities at the same time as they open others. Customs create "demands, expectations, rules, standards. These are not mere embellishments of forces which produced them, idle decorations of the scene. They are additional forces. They reconstruct. They open new avenues of endeavor and impose new labors. In short, they are civilization, culture, morality" (Dewey 1927, 57).

The propertied spatial habit whereby gardeners tend not to plant vegetables in their front garden or hack back "encroaching" vegetation, therefore, can be thought of in relation to custom, a uniformity of action. However, Dewey would not want to make metaphysical statements about such customs. It is wrong to characterize custom as law and actions of individual homeowners as somehow not law. Both are habit, differently organized. To say that habit "will be obeyed, that custom makes law, that *nomos* is lord of all, is after all only to say that habit is habit" (Dewey 1927, 54).

## HABIT AND SOCIAL CHANGE

For many critical legal geographers, alert to the workings of social power, such an account is insufficient, I suspect. To open the door to custom is to demand an analysis of power, of resistance, and of hegemony. Indeed, critics charged Dewey with having an undeveloped or naive conception of social power. C. Wright Mills, for example, criticized him for a failure to take on entrenched forms of power. From a different angle, Steven Lukes points to the workings of power in distorting people's true interests and feelings, thus masking domination and normalizing hierarchy (cited in Hildreth 2009). Yet Dewey was a social critic, taking on militarism and capitalism, and a meliorist who saw growth, a process of learning through experience, as the only moral end for social life. However, his non-foundationalist account of habit provides a distinctive and thoughtful interpretation of power, social criticism, and the possibilities of social change that critical legal geographers may find worth exploring, particularly given the tendency of some "critical" scholarship to be surprisingly unreflective about its own commitments (Blomley 2006). Again, Dewey's pragmatism resists essentialist logics and foundationalist accounts of power.[11] Rather than an architectural logic of big things, he brings us back to habit as a productive and enabling site of power. It is here, he insists, that we must look for progressive possibility, and it is here that we must guard against its negation.

How, then, are we to judge the merits of habit, such as those of my neighbor, as they relate to the geographies of law? Dewey eschews universalistic claims, insisting that there is no one correct habit. All we can work with, he notes, is "an honestly modest theory" that will be alert to the consequences of habit while never assuming that an absolute moral judgment can be made: "We have just to do the best we can with habits, the forces most under our control" (Dewey 1922, 38). For we cannot abandon habit, because to do so, of course, is to abandon the self. There is no outside to habit: "To view institutions as enemies of freedom, and all conventions as slaveries, is to deny the only means by which positive freedom in action can be secured" (Dewey 1922, 115).

Custom needs to be treated with caution too. This is not because custom may replace some foundational "real interest" with a false consciousness generated by elites. Dewey's account necessarily rejects a pregiven set of "real" interests (for a pragmatist, remember, it's context all the way down). In its place, however, he argues for the value of forms of experimental inquiry or intelligence, essential for the learning through experience that, ideally, opens up future possibilities for learning. While all habit is, in part, unreflexive, it is the "inert, stupid quality of current customs" that can lead to "conformity, constriction, surrender of scepticism and experiment" (Dewey 1922, 47). For Dewey, "What makes a habit bad is enslavement to old ruts" (48). Given that the environment is constantly changing, habits must also change. His is an anticonservative impulse: he resists deifying custom as eternal or immutable and as immune from revision. His emphasis on the social nature of habit means that he is highly attentive to the articulations between the self and the society of which it is a part. His *Public and Its Problems* (1927) takes this seriously, noting that the practical success or failure of one's habits depends to a considerable extent on others. This may foster a measure of conformity. If most people regard private property as a means for securing privacy and autonomy, and if I choose to act in those ways, then it is likely I will place myself in a productive and cooperative relationship with others. Thus, "if I live in a generally law-abiding society then it is safe to say that the social resources that are available to me as a law-abiding citizen will be greater than those that are available to me as an outlaw" (MacGilvray 2010, 37).

The critic may see this is an argument for social conservatism. Yet Dewey seeks a richly democratic public that can engage in collective communication and inquiry into its shared ends, including those served by law. The challenge, however, is that our current habits of collective action are often conservative and traditional. He is committed to an experimental approach to habit, akin to the model of inquiry within the natural sciences, centered on freedom of inquiry and the communication of ideas. Yet while such a method has been applied *to* human concerns, it is rarely put to work *in* them: "Application *in* life would signify that science was absorbed and distributed; that it was the instrumentality of that common understanding and thorough communication which is the precondition of the existence

of a genuine and effective public" (Dewey 1927, 174). Yet a "social pathology" con-
spires against effective inquiry into social institutions such as "the Constitution,
the Supreme Court, private property, free contract, and so on," which are treated
as quasi-religious institutions that are "not to be approached, save with ceremo-
nial precautions and by specially anointed officials" (Dewey 1927, 170). "Habits
of thought outlive modifications in habits of overt action," Dewey (1922, 77) also
notes. Thus, he is cautious about the possibilities of social transformation that
fails to recognize the work of habit, criticizing the "short-cut revolutionist" who
fails to realize the full force of institutions as embodied habits:

> Any one with knowledge of the stability and force of habit will hesitate to propose
> or prophesy rapid and sweeping social changes. A social revolution may effect
> abrupt and deep alterations in external customs, in legal and political institutions.
> But the habits that are behind these institutions . . . are not so easily modified.
> They persist and insensibly assimilate to themselves the outer innovations—much
> as American judges nullify the intended changes of statute law by interpreting
> legislation in the light of common law. The force of lag in human life is enormous.
> (Dewey 1922, 77)[12]

However, those who argue that social reform is impossible because of inherent
tendencies in human nature make a similar error, according to Dewey. Although
there may be some tendency to assimilate objects and events to the self, this does
not render current customs and habits of property, such those of my neighbor,
immutable or hardwired: "The need for appropriation has to be satisfied; but only
a calloused imagination fancies that the institution of private property as it exists A.D. 1921 is the sole or indispensable means of its realization" (Dewey 1927,
82–83). Human life, he insists, is an experiment:

> In the face of this elasticity, it requires an arrogant ignorance to take the existing
> complex system of stocks and bonds, of wills and inheritance, a system supported
> at every point by manifold legal and political arrangements, and treat it as the sole
> legitimate and baptized child of an instinct of appropriation. . . . We can conceive
> of a state of things in which the proprietary impulse would get full satisfaction by
> holding goods as mine in just the degree in which they were visibly administered
> for a benefit in which a corporate community shared. (Dewey 1927, 82–83).

Existing systems persist not because of an unalterable human nature, therefore,
but because of the inertia of established habit.[13] Habit persists until the environment rejects it. However, as he notes, there is the danger of a vicious circle—the
direction of native activity depends on acquired habits, but acquired habits can be
modified only by the redirection of impulses. Existing institutions impose their

stamp upon impulse and instinct. Thus it is, sadly, that my neighbor is unlikely to change his gardening habits.

Change, for Dewey, must necessarily take habit seriously. Dewey offers a few suggestions for change (true to form, he does not prescribe any particular end, other than his general meliorism). He points to the education of the young, in whom habits are more formative and flexible, as one arena (of significance to those of us who teach) while also noting that an increase in what he refers to as the complexity of culture can lead to the collision of habits, thus leading to new possibilities. Hildreth (2009) also develops Dewey's concept of the problematic situation, a moment at which habit is disrupted and the familiar becomes "not fully familiar" (Dewey 1925, 235; see also MacGilvray 2010; Shannon 2000)[14]. This, it is suggested, opens the possibility for "experimental inquiry," trying new combinations of actions and thought, and testing their results. The little flags my partner leaves on Larry's clandestine prunings may (perhaps) constitute such a problematic situation, disrupting legal geographies just as the squat of a privately owned building in the name of the commons may disrupt the habits of property. However, there is no certain outcome here. Pragmatism is nothing but open to contingency and ambiguity. As Allen (2008, 1616) notes, "Even though power may be exercised . . . with a purpose in mind, the difficulty of matching means to ends implies that the outcome of their actions is always likely to be in question. . . . What works best in any given situation cannot be known in advance, only *in practice.*"

## CONCLUSION

Pragmatism more generally offers legal geography (perhaps in its "postdisciplinary" manifestation) a number of useful insights: some of us may wish to draw from its pluralism and antifoundationalism, and from its commitment to experimentation, contingency, and democracy, for example. However, it should not be seen as a systematic theoretical blueprint, to be uncritically inserted into legal geography. Most immediately, it is not an idea so much as a set of tools for helping us think. And those tools clearly are more or less useful depending on circumstance. As forks are not usually helpful when eating soup, so particular concepts work best in particular intellectual settings. Dewey would insist that his suggestions not be thought of as the definitive tool, but as open to testing against the world, to revision, and to further conversation.

My purpose here has been rather more focused, with an emphasis on the practices of law and the relationships of those practices to legal spaces. This could include neighborly disputes over boundary lines but also much more. Law is experienced in multiple ways, formal and informal, whether in the practices of policing, judging, and enforcing; the enactments of sovereignty by the refugee, indigenous person, and border guard; and so on. It is spatialized through a web of boundaries, relationships, and codings. Legal geography regards such spatializations as important in shaping behavior and belief, but lacks an analysis of how these legal geographies get taken up by people. Habit, perhaps, may offer some salutary insights for thinking about the practices and dispositions associated with law's spaces.[15]

Most immediately, habit gives us a new place to begin. Rather than beginning with abstractions such as law and space, and the degrees in which these get "taken up" by actors, a Deweyan treatment of habit directs our attention to the experience of the world (including what we can call, provisionally, law). Habit, with its emphasis on transaction and event, points us to practices and action that are simultaneously spatial and temporal. We can imagine habits of territory, jurisdiction, property, and so on (although only insofar as such terms are taken as placeholders, not as essences).

If law is simply an empty formalism unless practiced and spatialized in the world, this seems a useful consideration. Rather than just asking in whose interests such legal spaces are made, habit asks us to inquire into how they are put together and stabilized, as well as changed. Rather than taking legal spaces as given in their effects, as in assertions that "boundaries mean" (Delaney et al. 2001, xviii), it becomes important to take seriously the ways in which we experience, experiment, and inhabit such spaces.

This is helpful, second, in encouraging us to be cautious of metaphysical or architectural thinking in relation to legal geographies; for example, that my fence is a manifestation of some larger phenomenon ("property") that operates at some higher level. As noted earlier, if we follow Dewey, all we have is habit. While some legal habits operate collectively, as custom, and other habits appear more rarefied (e.g., judging, as opposed to individual acts of boundary maintenance), law is no more than the habits of which it is constituted.[16]

Similarly, habit redirects our thinking to power as a creative capacity rather than as a form of instrumental "power-over." This is useful in encouraging us to think of power as always present, a relational effect of interaction and engagement with the world, rather than a prior capacity, waiting to be deployed (Allen 2008). It invites us to explore the experimental and creative ways in which people engage with legal geographies (Berk and Galvan 2009), as well as pointing us to the contingencies of power, such that outcomes cannot be read off any particular set of institutions or regulations. Law, put another way, is aspiration, not actuality. Rather than legal geographies calling up certain responses, an attention to habit redirects our attention to contingency, creativity, experimentation, contextuality, and alterity. Yet habit is not open ended: my fence habits are acquired within a social context that predisposes them to certain forms. Nonetheless, habits can be remarkably resistant to change. Dewey's way of thinking should not lead us to a Pollyannaish legal geography of play and possibility. As my neighbor's actions suggest, the habits of legal space are also (frequently) exclusionary, constraining, and self-interested.

The introduction to this collection encourages us to consider new theoretical resources in advancing legal geography. Here, I have dipped into an older tradition (which continues to develop on its own terms while also proving influential in the development of much contemporary social theory). To follow Dewey down the rabbit hole of pragmatism is both unsettling and liberating. In calm, measured, and accessible prose, he upends metaphysics and forces us to reconsider taken-for-granted conventions. He refuses the utopian blueprint while providing powerful critical resources. He rejects the notion of Truth while endorsing the idea of the true. In endorsing an experimental approach to collective life, he would approve, I hope, of the examination of the scholarly habits that constitute legal geography.

## NOTES

Many thanks for the comments of participants at the Buffalo conference, for the helpful advice of my pragmatic colleague, Meg Holden, and for the editorial advice of Irus Braverman.

1. This is not a form of relativism or an open-ended sort of social constructivism. While pragmatists argue that there is no unmediated access to the world, and that such a world is available to us only through culturally inflected beliefs and language, they insist that there is still a world out there. For James (1975, 283) a "notion of reality independent of either of us, taken from ordinary social experience, lies at the base of the pragmatist definition of truth. With some such reality any statement to be counted true, must agree." The distinction between actors and a world of objects they face is not an ontological divide inherent to the world itself, however, but "an analytical distinction that is warranted because it corresponds to the distinctive nature of the subject's perspective, i.e. the lived reality of resistance, negativity and contradiction that agents experience as they engage the world. The world of social objects and institutions, while every inch a social construction, confronts actors as an external, objective world that is handed down from past generations and is governed by mechanisms and rules of its own" (Konings 2010, 66).

2. We can see discussions of habit in the writings of other first generation pragmatists, including Peirce, who argued that "the essence of belief is the establishment of a habit, and different beliefs are distinguished by the different modes of action to which they give rise. . . . [W]hat a thing means is simply what habits it involves" (Dickstein 1998, 2–3).

3. "Scientific men, philosophers, literary persons, are not men and women who have so broken the bonds of habits that pure reason and emotion undefiled by use and wont speak through them. They are persons of a specialized infrequent habit" (Dewey 1927, 160). Irus

Braverman's contribution to this collection (Chapter 5) can be seen as an attempt to unpack some of the "specialized habits" of legal geographic scholars.

4. As far as I can tell, he does not go so far as to make a post-posthumanist argument for the agency of the world. Rather, his emphasis seems closer to the concept of performation (Callon 2007) or affordance (Rose, Degen, and Basdas 2010), predicated on the relation between human and nonhuman objects.

5. Valverde (1998), in her useful overview of habit more generally, and its application to sociolegal studies, similarly notes habit's utility in allowing us to go beyond the "structure versus agency" debate.

6. See the special issue of *Geoforum* (2009, vol. 29) on pragmatism and geography.

7. Given Dewey's abiding interest in education, it becomes helpful to think about the learning (and, presumably, the teaching) of the habits of legal spaces; "all distinctively human action has to be earned, and the very heart, blood and sinews of learning is creation of habitudes" (Dewey 1927, 160).

8. Dewey may also provide a useful set of pointers for thinking about law's spaces as transactional (i.e., as each as part of each other), not as separate (cf. Cutchin 2007, 2008).

9. As Barnes (2008, 1547) puts it, for pragmatism "the word 'and' trails along after every sentence. Something always escapes." Put another way, "The universe is plural; it hangs together, but in more ways than one" (Menand 2001, 377).

10. That there are temporalities to habit and custom is, I hope, clear, opening some interesting connections to those chapters in this collection that underscore the time-spaces of law.

11. Yet Dewey (1930, 100–101) fully recognized that not all have equal powers to act within the world: "The notion that men are equally free to act if only the same legal arrangements apply to all—irrespective of differences in education, in command of capital, and the control of the social environment which is furnished by the institution of property—is a pure absurdity, as the facts have demonstrated. The only possible conclusion, both intellectually and practically, is that the attainment of freedom conceived as power to act in accord with choice depends upon positive and constructive changes in social arrangements."

12. For William James (1890, 121), habit was the "enormous fly-wheel of society, its most precious conservative agent. It alone is what keeps us all within the bounds of ordinance, and saves the children of fortune from the envious uprisings of the poor. . . . It keeps the fisherman and the deck-hand at sea through the winter; it holds the miner in his darkness, and nails the countryman to his log-cabin and his lonely farm through all the months of snow."

13. Rather than making the argument that legal geographies are big lies, or untruths, we might abandon the idea of absolute truth, and consider legal geographies, like those of property, pragmatically true to the extent that they prove themselves successful at instantiating themselves in the world. Despite its detractor's claims, pragmatism is not committed to a formless relativism (at least in the looser sense) or to a philosophical skepticism but rather to a form of fallibilism, a conviction that belief, while never certain, is nevertheless provisionally secure. For Peirce, "your problems would be greatly simplified if, instead of saying that you want to know the 'Truth,' you were simply to say that you want to attain a state of belief unassailable by doubt" (in Westbrook 2005, 4). Here the model of scientific inquiry has proved appealing—no belief is secure until it has been scrutinized by a community of enquirers; it has proved itself "good in the way of belief." The truth of a belief,

therefore, is to be tested in practice. Does it enable human beings to accomplish their purposes? With a borrowing from Darwin, human intelligence is a capacity that emerged to secure human survival and success: "Pragmatism claims that human thinking and acting . . . are driven by the need to respond to problems: all thought and action are provoked by a tension between ourselves as needy organisms on the one side and, on the other, the environment that must satisfy these needs. We think and act in order to reduce that tension. . . . What we call the truth about reality is just a way of describing successful thinking" (Alan Ryan, quoted in Westbrook 2005, 5).

14. Dewey also emphasizes the potential for innovation and creativity when it comes to social change. Berk and Galvan (2009, 544) concur, characterizing institutional rules not as "a script or a schema, but a skill. . . . [A]ction always takes place in relation to prior rules and practices, which serve not as guides or constraints, but as mutable raw material for action. What we call the experience of living under rules is really an experience of living through rules." Legal custom can equally be productive, facilitative, and a site for creativity, often in unexpected ways, as illustrated by Berk and Galvan's discussion of property regimes in Africa (569–75).

15. Should we be so disposed, habit can be also hooked up to a number of contemporary scholarly concerns and concepts, including embodiment, actor-network theory, performativity, nonrepresentational theory, and flat or topological geographies.

16. This is not to say that the "things" of law are not relevant but rather to recognize, with Dewey, that legal habits are necessarily entangled with an environment.

## REFERENCES

Alexander, Thomas M. 1987. *John Dewey's Theory of Art, Experience, and Nature.* Albany: State University of New York Press.

Allen, John. 2008. "Pragmatism and Power, or the Power to Make a Difference in a Radically Contingent World." *Geoforum* 39: 1613–24.

Barnes, Trevor J. 2008. "American Pragmatism: Towards a Geographical Introduction" *Geoforum* 39: 1542–54.

Berk, Gerald, and Dennis Galvan. 2009. "How People Experience and Change Institutions: A Field Guide to Creative Syncretism." *Theory and Society* 38: 543–80.

Bernstein, R. J. 1983. *Beyond Objectivism and Relativism: Science, Hermeneutics, and Praxis.* Philadelphia: University of Pennsylvania Press.

Blomley, Nicholas. 2004. "Un-Real Estate: Proprietary Space and Public Gardening." *Antipode* 36 (4): 614–41.

———. 2005a. "The Borrowed View: Privacy, Propriety, and the Entanglements of Property." *Law and Social Inquiry* 30 (4): 617–61.

———. 2005b. "Flowers in the Bathtub: Boundary Crossings at the Public-Private Divide." *Geoforum* 36 (3): 281–96.

———. 2006. "Uncritical Critical Geography?" *Progress in Human Geography* 30 (1): 87–94.

Callon, Michel. 2007. "What Does It Mean to Say That Economics Is Performative?" In *Do Economists Make Markets? On the Performativity of Economics*, edited by Donald MacKenzie, Fabian Muniesa, and Lucia Siu, 311–57. Princeton, NJ: Princeton University Press.

Cutchin, Malcolm. 2007. "From Society and Self (and Back) through Place: Habit in Transactional Context." *Occupational Therapy Journal of Research* 27 (suppl.): 50–59.

———. 2008. "John Dewey's Metaphysical Ground-Map and its Implications for Geographical Inquiry." *Geoforum* 39: 1555–69.

Delaney, David. 2010. *The Spatial, the Legal, and the Pragmatics of World-Making: Nomospheric Investigations.* New York: Routledge.

Dewey, John. 1922. *Human Nature and Conduct.* Vol. 14 of *Middle Works, 1899–1924.* Edited by Jo Ann Boydston. Charlottesville, VA: InteLex.

———. 1925. *Experience and Nature* (The Collected Works of John Dewey, 1882–1953, Later Works, Vol. 1), edited by Jo Ann Boydston. Charlottesville, VA: InteLex.

———. 1925–27. *Essays, Reviews, Miscellany, and the Public and Its Problems.* (The Collected Works of John Dewey, 1882–1953, Later Works, Vol. 2), edited by Jo Ann Boydston. Charlottesville, VA: InteLex.

———. 1927. *The Public and Its Problems.* Denver, CO: Alan Swallow.

———. 1930. *Individualism Old and New.* New York: Capricorn Books.

Dickstein, Morris. 1998. "Pragmatism Then and Now." In *The Revival of Pragmatism: New Essays on Social Thought, Law and Culture*, edited by Morris Dickstein, 1–18. Durham, NC: Duke University Press.

Engel, David. 1998. "How Does Law Matter in the Constitution of Legal Consciousness?" In *How Does Law Matter?*, edited by G. G. Bryant and A. Sarat, 109–44. Evanston, IL: Northwestern University Press.

Hildreth, R. W. 2009. "Reconstructing Dewey on Power." *Political Theory* 37 (6): 780–807.

James, William. 1890. *Principles of Psychology.* Vol. 1. New York: Henry Holt.

———. 1907. *Pragmatism: A New Way for Some Old Ways of Thinking.* New York: Longman, Green.

———. 1975. *Pragmatism and the Meaning of Truth.* Cambridge, MA: Harvard University Press.

Konings, Martijn. 2010. "The Pragmatic Sources of Modern Power." *Archives of European Sociology* 51 (1): 55–91.

MacGilvray, Eric. 2010. "Dewey's Public." *Contemporary Pragmatism* 7 (1): 31–47.

Menand, Louis. 2001. *The Metaphysical Club: A Story of Ideas in America.* New York: Macmillan.

Nedelsky, Jennifer. 1990. "Law, Boundaries and the Bounded Self." *Representations* 30: 162–89.

Pottage, Alain. 2012. "The Materiality of What?" *Journal of Law and Society* 39 (1): 167–83.

Rose, Gillian, Monica Degen, and Begum Basdas. 2010. "More on 'Big Things': Building Events and Feelings." *Transactions of the Institute of British Geographers*, n.s., 35: 334–39.

Sack, Robert. 1986. *Human Territoriality: Its Theory and History.* Cambridge: Cambridge University Press.

Sullivan, Shannon. 2000. "Reconfiguring Gender with John Dewey: Habit, Bodies, and Cultural Change." *Hypatia* 15 (1): 23–42.

Valverde, Mariana. 1998. "Governing out of Habit." *Studies in Law, Politics and Society* 18: 217–42.

Westbrook, Robert B. 2005. *Pragmatism and the Politics of Truth.* Ithaca, NY: Cornell University Press.

# 4 EXPANDING LEGAL GEOGRAPHIES

## A Call for a Critical Comparative Approach

Alexandre (Sandy) Kedar

The project of expanding the horizons of legal geography must involve the adoption of a comparative outlook. Since the late 1980s, legal geography scholarship increased and deepened immensely, simultaneously broadening its topical scope (Blank and Rosen-Zvi 2010; Blomley 2009; Butler 2009; Delaney 2010; Kedar 2003; see also the introduction to this volume). Legal geographers have gradually moved beyond the binary treatment of law and space as two distinctive autonomous realms in favor of an understanding that they are "conjoined and co-constituted." Blomley (2003a) terms this spatiolegal integration *splice*, and Delaney (2004, 2010) calls it *nomosphere*.

Contemporary legal geographers look at "the ways in which the (socio)spatial and the (socio)legal are constituted through each other" imagined and performed (Delaney 2010, 23), in an impressive range of areas, as diverse as the human body, public housing, "spaces of exception" and the "international" (Blank and Rosen-Zvi 2010; Blomley 2001, 2009; Braverman 2009a, 2009b, 2012; Delaney 2004, 2010; Kedar 2001, 2003; Yiftachel 2006; Yiftachel, Kedar, and Amara 2012). Such projects are undoubtedly important, and legal geography needs more of them.

Yet the scholarship focuses mainly on and is produced by common law countries and scholars, typically North American, with some branches in Israel, Australia, the United Kingdom, and several European countries. As noted in the introduction to this volume, the legal geography project could be enriched by studies situated out of usual ambit of the largely urban, Global Northwest. Furthermore, as legal comparatists note, comparative law—and, I argue, also *comparative* legal geography—can serve as "a critical or 'subversive' discipline that can destabilize and undermine established beliefs and conceptions" (Reimann 2002, 682; see also Nelken 2010). Nevertheless, legal geographers hardly engage in sustained comparative research.

I have approached comparative law hoping to draw upon its rich tradition of legal comparisons in suggesting an agenda for comparative legal geography. As I explain later, I discovered that legal geography scholarship could contribute to comparative law as much as, if not more than, it has to gain from it, and thus I have found ample space for cross-fertilization. Yet to date, contemporary comparative law and legal geography remain separate academic spheres. This is remarkable, as "historically, the development of spatial concepts in law appears to have originated within comparative legal studies" (Economides, Blacksell, and Watkins 1986, 163) and legal comparatists are deeply involved in the classification and mapping of "legal families" across the globe and the tracing of the movement and transplantation of law between jurisdictions. Nevertheless, there are practically no academic articles addressing the terms *comparative law* and *legal geography* in unison; I have found no entries for *geography* or *legal geography* in the indexes of leading books on comparative law and the term *comparative law* is absent from the indexes of major books in legal geography. Legal comparatists and legal geographers virtually ignore each other's work.[1]

This chapter represents an initial attempt to discuss the benefits of adopting a critical comparative legal geographical (CCLG) approach. The first part of the chapter addresses comparative law scholarship. It demonstrates that while early comparatists engaged with geography, their interest in it waned with the institutionalization of the field at the beginning of the twentieth century. Until recently, the bulk of mainstream comparative law—to which I refer to as the "dominant outlook"—was mainly conservative and formalist, and did not interact much with other academic disciplines. The dominant outlook is recently undergoing what some define as a crisis, while even mainstream comparatists begin to understand that "co-operation with other disciplines is an *essential element* for the prospect of development in the future of comparative law" (Husa 2004, 37–38). Particularly interesting is the work of critical and postcolonial comparatists who challenge the dominant outlook, and a small number have even started to take space seriously. These scholars offer insights and research questions that should inform the construction of the comparative legal geography project and that simultaneously would greatly benefit from an acquaintance with legal geography.

The second part is a preliminary attempt to envision a comparative critical legal geography inspired by both critical legal geography (CLG) and comparative law scholarship. My purpose here is no more than to raise questions and suggest some possible research directions. I focus on colonial and postcolonial settings, interrogate processes of displacement and dispossession, and argue that they are important locations to engage in CCLG. I illustrate my argument with a short case study that investigates a legal-geographical triangle set within the British "legal family": Britain, Palestine/Israel, and India/Pakistan, showing how ideas and legal concepts embodied in British war legislation were transplanted to and transformed in post-partition India/Pakistan and Israel in the form of Evacuee

Property acts in India/Pakistan and Absentee Property legislation in Israel. These laws facilitated the taking and reallocation of refugee property and played a part in postindependence spatial transformations. The chapter concludes by suggesting some additional research directions and methods.

## THE TRAJECTORY OF COMPARATIVE LAW:
## FROM ENGAGEMENT WITH GEOGRAPHY TO
## DESPATIALIZATION AND BACK?

"Modern" comparative law begins with the work of French jurists and social thinkers such as Montesquieu, the "foremost precursor of modern comparative law" (Hug 1932, 1050; see also Fauvarque-Cosson 2006) and Pascal, who, according to Grossfeld (1984), were also the pioneers of legal geography. Unlike present-day comparatists' neglect of geography, these and other early modern scholars compared legal systems while simultaneously attributing determining influences to climate and physical geography, seeking to explain legal differences "in relation to the climate of each country, to the quality of its soil, to its situation and extent" (Montesquieu, quoted in Blomley 1994, 29; see also Donahue 2006; Zweigert and Kötz 1998).

Following these and additional precursors, academic comparative law developed during the nineteenth and twentieth centuries, primarily in France, Great Britain, and Germany, and later in the United States (Cairns 2006; Clark 2006; Fauvarque-Cosson 2006; Schwenzer 2006; see generally Reimann and Zimmermann 2006). The first congress of the French Société de Législation Comparée, held in 1900, is considered the "birthplace of comparative law" (Fauvarque-Cosson 2006, 36) and set optimistic and Eurocentric goals aiming to uncover the common legal core of "advanced nations" and to contribute thereby to world unity (Clark 2006; Cotterrell 2003; Zweigert and Kötz 1998).

The inception of academic comparative law during the age of colonialism, social Darwinism, classificatory scientific models, legal formalism, and dogmas of progress had much to do with the discipline's trajectory (Glenn 2006; Riles 2001). Comparatists classify national systems, comparing and ascribing them to "legal families." At the apex of this classification, one usually finds a particular European "family," such as civil (sometimes subdivided) or common law. During late nineteenth and early twentieth centuries, this evolutionary classification often justified colonization (Arminjon, Nolde, and Wolff 1950; Cairns 2006; David and Brierley 1985; Glenn 2006; Zweigert and Kötz 1998). The "legal families" classification has even generated a series of legal maps, such as the one John Wigmore (1929) published in *Geographical Review*. Furthermore, comparatists argue that the divergent heritage of European legal families left lingering traces in their former African colonies. This creates a particular, nonlinear legal geography: "There is still a deep divide between the previous French and Belgian colonies on the one hand, and those that were British on the others. This is why it is much easier for a lawyer from Ghana to understand a lawyer from Kenya, Uganda, or even from England, which are far away, than a lawyer from the Ivory Coast next door" (Zweigert and Kötz 1998, 67).

Although there is a growing criticism of "legal families," the concept still plays a dominant role in comparative legal studies (Glenn 2006; Menski 2006; Twining 2009), and as I argue in the conclusion, it can assist legal geographers in constructing comparative conceptual tools.

Following Günter Frankenberg (1985), critical comparatists have challenged the discipline's conservatism; its "keeping ideology out of comparative law analysis" (Kennedy 2012, 54); its lack of a solid critical agenda; and the "epistemological racism" of the dominant outlook, which "remains Eurocentric" (Watt 2006, 583, 597). They note that the "core" of "modern" law is still neocolonial, whereas comparative law complies with the politics of "organized amnesia of law as a form of conquest" (Baxi 2003, 49–50; see also Miller and Ruru 2009). An additional critique focuses on comparative law's fixation on official legal rules and its dated law-in-the-books conception of "the legal," which leads to its dearth of dialogue with other disciplines (Cotterrell 2003, 2006; ; Gross 2011; Harris 2001; Husa 2006; Merryman 1997; Riles 2006).

All this explains comparative law's neglect of legal geography and shows how much it can gain from engaging with critical legal geography. The time seems ripe, as the winds of change have begun to reach the strongholds of the discipline while the dominant outlook is experiencing what is some observers have referred to as "the crisis of orthodox comparative law" (Harris 2001, 443–44) and the "discipline's malaise" (Reimann 2002, 672). The annual meeting of the American Society of Comparative Law in 2008, devoted to "The West and the Rest in Comparative Law," aimed at "unveiling the master 'narrative' of the Western Legal Tradition as reflected in the comparative study of law." A recent plenary session held by two leading comparative law societies revealed a similar approach (International Academy of Comparative Law and American Society of Comparative Law 2010). Comparatists have started to acknowledge that cooperation with other disciplines is crucial for the future of comparative law. However, while legal comparatists have discovered interdisciplinary work, practically none directly engages legal geography scholarship.

Nevertheless, some come quite close. For example, William Twining (2009), who devotes a chapter to "mapping law," offers insights that resonate with spatial conceptions of cultural anthropologists such as James Ferguson and Akhil Gupta (see the introduction to this volume). While the dominant approach assumes that legal relations are neatly arranged in hierarchical concentric circles ranging "from the very local, through sub-state, regional, continental, North-South, Global and beyond to outer space," Twining (2009, 14–15) argues that the picture includes "empires, alliances coalitions, diasporas, networks, trade routes and movements . . . special groupings of power such as the G7, the G8, NATO, the European Union, the Commonwealth, multi-national corporations, crime syndicates and other non-governmental organizations and networks."

Twining maintains that the amount of interdependence, influences, and interactions among legal orderings will be greater when spatial or other proximities such as historical associations (of former colonies, established alliances, or trade routes) and legal traditions such as common or civil law exist. His embedded understanding of law, which includes social practices arising at particular times and in specific places, comes as close as any legal comparatist to that of legal geographers. Thus, important comparatists begin studying legalities as embedded in social, cultural, and especially *spatial* settings. Although there still has been no meaningful direct dialogue between comparatists and legal geographers, the ground is set for such encounters.

In the next section, I address a promising area of comparative law, which some comparatists consider "at the core of the comparative legal enterprise" (Twining 2005, 214), that, while currently suffering from a failure to consider legal-geographical literature, stands to gain the most from such rethinking: the scholarship on "legal transplants." Concurrently, comparatists addressing critically mainstream transplantation discourse, such as Twining and Upendra Baxi, offer insights and research questions that should inform the construction of the comparative legal geography project.

## LEGAL TRANSPLANTS AND DIFFUSION OF LAW

A dominant research stream in orthodox comparative law, originally introduced by Allan Watson, studies the movement—commonly termed *transplantation* by comparatists—of legal norms from one country to another.[2] Watson's (1974) publication of *Legal Transplants* and his subsequent work (e.g., 1993, 2000a, 2000b) have positioned legal transplants at the forefront of the comparative project (Graziadei 2003, 2006, 2009; Nelken 2003; Twining 2005).

Transplantation scholarship has begun without paying much attention to local conditions or "extralegal" factors, and without engaging with relevant geographical literature (Cotterrell 2006).[3] Watson and his collaborator Ewald assert that legal changes are mainly "internal" processes and that social influences on legal norms are relatively unimportant (Cotterrell 2003; Nelken 2003). With such positivist focus on formal legal rules, there is no need to dwell upon local socio-spatial characteristics or to engage in empirical study (Riles 2006; Twining 2005).

Critical comparatists critique Watson's transplant theory for ignoring questions of power relations between such zones as the metropolitan center, the semiperiphery and the colonial periphery (Mattei 2006) and point out that this scholarship has focused mainly on the transplantations of "Western inputs" (Menski 2006, 51). While some question the very possibility of such transplants (Legrand 1997, 2003), law can spread similarly to ideas, structures of thoughts, innovations, fashions, and policies (Twining 2005). Transplantation does not entail full adherence to the original meanings and functions, and the process "always involve[s] a degree of cultural adaptation, a 'domestication'" (Graziadei 2009, 728).

While there is a good deal of discussion of "transplantation, transposition, spread, transfer, import/export, reception, circulation, mixing and transfrontier mobility" of law, this scholarship usually does not engage with the social science literature on diffusion (Twining 2006, 510; see also Twining 2005). Twining (2005, 221) offers a set of basic questions on diffusion that could inspire legal geographers:

> What were the conditions of the process, and the occasion for its occurrence? What was diffused? Through what channel(s)? Who were the main change agents? To what extent were the characteristics of the change agents and their contexts similar or different? When and for how long did the process occur? Why did it start at that particular time? What were the main obstacles to change? How much did the object of diffusion change in the process? What were the consequences of the process and what was the degree of implementation, acceptance and use of the diffused objects over time?

Legal diffusion includes not only a "relationship between two countries involving a direct one-way transfer of legal rules or institutions" (Twining 2006, 511). Variants include a diffusion of law from a single exporter to multiple destinations, a single importer from multiple sources, and multiple sources to multiple destinations. While the standard case is from one national legal system to another, diffusion involves cross-level transfers. Pathways of diffusion include reciprocal interactions and reexport. Diffusion involves also informal or semiformal adoptions and legal phenomena or ideas such as ideologies, theories, and personnel (Twining 2006). In response to the dominant vision of law as a Northern, European, and Anglo-American creation diffused through the world via colonialism, trade, and postcolonial influences, there is a need to enrich this discourse and recognize that there are varied processes and directions of legal diffusion that do not necessarily converge. Finally, it is crucial to include, at the core of the comparative project, the legal traditions of the Other, particularly the marginal-ized South (Twining 2009, 6–7).

The study of transplants can be a powerful critical tool. Transplants occur in several ways, including "imposition of law through violence in one form or an-other" (Graziadei 2006, 456). Although much of the literature "treats diffusion of law as part of development, modernization, and convergence," there is a "discern-ible strand . . . that treats culture, tradition, local context, and resistance sympa-thetically. One obvious reason for this is that so much of diffusion of state law is associated with colonialism and imperialism and neo-colonial forms of capital-ism" (Twining 2005, 233). For instance, comparatist Upendra Baxi (2003, 61) re-counts from a critical perspective how the British Indian penal code traveled into many of Britain's African colonies, and how "the widely-exported colonial Indian Official Secrets Act renders criminal any spatial movement by the subject within an ascribed 'place' as notified, say by the executive. . . . Colonial penal legality . . . abounds in models of legislation that constitute the political *geographies of injus-tice*." Thus, "among the formidable challenges which await tomorrow's comparat-ist [and legal geographers] . . . are the tasks of tracing the sometimes improbable paths taken by migrating law, of investigating the ways in which they come to be assimilated, rejected or refashioned" (Munday 2003, 9).

The time seems ripe for a "spatial turn" in comparative law, a perspective found—in an environmental determinist version—in the scholarship of compar-ative law's precursors but lost with the institutionalization of the discipline. The reintroduction of spatiality and an engagement with CLG scholarship could assist comparative law in recovering from its current malaise and embarking on a new trajectory. Simultaneously, comparatists' insights, particularly those of critical and postcolonial scholarship could provide powerful, though limited, research tools and help expand legal geography's horizons.

In the next section, I examine processes of displacement and dispossession in colonial and postcolonial settings, which I conceive as important locations for en-gaging in comparative CLG. After introducing CLG scholarship on dispossession, I offer an example that shortly examines how ideas and legal concepts embodied in British war legislation were transplanted to and transformed in India/Pakistan and in Israel.

## CRITICAL COMPARATIVE LEGAL GEOGRAPHY
## OF DISPOSSESSION

While legal geography consists of several approaches, a powerful stream adopts a critical perspective. As the choice of title of Blomley's (1994) seminal book, *Law,*

*Space and the Geographies of Power* hints at and as the book demonstrates, attention to the interconnectedness and mutual constitution of law and space often entails a critical exposition of their frequent role in the production of oppressive power structures. Critical legal geography examines how spatial-legal alignments contribute to the legitimation and persistence of hierarchical social orders (Delaney 2010; Yiftachel 2006). It endeavors to unveil the constructed entanglements of the spatiolegal and to demonstrate that, although they are conventionally conceived as neutral and static, as integral components of the natural and unchangeable order of things, they are social constructions that "systematically favor the powerful: employers, men, whites, property owners, and so on" (Blomley 2003a, 30). Critical legal geography draws attention to neglected and hidden areas and boundaries, as well as to those that are "taken for granted," within which hierarchical social orders are forged (Kedar 2003). These contribute to the creation of a legal geography of power and powerlessness, of zones of security and those of insecurity, of legal and illegal presence, of emplacement and displacement.

Property, and especially landed property, is a central locus where such a power-space-law nexus is established and maintained (Blomley, 2003b; Delaney 2004; Kedar 2001, 2003). As Delaney (2004, 849) so aptly describes, while frequently the immediate displacement of the homeless, refugees, and indigenous peoples is effectuated by physical force, often "displacement is effected through the force of reason," by the enactment of statutes and the "canons of statutory interpretation, . . . [and] the submission before grammatical imperatives." Violences served "as a vector of colonial power. . . . Space, property and violence were performed simultaneously" (Blomley 2003b, 129). Critical legal geography has exposed how law is used to place and displace and "to produce the spaces of racial subordination (segregated spaces, native reserves, colonies). . . . As examples as varied as apartheid, Jim Crow, White Australia and indigenous reserves in different parts of the world demonstrate, racialization is commonly effected through processes of spatialization: separation, confinement, exclusion, expulsion, and forced removal" (Delaney 2009, 167–68).

Such processes of violent spatialization can serve as fertile ground for comparative CLG, and I now move to examine such an example.

## BRITAIN, INDIA/PAKISTAN, PALESTINE/ISRAEL

This case study investigates a legal-geographical triangle set within the British "legal family," showing how ideas and legal concepts embodied in the World War II–era British Trading with the Enemy Act (TEA) moved in space and were transplanted to and transformed in two of its former possessions: postpartition India/

Pakistan as evacuee property legislation and Palestine/Israel in the form of the Israeli absentee property legislation. These territories underwent partition, ethnic war, mass population movements, a radical restructuring of their human and physical landscapes, and a simultaneous creation of new property regimes and legal geographies.

As we have seen, comparatists contend that legalities are "transplanted" to novel settings. They move not only from "advanced Western" centers to recipient peripheries but also in varied diffusion patterns. In the process, they are transformed and sometimes reexported. Transplantation can be violent. Legal transplantations are more likely to occur between regimes in which spatial or other proximities exist, like former colonies, or between countries sharing legal traditions such as the common law.

The present case applies and interrogates these insights. Until the mid-twentieth century, the British Empire ruled much of the world, including India and Palestine. In this context, members of epistemic legal communities communicated with one another and legal actors were moving across regions, transporting with them legal conceptions, and implementing and adapting those in new locations, while leaving traces, traditions, and lines of communications that continued to influence former possessions long after the British left (see, e.g., Smandych 2010).

## Britain and Mandate Palestine

During World War II, most belligerents enacted or reapplied legislation limiting, freezing or confiscating enemy property (Domke 1943; Grathii 2006; McNair and Watts 1966). The British TEA (1939) provided that the Board of Trade could appoint a Custodian of Enemy Property (CEP) and vest in him enemy property (see Domke 1943, 385). Ordinarily, decisions to vest property in the custodian were taken on an individual basis and included only designated property (Domke 1943; Foreign and Commonwealth Office 1998). Vesting property in the custodian gave him almost unlimited powers with respect to that property (Greenspan 1959; McNair and Watts 1966).

As the legislation did not directly apply to Mandate Palestine, it was transplanted in the form of the Trading with the Enemy Ordinance (TEO) of 1939 and subsequent legislation that closely followed the British model.[4] In Palestine, the decision of whether to transfer specific properties to the custodian remained in the hands of the High Commissioner. While he issued specific vesting orders, many of them as a protective measure to safeguard property in Palestine of Jews under Nazi sway, unlike the future Indian, Pakistani, and Israeli legislation, most property of enemy nationals was not vested in the custodian (Kantrovitch 1943).

The custodian received stringent procedural and evidentiary powers, which the future Israeli legislation regulating absentee property essentially reproduced. A certificate issued by the custodian declaring "enemy property" or "with regard to matters within the scope of his duties" served as evidence of the facts stated in it (TEO Sec. 9(2)), "unless the Court directs otherwise for special reasons."[5] The vesting or transferal of a property by the custodian could not be invalidated simply on the grounds that the person declared by the custodian an enemy was discovered not to be one (Sec. 9(b)(4)).

Many of the trading-with-the-enemy arrangements were adopted in the future Israeli evacuee property legislation, such as the office of the Israeli Custodian of Absentee Property (CAP), the stringent powers accorded him, and the formal extinguishing of all former rights to the property vested in the custodian (Fischbach 2003, 21). Israeli legislation differed in three essential areas: First, unlike the British laws, Israeli law included persons who had never left their residence and were not nationals of enemy states. Second, unlike the British Mandatory legislation that required specific orders, Israeli legislation vested in the CAP all property belonging to anyone coming under the statutory definition of *absentee*. Last, while both the stated aims of Mandatory legislation and the practices associated with it presented it as a temporary economic weapon until hostilities end, the stated purpose of Israeli legislation remained vague, in practice serving as a tool for extensive expropriation of Arab land in Israel.[6] To find the sources of these arrangements, we have to turn to the Pakistani and Indian legislation.

## India/Pakistan

As was Israel, established about a year later, Pakistan and India were established in a context of intercommunal violence after a period of British colonial rule, with the partition of British-controlled India into the states of Pakistan and India on August 15, 1947 (Frazer 1988; Moore 1988). As a result, between 500,000 to 1 million people died and an estimated 14 million to 17 million people crossed the Indo-Pakistani border, leaving behind vast amounts of property (Naqvi 2007; Schechtman 1951; Talbot 2011; Talbot and Singh 2009, 61–62; Vernant 1953, 736–37; Zamindar 2007). While Indian and Pakistani lawmakers drew on the British TEA, their legislation incorporated new components that facilitated not only vesting but also transfer and reallocation of ownership.

On September 9 and 14, 1947, respectively, the governments of Pakistan and India issued ordinances creating custodians of evacuee property (Das Gupta 1958, 190). These ordinances were modeled after the British CEP (Vernant 1953, 739), but in the context of the massive population transfer, they served very different functions. Initially, the stated intention of the legislation was to preserve refugee properties (Das Gupta 1958), but Hindu and Sikh evacuees' property served as the major source for the resettlement in Pakistan of Muslim refugees from India, and land belonging to Muslim evacuees would serve to settle Hindu and Sikh refugees in India. On September 9, 1947, concurrently with the creation of the office of Custodian of Evacuee Property—ostensibly created to preserve property on behalf of its owners—Pakistan enacted an ordinance "to provide for the economic rehabilitation of West Punjab" (West Punjab Economic Rehabilitation Ordinance, No. IV of 1947, *West Punjab Gazette*, Lahore, September, 10, 1947, quoted in Das Gupta 1958, 191). This ordinance granted sweeping powers to the province's rehabilitation commissioner. For settling refugees, he could distribute land abandoned by evacuees (Das Gupta 1958; Schechtman 1951; Vakil 1950). A Hindu refugee could recover his property only if he physically returned to Pakistan. In light of the ethnic violence then raging, few Hindus ventured back into Pakistan (Schechtman 1951, 408; Vakil 1950). India issued similar ordinances (Das Gupta 1958, 193; Schechtman 1951, 411; Vernant 1953, 751).

The transplanted British TEA continued to transform as both India and Pakistan gradually enacted laws that broadened the definition of evacuees and vested in their custodians almost unlimited powers, with respect not only to evacuees but also to *intending evacuees*, a term referring to anyone contemplating migration from one country to the other (Das Gupta 1958, 200). Furthermore, Pakistani legislation permitted classifying as "evacuee" any landowner only visiting friends or family who had not even left Pakistan (Das Gupta 1958, 202; Vakil 1950, 109; Vernant 1953, 756). Such definitions, which included persons who had temporarily left their habitual place of residence, resembled the future Israeli legislation and the status of "present absentee."

## Israel/Palestine

On November 29, 1947, the United Nations voted in favor of the partition of Palestine. The 1948 War of Independence/Nakba that ensued resulted in the establishment of Israel; the flight, expulsion, and barred return of hundreds of thousands of Palestinian refugees; and the immigration of hundreds of thousands of Jews to Israel, including most Jews who had been living in Arab countries and Holocaust survivors (Morris 1987, 2008; Patai 1971; Said 1980). Israel initiated a process of land nationalization, settling Jews on former Palestinian land. The absentee property legislation and the Development Authority Act served as major legal instruments in this process (Jirys 1976; Kedar 2003; Morris 1987).[7]

Comparatists argue that "[t]ransplants are affected by the actors and the networks of individuals . . . that play a role in the diffusion of laws" (Graziadei 2006, 473), contending that "ideas about law and legal institutions migrate from one jurisdiction and social context to another as a result of the efforts of individual legal actors working in the service of their individual interests—their personal career interests, the interests of their families or class, or of their firms and organizations" (Riles 2006, 789). In this case, the key actor, and the major "nomospheric technician" (Delaney 2010, 157–95) was Zalman Lifshitz, the prime minister's advisor on land and border demarcation who served as a major architect of the legislation. Archival sources reveal that Lifshitz and other Israeli officials closely followed and adopted the Indian and Pakistani evacuee legislation and policies. Lifshitz regularly received copies of the legislation of evacuee property in India and Pakistan from local correspondents like Jain Book Agency in New Delhi, and Israeli experts minutely analyzed the legislation and frequent amendments to it (Counselor on Arab Affairs, 1949).

On March 30, 1949, Lifshitz (1949) submitted to Prime Minister Ben-Gurion the "Report on the Need for a Legal Settlement of the Issue of Absentee Property to Facilitate Its Permanent Use for Settlement, Housing, and Economic Recovery Needs." He asserted that countries in similar situations, such as India and Pakistan, had assumed vast powers to liquidate refugee property for state use and urged the Israeli government "to proceed in a similar manner," as "there [was] no lack of precedents" (5–6). Lifshitz surveyed the two-statute model that Pakistan had adopted a few months earlier and explained that while Pakistani lawmakers drew on the British Trading with the Enemy Act, their legislation incorporated new components facilitating expropriation, but also ownership transfer and reallocation. The first ordinance authorized a "custodian of evacuee property" to take refugee property and transfer it to a "rehabilitation authority." The Rehabilitation Authority, created by another ordinance the same day, was empowered to "pool and allot" property to others. These two statutes created an integrated system that enabled the taking of Sikh and Hindu evacuee property in Pakistan and the use of that same land for resettling Muslim evacuees from India. Lifshitz (1949, 10) proposed replacing the temporary absentee property emergency regulations "with a new law, similar to the above mentioned Pakistani regulations and based on the principles they contain"; see also Forman and Kedar 2004). Commenting on Lifshitz's proposal, the high-ranking legal counselor Aharon Ben-Shemesh, remarked:

> In the absence of a recognized international legislative institution, recognized
> international customs and arrangements have a compulsory power. From this

perspective, we should see in: (a) the date of the Ordinances (October 1948) (b) in the fact that the problems addressed by these ordinances stem, like with us from the birth of this Muslim country, (c) in the fact that this country belongs to the British Commonwealth and to the U.N., big advantages that make it a first rate international precedent and we should chose to use it without hesitation." (Ben-Shemesh 1949, 6–7)

In concluding, he wrote: "The Pakistani Ordinances are a first rate international legal precedent. Their date and the similar problems give it an advantage over other precedents. This is an example on how these problems are solved *today*. . . . We should take this paved road and adjust it to our needs without hesitations" (Ben-Shemesh 1949, 8).

In 1949, two bills resembling the Indian and Pakistani ordinances came before the Knesset. Like its British, Mandatory, Indian, and Pakistani counterparts, the Israeli custodian received stringent and encompassing administrative and quasi-judicial powers. Likewise, the evidentiary and procedural tools made available to him were powerful ones. The custodian could appropriate any property on the strength of his own judgment. All he needed to do was certify in writing that a person, body of persons, or property came under the status of "absentee" or "absentee property." The burden of proof then shifted upon the owner or person involved.

In the British TEA, vesting of "enemy property" in the custodian constituted an administrative act, exercised upon a specific individual on the basis of particular considerations. The Israeli legislation, like its Indian and Pakistani models, introduced fundamentally different arrangements. While using the British legislation, it dramatically transformed it into a powerful tool of dispossession and resettlement, according to which, all property of "absentees" was vested in the custodian without need for any further legal recourse. It applied retroactively, setting a specific date as a watershed. It included "present absentees," a concept resembling the "intending evacuees" of India and Pakistan. It served not only as an instrument of war but also, as in India and Pakistan, gradually evolved from a temporary to a permanent measure with the establishment of a "Development Authority" inspired by the Pakistani Rehabilitation Authority, and transferred to that authority the full and unencumbered ownership of absentees' property.

During the parliamentary debates over the legislation of the Evacuee Property Act, Finance Minister Eliezer Kaplan explained, "We have learned of the recent example of the Indian and Pakistani nations that have also faced the problem of refugees and a mass exchange of population. These two states faced the difficulty of abandoned property head on" (Divrei HaKnesset 1949, 139). These countries, too, saw fit to establish a Development Authority, he explained. "When one reads the Indian statute, one entertains the thought that after all we have nothing to be ashamed of in our statute, despite the fact that it is far from being an acme of perfection." Kaplan also likened the institution of the custodian of absentee property to the British Custodian of Enemy Property. The Knesset enacted the Absentees' Property Law in March 1950 and the Development Authority (Transfer of Property) Law in July 1950.[8] This legislation incorporated elements from the British TEA and TEO, as well as the Pakistani and Indian evacuee acts. It served as a cornerstone of the transformative Israeli spatiolegal machinery that facilitated the expropriation and reallocation of Arab land in the aftermath of 1948, and contributed to the enduring transformation of Palestinian and Israeli human geographies.

## CONCLUSION

"[T]he nomosphere is radically heterogeneous. How it is manifest in, say, rural Sumatra is vastly different than how it is manifest in midtown Manhattan" (Delaney 2004, 852). Moving ahead in legal geography entails a comparative project seeking to understand similarities and differences between nomospheres. It should integrate insights and concepts informed by both comparative law and legal geography into a critical comparative legal geographical investigation that is so conspicuously absent from current scholarship in both fields.

The concept of legal families could contribute to comparative legal geography, but this necessitates elaboration. For instance, we could develop a typology that would take into account traditional comparative law classifications such as "common law" and "civil law" while simultaneously paying attention to sociospatial factors. Comparative legal geography could investigate nomospheric situations such as indigenous dispossession in countries belonging to different legal families and assess the scope and endurance of distinctive legacies while they engage with local geographies and legalities, as well as with regional and international practices. This could assist in the development of a novel classification of nomospheric situations according to states' performances. We can envision similar classifications of other typical nomospheric situations, such as those concerning homeless persons, refugees, illegal immigrants, public housing, workplaces, public-private divides, wars, spaces of exceptions, nature, and the like. With sufficient research, and depending on states' performances in these situations, it might become possible to assess states according to a "nomospheric scale" or even to classify them into "nomospheric families." Such nomospheric families would differ from current formalist comparative law classifications and would take into account not so much law in the books as emplaced legalities and law in action.

At least as promising is research on the transplantation and mobilities of spatiolegal knowledge and institutions between states and empires and the role of different actors in promoting and resisting it. In the case study examined here, transplantation took place within the framework of the British Empire and its postempire colonies. However, the movement can take place between empires as well. For instance, French colonizers adopted structures developed by the British Empire such as the Torrens land settlement and registration system and used them in their own colonies in Tunisia, Madagascar, French Congo, West Africa, and Morocco, even though land registration in France was very different (Graziadei 2006). Why did this transplantation take place? How did it affect, and how was it affected by, local geographies?

In studying nomospheric movement, attention should be devoted to recent developments in the social science scholarship on mobility. In their editorial in the first volume of *Mobilities*, Hannam, Sheller, and Urry (2006) announced the dawn of a "mobility turn" in the social sciences and called for attention to mobilities, immobilities, and moorings. In a related article, Sheller and Urry (2006) proclaimed the emergence of a "mobility paradigm." The mobility paradigm stems from scholarship rooted in a number of social sciences fields, including anthropology, sociology, cultural, transport, migration, international and political studies, and geography (see also Cochrane and Ward 2012). This scholarship simultaneously emphasizes that "all mobilities entail specific often highly embedded and immobile infrastructures" (Sheller and Urry 2006, 210). This literature investigates therefore not only mobilities but also immobilities (McCann forthcoming).

This emergent paradigm has so far ignored legal mobility and been ignored by legal comparatists. Although much of it tracks movements of persons and objects, it also focuses on the mobility of ideas and policies. Such scholarship is especially inspiring for those interested in nomospheric transfers. McCann and Ward (2013, 3) notice the formulation of a multidisciplinary perspective "on how, why where and with what effects policies are mobilized, circulated, learned, reformulated and reassembled." This emerging scholarship embraces "critical genealogies of policy discourse; the tracking of policy networks, norms and actors; . . . and various forms of transnational, cross-scalar and relational comparativism" (Peck and Theodore 2010, 169). Policy transfer depends on networks of experts and additional protagonists, grounded in local conditions and serving as "links" that are embedded in material places and often in specific temporalities (Garrett, Dobbins, and Simmons 2008, quoted in Peck 2011). Similarly, we should look for nomospheric mobilities in concrete sites—offices of state attorneys; governmental planners; interdepartmental meetings; courts of law; local and international architectural, planning, and law firms; legally and spatially oriented nongovernmental organizations; law schools and planning departments; local governments; academic and professional conference halls—where nomospheric ideas, structures, and practices are constructed, conveyed, and transformed.

Furthermore, we should pay attention to the "dialectical reconstruction of policy landscapes. 'Mobile' policies . . . dynamically reconstitute the terrains across which they travel, at the same time as being embedded within, if not products of, extralocal regimes and circuits" (Peck 2011, 793). Indeed, "mobile policies rarely travel as complete 'packages' they move in bits and pieces—as selective discourses, inchoate ideas, and synthesized models—and they therefore 'arrive' not as replicas but as policies already-in-transformation" (Peck and Theodore 2010, 170). Simultaneously, they are "*co-produced* through concurrent processes of site-specific experimentation, purposeful intermediation, and emulative networking" (171). Mobilities scholarship instructs us not to look so much at incremental and orderly diffusion but instead to devote more attention to "moments of rupture, transition, and transformation" (Peck 2011, 791), such as the partitions, wars, and population transfers.

In the example of the British, Indian/Pakistani, and Palestinian/Israeli triangle offered earlier, we began to track the traces of trading-with-the-enemy legislation, which circulated, in bits and pieces, from London bureaus during World War II to specific offices and officials in postpartition India, Pakistan, British Palestine, and Israel while being restructured in the route. We unraveled a network linked by "immobile infrastructures" such as the Jain Book Agency in New Delhi and the office of Zalman Lifshitz in Jerusalem, which transferred knowledge and practices to Israel. Then in Israel, a local network of different nomospheric actors and technicians reformulated and reassembled that knowledge and thereby facilitated the radical restructuring of post-1948 legal, human, and political Israeli and Palestinian geographies.

Likewise, the legal geographies of settler and deeply divided multiethnic societies in general and between such states and their indigenous peoples in particular, can serve as important prisms for comparative critical legal geography of displacement (on the land disputes between Israel and its indigenous Bedouins, see Yiftachel, Kedar, and Amara 2012). By examining the role of law and legal technicians in creating and sustaining differential nomospheric zones and tools of displacement, we can begin forming generalizations about how such nomospheric zones are created and sustained. For instance, a comparative legal geography of the terra nullius doctrine (Daes 2001, Sec. 31; Miller and Ruru 2009) could be particularly promising, as this doctrine served as a prime instrument in displacing indigenous peoples while simultaneously denying the dispossession. Additionally, some countries, such as Canada, New Zealand, and Australia, as well as emerging international norms are moving away from this and adjacent doctrines and could serve as models for advancing nomospheric transformations.

Once we know more about nomospheric families, we may trace the diffusion and transplantation of specific ideas, institutions, and techniques that facilitated or hampered dispossession and domination within and between nomospheric families—terra nullius doctrines; classifications of "enemy," "evacuee," and "absentee"; settlement of title practices. Likewise, we can trace the movement of and resistance to other nomospheric conceptions, structures, personnel, and practices.

We should not only follow the movement but also compare how nomospheric ideas, concepts, and institutions developed in different settings. A comparative CLG could investigate the networks through which moved the regimes of separation barriers in East and West Germany, Israel/Palestine, India/Pakistan, North/South Cyprus, Northern Ireland, United States/Mexico, Spain/Morocco, and Malaysia/Thailand. What are the commonalities and differences between these mobility or immobility regimes (McCann forthcoming) once in place, and what can we learn from their local transformations? A comparison of legal geography of trees and afforestation is also a promising area. Trees serve as a prime tool in the struggle between Israeli and Palestinians, and earlier the British declared forest reserves to transform them into state lands in Palestine, India, and Cyprus (Braverman 2009b). Mawani (2007, 724) notices the role of colonial forest laws in dispossessing indigenous peoples "from Africa, to Australia, to North America."

With the accumulation of comparative legal geography scholarship, we could imagine a classification along a scale of urban or rural displacements and emplacement or look at the diffusion and transplantation of spatiolegal knowledge and practices between members of global municipal "families" in reaction to social protests such as the Occupy movement. However, hegemony is never complete, and such policies are marked by "contradictions and contestations" (Peck and Theodore 2010, 171). Thus, "anti-poverty movements in Toronto and Mexico City [serve] not only as spaces of resistance to neoliberal rule, but as sites for the production of alternative policy projects, visions and strategies" (171). Peck and Theodore ask whether these alternative models travel differently than those emulating the dominant paradigm, and legal geographers should ask how counterhegemonic, oppositional spatiolegal knowledge and practices move among social activists.

Comparisons should not solely focus on the dark heritage of colonial dispossession but also should look at some contemporary inspiring transformations, which can serve in planning reforms and imagining progressive solutions. Comparisons can contribute to the challenging of existing structures and the destabilization of nomospheric constellations. For instance, some international and national courts have rejected terra nullius (Daes 2001; *Mabo v. Queensland* 1992; Russell 1998;

Stavenhagen and Amara 2013; *Western Sahara Advisory Opinion* 1975), and the UN Declaration on the Rights of Indigenous Peoples (UN General Assembly 2007) offers a positive model for transforming nomospheric state-indigenous relations.

Quite a few chapters in this book suggest fascinating directions for comparative work such as studying differing entanglements of law, temporality, and space (Chapters 1 and 2) or the varied habits of territory, jurisdiction, and property (Chapter 3). We could compare the geolegalities of the Western (Chapter 6) and Soviet interventions in Afghanistan. We could study the ways legal disputes concerning the ordering of housing and workplaces for the poor in Mexico City (Chapter 7) compare with other megalopolises in the Global South or Global North and ask whether and how nomospheric knowledge and practices move between them. Similarly, we can compare the spatiolegal constructions of rurality in the United States (Chapter 8) and China. Likewise, we could ask how rules of engagement in civil law systems or in India compare with those described in Chapter 9, or how spatiolegal production of emotions at work looks in Indonesia or in Italy and trace networks and pathways of such know-how (Chapter 10)? We could conduct such comparative CLG while employing different methodologies, such as ethnography (Chapter 5).

A comparative CLG project demands proficiency in several academic disciplines and geographical regions. I suggest initiating collaborative comparative research projects. Working in teams of scholars, such as critical legal geographers and critical comparatists, fluent in the legal geographies of the studied regions, would facilitate comparisons based on local and cross-disciplinary knowledge.

Additionally, the project of expanding the horizons of legal geography could entail a much-needed expansion of comparative law. While a renewed infusion of spatiality and an engagement with legal geographical scholarship necessitates a paradigmatic shift in the dominant outlook, it could contribute to setting a new trajectory for comparative law and assist it in recovering from its current malaise and Eurocentrism. Simultaneously, insights of comparatists, particularly critical and postcolonial comparatists could help expand legal geography. At the very least, a timely dialogue between critical comparatists and critical legal geographers could contribute to both groups and to the initiation of a critical comparative legal geography project.

## NOTES

I would like to thank Irus Braverman, Nick Blomley, and David Delaney for their constructive comments, as well as Ely Aharonson, Shulamit Almog, Eugene McCann, David Nelken, Deborah Shmueli, Rinat Yitzhaki, and Jonathan Yovel, for their helpful suggestions and advice, as well as the participants of the Haifa Law and Society Forum and the participants of the International Conference of Comparative Law on Diffusion, June 3–4, 2013. For excellent research assistance, I thank Liat Leizer, Uri Sabach, and Irena Nuntenko. As always, my gratitude to Claudia Kedar for her love, wisdom, and support. The research was supported by the German Israeli Foundation Grant No. G-992-247.4/2007 and the Israel Science Foundation Grant No. 920/13.

1. A Lexis/Nexis search on March 5, 2012, in US and Canadian law reviews returned no article in which the terms *comparative law* and *legal geography* appeared in the same sentence, and only three such articles contained the terms in the same paragraph. A similar search on March 5, 2012, in ProQuest Central found only seven articles addressing both *legal geography* and *comparative law,* and only four of those dealt substantially with both concepts. The terms *Geography* and *legal geography* do not appear in the indexes of the following leading books in comparative law: Bussani and Mattei (2012); David and Brierley (1985); De Cruz (2007); Legrand and Munday (2003); Menski (2006); Reimann and Zimmermann (2006); Smits (2006); Zweigert and Kötz (1998). Likewise, the term *comparative law* is absent from the indexes of Benda-Beckmann, Benda-Beckmann, and Griffiths (2009); Blomley (1994); Blomley, Delaney, and Ford (2001); Braverman (2009); Butler (2012); Delaney (2004, 2010); Holder and Harrison (2003); Rosen-Zvi (2004); and Taylor (2006),

2. "The comparative study of transplants and receptions investigates contacts of legal cultures and explores the complex patterns of change triggered by them." Associated terms include *circulation of legal models, transfer, reception,* and *cross-fertilization* (Graziadei 2006, 441–44; Menski 2006; Twining 2005).

3. This seems to be a more general phenomenon. "Modern sociological accounts of diffusion and modern legal discussions of reception and transplants are a rather clear example of two bodies of literature seemingly addressed to similar phenomena that largely ignore each other" (Twining 2005, 203).

4. The legislation is reproduced in Blum and Roskin-Levy (1940); Gillis, Ball, and Lipschitz (1939); and Kantrovitch (1943), who also offered commentaries.

5. Amendment 1083 P.G 426, supplement no. 2 (March 13, 1941) (reproduced in Kantrovitch 1943).

6. Although "enemy persons" as a rule did not lose their property in the course of the war, some did do so because of the subsequent peace settlement (Mason 1951; McNair and Watts 1966).

7. Development Authority (Transfer of Property) Law, 5710-1950 (1950), *Laws of the State of Israel* 4: 151–53.

8. Absentees' Property Law, 5710-1950 (1950), *Laws of the State of Israel* 4: 68–82.

## REFERENCES

American Society of Comparative Law. 2008. *The West and the Rest in Comparative Law— 2008 Annual Meeting of the American Society of Comparative Law Event Program.* http:// web.archive.org/web/20121016192323/http://uchastings.edu/media-and-news/event/ docs/ascl-program.pdf.

Arminjon, Pierre, Boris Nolde, and Martin Wolff. 1950. *Traité de droit comparé.* Paris: Librairie Generale de Droit et de Jurisprudence.

Baxi, Upendra. 2003. "The Colonialist Heritage." In *Comparative Legal Studies: Traditions and Transitions,* edited by Pierre Legrand and Roderick Munday, 46–75. Cambridge: Cambridge University Press.

Benda-Beckmann, Franz von, Keebet von Benda-Beckmann, and Anne Griffiths, eds. 2009. *Spatializing Law: An Anthropological Geography of Law in Society*. Farnham, UK: Ashgate.

Ben-Shemesh, Aharon. 1949. "Opinion on the Ways to Solve the Problems of the Absentees Remaining in Israel." July 8. Israel State Archives GAL 17116/8 (Hebrew).

Blank, Yishai, and Issi Rosen-Zvi. 2010. "The Spatial Turn in Legal Theory." *Hagar* 10 (1): 37–60.

Blomley, Nicholas K. 1994. *Law, Space and the Geographies of Power*. New York: Guilford Press.

———. 2001. "Law and Geography." In *International Encyclopedia of the Social and Behavioral Sciences*, edited by Neil J. Smelser and Paul B. Baltes, 12:8461–65. New York: Elsevier.

———. 2003a. "From 'What?' to 'So What?' Law and Geography in Retrospect." In *Law and Geography*, edited by Jane Holder and Carolyn M. Harrison, 17–33. Oxford: Oxford University Press.

———. 2003b. "Law, Property, and the Spaces of Violence: The Frontier, the Survey, and the Grid." *Annals of the Association of American Geographers* 93 (1): 121–41.

———. 2009. "Law." In *The Dictionary of Human Geography*, edited by Derek Gregory, Ron Johnston, Geraldine Pratt, Michael Watts, and Sarah Whatmore, 414–15. 5th ed. Malden, MA: Wiley-Blackwell.

Blomley, Nicholas K., David Delaney, and Richard Thompson Ford, eds. 2001. *The Legal Geographies Reader: Law, Power and Space*. Oxford, UK: Blackwell.

Blum, Arno A., and I. Roskin-Levy. 1940. *The Law Relating to Trading with the Enemy*. Tel Aviv: Palestine Publishing.

Braverman, Irus. 2009a. "Loo Law: The Public Washroom as a Hyper-Regulated Space." *Hastings Women's Law Journal* 20 (1): 45–71.

———. 2009b. *Planted Flags: Trees, Land, and Law in Israel/Palestine*. New York: Cambridge University Press.

———. 2012. *Zooland: The Institution of Captivity*. Stanford, CA: Stanford University Press.

Bussani, Mauro, and Ugo Mattei. 2012. *The Cambridge Companion to Comparative Law*. Cambridge: Cambridge University Press.

Butler, Chris. 2009. "Critical Legal Studies and the Politics of Space." *Social and Legal Studies* 18 (3): 313–32.

———. 2012. *Henry Lefebvre: Spatial Politics, Everyday Life and the Right to the City*. New York: Routledge.

Cairns, John. 2006. "Development of Comparative Law in Great Britain." In *The Oxford Handbook of Comparative Law*, edited by Mathias Reimann and Reinhard Zimmermann, 131–73. Oxford: Oxford University Press.

Clark, David. 2006. "Development of Comparative Law in the United States." In *The Oxford Handbook of Comparative Law*, edited by Mathias Reimann and Reinhard Zimmermann, 175–213. Oxford: Oxford University Press.

Cochrane, Allan, and Kevin Ward. 2012. "Guest Editorial—Researching the Geographies of Policy Mobility: Confronting the Methodological Challenges." *Environment and Planning A* 44: 5–12.

Cotterrell, Roger. 2003. "Comparatists and Sociology." In *Comparative Legal Studies: Traditions and Transitions*, edited by Pierre Legrand and Roderick Munday, 131–53. Cambridge: Cambridge University Press.

————. 2006. "Comparative Law and Legal Culture." In *The Oxford Handbook of Comparative Law*, edited by Mathias Reimann and Reinhard Zimmermann, 709–38. Oxford: Oxford University Press.

Counselor on Arab Affairs. 1949. "Pakistan and India: Problems of Refugee Rehabilitation." Israel State Archives, GAL 17114/8 (Hebrew).

Daes, A. Erica-Irene. 2001. "Prevention of Discrimination and Protection of Indigenous Peoples and Minorities: Indigenous Peoples and Their Relationship to Land." Working paper prepared by the Special Rapporteur submitted to the Commission on Human Rights, UN Doc. E/CN.4/Sub.2/2001/21. http://www1.umn.edu/humanrts/demo/RelationshiptoLand_Daes.pdf.

Das Gupta, Jyoti Bhusan. 1958. *Indo-Pakistan Relations, 1947–1955*. Amsterdam: Djambatan.

David, René, and John Brierley. 1985. *Major Legal Systems in the World Today*. 3rd ed. London: Stevens.

De Cruz, Peter. 2007. *Comparative Law in a Changing World*. 3rd ed. Oxon, UK: Routledge-Cavendish.

Delaney, David. 2004. "Tracing Displacements: Or Evictions in the Nomosphere." *Environment and Planning D: Society and Space* 22: 847–60.

————. 2009. "Law and Law Enforcement." In *International Encyclopedia of Human Geography*, edited by Nigel Thrift and Rob Kitchin, 165–71. Amsterdam: Elsevier.

————. 2010. *The Spatial, the Legal and the Pragmatics of World-Making: Nomospheric Investigations*. New York: Routledge.

Divrei HaKnesset [Knesset Records]. 1949. 88th meeting of the 1st Knesset, November 22. 3:136–145.

Domke, Martin. 1943. *Trading with the Enemy in World War II*. New York: Central Book.

Donahue, Charles. 2006. "Comparative Law Before the Code Napoléon." In *The Oxford Handbook of Comparative Law*, edited by Mathias Reimann and Reinhard Zimmermann, 3–32. Oxford: Oxford University Press.

Economides, Kim, Mark Blacksell, and Charles Watkins. 1986. "The Spatial Analysis of Legal Systems: Towards a Geography of Law?" *Journal of Law and Society* 13 (2): 163–81.

Fauvarque-Cosson, Bénédicte. 2006. "Development of Comparative Law in France." In *The Oxford Handbook of Comparative Law*, edited by Mathias Reimann and Reinhard Zimmermann, 35–67. Oxford: Oxford University Press.

Fischbach, Michael R. 2003. *Records of Dispossession: Palestinian Refugee Property and the Arab-Israeli Conflict*. New York: Columbia University Press.

Foreign and Commonwealth Office. 1998. *History Notes: British Policy Towards Enemy Property During and After Second World War*. http://www.enemyproperty.bis.gov.uk/fcoreport.pdf.

Forman, Geremy, and Alexandre (Sandy) Kedar. 2004. "From Arab Land to 'Israel Lands': The Legal Dispossession of the Palestinians Displaced by Israel in the Wake of 1948." *Environment and Planning D: Society and Space* 22: 809–30.

Frankenberg, Günter. 1985. "Critical Comparisons: Rethinking Comparative Law." *Harvard International Law Journal* 26 (2): 411–55.

Frazer, T. G. 1988. "The Transfer of Power in Divided Societies: Partition in India, Ireland and Palestine." *Indo-British Review* 14: 61.

Gillis F., K. Ball, and H. Lipschitz. 1939. *The ABC of the Emergency Legislation of Palestine: Part I: Trading with the Enemy*. Tel Aviv: F. Gillis and K. Ball.

Glenn, Patrick H. 2006. "Legal Families and Legal Traditions." In *The Oxford Handbook of Comparative Law*, edited by Mathias Reimann and Reinhard Zimmermann, 421–40. Oxford: Oxford University Press.

Grathii, James Thuo. 2006. "Commerce, Conquest and Wartime Confiscation." *Brooklyn Journal of International Law* 31: 709–40.

Graziadei, Michele. 2003. "The Functionalist Heritage." In *Comparative Legal Studies: Traditions and Transitions*, edited by Pierre Legrand and Roderick Munday, 100–127. Cambridge: Cambridge University Press.

———. 2006. "Comparative Law as the Study of Transplants and Reception." In *The Oxford Handbook of Comparative Law*, edited by Mathias Reimann and Reinhard Zimmermann, 441–75. Oxford: Oxford University Press.

———. 2009. "Legal Transplants and the Frontiers of Legal Knowledge." *Theoretical Inquiries in Law* 10 (2): 723–44.

Greenspan, Morris. 1959. *The Modern Law of Land Warfare*. Berkeley: University of California Press.

Gross, Ariela J. 2011. "Race, Law, and Comparative History." *Law and History Review* 29 (2): 549–65.

Grossfeld, Bernhard. 1984. "Geography and Law." *Michigan Law Review* 82 (5–6): 1510–19.

Hannam, Kevin, Mimi Sheller, and John Urry. 2006. "Editorial: Mobilities, Immobilities and Moorings." *Mobilities* 1: 1–22.

Harris, Ron. 2001. "Why and How to Teach Comparative Law in Israel?" *Tel Aviv University Law Review* 25: 443–66 (Hebrew).

Holder, Jane, and Carolyn M. Harrison, eds. 2003. *Law and Geography*. Oxford: Oxford University Press.

Hug, Walter. 1932. "The History of Comparative Law." *Harvard Law Review* 45: 1027–70.

Husa, Jaakko. 2004. "Classification of Legal Families Today: Is It Time for Memorial Hymn?" *Revue Internationale de Droit Comparé* 56 (1): 11–38. http://papers.ssrn.com/sol3/papers.cfm?abstract_id=1865050.

———. 2006. "Legal Families." In *Elgar Encyclopedia of Comparative Law*, edited by Jan M. Smits, 382–93. Cheltenham, UK: Edward Elgar.

International Academy of Comparative Law and American Society of Comparative Law. 2010. *Program of the XVIIIth International Congress of Comparative Law*. July 25–August 1, Washington, DC. http://www.wcl.american.edu/events/2010congress/agenda.en.cfm.

Jiryis, Sabri. 1976. *The Arabs in Israel*. New York: Monthly Review Press.

Kantrovitch H., ed. 1943. *War Legislation in Force on the 15th Day of April 1943*. Tel Aviv: Mizpah.

Kedar, Alexandre (Sandy). 2001. "The Legal Transformation of Ethnic Geography: Israeli Law and the Palestinian Landholder 1948–1967." *NYU Journal of International Law and Politics* 33 (4): 923–1000.

———. 2003. "On the Legal Geography of Ethnocratic Settler States." *Current Legal Issues: Law and Geography* 5: 404–41.

Kennedy, Duncan. 2012. "Political Ideology and Comparative Law." In *The Cambridge Companion to Comparative Law*, edited by Mauro Bussani and Ugo Mattei, 35–56. Cambridge: Cambridge University Press.

Legrand, Pierre. 1997. "The Impossibility of 'Legal Transplants.'" *Maastricht Journal of European and Comparative Law* 4: 111–24.

———. 2003. "The Same and the Different." In *Comparative Legal Studies: Traditions and Transitions*, edited by Pierre Legrand and Roderick Munday, 240–311. Cambridge: Cambridge University Press.

Legrand, Pierre, and Roderick Munday, eds. 2003. *Comparative Legal Studies: Traditions and Transitions*. Cambridge: Cambridge University Press.

Lifshitz, Zalman. 1949. "Report on the Need for a Legal Settlement of the Issue of Absentee Property." March 18. Israel State Archives, Jerusalem (130) 2401/21 I (Hebrew).

*Mabo v. Queensland [no. 2]*. [1992] 175 C.L.R. 1. High Court of Australia.

Mason, Malcolm S. 1951. "Relationship of Vested Assets to War Claims." *Law and Contemporary Problems* 16 (3): 395–406.

Mattei, Ugo. 2006. "Comparative Law and CLS." In *The Oxford Handbook of Comparative Law*, edited by Mathias Reimann and Reinhard Zimmermann, 816–36. Oxford: Oxford University Press.

Mawani, Renisa. 2007. "Legalities of Nature: Law, Empire, and Wilderness Landscapes in Canada." *Social Identities* 13 (6): 715–34.

McCann, Eugene. Forthcoming. "Situated Knowledge on the Move? Reflections on Urban Policy Mobilities/Immobilities."

McCann, Eugene, and Kevin Ward. 2013. "A Multi-Disciplinary Approach to Policy Transfer Research: Geographies, Assemblages, Mobilities and Mutations." *Policy Studies* 34: 2–18.

McNair, Duncan, and Arthur Watts. 1966. *The Legal Effects of War*. 4th ed. Cambridge: Cambridge University Press.

Menski, Werner F. 2006. *Comparative Law in a Global Context: The Legal Systems of Asia and Africa*. New York: Cambridge University Press.

Merryman, John Henry. 1997. "Comparative Law Scholarship." *Hastings International and Comparative Law Review* 21: 771–84.

Miller, Robert J., and Jacinta Ruru. 2009. "An Indigenous Lens into Comparative Law: The Doctrine of Discovery in the United States and New Zealand." *West Virginia Law Review* 111: 849–918.

Moore, R. J. 1988. "The Transfer of Power: An Historiographical Survey." *Indo-British Review* 14: 108.

Morris, Benny. 1987. *The Birth of the Palestinian Refugee Problem, 1947–1949*. Cambridge: Cambridge University Press.

———. 2008. *1948: The First Israeli-Arab War*. New Haven, CT: Yale University Press.

Munday, Roderick. 2003. "Accounting for an Encounter." In *Comparative Legal Studies: Traditions and Transitions*, edited by Pierre Legrand and Roderick Munday, 3–28. Cambridge: Cambridge University Press.

Naqvi, Tahir Hasnain. 2007. "The Politics of Commensuration: The Violence of Partition and the Making of the Pakistani State." *Journal of Historical Sociology* 20 (1–2): 44–71.

Nelken, David. 2003. "Comparatists and Transferability." In *Comparative Legal Studies: Traditions and Transitions*, edited by Pierre Legrand and Roderick Munday, 437–66. Cambridge: Cambridge University Press.

———. 2010. *Comparative Criminal Justice: Making Sense of Difference*. Los Angeles: Sage.

Patai, Raphael, ed. 1971. *Encyclopedia of Zionism and Israel*. New York: Herzl Press.

Peck, Jamie. 2011. "Geographies of Policy: From Transfer-Diffusion to Mobility-Mutation." *Progress in Human Geography* 35: 773–97.

Peck, Jamie, and Nick Theodore. 2010. "Mobilizing Policy: Models, Methods and Mutations." *Geoforum* 41: 169–74.

Reimann, Mathias. 2002. "The Progress and Failure of Comparative Law in the Second Half of the Twentieth Century." *American Journal of Comparative Law* 50: 671–700.

Reimann, Mathias, and Reinhard Zimmermann, eds. 2006. *The Oxford Handbook of Comparative Law.* Oxford: Oxford University Press.

Riles, Annelise. 2001. "Introduction: The Projects of Comparison." In *Rethinking the Masters of Comparative Law,* edited by Annelise Riles, 1–18. Oxford, UK: Hart Publishing.

————. 2006. "Comparative Law and Socio-Legal Studies." In *The Oxford Handbook of Comparative Law,* edited by Mathias Reimann and Reinhard Zimmermann, 775–814. Oxford: Oxford University Press.

Rosen-Zvi, Issachar. 2004. *Taking Space Seriously: Law, Space, and Society in Contemporary Israel.* Aldershot, UK: Ashgate.

Russell, Peter. 1998. "High Courts and the Rights of Aboriginal Peoples: The Limits of Judicial Independence." *Saskatchewan Law Review* 61: 247–76.

Said, Edward W. 1980. *The Question of Palestine.* London: Routledge and Kegan Paul.

Schechtman, Joseph B. 1951. "Evacuee Property in India and Pakistan." *Pacific Affairs* 24 (4): 406–13.

Schwenzer, Ingeborg. 2006. "Development of Comparative Law in Germany, Switzerland and Austria." In *The Oxford Handbook of Comparative Law,* edited by Mathias Reimann and Reinhard Zimmermann, 69–106. Oxford: Oxford University Press.

Sheller, Mimi, and John Urry. 2006. "The New Mobilities Paradigm." *Environment and Planning A* 38: 206–26.

Smandych, Russell. 2010. "Mapping Imperial Legal Connections: Toward a Comparative Historical Sociology of Colonial Law." *Adelaide Law Review* 31: 187–228.

Smits, Jan M., ed. 2006. *Elgar Encyclopedia of Comparative Law.* Cheltenham, UK: Edward Elgar.

Stavenhagen, Rodolfo, and Ahmad Amara. 2013. "International Law of Indigenous Peoples and the Naqab Bedouin Arabs." In *Indigenous (In)Justice: Human Rights Law and Bedouin Arabs in the Naqab/Negev,* edited by Ahmad Amara, Ismael Abu-Saad, and Oren Yiftachel, 161–93. Cambridge, MA: Harvard University Press.

Talbot, Ian. 2011. "The 1947 Partition of India and Migration: A Comparative Study of Punjab and Bengal." In *Removing Peoples: Forced Removal in the Modern World,* edited by Richard Bessel and Claudia Haake, 321–49. Oxford: Oxford University Press.

Talbot, Ian, and Gurharpal Singh. 2009. *The Partition of India.* Cambridge: Cambridge University Press.

Taylor, William M., ed. 2006. *The Geography of Law: Landscape, Identity and Regulation.* Oxford, UK: Hart Publishing.

Twining, William. 2005. "Social Science and Diffusion of Law." *Journal of Law and Society* 32 (2): 203–40.

————. 2006. "Diffusion and Globalization Discourse." *Harvard International Law Journal* 47 (2): 507–16.

————. 2009. *General Jurisprudence: Understanding Law from a Global Perspective.* Cambridge: Cambridge University Press.

UN Development Group. 2008. *Guidelines on Indigenous People' Issues.* February. http://www.un.org/esa/socdev/unpfii/documents/UNDG_Guidelines_indigenous_FINAL.pdf.

UN General Assembly. 2007. *United Nations Declaration on the Rights of Indigenous Peoples.* Resolution 61/295. October 2. http://www.un.org/esa/socdev/unpfii/documents/DRIPS_en.pdf.

Vakil, C. N. 1950. *Economic Consequences of Divided India: A Study of the Economy of India and Pakistan.* Bombay: Vora.

Vernant, Jacques. 1953. *The Refugee in the Post-War World.* New Haven, CT: Yale University Press.

Watson, Alan. 1974. *Legal Transplants: An Approach to Comparative Law.* Charlottesville: University Press of Virginia.

———. 1993. *Legal Transplants: An Approach to Comparative Law.* 2nd ed. Athens: University of Georgia Press.

———. 2000a. *The Evolution of Western Private Law.* Baltimore: John Hopkins University Press.

———. 2000b. *Law out of Context.* Athens: University of Georgia Press.

Watt, Horatia Muir. 2006. "Globalization and Comparative Law." In *The Oxford Handbook of Comparative Law,* edited by Mathias Reimann and Reinhard Zimmermann, 579–607. Oxford: Oxford University Press.

*Western Sahara, Advisory Opinion,* I.C.J. Reports [1975]. http://www.icj-cij.org/docket/index.php?p1=3&p2=4&k=69&case=61&code=sa&p3=4.

Wigmore, John H. 1929. "A Map of the World's Law." *Geographical Review* 19 (1): 114–20.

Yiftachel, Oren. 2006. *Ethnocracy: Land and Identity Politics in Israel/Palestine.* Philadelphia: University of Pennsylvania Press.

Yiftachel, Oren, Alexandre (Sandy) Kedar, and Ahmad Amara. 2012. "Re-Examining the 'Dead Negev Doctrine': Property Rights in Arab Bedouin Regions." *Law and Government* 14: 7–147 (Hebrew).

Zamindar, Vazira Fazila-Yacoobali. 2007. *The Long Partition and the Making of Modern South Asia: Refugees, Boundaries Histories.* New York: Columbia University Press.

Zweigert, Konwrad, and Hein Kötz. 1998. *Introduction to Comparative Law.* Translated by Tony Weir. 3rd ed. New York: University Press.

# 5 WHO'S AFRAID OF METHODOLOGY?

## Advocating a Methodological Turn in Legal Geography

*Irus Braverman*

Since its inception in the early 1980s, legal geography has regarded questions of method as peripheral or even irrelevant. My chapter urges legal geographers to amend this by being more reflexive about how we research the world. A greater awareness of our methodologies will pay off in a range of ways, not least of which is an increase in our methodological diversity and, therefore, also in our interdisciplinarity. Specifically, attention by legal geographers to the craft of scholarship is likely to result in an expansion of the available tools in our methodological arsenal, thus enhancing the richness of legal geography as a tradition and its interdisciplinary potentials. For this to happen, we must engage in discussions about *how* we go about answering the questions we ask—namely, the art of craftsmanship.

Alongside the push to expand legal geography into new spaces and temporalities "out there," this chapter proposes an *inward* expansion: a reflection into the process of research rather than its goals and ends; a reflection on how we came to write what we write rather than where, when, and why we do so. The potential for such reflections on our highly routinized ways of working cannot be overstated. My own experience has convinced me that one's choice of methodology is hardly marginal or technical. Instead, it is probably the most significant component of our work, the substrate for establishing our knowledge of the world.

This chapter explores one methodological tool that I have employed (alongside others) over the past decade or so: ethnography. My reflections on the pitfalls and virtues of ethnography are presented here as a way of inviting other legal geographers to explore how they craft their own research, and perhaps to encourage them to undertake new ways of doing so in the future. Although I believe that legal geographers should experiment with a variety of methodologies, I here advocate the special relevance of ethnography for this tradition.

Legal geographers' familiarity with administrative structures and bureaucratic reasoning, as well as our affiliation and heightened access to professional experts and government schemes, uniquely situates us to perform what cultural anthropology has termed *studying-up*, *multi-sited*, *engaged*, and *para* ethnographies. We are familiar with legal language and are therefore "insiders" in the legal world. As a result, we are probably both better situated and better equipped than scholars in other disciplines to explore the intricacies of various administrative structures. It is likely for this reason that a large portion of legal geography studies already focuses on such institutional spaces and nomospheric figures (see, e.g., Susan Coutin's [2007] work on migrants, Steve Herbert's [2006] work on community policing and social control, Jennifer Hyndman's [2000] work on refugee camps, and Setha Low's [2004] study of gated communities). Then again, these few exceptions say more about the general rule: institutional and administrative ethnographies do not perform the important role that they deserve in our tradition.

This chapter reflects on my personal path as I have struggled to combine my research interests and concerns as a legal geographer with engaged, multi-sited, and para-ethnographies. In particular, the chapter unravels the complex methodological path of my research on zoos in North America, and how this path has transformed how I—as a legal geography scholar—have come to know and experience the world. Drawing on this personal account, I ask the following questions: Are there, or should there be, distinctive legal geography methods? And how can ethnography in particular enhance the legal geography project?

## WHAT IS METHODOLOGY? A WORKING DEFINITION

The *Oxford English Dictionary* defines *methodology* as follows:

> Originally: the branch of knowledge that deals with method generally or with the methods of a particular discipline or field of study; (*arch.*) a treatise or dissertation on method; (*Bot.*) †systematic classification (*obs. rare*). Subsequently also: the study of the direction and implications of empirical research, or of the suitability of the techniques employed in it; (more generally) a method or body of methods used in a particular field of study or activity.[1]

In other words, methodology is the *craft* of working through an inquiry or question. This is largely a discipline-specific endeavor, in the sense that different disciplines use, and are defined by, their distinct methodologies.

The idea of craftsmanship calls to mind ancient Greek philosophers' juxtaposition between *epistêmê* as pure theory and *technê*, or craft, as practice. In *Nicomachean Ethics*, Aristotle identifies five virtues of thought: *technê*, *epistêmê*, *phronêsis*, *sophia*, and *nous* (Aristotle 1139b15, quoted in Parry 2008). *Technê* is often translated as "craft" or "art," whereas *epistêmê* is generally defined as knowledge, and scientific knowledge in particular. Scientific knowledge is distinguished by its focus on eternal objects discovered through demonstration. The full account of *epistêmê* is found in Aristotle's *Posterior Analytics*, where he suggests that we think we know something without qualification when we think we know the cause of the thing, and that it is inevitably so (71b10–15, quoted in Parry 2008). *Technê* must also be known, although not by demonstration (1139b15–30) but through practical engagements (see also Chapter 3, in this volume). This classic divide between scientific knowledge and craft is still prevalent in contemporary academic discourse, which commonly distinguishes between the purely theoretical and the purely practical. Scientific knowledge is seen as concerning itself with the world of necessary truths, which stands apart from the world of everyday contingencies, the province of craft.

As the craft of research, methodology is how we find the answers to our research questions and how we make sense of the world in and around us through routine inquiry. A few types of methodology and their principal disciplines include interpretive or hermeneutic methods in law, religion, and literature; quantitative methods (statistical, mathematical, or computational) in social sciences such as psychology, economics, sociology, and political science; qualitative methods such as grounded theory, storytelling, and ethnography, commonly used in anthropology and sociology; and archival research in history.

## METHOD IN LEGAL GEOGRAPHY

The question is, then, not so much whether researchers in fact *have* a method—because every way of making sense of the world can be viewed as a method—but rather whether or not they are *reflexive* about it. The legal discipline, still the discipline of origin for many legal geographers, is arguably not as reflective as many other disciplines about its methods. Moreover, the question of method usually seems curiously irrelevant to the majority of legal scholars. Although hardly a representative sample, my own experience with journal submission helps illustrate this point: whereas methodological inquiries have come up in some form or another in every article I have submitted to social science journals, no methodology-related question has even once come up in my submissions to law reviews. One of my colleagues at SUNY Buffalo Law School explains the wariness of legal scholars to engage in methodological reflections per se:

> Regarding whether "the legal discipline" in general (does one really exist?) is not as reflexive about methodology as some other disciplines, I suppose that could be accurate if we take what you call a technical approach to methodology. While

law professors in some cases do take methodology very seriously, more often, as a group, they are much more skeptical about the proposition that methodology (defined as a set of rules for gathering information) is a test for and assurance of validity. They are very loath to hang their claims to validity on any given method, since they are quite aware (sometimes just instinctively) of the multiple ways that method can be used to fold in preferred outcomes. They tend to think that the truth of a proposition depends on many things, including the integrity of the person asserting it, the attentiveness to counterarguments or counter information—of whatever sort, the fit with other sources of knowledge, and so on. In other words, it's a kind of "craft," in your terminology (Errol Meidinger, personal communication, July 6, 2013; cited with permission).

Conversely, geographers, and especially physical geographers, tend to be quite explicit about their methodologies, usually working through complicated geographic information systems (GIS) and other quantitative methods. Moreover, ensuing debates about method can be proxies for disagreements over theory. In geography, for example, disagreements about whether research should be "nomothetic" or "ideographic," debates between positivists and postpositivists, humanists and "more-than-human" geographers and so forth are often methodological differences that then structure the theoretical underpinnings of various geography projects.

Because many legal geographers had their central disciplinary training in law schools, and because law schools rarely teach methodology, it is perhaps unsurprising that legal geographers, too, are often unreflective about their methods. The recent changes in legal geography and its branching out to new disciplines and territories, including anthropology and sociology (as the introduction to this volume illustrates), will hopefully enhance our methodological reflections, broaden our methodological choices, and strengthen our ability to carry out transdisciplinary conversations. If legal scholars and scholars of legal geography have been underattentive to questions of method, these questions have been at the core of anthropology, and of cultural anthropology in particular, for many decades. The following sections introduce a few central methodological tools from anthropology and consider their relevance to legal geography from the standpoint of my personal path as a legal geographer.

## ETHNOGRAPHY FOR BEGINNERS

Although ethnography is but one of several methodological choices that are open to legal geographers, I find it particularly well suited to our work for its explorations of power, its (recent) emphasis on engaging the subjects of research, its multi-sited fieldwork and projections, and its call to study administrative networks. In particular, ethnography can enhance legal geography by allowing practitioners to ask how people live, constitute, and imagine social space, place, and landscape as well as how people understand themselves as living, doing, and imagining the legal.

Finally, ethnography is also in accord with legal geography's increasing commitment to challenging the linear, monolithic, and rational definitions of space and time. David Fetterman (2008, 289) points out in this context that, "in contrast to a priori assumptions about how systems work from a simple, linear logical perspective—which might be completely off target—ethnography typically takes a phenomenologically oriented research approach." An ethnography that highlights the thingness of matters and the interrelatedness of subjects and objects (Brown 2001) would be particularly insightful for legal geographers, who often privilege abstract constructions of space over mundane materialities.

There are a variety of definitions of ethnography. I find the following definition by the Center for Ethnography at the University of California, Irvine, especially useful:

> Ethnography is perhaps the most important and most widely used qualitative mode of inquiry into social and cultural conditions. . . . There is no single definition of ethnography or uniform practice of ethnographic method, nor should there be: ethnographic practice responds and adapts to field research situations. As Marilyn Strathern has written, ethnography, through participant-observation, interviewing, and other qualitative techniques, is a "deliberate attempt to generate more data than the researcher is aware of at the time of collection," and is thus eminently suited to the study of unpredictable outcomes, complex emerging social formations, and technological and market change.[2]

The interplay between *emic* (insider) and *etic* (outsider) perspectives is crucial for the ethnographer's work. According to Fetterman, "The ethnographer is interested in understanding and describing a social and cultural scene from the emic, or insider's, perspective. The ethnographer is both story-teller and scientist; the closer the readers of an ethnography come to understanding the native's point of view, the better the story and the better the science" (Fetterman 2008, 288).

Ethnography is thus a loose method for exploring the world through an open-ended, experimental, and initially nonjudgmental mind to understand how it actually functions. Of particular interest to legal geographers is the commitment to "studying-up," a concept that was developed in the 1970s and that has more recently evolved and branched out into "engaged," "collaborative," and "para" ethnographies. The following sections present this evolution and contemplate its relevance for legal geographers.

## "STUDYING-UP" ETHNOGRAPHY

As early as 1972, legal ethnographer Laura Nader (1972, 284) challenged anthropologists to study the ways in which "power and responsibility are exercised" in their own society. Nader suggested that historically, ethnographic fieldwork has been produced through an imbalance of power: the anthropologist had privileged access to marginalized or disenfranchised populations. As a result, there has been plenty of work gathered on "the poor, the ethnic groups, the disadvantaged," but "comparatively little on the middle class and very little firsthand work on the upper classes" (Nader 1972, 289).

To address the need for an exploration of elite societies, Nader (1972, 293) argued for a "studying-up" approach: "a reinvented anthropology should study power institutions and bureaucratic organizations." To reinvent anthropology, in other words, Nader suggested that anthropologists should study the colonizers, "the culture of power rather than the culture of the powerless, the culture of affluence rather than the culture of poverty" (289). Nader acknowledged that there are real impediments to studying-up. For example, those in power do not want to be observed and have elaborate systems of protection in place to guard their privacy. Although typically barred from using the participant observation method—which is the primary means open to an anthropologist, according to Nader—anthropologists can draw from financial and legal documents, memoirs, and personal documents.

Although I agree with Nader that documents offer insights into how institutions and government officials function (Riles 2006), I disagree with her statements regarding the heightened obstacles for direct ethnographic engagements with those in power. As I illustrate shortly, the elites I have studied actually *loved* talking about themselves. As a result, my experience has been that direct interviews and observations are highly relevant in this context. Additionally, Nader's idea of studying "up" may be too simple and binary. Are there not plenty of situations in which our subjects of study are neither "up" nor "down"? Perhaps this should elicit a "studying-sideways" ethnography? And what about studying administrative networks that are both up and down, and in fact *everywhere*? For example, some of the professional networks that I have been researching encompass a multitude of geographies and social milieus: they include high level scientists and zoo designers who work on conservation projects ranging from Rwanda to India and China; zookeepers who work with specific animals in small zoos in Louisville, Kentucky, and Buffalo, New York; and low-level administrators from a variety of socioeconomic backgrounds. Conducting ethnographic studies on these multi-sited scales is especially important for excavating the working of complex power apparatuses.

Despite these misgivings, I suggest that Nader's emphasis on studying bureaucracies and administrative networks is now more relevant than ever, and that this is especially true for legal geographers. Because legal geographers are familiar with legal discourses, we are insiders, or at least "halfies" (Abu-Lughod 1991), in the legal world. One might suggest, moreover, that legal geographers are actually "twosies," in that our interests bring together concerns over space and materiality alongside those about how power relations manifest through various forms of legality. In other words, legal geographers have a special vantage point from which to engage humans and nonhumans who operate within regulatory networks.

As a result, legal geographers are probably better suited than scholars in other disciplines to explore the intricacies of various administrative structures and their material manifestations in the world. The importance of documenting how professional and expert networks actually work cannot be overemphasized, especially at this time. As power structures become more sophisticated and dynamic and harder to pin down, it becomes necessary to employ tools that can effectively penetrate them in order to gain insights into their operations. This is an important undertaking, especially for *critical* legal geographers, who have long been committed to exposing and challenging hegemonic power dynamics (see the introduction to this volume).

## "MULTI-SITED" ETHNOGRAPHIES

An additional common ground between legal geography and ethnography is the attention that both traditions have paid to space and place. One manifestation of this orientation in anthropology is the development of "multi-sited" ethnography. Alongside the need to expand ethnography into multiple *social* spaces, there was also the need to expand ethnography into multiple *physical* sites. According to the prominent cultural anthropologist George Marcus, who coined the term, multi-sited anthropology "does away with much criticized study of a bounded locality; it allows one to follow webs of power that connect, for example, an isolated indigenous community and transnational actors such as the World Bank" (Marcus 1998, quoted in Hale 2006, 102). Marcus further points out that multi-sited ethnography has developed out of a sense that single-sited study is inadequate because it cannot account for a "world system perspective." Taking up the traditional elements, "concerns with agency, symbols, and everyday practices," but tracking these in "a differently configured spatial canvas," is the heart of the multi-sited approach. In this mode, ethnographers "examine the circulation of cultural meanings, objects, and identities in diffuse time-space" (Marcus 1995, 96; see also Rabinow 2002).

The recent attention by ethnographers to multi-sited anthropology fits well with critical legal geography's influence by the neo-Marxist and deconstructionist critical legal studies (CLS) scholarship, which has been concerned with exposing power relations and exploring their manifestations through various temporalities and in multiple spaces (see the introduction to this volume). As legal geographers, we focus on place and materiality and are increasingly paying attention to space-time relations. Hence, such an explicit engagement in multi-sited research by ethnographers is quite relevant for our work. The benefit of adopting a multi-sited *ethnography* (in comparison to, say, a multi-sited secondary data method) is that when researchers engage in a dialogue with their human and nonhuman quasi-subjects and quasi-objects, to borrow from Bruno Latour (1993, 225), complicated networks that are not always apparent "on the books" become visible.

Reciprocally, the sensitivity of legal geographers to spatial and material concerns and our recent explorations of space-time relations (see Chapters 1 and 2 in this volume) can prove helpful for cultural anthropologists. Specifically, legal geography can bring richer understandings of spatiality and materiality to what seems, at first glance at least, to be a rather thin approach to such matters in the cultural anthropology literature. For example, legal geographers may offer more nuanced interpretations of the term *site*. Although by their training anthropologists tend to be very sensitive to location, they commonly regard it as a flat and static surface rather than one that is bound with culture (Westbrook 2008). The following is legal scholar David Westbrook's similar call to ethnographers to think about space and place differently:

> [C]ultural anthropologists are not on an island that, however remote, remains an identifiable place with its own coordinates and indeed its own culture, and that is easily distinguishable from other places with their own cultures. Instead of landing in some archipelago, cultural anthropologists are continuously at sea, always some place, but where? Indeed, cultural anthropologists (and ethnographic subjects) are always connected with all other parts of the ocean of global society, but in what direction, at what distance, tugged upon by what great currents? The significances that constitute present situations are socially defined, difficult to be sure of, and likely to shift—it is difficult to perceive where one is. Navigation is required. (Westbrook 2008, 46–47; see also Tsing 2005)

Because of its complex global dimensions, multi-sited ethnography can be a particularly effective means of pursuing research in environmental law. In the words of anthropologist Peter Brosius (1999, 278):

Studies of environmental movements, rhetorics, and representations provide a tremendously fertile site for exploring and extending any number of current theoretical discussions within and beyond the discipline of anthropology: how we approach the task of ethnographic writing in multi-sited contexts . . . , how we discern articulations between the local and the global . . . , how we understand emerging forms of political agency . . . , how we view the intersections between issues of identity and notions of hybridity and authenticity . . . , and how we analyze systems for the production of knowledge.

Research on environmental law—which is, arguably, closely affiliated with legal geography—may be greatly enriched by such self-reflections through multidisciplinary perspectives. In what follows, I present my own methodological path for the insights that it may offer to legal geographers who may want to experiment with different methods, and with ethnography in particular.

## LEGAL GEOGRAPHY AND ZOO ETHNOGRAPHY

From the start of my academic career, I have been drawn to both one-on-one interviews and field observations as research tools. Growing up in a highly contested physical space, I was quite intrigued by the interrelations of space, power, and law. Both interests were probably a result of my longtime training as a community organizer and my work with disempowered communities in Israel/Palestine. As a master's student in criminology, I received little to no professional guidance on how to conduct interviews and observations. For example, only after finishing my thesis on house demolitions in East Jerusalem and its underlying bureaucratic regime did my thesis adviser discover that I should have obtained institutional permission to study "human subjects," which resulted in an emergency appeal to the relevant institutional review board.[3]

Some years later, my book *Planted Flags* relied extensively on ethnographic research—interviews and participatory observations—this time to describe the land wars that take place in Israel/Palestine through tree planting and uprooting (Braverman 2009). Although a few of my interviewees were Palestinian farmers and radical Jewish settlers (both minority groups, and at least one also a "native" in the traditional ethnographic sense), a large part of my research in the Israeli-Palestinian context consisted of interviews with high-level bureaucrats and military officials, as well as observations of administrative and military operations.

Despite learning about Nader's concept of studying-up only much later, our insights were probably similar. For me, these insights were mostly founded on Michel Foucault's scholarship. Drawing on Foucault's (1977) early work, I was interested in uncovering how certain institutions exert their power. I was especially interested in disciplinary and panoptic regimes: alongside the visible national structures, these regimes offer less visible subcultures that interact with the hegemonic culture and render it meaningful.

My position as a "halfie" (Abu-Lughod 1991)—as both an insider of and an outsider to some of the governmental and semigovernmental institutions in Israel/Palestine—assisted me in gaining access to people, documents, and site observations that outsiders would rarely be trusted to enter. My identity as a Jewish-Israeli woman who had served in the Israeli army and my work as a state criminal prosecutor and environmental lawyer were especially helpful in establishing my credibility. In fact, I was often surprised at how easily high-level military officials in the Israeli Defense Forces were willing to speak to me about checkpoints and borders and how readily they explained their points of view. Similarly, when working on *Planted Flags*, I often wondered why Jewish National Fund officials and experts would dedicate so much time and effort to offer me a glimpse into their world. Finally, even as I was working on the topic of zoos in Israel/Palestine, zoo professionals and scientists were extraordinarily honest about their beliefs and very open to discussing their work. These experiences counter Nader's argument that governmental actors are generally reluctant to speak about themselves.

In light of my experience in Israel/Palestine, I expected little to no resistance when studying a seemingly less conflicted terrain: zoos in North America. Focusing on zoos as bureaucratic institutions, I set out to interview zoo officials in North America, where I have been living since 2006. Surprisingly, the North American zoo community proved to be the most insular community I have researched. After years of dramatic struggles with animal rights activists, American zoo personnel have become wary of strangers asking provocative questions. Institutional barricades have been set up to prevent easy access to zoo personnel, including internal procedures that require advance permission from public relations departments for any interview.

Here, I was more of an outsider than ever before. Although zoo personnel considered me a professional and expert in my own field, I did not qualify as a scientist and was certainly not an insider to the zoo community. My not being American may also have played a role in my alienation. Hence, my prospective subjects often wore a puzzled expression when I explained what I was interested in. "Why would the administrative culture of this institution be of interest to an outsider?" they often wondered aloud. Actually, my embarrassing ignorance about animals turned out to be quite handy for convincing my interviewees that I was not an animal rights activist. I can still recall the shock—the horror, even—on the face of one of my interviewees when I casually asked her whether the penguin was a bird or a mammal.

Although I was an outsider to my interviewees in the organizational sense, I was more or less an equal on the social front with the conservation biologists, zoologists, animal psychologists, and anthropologists. In many ways, we were peers: we shared similar socioeconomic backgrounds, attended similar schools and then conferences, and had common concerns and life views. Like me, many of them hold academic positions in universities. Because of the nature of this project, my two young daughters were present for many of my on-site observations and, as a result, my more regular interviewees got to know my family. Although this was an unplanned occurrence, it proved quite helpful for bridging institutional gaps.

But at times, the commonalities were not enough. In numerous instances, the interviewees asked me to define my position with regard to the legitimacy of contemporary zoos: "Are you *for* or *against* zoos?" they insisted. Because I was unwilling to stake out a position within this schism, I found that I was denied access to certain personnel, documents, and data.[4] With some exceptions, the closer I got to the heart of zoo administration and the higher I reached in the zoo network, the easier it was to build credibility and to gain access to interviews and observations. At the same time, the American Association of Zoos and Aquariums (AZA) was an especially difficult organization to penetrate. Since its inception, the AZA has been a direct target of many animal rights groups. Consequently, its administrators have become quite wary of outsiders. Even when they were willing to talk, many refused to share their policy or working papers, and some were reluctant to grant me permission to record our conversations.

After a few failed trials, I learned that the way to establish trust with zoo professionals was to forge real relationships with them that would then translate into referrals to their colleagues. This was not a calculated endeavor; rather, it occurred because I found I had genuinely shared interests and concerns with so many of my interviewees. One particular person with whom I carefully built such trust and credibility, and who subsequently shared with me many of her connections, is the director of a northeastern zoo.[5] Although this relationship was indispensable to my access to the culture of North American zoo administration, I soon learned that it was fragile and required constant maintenance.

Initially, at least, my zoo research was defined in terms of legal geography: How do the relations between law and spatiality—between an array of legal norms, including industry standards and guidelines, and exhibit design goals and strategies—play out at the zoo? How are the materialities of animals embodied in, and negotiated through, the legal texts that pertain to zoos, and vice versa, how do legalities bring animal bodies into existence? To answer these questions, the director introduced me to the zoo's architect and to her documentation of a recent master plan process. On the basis of several in-depth interviews and on-site tours, I wrote my first zoo-related article about zoos' visible and invisible spaces and natures (Braverman 2011). I was intrigued to discover how local zoning laws, environmental laws, fire codes, animal welfare standards, animal bodies and human bodies, principles of immersion design, and those of historical preservation all intersect and correspond in and through this space (Braverman 2012a).

Following my curiosity about the relationship between zoo laws and zoo design, my ethnographic method enabled me to "stumble" upon additional inquiries and insights. For example, during an interview with the zoo's curator about zoo design, his office mate offered enough comments that I turned to her and asked whether she would be willing to set some time aside for an interview with me. As it turns out, this was the zoo's registrar, who subsequently introduced me to the sophisticated archival apparatuses in zoos. The role of the registrar has rarely, if ever, been acknowledged in zoo literature; she is an invisible yet crucial figure in contemporary zoo culture in North America and performs an important legal and administrative role in this institution's operations (Braverman 2010; 2012a, chapter 5).[6]

Such in-depth, semistructured interviews enabled me to discover valuable information that might have not been available to me had I limited my study to written documents. Although this method has lent my research an eclectic quality that made advance planning (and ultimately, writing) difficult, it also created a project that was dynamic and flexible enough to easily detour to unforeseen grounds.

But there were also many challenges to this open-ended, engaged interview process. It often made me uncomfortably visible to the (human) subjects of my study, who were then able to observe, even inspect, my work alongside my observation and inspection of theirs. A book manuscript workshop organized for me by the Baldy Center for Law and Social Policy at SUNY Buffalo Law School illustrates this point. The Baldy Center invited scholars from multiple departments to help me grapple with my neologism *zooveillance*, which was then central to my thinking about zoos. Shortly before this event, I had learned that several zoo personnel planned to attend the workshop. Although I had never kept my thoughts a secret, the interviewees had yet to hear my overall framing of their work and I was concerned that they might interpret it as being overly critical.

My concerns were soon confirmed. The zoo's public relations manager seemed uncomfortable during the presentation and left the room abruptly before it was over. After the workshop, I was confronted by a furious zoo veterinarian who accused me of undermining his life's work. He was not in this business to control or manage zoo animals but to *care* for them, he explained with much frustration. I had already received similar remarks from several other zoo supporters and had begun to grasp that the surveillance framework might be culturally alienating to my North American interviewees. Although she was not at the workshop, I soon heard from the zoo director as well. Her self-confidence surprised me: she instructed her staff that as long as my presentation was fair, it was important to let it be heard. In light of this support, the following occurrence came to me as a complete surprise.

The director did not ask that I send her my book manuscript; I was the one who asked her if she would be willing to read through the draft to ensure that it was scientifically accurate. She agreed. Several weeks later I received her response:

> Throughout the book, you use highly inflammatory language, which will offend many of my friends and colleagues who were reluctant to talk to you. I put my reputation on the line to assist you and feel betrayed. You frequently use the word "legitimize" in a negative manner to depict zoo motives. . . . I respect your right to be provocative, but I am extremely disappointed and hurt by your decision to portray [our zoo] in such a derogatory manner. . . . I have been extremely fair to you during the entire process introducing you to my AZA colleagues, sharing resources and giving you extensive access to me, my staff and facilities, even providing copies of graphics which are now used against us. (E-mail communication with zoo director, November 14, 2011).

The director's comments stretched over six single-spaced pages, including detailed discussions of my word choices.

An example of a term that I had used without realizing that it would sound offensive to the ears of zoo personnel was my reference to certain zoo animal names as "pet" names. I had used this term when explaining the multiple systems of naming that occur at the zoo and that enable zoo professionals to identify their animals and to manage complex information about their lives and deaths. Timmy the gorilla, for example, had at least five names, including an institutional number in the zoo database system; a radio-frequency identification (RFID) number on a chip inserted into his body for identification purposes; and his public and house name, "Timmy." Since the last type of naming reminded me of how humans name their pets to strengthen their bond with them (but also as a form of power and control), I called it a "pet" name. Yet according to the director, my "choice of the word 'pet' names for 'house' names is not appropriate. . . . It tacitly implies that zoos keep the animals for their exclusive enjoyment and not for educating the public." She strongly suggested that I use "the more accurate term—'house name'" throughout the book. I found this sensitivity to names to be fascinating and ended up documenting the ensuing debates over this and similar issues in the book's main text and footnotes.

The director also had more general comments. "I believe that it would be in your best interest to tone down the rhetoric," she said. "Otherwise, you risk having the book tossed in the heap of those written by anti-zoo activists, which would be a shame. You have a unique opportunity to write a book that would be recognized as fair and balanced by both zoo professionals and their detractors." And she concluded, "I hope you are willing to make the changes I have requested. . . . I have included a copy of the requested changes using track changes within Word. I also hope you will give me a chance to read your final draft."

I was confronted with a clear choice. Because the interview process was formally over—and it was well documented and performed with all the necessary permissions—I could have simply forged ahead, despite the director's disapproval. But I chose to go down another path: instead of shutting off communications, I entered into detailed communications about the contents of the manuscript not only with the director but also with a few additional interviewees who, up to that point, had not played an active role in constructing the written text. The interviewees gave me their professional and scientific perspective, pointed to some of the nuances that I did not pick up on, and made suggestions where certain statements could be misunderstood or misconstrued.

I did not accept all of the interviewees' comments and suggestions. For example, a few resented my use of the term *captivity* when referring to wild animals living in zoos. *Captivity* triggers a host of negative associations, they explained, suggesting that I refer to these animals as wild animals "in human care." One of my interviewees from the Toronto Zoo even threatened that if I declined to change the book's subtitle (*The Institution of Captivity*), she would retract the permission she had granted me to use images she had sent me earlier in the process. I decided to further engage with a few of my interviewees on this issue. One of my newer contacts responded as follows: "Some zoos want to paint a different picture. . . . Even though their animals are captive, they don't want to say that. Part of the issue is slightly more legitimate than it sounds, because, internationally, when you translate that it means 'jailed,' or something harsher than captivity" (interview, August 1, 2012). Again, I was unaware of the level and layers of sensitivity when deciding on the book's subtitle, which I eventually left intact. These interactions thus served as a window through which I could more clearly understand my subjects' perspective and their strong emphasis on "care" (more on this theme later).

What ensued was an intense revision project that radically changed the tone of my book. One might infer that I was forced to "tone myself down" and that this process undermined my academic integrity, along the lines of: "I was told that it will be a very sad day for anthropology when we let our subjects dictate our ethnographies" (Davis 1993, 34). But I would like to offer that something subtler was going on: through the dialogue that ensued about my text, I was transforming my own understanding of what I had observed and recorded. I also came to realize that "our analytical language makes it difficult to describe . . . without using negative, value-laden words, even when we especially wish to sound as neutral, descriptive, and objective as possible" (Jacobson 1989, 138).

What seemed to trigger the strongest resistance among zoo professionals and supporters was my neologism *zooveillance*. The term *surveillance*, I soon found out, has an Orwellian connotation for many Americans—especially those unfamiliar with Foucault—and *zooveillance* smelled more or less the same. Although I put much effort into divorcing *surveillance* from state actions and from morally negative implications, I encountered a thick wall of resentment on this front from the vast majority of my interviewees. What was it that I was missing? I asked myself. After numerous conversations, I realized that zoo personnel are strongly motivated by care for animals and that this sentiment, also referred to by some of the interviewees as "stewardship," did not find a clear expression through my use of the term *surveillance*.

Although the book was already written from a "zooveillance" perspective (as expressed in Braverman 2012b), I decided to search for a concept that would capture many of my interviewees' emotional devotion toward animals, on the one hand, and their domination of, and power over, those animals, on the other hand. Although care and power may seem mutually exclusive, my book thus rethought both in such a way that revealed their interdependency. From the perspective of zoo professionals, the extensive power to govern zoo animals is driven by a desire to care for and save animals, both in zoos and in the wild.

The intertwined properties of care and power are emphasized in Michel Foucault's notion of pastoral power. It was this intertwined nature that drew me to Foucault's analysis to explain what I was experiencing, rather than to myriad other explorations of care, especially in feminist studies. Pastoral power—probably Foucault's least-quoted technology of power—was developed in the recently translated lectures *Security, Territory, Population* (Foucault 2007, 117). However, this "solution" to my framing problem still sounded problematic to some of my interviewees: it had religious connotations, and they were scientists. This resistance in turn prompted me to also explore the religious elements at work in the contemporary zoo. I contemplated the zoo as a spiritual institution and pastoral power as enacted for the salvation of mankind.

The alteration of my terminology to reflect the discursive process I was engaging in has also changed the tone of my communications with the interviewees: involvement and enthusiasm replaced suspicion and alienation. Here, for example, is an excerpt from the director's comments during the writing process:

I really like the revised Introduction. It includes a much better explanation of the term panopticon. Now I understand why the analogy is appropriate for zoo management, especially with our increasing use of cameras for viewing the animals in off-site areas (by keepers or the public). I think most people may have thought using the prison analogy was negative portrayal of zoos (and some may still) but your explanation shows that it is more about the design of the prison that lets you see what's going on. (E-mail communication, November 18, 2011)

Toward the end of the same communication, the director further commented:

I really enjoy your writing style. It's like reading the account of an expert naturalist describing some primate society in great detail. You accurately capture the culture and practices of Zooland while remaining an objective observer neither advocating for or against zoos. (E-mail communication, November 18, 2011)

Obviously, happily-ever-after endings exist only in Hollywood. In all other settings, endings tend to be somewhat more complex (or so one would hope) and lack of resolution is common. The engagement with my interviewees involved and *still* involves multiple "growing pains"—it eroded boundaries that were sheltering. I felt, and surely will continue to feel, quite exposed, especially with the publication of my book. But I also feel much more confident in the voice that I have developed through this process. Reflecting back, I made a decision that respects the dignity and intelligence of my interviewees. True, these interviewees are not the typical disempowered and oppressed "natives" that many engaged ethnographers study. Instead, most of my natives were scientists and high-level administrators. Nonetheless, engaging one's subjects of inquiry can and probably should happen on these social scales, a political insight that is particularly acute for legal geographers and that I further discuss in the context of para-ethnography.

My experimental methodology also made it easier to trace various networks that were not site specific. I observed, accordingly, that for the purposes of reproducing zoo animals, all accredited North American zoos function as a single megazoo, which I referred to as *zooland*. From a single-site exploration of one particular zoo, I was thus able to discover a multi-sited and global zoo animal network. Zoo animals are documented and recorded by global systems such as the new Zoological Information Management System (ZIMS) database that enable their frequent and global transfers with the goal of sustaining optimal genetic diversity within the zoo animal population. As a result of my multi-sited ethnographic approach, I ended up interviewing zoo officials in Israel, Palestine, the Netherlands, Austria, Switzerland, and Norway as well as landscape designers who design zoos across the developing world, including India, Indonesia, China, and Afghanistan.

To summarize some of these reflections: although not framed explicitly as such, *Zooland* explores the legal geography of zoos. It focuses on the respatialization of zoos over time, their changing exhibit design and spatial relationship to the city and nature, the reconfiguration of individual zoos into a regional network, the different scopic regimes that occur in their various spaces, and their operation on various geographic scales. *Zooland* investigates these respatializations in light of dynamic and plural legalities: rules, regulations, industry standards, guidelines, and altering conceptions of animal rights.

Without its ethnographic component, *Zooland* would have been a very different project. Not only would it have been less alive, open, and nuanced; there would not have been an opportunity for the "natives" to read my work and "talk back." In the next and final section, I explore this aspect of engaged ethnography—namely, what happens when "they" read what "we" write. Although legal geographers usually do not relate to their subjects of inquiry through an explicit ethnographic framework, many nonetheless engage with various humans in their work (see, e.g., Nicholas Blomley's discussion of Larry in Chapter 3, and Lisa Pruitt's discussion of rurality from the judicial perspective in Chapter 8). It is my hope that the following section may prove helpful to our meditations on how we, as legal geographers, craft our work.

## "WHEN THEY READ WHAT WE WRITE"

I thought that I was pretty much inventing the wheel with my newly found collaborative methodology. But shortly after finishing my book, I discovered *When They Read What We Write*, edited by Caroline B. Brettell (1993). It turns out that ethnographers have been struggling with similar issues for the past twenty-five years at least. Already in 1986, George Marcus and Michael Fischer wrote, "Presumably, members of other societies, increasingly literate, will read ethnographic accounts that concern them and will react not only to the manifest descriptions of their own societies, but also to the premises about our society that are embedded in the double vision of any ethnographic work" (Marcus and Fischer 1986, 163). As mentioned, this is also highly relevant to legal geographers, who constantly engage with various subjects, especially legal actors, in a double vision effort to reimagine the interrelations of space and law.

Along these lines, the editor of *When They Read What We Write* explores what happens when the distance between the audience of colleagues and the audience of informants has been eroded (Brettell 1993, 3). Often, this involves unexpected and painful situations. One of the contributors to the volume describes, for example, how she "returned to her fieldsite to discover that many of her informants/

friends felt betrayed," and that "this sense of betrayal sometimes revolved around the use of a word or phrase that [she] had interpreted differently than the woman who had originally spoken it" (Brettell 1993, 4). Legal geographers, too, may encounter conflicts when they "report back" from the field in ways that reinterpret their subjects' understanding of space and law.

A study that identifies three possible reactions by anthropologists to the challenge of what they refer to as "native readers" might prove helpful to legal geographers as well. One is the "chicken little reaction": the experts hear the natives talk back and "react assertively by emphasizing the rightness of their interpretation and the wrongness of the native's response." Second is the "two-worlds reaction," a response emphasizing the belief that academics and their subjects speak two different languages that can never meet. The third, "one conversation reaction," emphasizes the insights that can be gained from attentiveness to native responses (Brettell 1993, 20–21). This last reaction (which was, arguably, also mine) can take different forms. Some choose to add an appendix to their ethnographies (or a separate section in the book) that spells out the objections to their work by those they have written about. Still others focus on the coproduction of texts in an interactive dialogue. I chose to use footnotes for this purpose. Anthropologists have suggested along these lines that, "If we insist upon interpreting other people's interpretations, at the very least, we are obligated to allow them space to respond. At the very most, we stand to learn far more than we ever bargained for" (Lawless 1992, 313).

At the end of the day, however, ethnography is by its very nature intrusive; "it entails a certain amount of symbolic and interpretive violence to the 'native' peoples' own intuitive, though still partial, understanding of the world" (Scheper-Hughes 2000, 127). Indeed, both the danger and the value of this method lie "in the clash and collision of cultures and interpretations as the anthropologist meets her subjects in the spirit of open engagement, frankness and receptivity" (Scheper-Hughes 2000, 127; see also Lamphere 2003; Low and Merry 2010; Metzo 2009, Myers 1988). Similarly, legal geographers can benefit, and indeed have benefited, from direct engagements with the dominant imaginings of space and law.

The final concept that I would like to introduce in this context is para-ethnography. According to George Marcus and Douglas Holmes, this concept was formulated to address the particular challenges of doing fieldwork "in settings dominated by scientific knowledge and/or a technocratic ethos," which present the following problem:

> How do we pursue our inquiry when our subjects are themselves engaged in intellectual labors that resemble . . . our own methodological practices? Para-ethnography answers this question by proposing an analytical relationship

in which we and our subjects—keenly reflexive subjects—can experiment collaboratively with the conventions of ethnographic inquiry. . . . By treating our subjects as collaborators, as epistemic partners, our analytical interests and theirs can be pursued simultaneously, and we can share insights and thus develop a common analytical exchange. (Holmes and Marcus 2008, 595).

Marcus's vision of the anthropologist as a collaborator means that rather than studying other people, anthropologists should work with them and treat them as co-researchers (Khazaleh 2008). Para-ethnography is thus very much a political attempt to find new ways of studying complex societies, administrations, and networks that operate on multiple time-space scales. It was highly relevant to my work on zoos, and it can be highly relevant to other legal geographers in their work.

## CONCLUSION: TOWARD A METHODOLOGICAL
## TURN IN LAW AND GEOGRAPHY

For the most part, legal geographers have been woefully unreflective about their methodologies. Now that our tradition has matured and become richer and more influential in many ways, the time is ripe to reflect on the craftsmanship of our work. In addition to the importance of self-reflection for producing more thorough, careful, and accurate accounts of our research, I have offered that such self-reflection will allow us to expand, diversify, and enrich our substantive and unique contributions as legal geographers.

Engaging in methodological reflections will also make legal geography more interdisciplinary in that it will more productively engage with the rich methodological traditions developed by other disciplines. Put differently, engaging in mutual conversations about methodology enhances interdisciplinary dialogue and may help to bridge the otherwise fraught waters that run between disciplinary divides.

In the interest of methodological self-reflection and experimentation, I have argued here that it might make sense to borrow from disciplines that have been concerned with these questions for years. I have offered, more precisely, that the distinctive issues raised in our work as legal geographers are intrinsically tied with many ethnographic concerns. Much of our work involves reimagining space and law in ways that call into question the conventional interpretations of these terms, thus surfacing the tensions between emic (insider) and etic (outsider) relations, a process that is also highly relevant to ethnographers. In addition, our work often involves engagement with expert subjects who are very much like us (in ethnography: studying-up), work in multiple-scale operations (multi-sited ethnographies), are highly informed about their rights, and are eager to "talk back" (para-ethnography). For these reasons, I think we can learn much from the craft of ethnography.

This chapter has drawn on experimental literature in cultural anthropology to reflect on my own research on North American zoos. On this path, which I traveled as a legal geographer, such self-reflections led me to adopt a studying-up, multi-sited, engaged, and para-ethnography. These methodological tools are important for the contemporary legal geography project, I have argued here, precisely because they enable the exposure of complex administrative and bureaucratic structures on a variety of temporal and spatial scales. I have proposed, furthermore, that because of our associations with some of these professional and expert networks, legal geographers hold an enhanced responsibility to decipher and document their operations.

Rather than expanding the spaces of law into novel places, domains, and even temporalities "out there," I have proposed an *inward* expansion: a reflection on how we think, work, and engage with our world, on *how* we come to write what we write. I am not suggesting here that legal geographers should dump all other methodologies and utilize instead only engaged, multi-sited, studying-up ethnographies. Quite the contrary, I am proposing a self-reflective process of diversification—a playful experimentation—that engages a variety of ways for crafting our research. Such self-reflection on methods includes considering ethnography seriously, for its close linkages and associations with legal geography.

## NOTES

I would like to thank David Delaney, Nick Blomley, and Errol Meidinger for their comments on this chapter and Jack Schlegel for encouraging me to document my methodological path and its challenges. As always, Gregor Harvey provided invaluable editorial assistance.

1. *Oxford English Dictionary*, s.v. "Methodology," http://www.oed.com/view/Entry/117578.

2. "Welcome," University of California, Irvine, Center for Ethnography, http://www.ethnography.uci.edu.

3. For a thorough account of the institutional review board (IRB) process in the social sciences, see Schrag (2010). Feeley (2007, 757) argues that legal scholars usually see themselves as excluded from the IRB process, although he suggests that their use of IRB processes is on the rise and views this as a welcome change.

4. On the other end of the ideological spectrum, an animal photographer refused to grant me permission to use her striking photos for my work because I was not willing to declare an antizoo agenda.

5. After some deliberation, I decided not to identify my subject by name (despite her permission). Because this sort of analysis of the behind-the-scenes communications is not

traditionally a topic for scholarly study, I felt that she might have not expected to be cited in this context.

6. But see a different take by a reader in review on Goodreads: "Then I read the author's bio and found out it was written by a lawyer. That explains the endless coverage of policy and administrative details. There was even a chapter about registrars . . . and the registrar interviewed mentions how boring that subject is!" "Zooland, Community Reviews," *Goodreads*, February 23, 2013, http://www.goodreads.com/review/show/542305539.

## REFERENCES

Abu-Lughod, Lila. 1991. "Writing against Culture." In *Recapturing Anthropology: Working in the Present*, edited by Richard Fox, 137–62. Santa Fe, NM: School of American Research Press.

Braverman, Irus. 2009. *Planted Flags: Trees, Land, and Law in Israel/Palestine*. New York: Cambridge University Press.

———. 2010. "Zoo Registrars: A Bewildering Bureaucracy." *Duke Environmental Law and Policy Forum* 21 (1): 165–206.

———. 2011. "Looking at Zoos." *Cultural Studies* 25 (6): 809–42.

———. 2012a. *Zooland: The Institution of Captivity*. Stanford, CA: Stanford University Press.

———. 2012b. "Zooveillance: Controlling Zoo Animals to Conserve." *Surveillance and Society* 10 (2): 119–33.

Brettell, Caroline B. 1993. *When They Read What We Write: The Politics of Ethnography*. Westport, CT: Bergin and Garvey.

Brosius, J. Peter. 1999. "Analyses and Interventions: Anthropological Engagements with Environmentalism." *Current Anthropology* 40 (3): 277–88.

Brown, Bill. 2001. "Thing Theory." *Critical Inquiry* 28 (1): 1–22.

Coutin, Susan Bibler. 2007. *Nations of Emigrants: Shifting Boundaries of Citizenship in El Salvador and the United States*. Ithaca, NY: Cornell University Press.

Davis, Dona L. 1993. "Unintended Consequences: The Myth of 'The Return' in Anthropological Fieldwork." In *When They Read What We Write: The Politics of Ethnography*, edited by Caroline B. Brettell, 27–36. Westport, CT: Bergin and Garvey.

Feeley, Malcolm. 2007. "Legality, Social Research, and Institutional Review Boards." *Law and Society Review* 41 (4): 757–76.

Fetterman, David M. 2008. "Ethnography." In *The Sage Encyclopedia of Qualitative Research Methods*, edited by Lisa M. Given, 289–93. Thousand Oaks, CA: Sage Publications.

Foucault, Michael. 1977. *Discipline and Punish: The Birth of the Prison*. Translated by Alan Sheridan. New York: Vintage.

———. 2007. *Security, Territory, Population: Lectures at the College de France, 1977–1978*. Edited by Michel Senellart. Translated by Graham Burchell. New York: Picador.

Golder, Ben. 2007. "Foucault and the Genealogy of Pastoral Power." *Radical Philosophy Review* 10 (2): 157–66.

Hale, Charles R. 2006. "Activist Research v. Cultural Critique: Indigenous Land Rights and the Contradictions of Politically Engaged Anthropology." *Cultural Anthropology* 21 (1): 96–120.

Herbert, Steve. 2006. *Citizens, Cops, and Power: Recognizing the Limits of Community*. Chicago: University of Chicago Press.

Holmes, Douglas R., and George E. Marcus. 2008. "Para-Ethnography." In *The Sage Encyclopedia of Qualitative Research Methods*, edited by Lisa M. Given, 596–98. Thousand Oaks, CA: Sage Publications.

Hyndman, Jennifer. 2000. *Managing Displacement: Refugees and the Politics of Humanitarianism*. Minneapolis, MN: Minnesota University Press.

Jacobson, Jean. 1989. "Is There a Way to Talk about Making Culture without Making Enemies?" *Dialectical Anthropology* 14: 127–43.

Khazaleh, Lorenz. 2008. "George Marcus: 'Journals? Who Cares?'" *Antropologi.info*, October 25. http://www.antropologi.info.

Lamphere, Louise. 2003. "The Perils and Prospects for an Engaged Anthropology: A View from the United States." *Social Anthropology* 11 (2): 153–68.

Latour, Bruno. 1993. *We Have Never Been Modern*. Translated by Catherine Porter. Cambridge, MA: Harvard University Press.

Lawless, Elaine, J. 1992. "'I Was Afraid Someone like You . . . an Outsider . . . Would Misunderstand': Negotiating Interpretive Differences between Ethnographers and Subjects." *Journal of American Folklore* 105 (417): 302–14.

Low, Setha M. 2004. *Behind the Gates: Life, Security, and the Pursuit of Happiness in Fortress America*. New York: Routledge.

Low, Setha M., and Sally Engle Merry. 2010. "Engaged Anthropology: Diversity and Dilemmas: An Introduction to Supplement 2." *Current Anthropology* 51: S203–26.

Marcus, George E. 1995. "Ethnography in/of the World System: The Emergence of Multi-Sited Ethnography." *Annual Review of Anthropology* 24: 96–117.

————. 1998. *Ethnography through Thick and Thin*. Princeton, NJ: Princeton University Press.

Marcus, George E., and Michael M. Fischer. 1986. *Anthropology as Cultural Critique: An Experimental Moment in the Human Sciences*. Chicago: University of Chicago Press.

Metzo, Katherine. 2009. "Collaboration and Co-Authorship." *Podcasts from the SfAA*. April 22. http://sfaapodcasts.net/2009/04/22/.

Myers, Fred R. 1988. "Locating Ethnographic Practice: Romance, Reality, and Politics in the Outback." *American Ethnologist* 15 (4): 609–24.

Nader, Laura. 1972. "Up the Anthropologist: Perspectives Gained from Studying Up." In *Reinventing Anthropology*, edited by Dell Hymes, 284–311. New York: Random House.

Parry, Richard. 2008. "*Episteme* and *Techne*." *Stanford Encyclopedia of Philosophy. Fall 2008 ed.* Edited by Edward N. Zalta. http://plato.stanford.edu/archives/fall2008/entries/episteme-techne/.

Rabinow, Paul. 2002. "Midst Anthropology's Problems." *Cultural Anthropology* 17 (2): 135–49.

Riles, Annelise. 2006. *Documents: Artifacts of Modern Knowledge*. Ann Arbor: University of Michigan Press.

Scheper-Hughes, Nancy. 2000. "Ire in Ireland." *Ethnography* 1 (1): 117–40.

Schrag, Zachary M. 2010. *Ethical Imperialism: Institutional Review Boards and the Social Sciences, 1965–2009*. Baltimore: John Hopkins University Press.

Tsing, Anna L. 2005. *Friction: An Ethnography of Global Connection*. Princeton, NJ: Princeton University Press.

Westbrook, David. 2008. *Navigators of the Contemporary: Why Ethnography Matters*. Chicago: University of Chicago Press.

# 6 STATES THAT COME AND GO

## Mapping the Geolegalities of the Afghanistan Intervention

Michael D. Smith

Law cannot help but be armed, and its arm, par excellence, is death; to those who transgress it, it replies, at least as a last resort, with that absolute menace. The law always refers to the sword. (Foucault 1990, 144)

Law has become a force multiplier for commanders. (Pitzul 2001, 321)

Camp Belambay is a Green Beret outpost situated in the Panjwai district of Afghanistan's Kandahar province, about fifteen miles outside of Kandahar City. The district lies in a region long considered the "Taliban heartland" and has in recent years been the scene of intense fighting between Taliban insurgents and the forces of the International Security Assistance Force (ISAF), the UN-mandated operation led and largely conducted by the United States and its NATO allies to reestablish security and stability in Afghanistan. The camp was part of a network of "village stability platforms," smaller US bases located in strategically important and contested rural areas in an effort to root out the Taliban, earn the trust and allegiance of local Afghans, and extend the reach of nascent Afghan state institutions (Wendle 2012). Such operations to "clear, hold and build" were part of a broader recalibration of Afghanistan strategy initiated in 2009 by the newly elected President Obama, who hoped that a troop surge and redoubled counterinsurgency (COIN) effort focused on "winning hearts and minds" could stem the tide of a Taliban resurgence and lay the groundwork for eventual US-NATO withdrawal and transfer of security responsibilities to a weak and troubled Afghan government (Baker 2009; Jones 2008).

In the early hours of March 11, 2012, an American soldier left Camp Belambay and walked south a short distance to Alkozai, a neighboring village. He moved deliberately among the mud houses, trying door handles and eventually breaking down the door of one dwelling, where he shot ten people. He then returned to the base, before leaving again to break into two more houses in Najibian, another nearby village. There he killed twelve people, eleven of them members of the same family, and attempted to burn some of the bodies. By the time a US patrol intercepted him as he returned to base, he had killed sixteen people, nine of them children, and wounded another six. His killing spree sparked immediate and understandable furor both within Afghanistan and internationally. Camp Belambay, once envisioned as the local linchpin of stabilization through a "partnership with the populace," suddenly became the focus of outraged protests and anguished relatives bearing the charred bodies of their loved ones. Recognizing the so-called Panjwai massacre as a potential tipping point for the Afghanistan mission amid increasing calls for accelerated or even immediate withdrawal, President Obama and other senior US and NATO officials scrambled to contain the damage, issuing the usual statements expressing deep sorrow and promising a full investigation. "We will follow the facts wherever they lead us," Obama intoned, "and we will make sure that anybody who is involved here is held fully accountable with the full force of the law" (AFP 2012).

*But under whose law, and where?* Given the complex, fragmented, and qualified nature of state sovereignty in the context of a multinational intervention, the territorial scope, content, and application of law became a political—but also a *geo*political—question. The lower house of the Afghan parliament issued a statement demanding that a public trial of the alleged killer be held in Afghanistan and called on the Karzai government to cease all negotiations with the United States on future security arrangements until this was ensured. Some called for a trial under Afghan law, since the victims were civilians, and the soldier had acted outside the scope of US military authority, so the legal immunities the United States commonly demands for its troops should not apply. For its part, the US military insisted that any trial would be conducted under US military law, though initially there were conflicting messages on whether or not a court-martial would be held in Afghanistan. Within days of the massacre, however, US authorities, citing safety concerns and "legal considerations," had moved the soldier out of Afghanistan, first to Kuwait, then to a military detention facility in Kansas. Even before the soldier—eventually identified as Sgt. Robert Bales of Joint Base Lewis-McChord near Tacoma, Washington—was formally charged with multiple counts of murder and attempted murder, US Defense Secretary Leon Panetta pointedly noted that that he could well face the death penalty (Simendinger 2012; Vogt and Jelinek 2012).[1]

This horrific episode can be read in many ways, but it clearly exemplifies the central, instrumental, and political role that law continues to play in the US-led intervention in Afghanistan. The deployment of an American soldier to support counterinsurgency in Kandahar, his subsequent rampage, and his hasty removal to face military justice in the United States were all made possible by an interventionist apparatus whose mobilization, operations, and legitimation across space and time is constituted in vital ways through law. Such large-scale, multinational incursions led by the major powers of the Global North in Afghanistan and elsewhere in the Global South reveal a complex interplay of "states that come and go"—a formulation inspired by the Benda-Beckmanns' suggestive notion of "places that come and go" (see Chapter 1 of this volume)—and law plays an important, ordering role in their mobile and mutable relations. This chapter explores the relationship between the martial and the legal in the context of contemporary Western interventionism as a way of opening up a number of avenues of inquiry for a renewed project of critical legal geography. This exploration asks, what spatializations of law underpin and enable multinational interventions, and what legal geographies do they produce? My overarching claim is that legal geography should attend more to the international and transnational, to the ongoing rescaling of the state and the transformations of state sovereignty, and to the hybrid—and often violent—legal geographies associated with political and economic globalization.

The discussion is divided into three main parts: the first situates my analysis within the prevailing modes and thematic orientations of an expansive legal geography that the editors chart in their introduction and offers two concepts—geolegality and martial law—that can help broaden this critical project. The second section highlights some of the geolegalities of martial law, suggesting that the spatiotemporalities of law are essential to grasping the hybrid political and economic formations associated with Western interventionism of the post–Cold War period. The third section focuses on some of the specificities of the Afghanistan intervention, sketching a provisional and admittedly schematic framework for mapping the geolegalities of contemporary Western war making and occupation. By examining Western intervention synoptically in terms of four different but overlapping moments—invasion, occupation, pacification, and autonomization—we can begin to discern how the spatiotemporalities of law are crucial to the oscillating sovereignties and violent passages of these "states that come and go."

## EXTENDING THE SPACES OF LAW:
## GEOLEGALITY AND MARTIAL LAW

This chapter investigates what the editors of this volume characterize as "new spaces" and "new connections" for legal geography, and aims toward the postdisciplinary, or even postlegal geographic direction they describe. My analysis of the multinational intervention in Afghanistan and the legal geographies of Western war certainly shifts the focus beyond the urban milieus of the dominant countries of the Global North that have tended to preoccupy legal geography until relatively recently (for notable exceptions, see, e.g., Braverman 2009; Kedar 2003). It also builds on the small but valuable body of scholarship on the geographies of international law, an area that deserves much greater attention (see Mahmud 2010; Pearson 2008). It does so, however, not simply by taking US, Afghan, or even international law in isolation, but by highlighting their interplay in the dynamic and hybrid spatiolegal relations arising from a Western-led intervention that is at once a combat operation, a development program, a state-building exercise, and a legal transformation.

Thus, even as legal geographers have properly moved to "provincialize" Western law and legal systems to expose their particularity and challenge their universalist pretensions, it is useful to recall that even in this putatively postcolonial era, Western legality retains the capacity, and indeed perhaps the imperative, to globalize, even by violent means. Clearly, as a legal and geographical phenomenon, intervention would seem to represent an exemplar of what the Benda-Beckmanns term a "plural legal constellation" (Chapter 1), a condition of polylegality in which the transplantation or imposition of law produces spaces and places crosscut by multiple, overlapping legal orders (see also Benda-Beckmann and Benda-Beckmann 2009). To this extent, my inquiry has affinities with both the legal anthropology literature on legal pluralism and that strand of comparative legal scholarship that tracks the traffic of law and legal systems between states and across boundaries (as Kedar describes in Chapter 4 of this volume). Moreover, intervention's transformative and transitional nature, with its innumerable milestones, metrics, phases, and timetables for spatial extension, pacification, reconstruction, and eventual withdrawal, underscores the fact that, as Valverde reminds us (see Chapter 2 in this volume), its legalities are fundamentally temporal as well as spatial. In the remainder of this section, I briefly introduce two concepts, geolegality and martial law, that can help us not only survey some of the complex legal geographies of the Afghanistan intervention but also take the analysis of the law-space nexus—or law-space-time-power—in new directions.

## Geolegality

So what do I mean by *geolegality*? According to the *Oxford English Dictionary*, *geo*, of course, means "of or relating to the earth" and *legal* means "of, based on, or concerned with the law," where *law* is defined as "the system of rules that a particular country or community recognizes as regulating the actions of its members and may enforce by the imposition of penalties."[2] So at its root, *geolegality* designates the myriad forms of "earth ruling," just as geography at its most literal is a mode of "earth writing." Reflecting on this latter etymology, Matthew Sparke (2007, 338) has argued that we must attend to "how the 'geo' of any particular geography is 'graphed,' which is to say produced, by multiple, often unnoticed space-making processes and space-framing assumptions." So too with geolegality, which calls attention to practices, processes, and discourses involved in both the worlding of rules and the ruling of worlds. This is, of course, familiar terrain. Scholars across a range of disciplines who have engaged in some variation of legal geography have used a variety of concepts to capture the reciprocal relationship of law and space, including the law-space nexus, the spatiolegal, legal spatiality, and law-space-power (Benda-Beckmann and Benda-Beckmann 2009; Blomley 1989; Delaney 2010; Raustiala 2005). In an effort to overcome the residual dualism reflected in these otherwise serviceable formulations, some have proposed new terms that underscore how the legal and the spatial are, as the editors suggest in their introduction, "conjoined and co-constituted." Blomley (2008), for example, offered splicing as a term that might better emphasize the inescapable fusing of space and law, and more recently and ambitiously Delaney (2010) outlined the elements of a sophisticated analytical tool kit revolving around his core concepts of the nomic and nomospheric.

Like these latter terms, *geolegality* signals the indissoluble relations between law and space. But for my purposes its embrace of the "geo" helps forge, and foreground, a connection between the spatiolegal, on the one hand, and two other concepts that name important discourses and domains of contemporary social life in a "glocalizing" world: geopolitics and geoeconomics. These are undoubtedly complex and contentious terms with checkered careers that align them uncomfortably with histories and geographies of oppression and exploitation. In its traditional form, *geopolitics* refers, of course, to the discourses, strategies and statecraft of nation, people, and territory animating major power politics historically and in the present; but it has also assumed a more contrarian and progressive form in the critical and feminist geopolitics of the past two decades, which have problematized the geographical premises, tropes, and practices underpinning prevailing geopolitical narratives (Hyndman 2004; O'Tuathail and Agnew 1992). Geoeconomics is a newer concept that focuses attention on the spaces and flows of economic globalization, especially as they remake sovereignty and reshape the structures, boundaries, and power dynamics of nation-states and the interstate system (Sparke 2007). For Cowen and Smith (2009, 24), the emergence of geoeconomics as a "political-geographic logic of economy, security and power," spurred on by decolonization and US imperial aims, marks the ascendance of "a geoeconomic conception of space, power and security, which sees geopolitical forms recalibrated by market logics." While I am broadly sympathetic with their argument, they underplay the essential role of the geolegal in the still unfolding transition they chart from a geopolitical to a "geoeconomic social" (Cowen and Smith 2009, 23). Though inquiries into the spatialization of these three domains— geopolitics, geoeconomics, geolegality—have generated rich bodies of scholarship, the relations among them have not been thoroughly explored, and they are seldom analyzed together. This is somewhat surprising, since in practice they are often so clearly intertwined, whether—to take just a few examples—in the international climate politics surrounding the Kyoto Protocol, the ongoing efforts to thwart supposed Iranian nuclear ambitions through trade and investment sanctions, the competition over Arctic sovereignty claims under the governing framework of the UN Convention on the Law of the Sea, or the debates surrounding international regulatory reform of globalized banking and finance following the 2008 economic meltdown. With some exceptions (see, e.g., Dodds 2010; Elden 2010; Jeffrey 2009), critical geopolitics has given scant attention to law, even though the persistent intersections of international law and politics would seem to underscore the need for what we might call a critical legal geopolitics. Similarly, as Barkan (2011, 591) notes, political and economic geographers' accounts of capitalist globalization and state rescaling have tended to marginalize the legal dimension of these processes, but the reverse is also true: legal geography has had only a limited engagement with international politics, on the one hand, and the global or even national dynamics of capitalist accumulation, on the other.

An alternate framing may serve to bridge these divides. Viewed as forming a triangle with geopolitics and geoeconomics, a triangulation, the *geo* in geolegality helps reorient our perspective toward scales and spatiotemporal processes working beyond—but also within, through, and across—the territorial container of the nation-state. At the same time, by emphasizing the legal, which implicates the state form and juridical apparatus, it underscores the continuing salience of the state-space of the national and subnational scales in a networked, mobile, but still far-from-borderless world. Yet it also posits simultaneously law's integral relations with the political and the economic and invites attention to the ways in which this triad of state, law, and market jointly produces, structures, and delimits our lived geographies—though this does not mean that these elements are always and everywhere equally salient. Geolegality, then, inflects our understanding of the law-space nexus toward the inside/outside of the nation-state and its complex and shifting spatializations under the neoliberal hegemony of globalizing capitalism.

## Martial Law

This formulation of geolegality is especially helpful when we begin to think about war. For we cannot properly analyze the geolegalities of Western war making and intervention without recognizing the forces and dynamics—both geopolitical (state sovereignty and security) and geoeconomic (globalizing capitalism)—that shape the conduct of war. Nor, however, can we grasp the geopolitics and geoeconomics of war and intervention without analyzing their constitutive geolegality. Thus, we need an analytical frame that can encompass the lethal conjunction of the "geolegal complex"—to add a spatial gloss to Valverde and Rose's (1998, 542) productive term—and the military industrial complex. This leads me to the second concept I want to propose, *martial law*. In its conventional definition martial law refers to military government, a "state of emergency" in which ordinary law is suspended and replaced by military rule of a civilian population. Here, however, I want to invoke an alternate, more expansive meaning—*martial* in the sense of "warlike" or "pertaining to war"—to evoke the intimate connections between law and war, legality and violence, regulation, and coercion. Of course, these links have been explored before (see, e.g., Agamben 2005; Cover 1986). To elaborate on this expanded conception of martial law, one useful starting point is Walter Benjamin's influential 1921 essay "Critique of Violence," a touchstone for much subsequent writing. Benjamin (1978, 295) makes an important distinction between violence that is law making (designating "*what* is to be established as law") and law preserving (subordinating citizens to a law already established). This distinction helps us to see the dual nature of Western intervention: a form of *lawmaking violence*— violence aimed at the establishment, or rather reestablishment, of law—but with the ultimate aim of reconstituting a legitimate local authority that can maintain law and order, security, and stability, through *law-preserving violence*. Benjamin also observes that military violence, being "paradigmatic and primordial," has an inherent "lawmaking character" (283). Although my focus here is martial legality in the context of war, Benjamin reminds us how martial law—legalized violence— is the foundation of all state law, or to put it differently, how all state law is in some sense martial, since its ultimate guarantor is police or, in extremis, military power. But the concept of martial law also seeks to emphasize the pervasive role of law in the regulation of state violence. "Law is the code of organized public violence," as another Marxist theorist, Nicos Poulantzas (2000, 77), memorably put it. Like Benjamin, Poulantzas identified the state's reliance on the law-preserving role of violence, but importantly, he also emphasized how law in turn regulates violence, "designating its modalities" and "structuring its devices" (77).

Martial law, like all law, has its geographies, and so we must also attend to the diverse spatializations of legalized violence. Nicholas Blomley (2003) has provided an incisive survey of the literature on the law-violence nexus and has examined the constitutive violence of law in control of land and the creation and preservation of property. Elsewhere he has recognized the spatiolegalities of war:

"War is also a splice: it is underpinned by and partly regulated by legal notions such as sovereignty, yet it is also clearly spatialized, reliant on spatial practices, categories and arrangements" (Blomley 2008, 162). In the aftermath of 9/11, with the onset of the interminable "long war" against global terrorism and its proliferation of new and more repressive security paradigms and measures, law has become ever more integral to the conduct of war. Notably, it is political rather than legal geographers who have tracked many of these mutations. Derek Gregory (2006, 2010, 2011a, 2011b) has done much to illuminate the regulatory black holes and killing spaces of an emergent or potential "everywhere war," and has paid close attention to what he calls its "legal armatures" (Gregory 2006, 242). Still others have explored the intersections of law and international politics utilizing the concept of lawfare—law as a weapon of war—to analyze the actions of the Israeli military in Gaza (Weizman 2009) and the US state in the Middle East (Morrissey 2011).

An expanded notion of martial law underscores the range and complexity of contemporary warfare and its legal entailments. Among other things, it highlights the welter of legal subjects and relations underpinning the deployment of organized violence both within and beyond the territorial bounds of the national state—the international, transnational, and multinational, with all their attendant legal, temporal, and scalar complexities—and it is to some of these geolegalities, in the context of Western intervention, that I now turn.

## GLOBAL POLICING: THE GEOLEGALITIES
## OF WESTERN INTERVENTION

We can better understand the Afghanistan war and its geolegalities if we view it within the larger context of the serial interventions of the post–Cold War era, a seemingly endless parade of states, governments, coalitions, and transitional authorities that "come and go." This includes the Gulf War (1991), Somalia (1992–93), Rwanda (1994–95), Haiti (1994 and 2004), Sierra Leone (1997–98), Kosovo (1999), East Timor (1999 and 2006), Liberia (2003), Iraq (2003), Côte d'Ivoire (2003), Libya (2011), and most recently Mali (2013) (Chandler 2002; Orford 2003). These missions have operated under various labels—humanitarian interventions, stability operations, civil-military operations, peace support operations, military operations other than war (MOOTW)—and have assumed multiple and complex forms. Their proponents view them as noble ventures aimed at spreading development and universal human rights, necessary steps on the halting path of progress toward a cosmopolitan vision of global prosperity and liberal governance. For critics, however, they mark a new form of US (and Western) imperialism— what the collective Retort (2005, 103) called "military neoliberalism"—aimed at preserving and deepening the dominance of the Global North over the Global South, rich over poor, and containing the disorder that accumulation on a world scale produces in the global peripheries and borderlands (Bauman 2002; Douzinas 2003; Duffield 2007; Harvey 2003). Commonly cast as global policing operations to neutralize emergent threats and install or restore the rule of law, democracy, and market freedom in so-called failed or failing states—warfare as law enforcement—these missions blur the traditional inside-outside divisions of state sovereignty—"the engrained ideological separation between military (external) and police (internal) assertions of social security" (Cowen and Smith 2009, 24)—so that policing is no longer limited to maintaining domestic law and order, if indeed it ever was (Dean 2006; Neocleous 2011a). But this is not the only way that interventions blur conventional boundaries, so I want to highlight several features that are important for understanding the changing martial and geolegalities that Western intervention entails.

The first concerns certain *doctrinal shifts in international law* relating to state sovereignty, war, and occupation. As Elden (2010) argues, the post-9/11 period has accelerated changes in the prevailing conceptions of sovereignty that were already under way. Whereas territorial sovereignty traditionally encompassed the twin principles of territorial integrity (the sanctity of borders) and sovereign equality—the notion that within their own borders states were supreme and other states could not interfere—the link between them has gradually loosened, if not dissolved. Thus, while the integrity of international borders is maintained in the name of preserving stability, the internal sovereignty of weak states (usually but not always in the Global South) is rendered conditional. Sovereignty entails rights, but also responsibilities, and the failure to discharge them opens up the possibility of outside intervention to preserve regional and global order and stability. This also entails a concomitant expansion of the legal grounds for waging war—the *jus ad bello*—so that intervention may be justified both to protect civilians on human rights or humanitarian grounds (i.e., "the responsibility to protect") or to defend prophylactically against terrorist or other emergent threats. This latter rationale, in the form of the highly contentious and elastic doctrine of preemption, supplied the legal basis for the 2003 Iraq invasion under George W. Bush, and it serves now as the legal foundation for Obama's drone wars and other clandestine operations in the fragile states and "ungoverned spaces" of the Afghanistan-Pakistan borderlands, Africa, and elsewhere (Pincus 2012; Turse 2012).

These changing conceptions of sovereignty and war are linked to corresponding changes in the law of armed occupation, a subset of the law of war. Whereas an occupying power was traditionally conceived as a temporary custodian obliged largely to preserve the status quo in a defeated state, contemporary

Western interventionism envisions a new model of multilateral occupation that is less preservative than transformative (Roberts 2006). Since its aims frequently involve so-called state building and reconstruction, intervention often brings with it "revolutionary regimes, designed to eliminate existing laws, property relations and political cultures deemed illegitimate" (Orford 2010, 2). In some cases, change may be imposed directly and over a sustained period within the dictatorial framework of "international territorial administration"—government by fiat of international officials—but perhaps the preferred model is to implement sweeping change in conjunction with newly constituted "transitional" authorities. This fosters the appearance of autonomy and self-government, and it recasts transformation—generally calibrated in neoliberal logics concerned with "securing private property and entrenching contractarian market relations" (Krever 2010, 149)—as the path to a reclaimed national sovereignty and economic prosperity. Under either model, occupation may often serve as a form of what David Delaney (2010, 148–51) has called a "transformative nomospheric project," a form of legal "re-worlding," which demonstrates, as Orford (2010) underscores, unsettling continuities with the authoritarian and exploitative rule of the colonial era.

Notably, intervention has also propelled policy, institutional, and legal changes in the dominant Western states that initiate, organize, and implement these incursions. Institutionally, interventions are increasingly hybrid affairs that manifest novel linkages between, and even the fusing of, security and development programs, military and civil functions, public and private entities, state officials and private contractors (Duffield 2001, 2007; Reid-Henry 2011). Thus, the transformation of Western war making into *global policing* goes beyond a mere conceptual change. Under the rubric of "integrated," "comprehensive" or "whole-of-government" approaches, the dominant powers of the Global North have engaged in ongoing reformulation of laws, policies, practices, and institutions to promote security, stability, and reconstruction in weakly governed conflict zones. Such initiatives have developed at the national, international and supra- and transnational (United Nations, NATO, European Union) levels, and they reflect an understanding that achieving stability in "weak" or "failed" states—especially when faced with insurgencies as in Afghanistan and Iraq—requires bridging the civil-military divide and coordination and integration of security and development agendas across a complex assemblage of state institutions, nongovernmental organizations, and private corporations. As Bell and Evans (2011, 372) note, "Insurgency mobilizes the multidimensional management of complex emergency. Instantiating control over lived space occurs not through exclusion, but through the incorporation of life into the technologies of management."

The key point, for present purposes, is that geolegality plays a crucial—and underexamined—role in these composite missions. In the military sphere, this is perhaps best illustrated by the rapid emergence, institutionalization, codification, and diffusion among Western powers of a new, hybrid body of law: so-called operational law (in military jargon, OPLAW) (Warren 1996). There is no space here to trace in any depth the genealogy of this development, but suffice it to say that it is an American invention that emerged in the aftermath of Operation Urgent Fury, the 1983 invasion and occupation of Grenada (Graham 1987). By the late 1980s Canada and other US allies were drawing on US innovations, and the US military now publishes an annual operational law handbook to guide military lawyers during military operations (US Department of Army 2013). Graham (1987, 10) recites an early definition of operational law that captures the breadth and hybridity of this martial legality:

> Domestic and international law associated with the planning and execution of
> military operations in peacetime or hostilities. It includes, but is not limited
> to, Law of War, law related to security assistance, training, mobilization,
> predeployment preparation, deployment, overseas procurement, the conduct of
> military combat operations, anti- and counter-terrorist activities, status of forces
> agreements, operations against hostile forces, and civil affairs operations.

Operational law is a subset of military law and intersects with its other components—military justice, for example, and military administration—but it also blurs the boundary between national and international law (or at least national interpretations of international law). Its hybrid content reflects the multifaceted nature of contemporary military operations, but also the intersections of geolegality with geopolitics (status of forces agreements, counterterrorism, security assistance) and geoeconomics (e.g., overseas procurement). Operational legality is fundamentally shaped by strategic considerations; in other words, the mission objectives dictate to a substantial degree what is authorized. Seen in this light, like war itself, OPLAW is politics continued by other means, and the geopolitics of this martial legality are never far from the surface. This is apparent if we recall that law not only orders but also legitimates military violence, a vital function in a media-saturated era in which Western wars are always already public relations campaigns. Thus, OPLAW provides a justificatory arsenal in the battle for hearts and minds in the conflict zone but also among various domestic and international publics. As Demarest (1995, 7) notes, "International law is a premier format of international propaganda" such that "the propagandist and the operational lawyer must synchronize completely."

This brings me to a final point regarding the geolegalities of intervention. The multinational character of most stability operations makes coordination of their "floating coalitions" and "confluent alliances" essential (Bauman 2002, 85). Thus, a key—if often elusive—imperative for the militaries of the Global North is the drive to achieve so-called interoperability—"the ability to act together coherently, effectively and efficiently to achieve Allied tactical, operational and strategic objectives" (NATO 2013, 2-I-8). As Walsh (2005, 316–17) indicates, interoperability is not merely a technical question concerning equipment design and interchangeability; it encompasses the synchronization of doctrine and procedure, and here operational law plays an essential ordering role. David Kennedy (2006, 63) conveys this point concretely:

> Operating across dozens of jurisdictions, today's military must comply with innumerable local, national and international rules regulating the use of territory, the mobilization of men, the financing of arms and logistics, and the deployment of force. If you want to screen banking data in Belgium, or hire operatives in Pakistan or refuel your plane in Kazakhstan, you need to know the law of the place.

Multinational stability operations thus put a premium on interoperability but also display an unavoidable *interlegality*. The term originates in a pioneering article by Boaventura de Sousa Santos (1987), but Valverde (2009, 141) has offered her own astute gloss: "the constant interaction among different legal orders—each of which has its own scope, its own logic, and its own criteria for what is to be governed, as well as its own rules for how to govern." Multinational interventions not only install multiple legal orders within the same space—orders that may feature distinct and sometimes conflicting spatiotemporal logics—but also stretch those orders across, or even recast, prevailing spatial and jurisdictional boundaries. The challenge of interoperability, of course, is to coordinate this legal multiverse in pursuit of the strategic objectives of a given operation, a task that concerns not just the intertwining of legal orders among coalition members but also the legal system of the host nation (Blank 2012). This is a field, par excellence, of what legal anthropologists call legal pluralism (Benda-Beckmann and Benda-Beckmann, 2009).

## RULING AFGHANISTAN

Taking these observations about geolegality, martial law, and Western intervention as coordinates, we can now turn our attention to the Afghanistan war. By any measure, it has been a protracted, costly, and highly lethal intervention. By the end of 2014, when the US and ISAF withdraw the bulk of their forces and the Afghan state assumes full responsibility for security, the war will have lasted more than thirteen years, cost the coalition countries upward of $1 trillion, and produced thousands of military and civilian casualties. Although the United States and its NATO allies appear to have succeeded in their original aim of "degrading" the threat posed by Al Qaeda, the promises of effective government and reconstruction remain largely unfulfilled, and there are real fears that the post-withdrawal period might see a return to civil war. With the majority of the Afghan population still facing abysmal living standards by most conventional measures—male and female life expectancy, access to drinking water, literacy, poverty, displacement—it is plausible to ask, as Pounds (2012) does, "What ten years, 46 nations, 130,000 troops and half a trillion dollars have done to help the Afghan people build a strong and peaceful democratic society?" To analyze some of the martial and legal geographies underpinning this dismal enterprise, I offer a conceptual map—admittedly partial and schematic—of the geolegalities of this intervention, a brief synopsis of the West's effort to remake rule in Afghanistan. For heuristic purposes we can distinguish four moments: invasion, occupation, pacification, and autonomization. Though we might notionally distinguish the military dimension (invasion-pacification) from the civilian (occupation-autonomization), there is no clear sequencing or division between these moments; they bleed—perhaps all too literally—into each other.

## Geolegalities of Invasion

One of the central questions animating the work of legal geographers and sociolegal scholars is, as the editors of the *Legal Geography Reader* put it, "Where is law?" (Delaney, Ford, and Blomley 2001), and these inquiries have extended to the "where" of international law (Pearson 2008). But there have also been recent calls for greater attention to the "how" of law, to take seriously both its technicalities (Valverde 2009) and the world-making practices of lawyers (Martin, Scherr, and City 2010). It is useful to pose these questions in the context of the complex, international, and multiscalar institutional network through which the Afghanistan war was initiated. Put simply, Where, when, and how do wars start? Where is war law? What geolegal processes authorize and enable states to "come and go"?

One starting point would be the various national and international legal procedures invoked to authorize the resort to armed force, a process that illustrates the integral links between geopolitics and geolegality in its martial form. Thus, for example, on September 12, 2001, in Brussels NATO signaled its mobilization for war by invoking article 5 of the North Atlantic Treaty, the collective self-defense provision (with the geographical caveat that it would only apply if it was determined that the 9/11 attacks were launched from abroad). On September 14, 2001, the US Congress granted President Bush an Authorization to Use Military Force (which even now serves as the domestic legal foundation for Obama's counterterror operations in Afghanistan, Pakistan, and elsewhere). On October 7, 2001, in New York the British and US governments provided the requisite notice to the UN Security Council of their pending action against Afghanistan pursuant to the inherent right of self-defense. On that date, too, the UN Security Council issued the first of a series of resolutions denouncing the terror attacks, recognizing the inherent right of self-defense, and endorsing "all necessary steps" to combat terrorism and preserve international peace and security, thereby providing its imprimatur for the invasion of Afghanistan. Thus, the organization and commencement of a coalition military operation undertaken for geopolitical aims of national and international security worked in important ways through law. Moreover, even apart from these more visible and formal legal procedures, mobilization for war obviously involves an array of sites, actors, and activities—basing, logistics, communications, transport, provisioning, financing, diplomacy—across a broad range of state and nonstate institutions to prepare and activate the war machine, all of which are "governed by law" (Rose and Valverde 1998). Operational law has emerged, it seems, precisely to meet the challenges of coordinating national and multinational action across all these spheres.

## Geolegalities of Occupation

For the US-led coalition the invasion of Afghanistan, it turns out, was the easy part (as it would be again in Iraq). The bombing of Afghanistan began on October 7, 2001, with the launch of US Operation Enduring Freedom (OEF). Within several weeks the United States and its coalition and Afghan allies in the Northern Alliance had retaken most of Afghanistan's major cities, including the capital, Kabul, and by December 2001 had largely vanquished the governing Taliban regime—another state to come and go—the remnants of which withdrew across the ill-defined, contentious, and porous Afghanistan-Pakistan border to regroup (see Ali 2008; Rashid 2008). The occupation that followed the—it turns out illusory—Taliban defeat was a lawmaking assemblage (and "plural legal constellation") that illustrates the convoluted dynamics of coordinating an ad hoc coalition and Afghan state formation across time and space. The coalition, for all its emphasis on interoperability, produced its own byzantine structures and bewildering interlegalities, a crazy quilt of "combined" (multinational), "joint" (interservice) and "interagency" (civil-military) units, overlapping command structures, and multiscalar organization with a complex territorialization (Ricks 2012; Trevithick 2012; Zaman 2010).

Here three aspects deserve emphasis. First, from the beginning the Afghanistan intervention comprised not one but two missions, the US OEF, and ISAF led by NATO under UN auspices. In the years following the 2001 invasion, the US OEF was largely a combat mission focused on defeating the Taliban and counterterrorism, mostly in the south and east of the country. In contrast, ISAF tended to focus on maintaining security and supporting reconstruction, initially in the Kabul region (from 2003) and then gradually beyond as it pursued a phased geographical expansion that by 2006 encompassed all of Afghanistan (NATO 2012). The result was a regional command structure deploying "mini-coalitions" composed of NATO and non-NATO militaries in each of the six regions. Second, though nominally and organizationally distinct, there is unsurprisingly substantial overlap between the US and NATO missions, as NATO countries at times provide forces to US OEF and US forces are deployed with ISAF forces in several of the regional commands. The United States is the dominant member of the NATO alliance, and its most senior officers are "double-hatted" as commanders of both OEF and ISAF (Zaman 2010). Third, despite this overlap the coordination both within and between the two missions has proved a constant challenge. This owes, in no small part, to the bifurcated nature of "command and control." In a combined operation, the coalition has operational control of troops in the field, but ultimate command remains with the national government of the sending state. In Afghanistan, many of the coalition countries have maintained "national caveats" that impose limits on the permissible deployment and activities of their forces. These have been a regular source of friction within the alliance, as some member states—the United States, Canada, Britain, among them—have played a much greater combat role and suffered much heavier casualties (Saidemann and Auerswald, 2012). As Bensahel (2012) notes: "Clausewitz's famous dictum applies as much to military coalitions as it does to individual states. Coalition warfare is still the continuation of politics by other means—but politics in the international system requires bargaining and compromise among sovereign states." Thus, the geopolitics of a coalition play out on the ground in Afghanistan in the geolegalities of national caveats as expressions of national law and sovereignty.

The other important, and similarly convoluted, element in this plural legal constellation is the fledgling Afghan state. Here too we can discern the import of geolegality, interlegality, and geopolitics in the political-legal procedures through which the Afghan state apparatus has been (re)constituted following the defeat of the Taliban government. The initial state-building process—which unfolded in stages between December 2001 and mid-2005—involved a complex interplay of US, UN, NATO, and Afghan internal politics as the coalition sought to rebuild state institutions throughout the country, consolidate the territorial reach of the central government, and promote the appearance and reality of Afghan self-government even as the Taliban resurgence from 2005 onward made an assertive coalition military presence an ever-greater necessity. The new state apparatus remains weak, given its dependence on foreign financing and military support, and is plagued by allegations of endemic corruption and electoral fraud. Yet its existence creates the trappings of sovereignty—the sort of partial or contingent sovereignty that Elden (2010) describes—and distinguishes it, at least in juridical terms, from the international territorial administration discussed earlier.

Moreover, quite apart from its dependent relationship with the US and ISAF forces, the Afghan state itself embodies a complex legal field, comprising as it does local customary law, Sharia law, still-extant forms of state law from previous incarnations of the Afghan government, as well as the new laws promulgated by Hamid Karzai's fledgling Islamic republic (Barfield 2008). Political conflicts have erupted periodically between the Afghan government and its coalition sponsors when it has enacted laws, or taken administrative actions, that conflict with Western conceptions of civil and political rights, as well as norms of gender equality. Even more vexing is the fact that, as the Taliban have regained effective control in some areas, they have increasingly established a virtual shadow state with a parallel legal system that—despite its puritanical severity—increasingly competes with, and subverts, the territorial reach of a Kabul government perceived as ineffectual and venal (Giustozzi 2011).

## Geolegalities of Pacification

Pacification here refers somewhat narrowly to the project of restoring the state's monopolization of violence, Benjamin's lawmaking violence (cf. Neocleous's [2010, 2011b] broader but not incompatible conception of pacification as "securing insecurity"). From mid-2005, as the Taliban reasserted themselves in the south and east of the country, coalition forces found themselves facing an insurgency that challenged their plan to reestablish a monopoly of legitimate force and consolidate a new regime of "law and order" within the national territory (whose uncertain extent and permeable border with Pakistan made this objective all the more difficult). The evolving coalition efforts to mount an effective counterinsurgency (COIN) campaign have a number of important geolegal dimensions—rules governing, for example, the detention of suspected insurgents, the use of air strikes, and targeted killing via drones—but I focus here on one crucial aspect of this martial legality, the rules of engagement (ROE), because they demonstrate the close relations between geolegality and geopolitics, and the ways that military violence is governed by law.

In general, NATO (2013, 2-R-10) defines its ROE as "directives issued by competent military authority which specify the circumstances and limitations under which forces will initiate and/or continue combat engagement with other forces encountered." In essence, the ROE represent a set of "spatiotemporalized" rules regulating the application of lethal violence: they direct military personnel on what force may be used, where, when, how, and against whom. They are time and place specific, and they have a complex geography, not least because the application of rules in the combat zone is but one node in a network of command authority, policy development, and military training that, in a coalition operation, reaches back to coalition headquarters but also to national governments (which, as mentioned earlier, may set caveats to limit the nature and scope of their combat engagements). Since multinational coalitions may feature complex demarcations of operational and tactical control, US forces may operate under US ROE, the coalition ROE, or a "common" ROE negotiated between the various forces involved (US Department of Army 2013, 89–90). Like the operational law of which it forms an essential element, the ROE derive from various sources: political and policy directives, operational imperatives of a specific mission, and domestic and international law governing the permissible use of force and the protection of civilians. As Demarest (1995, 5) puts it, in the case of the United States, ROEs represent an "evolved expression of American legal culture"; but in Afghanistan they also reflect the balance of (geo)political forces both within the coalition and in its relations with the Afghan state.

The COIN context alters the calculus and consequences of the use of deadly force fundamentally, since, as Gregory (2010) and others have observed, "war among the people" blurs vital distinctions—between war and peace, combatant and civilian, battlefield and peaceful habitation, soldier and aid worker—even as the "battle for hearts and minds" renders the protection of the civilian population a strategic imperative. The ROE represent a form of biopolitics in action—Foucault's (1990, 254–55) "killing in order to go on living" here means killing suspected insurgents to remake life for the Afghan civilian population. But US and ISAF forces continue to kill and injure, in alarming numbers, the Afghan civilians they are ostensibly there to protect. This lethal toll—whether by regular forces, private military contractors, or air strikes—has been a constant source of friction with the Afghan population and the Karzai government, particularly since the coalition forces have tended to enjoy relative operational freedom and—by virtue of status of forces agreements with the Afghan state—legal immunity under Afghan law (see Morrissey 2011).

These challenges led in 2009 to a revision of US and ISAF COIN strategy to grant civilian protection even higher priority and resulted in the adoption of more restrictive rules governing the conduct of house-to-house searches and, especially, the use of close air support.

In light of this complexity, some commentators have suggested that meeting the dual objectives of defeating the insurgents and protecting the population requires further spatiotemporal refinements to the ROE to distinguish subcategories of targets and the range of permissible force. For example, an individual providing occasional and indirect assistance to the Taliban would be a "legitimate target of detention" but not an "open fire" order; "transitory" and "recurring" targets could be targeted only while actively participating in hostile action, whereas those active insurgents who are continuously engaged in hostilities could be killed at any time (Blank and Guiora 2011). All this illustrates that, in the Afghanistan intervention, legal interpretation literally "play[s] out on the field of pain and death" (Cover 1986, 1606–7), but the imperatives of counterinsurgency render the hermeneutics of this martial legality ever more complicated (Tyson 2009).

## Geolegalities of Autonomization

By *autonomization* I mean coalition efforts to build the governing capacity of Afghan state institutions and promote reconstruction and economic development. There is a wide range of such activities undertaken by the military, civilian government departments, international organizations, development agencies (e.g., US Agency for International Development), for-profit private military contractors, and nongovernmental organizations. Here I want to focus on coalition efforts to build institutional capacity in the justice system as a geolegal strategy to promote geopolitical aims. Justice and the rule of law were early priorities following the 2001 invasion. The 2001 Bonn Agreement made the "rule of law sector" one of its priorities, and the UN Development Program's blueprint for international aid and Afghan reconstruction, the 2008 "Afghanistan National Development Strategy," also identified promotion of the rule of law and justice system as key development tasks and included detailed plans for development of the justice system over a five-year period (Government of the Islamic Republic of Afghanistan 2008a, 2008b; see also Fidler 2007). Faced with the perceived corruption and weakness of the Afghan state, coalition forces increasingly recognized the need to build its capacity and adherence to the rule of law in order to win the battle for legitimacy in the eyes of the Afghan population. In 2010, the US State Department published the "Rule of Law Strategy for Afghanistan," which has the explicit aim of bolstering the Afghan state justice system while thwarting the expansion of competing Taliban justice (Hagerott, Umberg, and Jackson 2010). One of its chief proponents identified the essential geopolitical role that this geolegal strategy was intended to serve:

By building legal institutions that have credibility and authority, wielders of COIN lawfare serve the ends at once of helping protect the population and of holding all of the other COIN instruments—conventional warfare, counterterror operations, security force capacity building, intelligence collection, physical security measures, public information, cyber security and warfare, economic development, electoral and other initiatives to connect government to the people—to purposes and methods that comply with law and advance the project of unhinging the enemy on a political level. That is, of course, the level where an insurgency must always ultimately be defeated. (Martins 2010)

In this view, law and its institutions legitimize, but are also effectively subsumed within, the arsenal of "COIN instruments" that serve a larger military strategy of building popular allegiance to the government and undermining support for the Taliban. Lawfare—a term the US military once used only to denigrate its opponents' illegitimate resort to law as a weapon of war (Gregory 2010, 178)—is recast as COIN lawfare to become an effective mode of counterinsurgency. It is also a prime example of what I have termed *martial law*.

Yet COIN lawfare is not only a military but also inevitably a spatiotemporal strategy. The task of "connecting government to the people" requires the use of military power to extend the reach of nascent security and justice institutions and solidify the new legal order. This is evident, first, in the emphasis the coalition has placed on so-called security sector reform. The recruitment and training of Afghan security forces, both the Afghan National Army and the Afghan National Police Force, remains a crucial priority, particularly given the planned transfer of security responsibility to the Afghan government in 2014. Two US officers involved in NATO's training efforts stress the need to have police distributed throughout Afghanistan to protect the population, enforce the law, and build the legitimacy of the Kabul government: "an effective police force is critical to achieving Afghan aspirations for stability and U.S. strategic objectives in Afghanistan. As the most visible representation of the government in towns and villages across the country, police capacity must be the highest priority of the Government [of Afghanistan] and international community" (Caldwell and Finney 2010, 121). In this prioritization of Afghan policing as US strategic objective, we may discern a desire to restore the link between legitimate sovereign authority and monopolized violence—between law and force—but also to forge a spatiolegal and institutional division between the lawmaking power of the US military and the law-preserving power of the Afghan police.

As another element of this COIN lawfare, the coalition has increasingly turned to what it calls "rule of law operations." These focus not only on building justice infrastructure, and training personnel, but also on ensuring that coalition and Afghan forces observe the rule of law in their own operations. Crucially, however, they reflect a recognition that, with the Taliban forces gaining strength, military force is required to protect the legal institutions charged with extending the rule of law. In various ways, then, coalition forces have pursued militarized spatio-temporal strategies for extending the reach of the Afghan state and building the legitimacy of its legal institutions. In a counterinsurgency war, as Foucault (1990, 144) told us long ago, the "law cannot help but be armed," but so too the sword must refer to the space-times of law.

## LAWS OF WAR, WARS OF LAW

This chapter has highlighted some new connections and spaces for legal geography. In particular, it suggests that legal geography might usefully expand its horizons in several directions: geographically, by extending its purview beyond the territorial container of the nation-state and the conurbations of the Global North; conceptually, by following the lines of inquiry suggested by the terms geolegality and martial law; and thematically, by exploring in greater depth the intersections of law, geopolitics, geoeconomics and war. It also offered an exploratory mapping of some of the spatiolegal dimensions of late-modern war and Western interventionism.

There are ample reasons to expand the spaces of law in these directions. We live in a world where the geopolitical and geoeconomic common sense of at least a half-century is undergoing dramatic change. The core rich states of the Global North have recognized that the future of warfare may be less about interstate conflict and more about stabilization operations to secure the affluent core against threats emanating from ungoverned spaces on the global fringes. In his 2009 book *Violence*, Slavoj Žižek provides some insights that may serve to crystallize the points I have tried to convey about the geolegalities of martial law. Remarking on the unsettled feeling he experiences on visits to Israel, he describes that "strange thrill of entering a forbidden territory of illegitimate violence." "But," he proceeds, "what if what disturbs me is precisely that I find myself in a state which hasn't yet obliterated the 'founding violence' of its illegitimate origins, repressed them into a timeless past. In this sense, what the state of Israel confronts us with is merely the obliterated past of *every* state power" (Žižek 2009, 117). In our still-colonial present (Gregory 2004), such founding violence is by no means unique to Israel. Western military interventions—like those launched in the Balkans in the 1990s, in Iraq and Afghanistan after 9/11, and more recently in Libya and Mali—are *wars of law, through law, and for law*. They are wars of law insofar as they are organized, instituted, and waged by the ostensibly liberal democracies of the Global North; they are wars through law in that, as I have tried to show, they are pervasively "governed by law" (Valverde and Rose 1998); and they are wars for law, as they aim to establish stable, liberal, or quasi-liberal regimes in which potential threats can be mollified through development or neutralized through lawfully monopolized force. In this sense, we might also view them as wars of "pacification" (Neocleous 2011b). Thus, the court martial of Sgt. Robert Bales in the United States, whatever the outcome, can do little to alter the fate of the murdered villagers of Panjwai. They form part of the global cohort of what Duffield (2007, 216–18) calls "non-insured life," and they join the constantly swelling ranks of those who are killed and injured in the Global North's manifold "wars that come and go," wars that are always fought in the name of global peace, security, and the rule of law.

## NOTES

I am grateful for the incisive comments of the Buffalo workshop participants, Derek Gregory, and especially, the editors.

1. In June 2013, Bales pleaded guilty to multiple counts of murder, attempted murder, and assault, thereby avoiding the death penalty, but at the time of writing he had yet to be sentenced. The account of his rampage is based on contemporaneous reports in Western media, but many details remain unclear and controversial (see Sanger 2012; Shah and Bowley 2012; Vogt and Jelinek 2012).
2. *Oxford English Dictionary*, 2013, http://www.oxforddictionaries.com/definition/american_english/.

## REFERENCES

AFP. 2012. "Obama Seeks to Calm Afghan Massacre Fallout." *Al Arabiya News*. March 13, 2012. http://english.alarabiya.net/articles/2012/03/13/200491.html.

Agamben, Giorgio. 2005. *State of Exception*. Translated by Kevin Attell. Chicago: University of Chicago Press.

Ali, Tariq. 2008. "Afghanistan: Mirage of the Good War." *New Left Review* 50: 5–22.

Baker, David. 2009. "How Obama Came to Plan for 'Surge' in Afghanistan." *New York Times*, December 5.

Barfield, Thomas. 2008. "Culture and Custom in Nation-Building: Law in Afghanistan." *Maine Law Review* 60 (2): 348–73.

Barkan, Joshua. 2011. "Law and the Geographic Analysis of Globalization." *Progress in Human Geography* 35 (5): 589–607.

Bauman, Zygmunt. 2002. "Reconnaissance Wars of the Planetary Frontierland." *Theory, Culture and Society* 19: 81–90.

Bell, Colleen, and Brad Evans. 2011. "Terrorism to Insurgency: Mapping the Post-Intervention Security Terrain." *Journal of Intervention and State-Building* 4 (4): 371–90.

Benda-Beckmann, Franz von, and Keebet von Benda-Beckmann. 2009. "Space and Legal Pluralism." In *Spatializing Law: An Anthropological Geography of Law in Society*. Edited by Franz von Benda-Beckmann, Keebet von Benda-Beckmann, and Anne Griffiths, 1–29. Farnham, UK: Ashgate.

Benda-Beckmann, Franz von, Keebet von Benda-Beckmann, and Anne Griffiths, eds. 2005. *Mobile People, Mobile Law: Expanding Legal Relations in a Contracting World.* Farnham, UK: Ashgate.

Benjamin, Walter. 1978. "Critique of Violence." In *Reflections: Essays, Aphorisms, Autobiographical Writings*, edited by Peter Demetz, 277–300. Translated by Edmund Jephcott. New York: Harcourt Brace Jovanich.

Bensahel, Nora. 2012. "Annals of C2(IV): Here's Why Coalition Command Structures Are So Ungainly." *Best Defence* (blog). http://ricks.foreignpolicy.com/posts/2012/03/28/annals_of_c2_vi_heres_why_coalition_command_structures_are_so_ungainly.

Blank, Laurie R. 2012. "Complex Legal Frameworks and Complex Operational Challenges: Navigating the Applicable Law Across the Continuum of Military Operations." *Emory International Law Review* 26: 87–135.

Blank, Laurie, and Amos N. Guiora. 2011. "Updating the Commander's Toolbox: New Tools for Operationalizing the Law of Armed Conflict." *Prism* 1 (3): 59–78.

Blomley, Nicholas K. 1989. "Text and Context: Rethinking the Law-Space Nexus." *Progress in Human Geography* 13: 512–34.

———. 2003. "Law, Property and the Geography of Violence: The Frontier, the Survey, and the Grid." *Annals of the American Association of Geographers* 93 (1): 121–41.

———. 2008. "Making Space for Law." In *Handbook of Political Geography*, Edited by Kevin Cox, Murray Low, and Jennifer Robinson, 155–68. London: Sage.

Braverman, Irus. 2009. *Planted Flags: Trees, Land and Law in Israel/Palestine*. Cambridge: Cambridge University Press.

Caldwell, William B., IV, and Nathan K. Finney. 2010. "Building Police Capacity in Afghanistan: The Challenge of a Multilateral Approach." *Prism* 2 (1): 121–30.

Chandler, David. 2002. *From Kosovo to Kabul: Human Rights and International Intervention.* London: Pluto.

Cover, Robert. 1986. "Violence and the Word." *Yale Law Journal* 95 (8): 1601–29.

Cowen, Deborah, and Neil Smith. 2009. "After Geopolitics? From the Geopolitical Social to Geoeconomics." *Antipode* 41: 22–48.

Dean, Mitchell. 2006. "Military Intervention as 'Police' Action?" In *The New Police Science: The Police Power in Domestic and International Governance*, edited by Markus Dubber and Mariana Valverde, 185–206. Stanford, CA: Stanford University Press.

Delaney, David. 2010. *The Spatial, the Legal, and the Pragmatics of World-Making: Nomospheric Investigations.* London: Routledge/GlassHouse.

Delaney, David, Richard T. Ford, and Nicholas Blomley. 2001. "Preface: Where Is Law?" In *The Legal Geographies Reader: Law, Power and Space*, edited by Nicholas K. Blomley, David Delaney, and Richard T. Ford, xiii–xxii. Oxford, UK: Blackwell.

Demarest, Geoffrey. 1995. "The Strategic Implications of Operational Law." Foreign Military Studies Office Publications. http://fmso.leavenworth.army.mil/documents/oplaw.htm.

Dodds, Klaus. 2010. "Flag Planting and Finger Pointing: The Law of the Sea, the Arctic, and the Political Geographies of the Outer Continental Shelf." *Political Geography* 29: 63–73.

Douzinas, Costas. 2003. "Humanity, Military Humanism, and the New Moral Order." *Economy and Society* 32: 159–83.

Duffield, Mark. 2001. *Global Governance and the New Wars: The Merger of Development and Security.* London: Zed Books.

————. 2007. *Development, Security and Unending War: Governing the World of Peoples.* Cambridge, UK: Polity.

Elden, Stuart. 2010. *Terror and Territory: The Spatial Extent of Sovereignty.* Minneapolis: University of Minnesota Press.

Fidler, Didier. 2007. "Counterinsurgency, Rule of Law Operations, and International Law." *ASIL Insights* 11 (24). http://www.asil.org./insights070919.cfm.

Foucault, Michel. 1990. *The History of Sexuality: An Introduction.* New York: Vintage.

Giustozzi, Antonio. 2011. "Hearts, Minds and the Barrel of a Gun: The Taliban's Shadow Government." *Prism* 3 (2): 71–80.

Government of the Islamic Republic of Afghanistan. 2008a. *Afghanistan National Development Strategy.* Kabul: Government of Afghanistan.

————. 2008b. *Justice & Rule of Law Sector Strategy.* Kabul: Government of Afghanistan.

Graham, David E. 1987. "Operational Law—A Concept Comes of Age." *Army Lawyer*, July, 9–12.

Gregory, Derek. 2004. *The Colonial Present: Afghanistan, Palestine, Iraq.* Oxford, UK: Blackwell.

————. 2006. "The Black Flag: Guantanamo Bay and the Space of Exception." *Geografiska Annaler B* 88 (4): 405–27.

————. 2010. "War and Peace." *Transactions of the Institute of British Geographers* 35: 154–86.

————. 2011a. "The Everywhere War." *Geographical Journal* 177 (3): 238–50.

————. 2011b. "From a View to a Kill: Drones and Late Modern War." *Theory, Culture and Society* 28 (7–8): 188–215.

Hagerott, Mark R., Thomas J. Umberg, and Joseph A. Jackson. 2010. "A Patchwork Strategy of Consensus: Establishing the Rule of Law in Afghanistan." *Joint Forces Quarterly* 59 (4): 143–46.

Harvey, David. 2003. *The New Imperialism.* Oxford: Oxford University Press.

Hyndman, Jennifer. 2004. "Mind the Gap: Bridging Feminist and Political Geography Through Geopolitics." *Political Geography* 23: 307–22.

International Security Assistance Force. 2012. "History." http://www.isaf.nato.int/history.html.

Jeffrey, Alex. 2009. "Justice Incomplete: Radovan Karadzic, the ICTY, and the Spaces of International Law." *Environment and Planning D: Society and Space* 27: 387–402.

Jones, Seth G. 2008. *Counterinsurgency in Afghanistan: RAND Counterinsurgency Study No. 4.* Santa Monica, CA: Rand.

Kedar, Alexandre. 2003. "On the Legal Geography of Ethnocratic Settler States: Notes Towards a Research Agenda." *Current Legal Issues* 5: 401–41.

Kennedy, D. 2006. "Modern War and Modern Law." *International Legal Theory* 12: 55–97.

Krever, Tor. 2010. "Calling Power to Reason?" Review of *Homo Juridicus: On the Anthropological Function of Law*, by Alain Supiot. *New Left Review* 65: 141–50.

Mahmud, Tayyab. 2010. "Colonial Cartographies, Postcolonial Borders and Enduring Failures of International Law: The Unending Wars along the Afghanistan-Pakistan Frontier." *Brooklyn Journal of International Law* 36 (1): 1–74.

Martin, Deborah, Alexander W. Scherr, and Christopher City. 2010. "Making Law, Making Place: Lawyers and the Production of Space." *Progress in Human Geography* 34 (2): 175–92.

Martins, Mark. 2010. "Reflections on 'Lawfare' and Related Terms." *Lawfare* (blog). November 24. http://www.lawfareblog.com/2010/11/reflections-on-"lawfare"-and-related-terms/.

Morrissey, John. 2011. "Liberal Lawfare and Biopolitics: US Juridical Warfare in the War on Terror." *Geopolitics* 16 (2): 280–305.

NATO. 2012. "About ISAF: History." http://www.isaf.nato.int/history.html.

———. 2013. *AAP-06—Edition 2013: NATO Glossary of Terms and Definitions* (English and French). Brussels: NATO. http://nsa.nato.int/nsa/zPublic/ap/aap6/AAP-6.pdf.

Neocleous, Mark. 2010. "War as Peace, Peace as Pacification." *Radical Philosophy* 159: 8–17.

———. 2011a. "The Police of Civilization: The War on Terror as Civilizing Offensive." *International Political Sociology* 5: 144–59.

———. 2011b. "'A Brighter and Nicer New Life': Security as Pacification." *Social and Legal Studies* 20 (2): 191–208.

Orford, Anne. 2003. *Reading Humanitarian Intervention: Human Rights and the Use of Force in International Law.* Cambridge: Cambridge University Press.

———. 2010. "Book Review Article: International Territorial Administration and the Management of Decolonization." *ICLQ* 59: 227–49.

O'Tuathail, Gerard, and John Agnew. 1992. "Geopolitics and Discourse: Practical Geopolitical Reasoning and American Foreign Policy." *Political Geography* 11: 155–75.

Pearson, Zoe. 2008. "Spaces of International Law." *Griffith Law Review* 17: 489–514.

Pincus, Walter. 2012. "Has Obama Taken Bush's 'Pre-Emption Strategy' to Another Level?" *Washington Post*, January 19.

Pitzul, Jerry S. T. 2001. "Operational Law and the Legal Professional: A Canadian Perspective." *Air Force Law Review* 51: 311–21.

Poulantzas, Nicos. 2000. *State, Power, Socialism.* London: Verso.

Pounds, Ian. 2012. "The American Agenda in Afghanistan: A Civilian's Review." *Counterpunch* (blog), May 30. http://www.counterpunch.org/2012/05/30/the-american-agenda-in-afghanistan-a-civilians-review/.

Rashid, Ahmed. 2008. *Descent into Chaos: The United States and the Failure of Nation Building in Pakistan, Afghanistan, and Central Asia.* New York: Viking.

Raustiala, Kal. 2005. "The Geography of Justice." *Fordham Law Review* 73: 2501–60.

Reid-Henry, Simon. 2011. "Spaces of Security and Development: An Alternative Mapping of the Security-Development Nexus." *Security Dialogue* 42 (1): 97–104.

Retort. 2005. *Afflicted Powers: Capital and Spectacle in a New Age of War.* London: Verso.

Ricks, Thomas. 2012. "Wartime Command Structures: Why Are We So Bad at Designing Effective Ones?" *Best Defence* (blog), March 15. http://ricks.foreignpolicy.com/posts/2012/03/15/command_structures_for_wartime_why_are_we_so_bad_at_designing_effective_ones.

Roberts, Adam. 2006. "Transformative Military Occupation: Applying the Laws of War and Human Rights." *American Journal of International Law* 100: 580–622.

Rose, Nikolas, and Mariana Valverde. 1998. "Governed by Law?" *Social and Legal Studies* 7 (4): 541–51.

Saideman, Stephen M., and David Auerswald. 2012. "Comparing Caveats: Understanding the Sources of National Restrictions on NATO's Mission in Afghanistan." *International Studies Quarterly* 56: 67–84.

Sanger, David. 2012. "Attacks May Derail Effort to Force Taliban into Talks." *New York Times*, March 11.

Santos, Boaventura de Sousa. 1987. "Law: A Map of Misreading—Towards a Postmodern Conception of Law." *Journal of Law and Society* 14 (3): 279–302.

Shah, T., and G. Bowley. 2012. "US Sergeant Is Said to Kill 16 Civilians in Afghanistan." *New York Times*, March 12.

Simendinger, Alexis. 2012."Obama Holds Firm on Afghan Strategy Despite Massacre." *RealClearPolitics*, March 13. http://www.realclearpolitics.com/articles/2012/03/13/ obama_holds_firm_on_afghan_strategy_despite_massacre_113465.html.

Sparke, Matthew. 2007. "Geopolitical Fears, Geoeconomic Hopes, and the Responsibilities of Geography." *Annals of the American Association of Geographers* 97 (2): 338–49.

Trevithick, Joseph. 2012. "Annals of Command and Control (IV): Untangling the Structure in Afghanistan." *Best Defence* (blog), March 21. http://ricks.foreignpolicy.com/ posts/2012/03/21/annals_of_command_and_control_iv_untangling_the_structure _in_afghanistan.

Turse, Nick. 2012. "The New Obama Doctrine: A Six-Point Plan for Global War." *Tomdispatch* (blog), June 14. http://www.tomdispatch.com/blog/175557/tomgram%3A _nick_turse,_the_changing_face_of_empire.

Tyson, Ann Scott. 2009. "In Afghanistan, a Test of Tactics Under Strict Rules to Protect Civilians, Marines Face More Complex Missions." *Washington Post*, August 13.

US Department of Army, JAG Legal Center and School. 2013. *Operational Law Handbook 2013*. Charlottesville, VA: Center for Law and Military Operations.

Valverde, Mariana. 2009. "Jurisdiction and Scale: Legal 'Technicalities' as Resources for Theory." *Social and Legal Studies* 18 (2): 139–57.

Vogt, Heidi, and Pauline Jelinek. 2012. "Accused US Soldier Flown out of Afghanistan." *San Francisco Chronicle*, March 14. http://news.yahoo.com/accused-us-soldier-flown -afghanistan-193617318.html.

Walsh, Gary. 2005. "Interoperability of United States and Canadian Armed Forces." *Duke Journal of Comparative and International Law* 15: 315–31.

Warren, M. 1996. "Operational Law—A Concept Matures." *Military Law Review* 152: 33–73.

Weizman, Eyal. 2009. "Lawfare in Gaza: Legislative Attack." *Open Democracy*, March 1. http://www.opendemocracy.net/article/legislative-attack.

Wendle, John. 2012. "Timing and Location of an Afghan Massacre Threatens US Strategy." *Time*, March 14. http://content.time.com/time/world/article/0,8599,2109044,00.html.

Zaman, Arshad. 2010. "US/ISAF Chain of Command in Afghanistan." *Afpak.com* (blog), June 23. http://afpakwar.com/blog/de/archives/5779.

Žižek, Slavoj. 2009. *Violence*. London: Verso.

# 7 THE EVERYDAY FORMATION OF THE URBAN SPACE

## Law and Poverty in Mexico City

*Antonio Azuela and Rodrigo Meneses-Reyes*

Recent explorations on law and geography have revealed how law and space shape each other. Under this line of thought, law has been defined as a tool to provide the essential order that will regulate the arrangement of things and people on the street (Blomley 2007, 60); a central element to the construction of a broader binary between public and private spheres (Cooper 2001); or a social framework that constantly shapes our everyday conceptions of authority, obligation, justice, and rights (Blomley, Delaney, and Ford 2001, xiv). But law is, as we will show, always a complex and often contradictory way of defining the social meaning of the space. On the one hand, law does mediate existent sociospatial relations from the governments' point of view, to regulate and exclude those activities and persons considered to be "out of place" (Mitchell 2003); on the other hand, law mediates those social relations through legal forms, which impose again and again inhibition upon the action of the rulers (Thompson 2001, 438).

Official legal systems are not different from any other formal or informal organization in the ways they have ongoing conflicts among groups pushing different versions of how space and society should be regulated. However, to say that law may be created, contested, or negotiated in multiple sites does not mean to presume its greater flexibility or indeterminacy. As Nicholas Blomley (2003, 29) has put it, "This becomes clear when we recognize [that] the world is not given to us, but actively made through orderings which offer powerful 'maps' of the social world, classifying, coding, and categorizing. In so doing, a particular reality is created." In this sense, we argue that an emphasis on how certain spatial formations have been given meaning through legal practices could illustrate the ways in which the law serves as a means to produce and reproduce an imaginary spatial cohesion in an urban space of conflicting values and expectations. This imaginary spatial cohesion refers to the way in which the urban poor had to mobilize the law and invoke postrevolutionary ideals in order to find a place in an urban landscape that was planned without them. In the remainder of this chapter, we seek to illustrate this process by focusing our analysis on two related episodes of legal-spatial transformations: the constitution of a workplace for the urban poor and the regulation of land as a means for locating the poor.

More precisely still, this chapter analyzes how two developments in the nomospheric transformation of Mexico City were shaped, contested, or resisted among different legal disputes in the wider context of the formation of the postrevolutionary state in Mexico City (1930–50), a particular time frame in which both the Mexican capital city and its legal system were in the midst of a transition. On the one hand, for nearly two decades after the revolutionary disruption in 1910, Mexico City experienced strong waves of migration and periodic episodes of economic instability, as well as increased rates of urbanization. Whereas in the two decades prior to the 1920s the population of Mexico City grew by 36 percent and then by 30.7 percent, between 1921 and 1930 it expanded by 67 percent, from 615,367 inhabitants to more than 1,029,068 (Davis 1994, 85–86).

On the other hand, these changes experienced in the urban life were happening in the context of a "new legal moment" in Mexico's legal history: the 1917 Constitution (Sayeg 1996), the cornerstone of the postrevolutionary regime that sought to reach compromise between the values of traditional liberal constitutionalism and the recognition of the popular demands that justified revolution itself. However, in the urban context, this process was problematic in several ways. Although it is true that the 1917 constitution did recognize the legitimacy of the popular demands, this acknowledgment was restricted to two different social categories: the peasants and the industrial workers. For the former, the new constitution did recognize their right to have access to land (Article 27). For industrial workers, the 1917 constitution dedicated a complete chapter, Article 123, to labor rights (Suárez-Potts 2009). In this context, there was no room for the emergent urban masses. They were not peasants or part of the formal labor force. They were just people looking for a place to live and a place to make a living in the postrevolutionary urban landscape. So, even if they could not be included in one of those novel social categories of the postrevolution, they were too many and too close to the geographical center of the national power to be ignored by the urban elite. Accordingly, these elites were forced to do something to ensure "the wise and proper distribution of humans and things, and their relations and movement, within the territorial confines" of the city (Dean 2010, 89), through a series of administrative regulations and procedures, which, from time to time, were challenged in courts.

By weaving together these two historical trends, this chapter intends to contribute to and provide new evidence for a debate on the legalities of the space prompted by the law and geography turn in sociolegal studies. The remainder of the chapter is organized around the idea that the impact of the law and geography movement can be enhanced if it locates its findings within a wider context, such as that of the (trans)formation of the state. We see it as obvious that the long-term consequences of legal practices are much better understood when seen in relationship with government policies, social mobilization, and the workings of the political system, among other issues that belong to the domain of the state. Indeed, there is a growing body of literature that emerged from a certain disappointment among historians about traditional notions of the state—the starting point being a seminal paper by Philip Abrams in 1988. Since then, following the inspiration of the Foucauldian and the Gramscian traditions, a number of authors have tried to avoid the idea of the state as a fixed set of institutions that "unfolds" upon society in a consistent and inexorable way (e.g., Joseph and Nugent 2002; Migdal 2001). Instead, these authors have been trying to understand the state as the product of a myriad of *localized interactions*.

By connecting these two different strains, we do not intend here to give an account of the many implications of the new "anthropology of the state" that has emerged from this movement.[1] However, for the purpose of this chapter it is important to highlight two of the salient features of this literature. In the first place, it stresses the *localized* character of social interactions through which the state is being continually reenacted in a vast variety of contexts—from the courtroom to the border post—an emphasis that shows an interesting awareness about the importance of geographical issues (Joseph and Nugent 2002). In the second place, this literature rejects the usual view of law as a taken-for-granted element of the state. Instead, it sees in the law a problematic field within the state, with its own and often unpredictable logic—as in the work of E. P. Thompson (2001). These two features should be seen as an invitation for law and geography scholars to join in the project of looking at processes of state formation.

Although the focus of this literature has been on rural issues (Joseph and Nugent 2002), especially in what authors call the "margins of the state" (Agudo-Sanchíz and Estrada-Saavedra 2011; Scott 2009), it seems more than adequate to think about urban processes as part of the same problematic, especially when societies have undergone profound changes precisely because they have become predominantly urban. Because of its complexity, Mexico City appears as an almost impossible field of inquiry, and we do not intend to offer a comprehensive account of its role in the (trans)formation of the state in this part of the world. However, by looking at the way the urban poor found a place in the city through a complex set of legal practices, we expect to make some sense of how the "legal geographies" of the ordinary people, as well as their strategies within the scope of a fragmented set of rules and institutions, become part of the historical formation and transformation of the state. Analyzing this conflictive character of the urban space by incorporating specific legal settings (i.e., the court) suggests the importance of connecting particular legal experiences to the broader social and institutional context in which they occur; and it also facilitates understanding how courts can project a version of reality back onto the social setting from which these conflicts emerged (Engel 2001, 17).[2] Therefore, by analyzing how the links among law, space, and poverty have been shaped among different judicial decisions, this chapter seeks to illustrate a particular face of a more wider process: that of the (trans)formation of the postrevolutionary state in Mexico City.

## MAKING A (MARGINAL) CITY FOR THE POOR

As a now-voluminous literature demonstrates, after the Mexican Revolution (1910–20), Mexico City provided a space for those who were displaced by the revolutionary outburst. Beggars, panhandlers, homeless, and so on were a common sight in the postrevolutionary city. It was not a spontaneous phenomenon. As Ochoa (2001) has noted, for nearly two decades after the revolutionary disruption in 1910, Mexico City experienced strong waves of migration and periodic episodes of economic instability. Although the economy was rebounding by the mid-1920s, the 1929–30 US stock market crash plunged Mexico into depression.[3] Such rapid migration, coupled with economic instability, made it difficult for people to find jobs and housing (Barbosa 2008; Davis 1994; Eckstein 1988; Ochoa 2001; Piccato 2001). There is still a debate over how the absence of employment and housing opportunities exactly affected the spatial configuration of Mexico City. However, we do know that most homeless and unemployed used to live in the downtown area, also known as the inner-city slum (Eckstein 1988, 40–41). By the 1930s, urban elites had become quite troubled by this. If a revolution could eliminate a dictatorial regime, it should also serve to abolish urban disorder and its everyday-life manifestations, at least for the sake of political image. The presence and visibility of the poor in the city clearly threatened those ideas of social justice that gave legitimacy to postrevolutionary governments (Olsen 2005).

Increased urbanization and its polarizing effects thus fueled the long-standing anxieties of elites toward the poor. This was expressed through heightened observations about the growing number of beggars, homeless, prostitutes, and street workers in the downtown area.[4] In response, local authorities developed a series of poor laws and administrative "strategies" attempting to clear the public space of homeless, beggars, hawkers, and vendors, and to move the poor to orphanages and almshouses (Ochoa 2001). Although the enforcement of these laws against the poor was inconsistent, they led to large-scale arrests of people caught in the act of being out in public and people who simply "looked like beggars."[5] Most of these people were captured in the downtown area, where the urban poor used to plea to the generosity and solidarity of their upper-class *paisanos*.[6] According to Ochoa (2001), while this strategy was established to deal with the large number of people detained, myriad logistical problems thwarted the efforts: the city was not equipped to deal with such an extensive population, and the police and administrative officers did not receive adequate training. This seems to indicate that the postrevolutionary regime accepted its defeat. Poverty, as a constitutive element of the postrevolutionary city, could not be eradicated at all, but it could be tamed and restricted in certain spaces and zones of the city, notably, in the historical downtown core (Barbosa 2008; Bliss 2001; Piccato 2001).

## FINDING A (WORK)PLACE FOR THE POOR

Throughout the first half of the twentieth century, municipal authorities tried to answer a very preliminary question: where and how to accommodate street-level livelihoods in Mexico City. Two strategies of accomplishing this included segregating unwanted activities from the downtown area and licensing stationary uses in the rest of the city. These types of ordinances were directed toward a number of street workers who increasingly used the public space of the historical city center for survival activities.[7] Accordingly, at the very beginning of the 1930s, the urban authority issued a new regulation to displace the street vendors from public space, prohibiting any form of street-vending activities in the historical downtown core to protect the urban-formal economy and improve traffic around the area (Meneses 2011).

From a historical perspective, it could be argued that this regulation represented the first step of the legal dispute toward defining the new regulatory boundaries of the city's downtown core.[8] Indeed, in a highly publicized strategy, one group of organized street vendors attempted to repeal this restrictive ordinance by demanding an *amparo* to the Federal Supreme Court (Suprema Corte de Justicia de la Nación, or SCJN) (Meneses 2013; E. Vázquez 1998).[9] This judicial dispute included issues that would continue to challenge the power of the urban authority for years to come, such as the limits of the right to work, the need of access to the public space for those who trade on the streets, and the discretionary application of administrative rules.[10] Federal courts responded to such issues by upholding administrative ordinances that restricted the uses of the downtown streets and the constitutional right to work, arguing that the urban poor still had the rest of the city to exercise their rights,[11] and thereby reinforcing a particular sociospatial order in which the urban poor could occupy a place on the pavements only at the margins of the city:[12] "This regulation seeks to facilitate traffic in the downtown core, and the municipal authority should enforce it in order to protect the public interest . . . because [street vendors] can trade elsewhere, in other place different than the downtown core."[13]

As in similar experiences (Hubbard and Colosi 2012), in this case the discretion given to municipal authorities to ban street vending in the downtown core represented a seminal example of how law would be used to shape both the space and the public in Mexico City. To gain access to a place at the margins of the city, street workers were required to keep out of the downtown core and to register with an organization affiliated with the official political party in order to get a license.[14] Licensing represented a specific municipal technique focused on shaping specific ways of being in the streets, for example, by requiring street vendors to not obstruct traffic (Meneses 2013). From a judicial perspective, however, licensing was addressed in granting a privilege, and the Supreme Court repeatedly upheld this principle arguing that "a license to work on the street was only a privilege and not a right . . . , a selective privilege represented into a written document that constituted the best tool to administrate the right to work on the urban street."[15]

Of course, it is possible to state that in a world where being governed meant "to be noted, registered and counted" (Proudhon, cited in Scott 1998, 183) licensing could became an imperative practice in the interaction between the state and the urban poor, in the sense that it represented, at the least, an institutional option to accommodate street-vending activities into a given urban reality (Meneses 2013). Nonetheless, it seems that the growth of both licensed and unlicensed street vendors caused them to disperse to contiguous streets and avenues surrounding the downtown core. As a consequence, the municipal authority was forced to offer new closed and legalized sites to trade, which represented both regulatory changes and a more rigorous legal enforcement. Accordingly, between 1946 and 1952 alone, the local government constructed more than twenty-two "emergency markets," at the periphery of the downtown core, to relocate thousands of merchants from the streets to enclosed spaces (I. Vázquez 1991). This was the first of numerous publicly funded markets for street commerce that had developed by the mid-twentieth century (Cross 1998; Crossa 2009; Eckstein 1988). Therefore, between the 1950s and early 1970s, new spatial divisions and marketplaces were built "to protect [mainly] downtown commerce and revive the moral, civic, and eminently public quality of life that the city once promised" (Davis 2004, 214).

This new strategy was conceived after World War II, when a new regulation, the Reglamento de Mercados para el Distrito Federal (1951), enabled local authorities to establish an innovative project of special vending zones and marketplaces in which the urban poor could supposedly work without strong restrictions

(Davis 2004; Meneses 2013). The only absolute prohibition was, again, vending in the downtown area and placing stalls within three meters of a street corner (Departamento del Distrito Federal [DDF] 1951, Articles 63 and 64). Other limitations, such as a section that forbade "obstructing traffic," were specifically designed to be administratively interpreted (Cross 1998). From a spatial perspective, this process represented a new and accelerated reconfiguration of the urban-commercial grid. In fact, as the official records of the city indicate, between 1957 and 1966, 174 markets were constructed or modified to accommodate more than fifty-two thousand merchants, raising the number of public markets and vending zones in Mexico city from 44 to more than 200 (I. Vázquez 1991). Such an accelerated transformation also reconfigured the legal relationships between the local authority and the people who used the street for commerce.

On the one hand, this process imposed new forms of organization among street vendors. To gain access to the newly built markets, street vendors were required to register with a street-vending organization that had more than a hundred members (DDF 1951, Article 77). On the other hand, only "recognized" groups would have an enclosed space constructed for them (Pyle 1968). In other words, although the process permitted the relocation of more than fifty-two thousand merchants from the streets to enclosed market structures, another uncounted number of subjects who were still on the streets faced a more repressive and discretional power, just for being in public and obstructing traffic (Cross 1998; Eckstein 1988). This spatiolegal transformation, however, replicated and even reinforced the dual geography of street vending: inside and around the closed market street trading was an accepted activity, whereas outside it was illegal. At the same time, on a larger scale, the character of the downtown streets as an illegal place for street vendors was reinforced, and the periphery became a "tolerated" space (though not always a legal one).[16]

Nevertheless, for the purposes of this chapter, what seems important to note is that the articulation of administrative rules, judicial interpretations, and the constitution of specific spatial formations (e.g., vending zones, closed markets) did not only affect the spatial configuration of the city and structural relations between street vendors and the state. It also represented a new system for organizing the city and the relations between the rulers and the population (Meneses 2011). On the one hand, urban authorities used licenses, rules, and the building of markets to control people they found difficult to discipline on the streets, for instance, by imposing regular hours, homogenizing the types of goods and services they sold there,[17] and even establishing specific and standardized processes to administer the everyday exercise of the constitutional right to work in the urban realm (Meneses 2013). On the other hand, such control entailed new rules and limits on public space, transforming the norms that governed street vending into an increasingly private and stratified entity, moving the popular spaces of work and sociability into closed and private pieces of property, and in essence re-creating the urban space.

This process, however, also contributed to conditioning or forcing street vendors to deal with the law during their everyday work life, through police and punishment (Crossa 2009). Up until the middle of the twentieth century, the less flexible limitation to engage in commerce in public spaces would fall directly upon those merchants who were not found in the interior of the markets but were wandering on the streets. For them, a special regime was created such that it would annul the benefit of being in the interior of the market, benefits such as the possibility of being protected from the rain or cold, and would exchange them for a series of controls and restrictions that would go beyond the immediate environment of the market (Meneses 2013). As Eckstein (1988) suggests, this was a rather remarkable feature in the history of street vending. For the vendors who decided or were forced to stay in the streets, being arrested became an occupational hazard of living and working on the streets (Eckstein 1988, 171).

Thus, through time, interaction with police and other quotidian representations of the law became a long-standing, growing experience that would not deter street vending but could change the vendors' conceptions of space and authority (Meneses 2013). In other words, as noted by Eckstein (1988, 51–52), these sociospatial experiences show that the state's intervention in the urban space had important social and political implications for the everyday practice of street vending in Mexico City. Even the community as a whole benefited from the process: "Rats much less frequently scurried through the streets, traffic moved freely" (Eckstein 1988, 51–52). However, with the growth and development of the city, such locations turned into ideal places for the street vendors, mainly because the construction rate for new markets was not sustainable. New merchants constantly emerged, and they needed to find their sustenance on the streets, but the cost of building and maintaining the markets was too high.[18]

Thus, it seems that the inability of the state to ensure and construct new enclosed spaces assigned to vendors caused clearing the streets to arrest vendors to become the most popular practice to prevent the public presence of street vendors. But it was still ineffective. Therefore, while the existing markets currently present a state of real abandonment in terms of infrastructure,[19] the average monthly number of detained merchants, only in the downtown area, was 4,890 in 2009 (Meneses 2011). Furthermore, from a more general perspective, the authority's refusal to build new marketplaces also enacted among vendors new forms and organized strategies to take a place in the city to survive. In some cases, these organized forms were defined as "street takeovers," in which hundreds of people would patiently sit, or "squat," in the spot they sought to claim, without selling merchandise but hoping in the interim to build up a particular clientele and waiting to successfully negotiate their rights to the street with the city (Eckstein 1988, 200–201). In some others, street vendors and municipal authorities, through an administrative process, were forced into a negotiation of the streets, thereby creating new tolerance zones but enhancing the same goal: relocating street trade from the center to the periphery.[20]

## LAND FOR LOCATING THE POOR

The spatiolegal restrictions, working at the boundaries of the historical downtown core through the first half of the twentieth century, clearly represented the occasion to introduce new strategies for controlling and (re)distributing the presence of the urban poor through the city. Indeed "most of those [vendors] who formerly slept in their stalls were left homeless. . . . [T]hey took flight to the outlying areas of the city depopulated area—some, with the government permission, to the then recently settled but still illegal squatter settlements" (Eckstein 1988, 50). There is still a debate as to the extent to which the two processes were deliberately tied together. What is more or less clear is that they did work in a mutually reinforcing way to offer a place for the poor at the margins of the city.

As a matter of fact, in 1951, the Mexican Supreme Court issued a decision on a takings case in the village of Magdalena de las Salinas, at the outskirts of Mexico City,[21] declaring that the use of eminent domain was unconstitutional when the purpose was to provide land for the creation of new neighborhoods (settlements) for the poor. We consider this as a landmark decision not only because the government never tried to use eminent domain power for that purpose again but also because it is at the center of the question we address here: the place of the urban poor within the urban order.

Whereas the *Magdalena* decision has gone completely unnoticed by mainstream legal texts, its subject matter has been recognized in urban studies as a central feature of twentieth-century urbanization in Mexico (Azuela 1987; Connolly 1985; Duhau and Giglia 2008); that is, the process of formation, recognition, and consolidation of *colonias populares*, an expression that corresponds to the international (UN-like) category of "low-income settlements." Here we use the Mexican name, in order to stress that changes in the way of labeling these urban spaces reflect changes in the place of the poor in Mexican public life. The point is, for the moment, that *colonias populares* represent the type of urban habitat that has been the only alternative for those who do not have access to formal housing schemes.

To give an idea of the importance of Mexico City's *colonias populares*, it suffices to say that, after three decades of unprecedented urban growth, by the end of the 1950s they housed around half of the city's population, which by then had reached three million (Sánchez-Mejorada 2005, 262). Apart from the sheer size of *colonias populares* as a proportion of urban development, their formation implies a complex set of interactions as a result of which the popular masses are accorded a certain status as well as a concrete physical space in the city. As in other parts of the world, the legal definition of these "settlements" is essential in the way their occupants are included (or excluded) from the wider social order. In fact, the marginal character of *colonias populares* is complex in two senses: first, they are part of the city, but they are excluded from most of the benefits of urban life (e.g., access to public goods and services). Second, because of the definition of illegality that is imposed on them, they are also at the margins of the state, which does not mean being completely disconnected from its institutions but in an ambiguous situation in relation to them. As will be seen, residents of colonias populares were connected to the political system through their incorporation into the official party, even if they lived in areas that were labeled "irregular."

Now the "labeling" of illegality that is imposed on *colonias populares* is not a straightforward one; rather, it is part of a process of urban transformation and growth whose legal definition is produced in the context of a series of interactions among landowners, settlers, settlers' leaders, government officials, and judges. A crucial aspect is that access to land implies coming to terms with a preexisting landownership arrangement. To understand this, it is important to recall that during the period we cover in this chapter (1930–50) Mexican society was undergoing two major transformations. First, as in many other parts of Latin America, cities were expanding at unprecedented rates, and a huge proportion of the new urban population did not have the means to buy or rent a house in the formal market. Second, agrarian reform, one of the promises of the Mexican Revolution, implied almost by definition a permanent instability of property relations in the rural world. Leaving aside the fact that both processes co-occurred in urban peripheries, those two sets of issues were the context in which our story about *colonias populares* begins.

Since the early 1930s, several local governments throughout the country had begun to use their eminent domain power to give access to land to the urban poor through the formation of what were then called *colonias proletarias*, a name that would be abandoned some three decades later. The very fact that government discourse used such a label gives us an idea of the dignity that those modest urban spaces could have *at that time* (Perló 1981). A large part of the legitimacy of the postrevolutionary state rested on its avowed commitment to social justice—in fact, Mexico became a worldwide reference for its project of social transformation at the time of the ascent of totalitarian regimes in Europe and elsewhere. Agrarian reform, the main component of that project, was based on the expropriation of large landholdings and their distribution among peasants. Expropriating lands for the poor in the urban context may have seemed consistent with the social goals of the regime, precisely when a large part of the population could not access housing and urban services through market mechanisms. Even if the Mexican Revolution defined itself as basically agrarian, the urban popular sector was an emergent social group with a clear identity: the *colonos*, a word that literally means "settlers" and has a similar implication, in the sense that these new social actors had to colonize a territory that for many years was a hostile one—not a land hard to till but an urban space hard to live in.

Another auspicious condition was the fact that, since 1936, legislation on eminent domain had authorized the expropriation of land for a wide series of purposes, such as creating new population centers or even distributing wealth concentrated in a few hands. In the political sphere, *colonos*' organizations became part of the official party (the Partido Revolucionario Institucional, or PRI). Since 1943, with the formation of the National Confederation of Popular Organizations (Confederación Nacional de Organizaciones Populares) the party adopted a corporatist structure with three sectors: peasants, workers, and "the popular sector." This new sector never gained the legitimacy of the other two, and it has been despised even by the "progressive" social science scholarship because of its association with populism and clientelism.[22] However, there can be no doubt that *colonos* gained a place in the political system, and it was from there that they could assert most of their demands.

In this context, the governors of at least three states throughout the country (Puebla, Veracruz, and Coahuila) used eminent domain powers to create *colonias proletarias* in the 1930s. Not surprisingly, the affected landowners resisted those expropriations through *amparo* suits. Against the general opinion according to which the Mexican postrevolutionary state did not allow any significant room for an independent judiciary (Carpizo 1978; González-Compeán and Bauer 2002), in many cases federal judges did rule in favor of the landowners. However, before establishing a clear stance against this sort of expropriations with the *Magdalena* decision in 1951, the Supreme Court had followed a rather erratic course for almost two decades.

In 1932 the Supreme Court upheld an expropriation to establish *colonias* in the city of Puebla and explicitly said that the state legislature had enough powers to enact laws for that purpose, because the creation of *colonias* benefited the city as a whole[23]—a strikingly similar argument to the one that the US Supreme Court used in *Kelo v. New London* seventy years later, in 2005. But this line of interpretation did not last for long. As early as 1937, in a new case in the port of Veracruz, the Supreme Court ruled that even if state legislation authorized taking land for the creation of *colonias*,[24] it would apply only for land in the "outskirts" of the city, not within it.[25] During the 1940s, conflicts around *colonias* gained a new political implication in Mexico City, as Mayor Javier Rojo-Gómez used eminent domain extensively to accommodate the poor in different areas of the capital's periphery.

When seen closely, the process looks more complex. In many cases, by the time the expropriation was issued, the land had already been taken by *colonos*. Even if the expropriation decree claimed that its intention was to *create* a new population center, the truth was that the government was acting as a mediator in the conflict between *colonos* and landowners.[26] At any rate, between 1940 and 1946 as many as 105 *colonias* were created, and this was the only period in which land was expropriated massively for housing the urban poor. Nevertheless, even in those days, this policy was never included in public discourse as having the same significance as agrarian reform, even if it could be considered an act of social justice.

Moreover, the fact that Rojo-Gómez tried to use the *colonos'* support for his own quest for the presidency of the republic (Sánchez-Mejorada 2005, 245) added to a negative image of the urban poor. Then, as now, *clientelism* and *manipulation* were the buzzwords for defining the place of the urban poor in the political system—and therefore in the state order.[27] The only voices that appeared in the public sphere were those in favor of the protection of private property. Prestigious lawyers would write articles in newspapers against the expropriation of land for the creation of *colonias*,[28] even if landowners did not necessarily want to get their property back, to obtain a compensation that would include the rents generated by the very process of urbanization. Litigation became more intense, but judges ruled in favor of landowners in only one of three cases (Sánchez-Mejorada 2005, 232).[29] Thus, by the mid-1940s the judiciary had not found a clear way of responding to this kind of expropriation.

In the following administration (1946–52) the government of Mexico City was far less sympathetic to the cause of *colonias populares*. Even though another fifty-two *colonias* were created as the result of a certain political and administrative inertia, in those days the term *colonia proletaria* was abandoned and a new way of naming *colonos* prevailed: *paracaidistas* (literally "parachuters," but people who come from God-knows-where). It was in the context of a growing hostility toward unruly *colonos*, both from the media and the government, that the Supreme Court adopted a criterion that has not since been abandoned. In the expropriation decree for the *Magdalena de las Salinas* case, the government had invoked the section of the Expropriation Act that authorizes the taking of land for "the betterment, growth and sanitation of urban areas, the building of hospitals, schools, parks, gardens, sport fields, airports, government offices and any other work for services of collective interest" (AR 1064/1950). The Supreme Court found that such provision does not explicitly allow the taking of land for the creation of *colonias*. Indeed, the government could have invoked other sections in the Expropriation Act, such as the one that provides for "the fair distribution of wealth hoarded or monopolized for the sole advantage of one or several persons, with prejudice for the collectivity as a whole or a [social] class in particular" (Ley de Expropiación, Article 1-VII). But even if those words were (and still are) part of the statute book, by the late 1940s the government had abandoned the rhetoric of social justice and was much more committed to a market economy. So it was unlikely that it would use that sort of language for mediating the disputes between landowners and *colonos*.

As expropriation ceased to be a legitimate mechanism for giving the poor a place in the city, *colonias populares* were created "outside" the law. This took a variety of forms that is worth bearing in mind. The first one was that of taking directly the land, commonly called "invasions," and this put *colonos* at risk of being evicted. Since the 1950s, such risk has increased. Whereas many *colonias* succeeded in remaining in place (mostly those in the less "desirable" areas of the city), they had to pay the price of political subordination and urban exclusion.[30] The second mechanism was that of unauthorized subdivisions. In this case *colonos* often were (and responded as) victims of landowners who sold them plots with the promise of providing urban services, a promise that was rarely kept. For different reasons, this mechanism became less important, and by the late 1970s, at least within the limits of the capital, it was very rare.[31]

The third mechanism, which was to become the most important way of creating *colonias populares*, was the illegal subdivision of agrarian communities' lands. Agrarian reform had adopted two basic forms: the recognition of land to *comunidades* (communities that existed before the 1910 revolution) and the granting of lands to *ejidos* (communities that were created after the revolution). It is impossible to explain here all the intricacies of the urbanization of peasants' lands (see Azuela 1987; Cruz 2001; Schteingart 1989; Varley 1998). For the purpose of this chapter, it suffices to say that, by and large, this was an extremely peaceful process. Peasants were selling lands that, according to the law, were inalienable, but they were never prosecuted for the sale because they provided an important political support to the government. At the same time, *colonos* did not complain because they enjoyed a peaceful possession of their plots, even if they had to wait for years (sometimes for decades) for the introduction of public services. Even if the label of "irregular settlements" was applied to all *colonias populares* regardless their origin, it is obvious that the three mechanisms gave rise to different social relations between owners and nonowners in the urbanization process. They were different ways of being "at the margins" of the state (Das and Poole 2004).

By the early 1970s, there were so many *colonias populares* that could be classified as irregular that regularization was considered an unavoidable task for the government. There are many things to say about land tenure regularization, as it had become the main "instrument of land policy" in Mexico for more than three decades, but its most salient feature resides in its political function: it converted *colonos* into a huge political clientele. This reached its climax in the early 1990s, when the president of the republic himself would attend massive concentrations in which *colonos* waived the property titles they had just received—in a folder with the name of the president on it (Varley 1998). So after years, and in some cases decades, of being stigmatized as "illegal occupants," *colonos* were converted into property owners by the direct (almost personal) intervention of the head of the state.

For the purpose of this chapter, the key aspect of regularization policies is the recognition of the rights of a previous owner over the rights of the current occupants of the land. Every law student knows about the age-old legal institution of usucaption (adverse possession), which has been explicitly recognized in the statute books of most liberal property regimes in modern states and makes possible that those who exert possession over a piece of land have access to property rights over time. A previous owner is thus obliged to recognize the rights that come with a continued possession. It is true that in the case of Mexico this is difficult when it comes to agrarian communities, as their property rights are considered *imprescriptibles*.[32] But authorities followed the same criteria even when the original owner was a private individual—and even when there were evidence that he was the one who had illegally sold the land to *colonos* in the first place.

There is a double operation in regularization procedures: first, *colonos* obtain their property rights (and therefore a legitimate place in the city) not because the law recognizes they have rights but as a result of a governmental largesse—and this is more effective if they are labeled "illegal," because that puts them in a subordinate position. Second, and to make the former possible, it is useful that there is a previous landowner, that is, someone who can be defined as having rights over the land. It does not matter the role that he or she might have played in the process, his or her rights will be put in the first place. Even if an expropriation is the legal mechanism to give title to settlers, its main function is to make clear that they were occupying someone else's land. Both private property and *colonos* thus have a place in the state order.

There can be no doubt that government policies were instrumental in maintaining *colonos* in a situation of subordination. However, judges played their part too, and not always in harmony with government agencies. By restricting the use of eminent domain for giving urban land to the poor, as in the *Magdalena* case, they actively contributed to the creation of a regime in which the landowners had rights, whereas *colonos* had gracious concessions from the government. Even if the spatial implications of this are different from those of the street vendors we analyzed in the previous section, it seems clear that both social groups were subject to the same condition in which political subordination was based on a legal definition.

## FINAL REMARKS

Against the general opinion according to which there was no room for an independent judiciary in the Mexican postrevolutionary state, in many cases federal judges did actively participate in the (trans)formation of the urban environment. It has been our contention here that the full meaning of these legal experiences is much better understood in the wider context of the process of state formation, taking into consideration the complex set of interactions between different actors who operate both inside and outside the legal field. However hard it is to know the real, material, and direct effects generated by the legal experiences here reported, an important consequence of them is that, tied together, they exemplify the role of the law in the organization of urban space. Thus, although a number of authors have stated that the "margins of the state" are social products enhanced by the people to "keep the state at distance" (Agudo-Sanchíz and Estrada-Saavedra 2011; Scott 2009), the geographic-juridical approach adopted here has been useful for understanding how the same official legal actors, institutions, and discourses have actively participated in the creation of those margins, at least in the case of Mexico City.

But as we stated before, law is always a complex and often contradictory way to define the social meaning of a space. Behind each decree, judicial ruling, administrative rule, and written document (e.g., property titles, licenses to work on the street) there was a clear intention of (re)creating the city and regulating the everyday life of the urban poor. No doubt, there was an imaginary of sociospatial coherence across all those legal devices. At the same time, they were part of a larger universe with multiple and often mutually opposing actors, practices, discourses, and representations. It is precisely on this plural and often contradictory face of the state that we have suggested the significance of incorporating the role of the judiciary in the constitution of the urban space, because, by doing so, it has been possible to illustrate that the legal formation of the space is, among other things, a competitive struggle in which different actors fight for "the technical competence to interpret [the limits of] a corpus of texts [and social practices]" (Bourdieu 1987, 817; see Houtzager 2005, 221).

Coming back to the 1951 decision in the *Magdalena* case, it would be an exaggeration to assert that it was the only (or even the main) "cause" that determined the condition of legal subordination of *colonos* in the second half of the twentieth century in Mexico. Many other (economic and political) factors contributed to produce that regime. But at the same time, considering the intensity of litigation and the tone of the debate in the newspapers of the time, it is difficult to deny that the law was a real arena for conflicts over urban spaces. There is no doubt that the way judges understood urban space, property rights, and government powers left an imprint in the definition of the place of *colonos* in the urban order. Following this line of thought, the legal experience of street vendors between the 1930s and 1940s can also be viewed as an example of how a specific set of rights and discourses, such as the right to work, was constantly (re)introduced into the urban environment by the urban poor, to resist a city planned without them. In both cases, however, it has been possible to see how judges imagined and outlined the urban space as a dual geography, with its center and its periphery, by a central and a marginal interpretation of the law. There was never an explanation of the reason for that distinction, but there must have been a strong spatial image in the justices' minds as they drew the line between a constitutional and an unconstitutional character of the strategies deployed by administrative agencies, depending on the location of the people and the pieces of land and pavement in dispute.

It is clear that the result of these processes is a spatial fragmentation between spaces of rights and spaces of privileges. To be sure, such spatial fragmentation has a socioeconomic origin that is the foundation of unequal access to public goods. Both the living conditions of *colonias populares* and the working conditions of street vending (spaces of privileges) stand in sharp contrast to those at the space of rights (the legal city). But it is even more interesting to note the way in which the border that divides both worlds was constructed and reinforced by legal practice. Political subordination is not an inherent feature of the urban poor; it is the result of myriad legal practices through which state agencies (including courts), in a rather consistent fashion, set the limits between the legal and the illegal city.

Looking at these developments in the wider context of the state implies, first and foremost, getting rid of the formalistic definitions of the state that have prevailed in legal positivism—notably the Kelsenian solution according to which the state is nothing but a legal order (Kelsen 1951),[33] and recognizing that the state is

the result of a vast array of different social processes: from the exercise of regulatory powers by bureaucracies to the production of social order through different forms of political mediation to the mobilization of resources by government
agencies and, of course, to judicial procedures. The social meaning of legal definitions of the place of the poor in the city is much better understood when viewed
as part of that complex universe.

As sociological research on Mexico City has shown, some of the most salient
features of the Mexican postrevolutionary state have to do with the ambivalent
position of the urban poor within it. It is a fragmented state, to the extent that
there are different sets of rules for what is defined as the "formal" and "informal"
economies, and such fragmentation manifests spatially in the contrast between
*colonias populares* and well-off areas, as well as in the "zoning" of streets where
working is permitted. Such re-spatializations underpin and give material expression to the fragmented state, the fragmented city, and the fragmentation of law as
such. Despite these social inequalities, there is a mobilization of public resources
to provide the poor with some basic services, through forms of political mediation
generally labeled as "clientelism." Last but not least, legal or quasi-legal categories
are used as a way of labeling the urban poor in ways that make clear their subordinate position vis-à-vis the state order (e.g., "informal" economy, "irregular"
settlements). All those are well-known characteristics of the Mexican state. The
difference with the perspective we have adopted here is that the state is viewed
not as an entity that preexists the urbanization process and imposes its logic at
will but as the product of myriad localized interactions among multiple actors.
Here we have focused on those who strive for a place in the city and those who
act from different levels and branches of state apparatuses, as well as an army of
intermediaries.

At the same time, it is easy to recognize that the urban poor, both as street vendors and as *colonos*, were not passive subjects of some predetermined state project.
In fact, they were active agents who played a role in the complex set of inclusion
and exclusion practices that determined their place in the city, a marginal place
that they have earned despite what the ruling elites would have chosen. And it is in
this context that the impact of legal developments is to be understood. No doubt,
these developments worked together with other aspects of the operation of the
state (e.g., political mediation, mobilization of government resources), but as we
have tried to show, judges performed an important and very specific role in defining the sort of rights to which the poor could aspire in the urban order. It remains
to be unveiled the specific way in which the logic of the law will combine with the
logic of other dimensions of the state to produce its social consequences.

## NOTES

1. Two useful readers are Hansen and Stepputat (2001) and Sharma and Gupta (2006).

2. As stated by Houtzager (2005, 221–22), "The power of judiciaries and other actors in the [juridical] field resides primarily in the symbolic effectiveness of their action—they are *signalers* par excellence. The outcome of court proceedings therefore is the product of interpretative struggles between actors (possessing unequal talents and juridical powers), not just inside the courtroom, but within a larger field of [sociolegal] practices."

3. "The stock market crash and the subsequent depression caused the real Mexican gross domestic product to decline 17.6 percent between 1929 and 1932, plunging many people into unemployment and underemployment. The official unemployment rate grew by over 350 [percent] between 1930 and 1932. In the countryside, depressed agricultural prices led to a reduction in wages for field workers. According to the agronomist Ramón Fernández y Fernández, the real wages of field workers fell by 17 percent in 1930 relative to 1929, and did not recoup their 1929 levels until 1934. Such a crisis prompted large numbers of rural people to migrate to Mexico City" (Ochoa 2001, 42).

4. Specific data regarding the presence and distribution of these unwanted populations through the streets of the historical downtown can be found in Barbosa (2008), Bliss (2001), Ochoa (2001), and Piccato (2001).

5. A category applied to those who showed their poorness, dirtiness, and illness in public. The participation of the street vendors in this heterogeneous universe was about 26 percent (Beneficencia Pública del Distrito Federal 1931).

6. To mention some data concerning the presence of the poor, sick, and unkempt in downtown Mexico City, between Tuesday May 22 and Sunday May 25, 1930, the authority registered the presence of 837 beggars on the street and 97 at adjacent churches. These numbers represented 16.7 percent of the total number of beggars estimated by the Police for the Federal District, with an average presence of 3.47 beggars per church and 133.5 beggars per square kilometer (Beneficencia Pública del Distrito Federal 1931).

7. In the turbulent days of the economic crash of 1929–30, for instance, there were about 1,500 authorized vendors operating in the area and distributed among three major organizations (E. Vázquez 1998).

8. In a survey developed to illustrate the growth of bylaws and codes enacted to regulate the urban space of Mexico City between 1910 and 1970, 60 percent of 279 bylaws and codes were developed between 1930 and 1940 (Meneses 2011).

9. "An amparo is an injunctive form of judicial relief granted to an individual who has applied to the federal court for the protection of the peoples' normally constitutional rights, if these were deemed to be in jeopardy because of the actions or mandates of a public authority" (Suárez-Potts 2009).

10. Amparo en Revisión 2477/1931, Segunda Sala de la Suprema Corte de Justicia de la Nación, Quinta Época. For a fuller account of these rulings, see Meneses (2012).

11. See, again, Amparo en Revisión 2477/1931, Segunda Sala de la Suprema Corte de Justicia de la Nación, Quinta Época.

12. According to several studies, this process experienced in Mexico City was mirrored in some other Latin American cities, such as Bogotá and Lima (Joffré 2004; Rincón 2006), through the 1930s and 1940s.

13. Amparo en Revisión 2477/1931, Segunda Sala de la Suprema Corte de Justicia de la Nación, Quinta Época.

14. As some have stated (Cross 1998; Davis 1994), many of these organizations were an essential part of the popular sector (CNOP) of the governing PRI party. Consequently, as time passed, the organizations grew in significance and became an important source of support for the party, gaining political leverage to negotiate with state institutions over a piece of the sidewalk, which, in the ideology of the Mexican Revolution, should be seen as the people's property.

15. AR 1622/1979, Tribunal Colegiado, Séptimo Circuito, Séptima Época; AR 3140/1944, Segunda Sala de la Suprema Corte de Justicia de la Nación, Quinta Época. For a fuller account of these rulings, see Meneses (2013).

16. We would like to thank to Sandy Kedar for this insightful comment.

17. For instance, an examination from 1960 of permits issued to vendors by the Department of Markets of Mexico City showed that about 40 percent of vendors dealt in fresh fruits, vegetables, and dried chilies; 13 percent sold meat; and 14 percent sold clothing and dry goods (Pyle 1970, 63).

18. Between 1953 and 1958 an amount of 350 million pesos was spent in the construction and conditioning of almost ninety markets (Cross 1998), and every refurbishment meant an average expense of 270,000 pesos for local authorities (Meneses 2011).

19. According to a diagnostic by the Secretaría de Desarrollo Económico del Distrito Federal (2007), the greatest lag was maintenance of water and drainage plumbing, for only 2 percent of the installations were in good conditions. The next greatest problem was the state of electrical wiring. In this case 92 percent of markets require corrective maintenance: the energy supply presents overcharge, is not properly placed, or simply does not exist. The physical aspect of sanitary facilities (71 percent), as well as the floors (51 percent) and ceilings (50 percent), are deplorable. The dirt and grime extend from the ground up, even considering trash containers, when these exist. And 54 percent of cases are such that they do not separate waste.

20. For instance, it is estimated that the number of licensed hawkers was about 2,770 between 2000 and 2007 (GDF-OIP 2009).

21. AR 1064/1950, Segunda Sala de la Suprema Corte de Justicia de la Nación. Quinta Época. Magdalena de las Salinas, in the sector of Gustavo A. Madero, close to the nascent industrial areas of Mexico City, was the name of the village (*ejido*) from which the government tried to take the land.

22. See recent debates over these subjects in the urban context in Latin America in Auyero (2001) and Merklen (2010).

23. AR 211/1932, Segunda Sala de la Suprema Corte de Justicia de la Nación, Quinta Época.

24. Expropriation in Veracruz (Act Number 323). "Regarding expropriations, the Supreme Court has adopted as a criterion that the new legal doctrine on property authorizes the use of eminent domain powers not only for the old and restricted concept of public use, but also for reasons of social interest or national interest. Now, it is self-evident that the subdivision of urban land for building houses for workers, which is defined by Act number 323 of the State of Veracruz as a cause of public interest, is based on social interest reasons, because the benefit of the expropriation is not only for those workers, but it also reaches the population in general, as far as the town is beautified and expanded; it favors the increase of businesses and frees the working classes form the hardship they suffer when they lack a home of their own; all of which means a real social benefit."

25. AR 48/1936, Segunda Sala de la Suprema Corte de Justicia de la Nación, Quinta Época. For a fuller account of these rulings, see Azuela and Herrera (2013).

26. Aerial photographs of that time allowed us to identify this kind of situations (Azuela and Cruz 1989).

27. Antiurbanism was a clear cultural bias at that time, and the urban poor were the worst face of urbanism for the Mexican elite (Rodríguez-Kuri 2003).

28. One of the fiercest legal texts against the nationalization of the oil industry in 1938 (Fernández del Castillo [1939] 1987) included a critique of the takings for housing purposes.

29. Significantly, that was the same proportion as nowadays, with an independent judiciary dealing with expropriations by the left-wing local government in Mexico City (Azuela and Herrera forthcoming).

30. We still do not have the definite historical reconstruction of this form of urbanization in Mexico City.

31. By then, most of the urban growth in peripheral areas took place in the neighboring State of Mexico.

32. Property rights held by agrarian communities (*ejidos* and *comunidades*) are explicitly defined as *imprescriptibles* by the Agrarian Act (or Ley Agraria), which means that no one can obtain property rights over them no matter how long they have occupied the land and even if it was sold by the original owner (Lemus-García 1996).

33. In Latin America this is not a trivial question. For Norberto Bobbio (1987), who is one of the more influential jurists in the region nowadays, the identification of the state with the law is a "precise" but forgotten thesis.

## LIST OF CASES AND STATUTES

Amparo en Revisión 2477/1931, Segunda Sala, Suprema Corte de Justicia de la Nación, Mexico, Quinta Época (1931).

Amparo en Revisión 211/1932, Segunda Sala de la Suprema Corte de Justicia de la Nación, Mexico, Quinta Época (1932).

Amparo en Revisión 3140/1944, Segunda Sala de la Suprema Corte de Justicia de la Nación, Mexico, Quinta Época (1944).

Amparo en Revisión 1064/1950, Segunda Sala de la Suprema Corte de Justicia de la Nación. Mexico, Quinta Época (1950).

Amparo en Revisión 1622/1979, Tribunal Colegiado, Séptimo Circuito, Mexico, Séptima Época (1979).

Departamento del Distrito Federal. 1951. *Reglamento de Mercados del Distrito Federal.* Mexico City: Departamento del Distrito Federal.

*Kelo v. City of New London*, 125 U.S. 2655 (2005).

Ley de Expropiación, November 25, 1936. *Diario Oficial de la Federación*, Mexico.

## REFERENCES

Abrams, Philip. 1988. "Notes on the Difficulty of Studying the State." *Journal of Historical Sociology* 1 (1): 58–89.

Agudo-Sanchíz, Alejandro, and Marco Estrada-Saavedra. 2011. *(Trans)formaciones del estado en los márgenes de Latinoamérica: Imaginarios alternativos, aparatos inacabados y espacios trasnacionales.* Mexico City: El Colegio de México and Universidad Iberoamericana.

Auyero, Javier. 2001. *La política de los pobres: Las prácticas clientelistas del peronismo.* Buenos Aires: Manantial.

Azuela, Antonio. 1987. "Low Income Settlements and the Law in Mexico City." *International Journal of Urban and Regional Research* 11 (4): 522–42.

Azuela, Antonio, and María Soledad Cruz. 1989. "La institucionalización de las colonias populares y la política urbana de la Ciudad de México (1940–1946)." *Sociológica* 9: 111–33.

Azuela, Antonio, and Carlos Herrera. 2013. "La propiedad que no se discute: Jueces y expropiaciones en la Ciudad de México." In *Expropiación y conflicto social en cinco ciudades latinoamericanas,* edited by Antonio Azuela. Mexico City: Instituto de Investigaciones Sociales and Lincoln Institute of Land Policy.

Barbosa, Mario. 2008. *El trabajo en las calles: Subsistencia y negociación política en la Ciudad de México a comienzos del siglo XX.* Mexico City: Universidad Autónoma Metropolitana.

Beneficencia Pública del Distrito Federal. 1931 *La mendicidad en México.* Mexico City: A. Mijares y Hermano Editores.

Bliss, Katherine. 2001. *Compromised Positions: Prostitution, Public Health and Gender Politics in Revolutionary Mexico City.* University Park: Pennsylvania State University.

Blomley, Nicholas. 2003. "Law, Property, and the Geography of Violence: The Frontier, the Survey, and the Grid." *Annals of the Association of American Geographers* 93 (1): 121–41.

———. 2007. "How to Turn a Beggar into a Bus Stop: Law, Traffic and the 'Function of the Place.'" *Urban Studies* 44: 1697–1712.

Blomley, Nicholas, David Delaney, and Richard Ford. 2001. "Where Is Law?" In *The Legal Geographies Reader,* edited by Nicholas Blomley, David Delaney, and Richard Ford, xiii–xxii. Oxford, UK: Blackwell.

Bobbio, Norberto. 1987. *Estado, gobierno, sociedad: Contribución a una teoría general de la política.* Barcelona: Plaza & Janés.

Bourdieu, Pierre 1987 "The Force of Law: Toward a Sociology of the Juridical Field." *Hastings Law Journal* 38 (5): 814–53.

Carpizo, Jorge. 1978. *El presidencialismo mexicano.* Mexico City: Siglo XXI Editores.

Connolly, Priscilla. 1985. "The Politics of Informal Sector." In *Beyond Unemployment: Poverty and the Informal Sector,* edited by Redclift Nanneke and Enzo Mignione, 55–91. London: Blackwell.

Cooper, Davina. 2001. "Out of Place: Symbolic Domains, Religious Rights and the Cultural Contract." In *The Legal Geographies Reader,* edited by Nicholas Blomley, David Delaney, and Richard Ford, 123–42. Oxford, UK: Blackwell.

Cross, John. 1998. *Informal Politics: Street Vendors and the State in Mexico City.* Stanford, CA: Stanford University Press.

Crossa, Veronica. 2009. "Resisting the Entrepreneurial City: Street Vendors' Struggle in Mexico City's Historic Center." *International Journal of Urban and Regional Research* 33 (1): 43–63.

Cruz, María Soledad. 2001. *Propiedad, poblamiento y periferia rural en la zona metropolitana de la Ciudad de México.* Mexico City: Universidad Autónoma Metropolitana, Azcapotzalco, and Red Nacional de Investigación Urbana.

Das, Veena, and Deborah Poole. 2004. "State and Its Margins: Comparative Ethnographies." In *Anthropology in the Margins of the State,* edited by Veena Das and Deborah Poole, 3–33. Santa Fe, NM: School of American Research Press.

Davis, Diane. 1994. *Urban Leviathan: Mexico City in the Twentieth Century.* Philadelphia: Temple University Press. (Published in Spanish: *El Leviatán urbano: La Ciudad de México en el siglo XX.* Mexico City: Fondo de Cultura Económica.)

————. 2004. "In Search of a Public Sphere: Local, National, and International Influences on Downtown Mexico City, 1910–1950." *Space and Culture* 2: 1–29.

Dean, Michael. 2010. *Governmentality: Power and Rule in Modern Society.* London: Sage.

Duhau, Emilio, and Angela Giglia. 2008. *Las reglas del desorden: Habitar la metropoli.* Mexico City: Siglo XXI Editores.

Eckstein, Susan. 1988. *The Poverty of the Revolution: The State and the Urban Poor in Mexico.* Princeton, NJ: Princeton University Press.

Engel, David. 2001. "Injury and Identity: The Damaged Self in Three Cultures." In *Between Law and Culture: Relocating Legal Studies,* edited by D. Goldberg, M. Musheno, and L. Bower, 3–21. Minneapolis: University of Minnesota Press.

Fernández-del-Castillo, Germán. (1939) 1987. *La propiedad y la expropiación.* Mexico City: Compañía Editora de Revistas.

González-Compeán, Miguel, and Peter Bauer. 2002. *Jurisdicción y democracia: Los nuevos rumbos del Poder Judicial en México.* Mexico City: Cal y Arena

Hansen, Thomas, and Finn Stepputat, eds. 2001. *States of Imagination: Ethnographic Explorations of the Post Colonial State.* Durham, NC: Duke University Press.

Houtzager, Peter. 2005. "The Movement of the Landless (MST), Juridical Field and Legal Change in Brazil." In *Law and Globalization from Below: Towards a Cosmopolitan Legality,* edited by Boaventura Santos and Cesar Rodríguez, 218–40. Cambridge: Cambridge University Press.

Hubbard, Peter, and Rachela Colosi. 2012. "Sex, Crime and the City: Municipal Law and the Regulation of Sexual Entertainment." *Social and Legal Studies* (October). doi: 10.1177/0964663912459292.

Joffré, Gabriel. 2004. "El guión de la cirugía urbana: Lima 1850–1940." In *Ensayos en ciencias sociales.* Lima: Fondo Editorial de la Facultad de Ciencias Sociales, Universidad Nacional Mayor de San Marcos.

Joseph, Gilbert, and Daniel Nugent. 2002. *Everyday Forms of State Formation: Revolution and the Negotiation of Rule in Modern Mexico.* Durham, NC: Duke University Press.

Kelsen, Hans. 1951. *Teoría general del estado.* Mexico City: Editorial Nacional.

Lemus-García, Raúl. 1996. *Derecho agrario mexicano.* Mexico City: Editorial Porrúa.

Meneses, Rodrigo. 2011. *Legalidades públicas: El derecho, los ambulantes y el espacio público en la Ciudad de México (1930–2010).* Mexico City: Universidad Nacional Autónoma de México, Instituto de Investigaciones Jurídicas, and Centro de Investigación y Docencia Económicas.

————. 2013. "Out of Place, Still in Motion: Shaping Immobility/Mobility through Urban Regulation." *Social and Legal Studies* (January 10). doi: 10.1177/0964663912469644.

Merklen, Denis. 2010. *Pobres ciudadanos: Las clases populares en la era democrática (Argentina 1983–2003).* 2nd ed. Buenos Aires: Editorial Gorla.

Migdal, Joel. 2001. *State in Society: Studying How States and Societies Transform and Constitute One Another.* Cambridge Studies in Comparative Politics. Cambridge: Cambridge University Press.

Mitchell, Don. 2003. *The Right to the City: Social Justice and the Fight for Public Space.* New York: Guilford.

Ochoa, Enrique. 2001. "Coercion, Reform, and the Welfare State: The Campaign against 'Begging' in Mexico City during the 1930s." *Americas:* 39–64.

Olsen, Patrice. 2005. "Revolution in the City Streets: Changing Nomenclature, Changing Form and the Revision of the Public Memory." In *Eagle and the Virgin: National and*

*Cultural Revolution in Mexico (1920–1940)*, edited by Kay Vaughan and S. Lewis, 119–34. Durham, NC: Duke University Press.

Perló, Manuel. 1981. *Estado, vivienda y estructura urbana en el cardenismo: El caso de la Ciudad de México*. Mexico City: Instituto de Investigaciones Sociales and Universidad Nacional Autónoma de México.

Piccato, Pablo. 2001. *City of Suspects: Crime in Mexico City 1900–1931*. Durham, NC: Duke University Press.

Pyle, Jane. 1968. *The Public Markets of Mexico City*. Ann Arbor, MI: University Microform Library Service.

———. 1970. "Market Locations in Mexico City." *Revista Geográfica* 73: 59–69.

Rincón, Análida. 2006. "Racionalidades normativas y apropiación del territorio urbano: Entre el territorio de la ley y la territorialidad de las legalidades." *Economía, Sociedad y Territorio* 5 (20): 673–702.

Rodríguez-Kuri, Ariel. 2003. "Simpatía por el diablo: Miradas académicas a la Ciudad de México 1900–1970." In *Los últimos cien años: Los próximos cien*, edited by Ariel Rodríguez-Kuri and Sergio Tamayo, 45–67. Mexico: Universidad Autónoma Metropolitana.

Sánchez-Mejorada, María Cristina. 2005. *Rezagos de la modernidad: Memorias de una ciudad presente*. Colección Cultura Universitaria Serie Ensayo No. 83. Mexico City: Universidad Autónoma Metropolitana.

Sayeg, Jorge. 1996. *El constitucionalismo social mexicano*. Mexico City: Fondo de Cultura Económica.

Schteingart, Martha. 1989. *Los productores del espacio habitable: Estado, empresas y sociedad en la Ciudad de México*. Mexico City: El Colegio de México.

Scott, James. 1998. *Seeing Like a State: How Certain Schemes to Improve the Human Condition Have Failed*. New Haven, CT: Yale University Press.

———. 2009. *The Art of Not Being Governed: An Anarchist History of Upland Southeast Asia*. New Haven, CT: Yale University Press.

Secretaría de Desarrollo Económico del Distrito Federal. 2007. *Diagnóstico sobre los mercados públicos*. Mexico City: Gobierno del Distrito Federal.

Sharma, Aradhana, and Akhil Gupta, eds. 2006. *The Anthropology of the State: A Reader*. Malden, MA: Blackwell Publishing.

Suárez-Potts, William. 2009. "The Mexican Supreme Court and the Juntas de Conciliación y Arbitraje, 1917–1924: The Judicialisation of Labour Relations after the Revolution." *Journal of Latin American Studies* 41 (4): 723–55.

Thompson, Edward. 2001. *The Essential E. P. Thompson*. New York: New Press.

Varley, Ann. 1998. "The Political Uses of Illegality: Evidence from Urban Mexico." In *Illegal Cities: Law and Urban Change in Developing Countries*, edited by in A. Varley and Edesio Fernandes, 177–90. London: Zed Books.

Vázquez, Esther 1998. *Organización y resistencia popular en la Ciudad de México durante la crisis de 1929–1932*. Mexico City: Instituto Nacional de Estudios Históricos de la Revolución Mexicana.

Vázquez, Ignacio. 1991. *El abasto en la Ciudad de México*. Mexico City: Departamento del Distrito Federal.

# 8 THE RURAL LAWSCAPE

## Space Tames Law Tames Space

*Lisa R. Pruitt*

A fundamental tenet of legal geographies scholarship is that law and space are mutually constitutive. This chapter deploys that framework to show how this feedback loop operates in rural contexts in the United States. In particular, I assert that formal law and rural spatiality are fundamentally at odds with each other because the presence of law as a force of the state—as an ordering force—is in tension with the material character of rurality, as well as with rurality's associated sociospatial features. The material characteristics to which I refer include low population density, small population clusters, and a dominance of what is perceived as nature over the built environment. These features serve to physically separate or remove rural residents from the state by distancing them from the state's agents and processes. At the same time, the manner in which legal agents and processes function effects a cognitive separation of rural livelihoods from the state because the less present, less robust, less powerful manifestations of law diminish rural society's expectations of law. The state—whose agents may be both literally and culturally "high up and a long way off" (MacKinnon 2005, 35)[1]—thus struggles to make meaningful the rule of law in rural and remote places.

Of course, some types of rural places—and the United States' rural past generally—have long been associated with disorder and a lack of human dominion over nature (Nash 2001). But I posit that rural places *remain* somewhat lawless not only because rural spatiality disables or impedes formal law and its functioning but also because formal legal actors—judges in their adjudications and law enforcement in their performance—constitute the rural as relatively lawless. That relative lawlessness is thus a manifestation of the mutual constitutivity of law and rural spatiality.

Furthermore, this construction of the rural as more dangerous, as less accessible to law, persists in spite of the technological advancements associated with modernity. Technology has no doubt wrought a "decline in the importance of the friction of distance" (Halfacree 1993, 28), enabling legal actors to more effectively police and impose the state's will on rural places and those present there.

Yet the friction persists (Wilkinson 1991). That is, the obstacle or burden that distance represents—indeed, the "tyranny of distance" (Blainey 1966)—remains a friction that frustrates formal law's work while also increasing the cost of that work. Karl Marx ([1939] 1973, 524) asserted that time annihilates space, but in relation to rural spatiality, this claim is hyperbole. Rurality may be conceptualized as the "counterpoint to modernity" (Woods 2011, 1), but rural spatiality remains a world-making force in the contemporary United States, somewhat managed by time and technology, but not annihilated.

I refer to the collective characteristics of the rural as they relate to law and legal processes as the rural lawscape (Philippopoulos-Mihalopoulos and FitzGerald 2008, 439–40). I assert that the very material characteristics that define rurality from an ecological or quantitative standpoint—small and sparse populations removed from urban areas—beget the social and cultural characteristics associated with the rural lawscape. For example, the material—the spatial removal from both human threats and human sources of assistance, whether public (the state) or private (other citizens)—invites a greater expectation of privacy while also enhancing vulnerability and, in turn, fostering an ethos of self-reliance. These and other features of rural sociospatiality mediate formal law's performance by rendering it less effective at ordering, monitoring, overseeing, and policing.

Unlike sociology and economics, which include somewhat robust subdisciplines exploring rural difference and the rural milieu, legal scholars and critical geographers have largely ignored the rural end of the rural-urban continuum. Critical geographers often include the words *city* and *urban* in their titles, openly declaring their focus. David Harvey published *Social Justice and the City* in 1973. Two decades later, Linda McDowell (1994, 152) observed a trend among cultural geographers to study questions about the "city and cultural life" and "how people experience and respond to the 'urban experience.'" The persistence of that trend—indeed, its apparent strengthening—is borne out by germinal geography books published since, including Lefebvre's *Writings on Cities*, first translated into English in 1996. Books published in the past decade include Don Mitchell's (2003) *The Right to the City: Social Justice and the Fight for Public Space*, Neil Brenner's (2004) *New State Spaces: Urban Governance and the Scaling of Statehood*, and Doreen Massey's (2007) *World City*. To consider just one book, Edward Soja's (2010) *Seeking Spatial Justice* includes the word *urban* ninety-five times, whereas the word *rural* appears only seven times. Most references to the rural in these works, as well as in the edited volume *The Legal Geographies Reader* (Blomley, Delaney, and Ford 2001), merely name rural as the foil to urban, failing to grapple with the character or consequences of rural sociospatiality in the contemporary developed world.

Critical rural studies, in contrast, comprises a relatively sparse and nascent enterprise. *The Handbook of Rural Studies* (Cloke, Marsden, and Mooney 2006) is a notable exception, along with the work of British geographers such as Jo Little (2006), Paul Cloke (2006; see also Cloke and Little 1997), and Keith Halfacree (1993, 2006). The first offering solely by US academics, *Critical Rural Theory: Structure, Space, Culture*, was published in 2011 (Thomas et al. 2011). Forays into what I have called legal ruralism are rare, but some recent scholarly activity indicates that the study of law and rural livelihoods is gaining a toehold as a subdiscipline (Boso 2013; Jerke 2011; Pruitt 2006).

This chapter engages legal geography to bring the rural into scholarly view. One goal is to broaden our understanding of the diffuse and localized operation of formal law in rural spaces of the United States. In theorizing the significance and force of rural spatiality in relation to law and legal processes, I challenge the urban normativity and metrocentricity of critical geography and law. I thus refute Soja's suggestion that "rusticity is not only idiotic but justifiably marginal and vestigial" (Creed and Ching 1997, 8), and that only the urban is worthy of critical attention. In exploring the rural lawscape, I deploy spatial tools or concepts not typically associated with legal geography and its metrocentric bent. Many legal geographers speak in terms of lines, crossings, territory, jurisdiction, confinement, and the like (Blomley 1994, 35, 56–57; Delaney 2010, 12, 26, 138). This ruralist project draws more prominently on other spatial concepts—distance, isolation, and density—theorizing their impact on sociolegal relations.

The "rural" is, of course, contested territory, literally and ideologically (Pruitt 2008a, 344–47). My focus here is on the contemporary rural United States, although realities and imaginaries associated with the rural past surely influence their present-day counterparts (Nash 2001, 143; Pruitt 2006, 169–72; R. Williams 1973). Specifically, I attend to sparsely populated and remote places, which are not necessarily synonymous with the small and even midsize towns that many think of as "rural."[2] I am contemplating places the US Census Bureau (2012a) refers to as open territory or open space, those outside even modest population clusters.

One reason legal geographers may have overlooked such places is that they have thought of them not as rural but perhaps as "wilderness" or, more generally, as "nature." Because wilderness is often conceptualized as lacking human presence (Nash 2001, xii, 7, 30; see also Cronon 1995), legal geographers may have failed to view such places as human habitat, with resultant implications for sociological study (but see Braverman 2014). This narrow view of wilderness, bereft of humanity, may have obscured the sociospatial complexity of the rural. Roderick

Nash's work on "wilderness" is helpful on this point because it acknowledges that term's relativity while also articulating a continuum between civilization and wilderness. Nash (2001, xii) associates wilderness with "the unknown, the disordered, the dangerous" and those "parts of nature not subject to human control." He explains that wilderness had no meaning for "nomadic Natives," for whom

> everything natural was simply habitat, and people understood themselves
> to be part of a seamless living community. Lines began to be drawn with the
> advent of herding, agriculture, and settlement. Distinctions between controlled
> (domesticated) and uncontrolled animals and plants became meaningful, as did
> the concept of controlled space: corrals, fields, towns. (Nash 2001, xi)

According to Nash (2001, 244), "civilization" was pastoral before it was urban, making pastoral an early counterpoint to wilderness. But this dichotomy is dated—and misleading. Wilderness and the pastoral are arguably more alike than different; they are both variations on the rural. Pastoral may have been an early counterpoint to wilderness, but like wilderness, pastoral is now more a counterpoint to urban. Pastoral is a version of the rural. Indeed, wilderness and the pastoral are very often physically and ideologically contiguous, the line between them often indistinct and shifting.[3] While both rural and urban can be civilized in Nash's (2001) analysis, rural folks typically live and work in closer proximity to—and sometimes within—that which is popularly perceived as wilderness.[4] It is these rural livelihoods, more remote from the metropolis and even the "small town," more intertwined with "nature" and "wilderness," which are my focus.

## THE MUTUAL CONSTITUTIVITY OF LAW AND SPACE

That spatiality and society are mutually constitutive is a core idea of legal geography. This central tenet is expressed in a range of ways. Soja (1985, 92–93) explains that the "process of 'spatiality' is the idea of space as socially produced." Space both contains and actively shapes social processes, as "social phenomena are necessarily spatial phenomena" (Jones and Kodras 1990, 24–25). Institutions, networks, and individuals are all spatiality's agents (Teather 1994, 33–34), engaged in ongoing "struggle, conflict and contradiction" (Soja 1985, 97). Indeed, Neil Smith (1984, 77, 85) asserts that "we do not live, act and work 'in' space so much as by living, acting and working we produce space." Space and time are similarly mutually constitutive. Soja (1985, 94) observes:

> Spatiality and temporality, human geography and human history, intersect in a
> complex social process which creates a constantly evolving historical sequence

of spatialities, a spatio-temporal structuration of social life which gives form not only to the grand movements of societal development but also the recursive practices of day-to-day activity.

Complimentary to the notion that the social, the spatial, and the temporal are mutually constitutive is the idea that the legal and the spatial also constitute one another (Delaney 2010, 8; Martin, Scherr, and City 2010, 177). Igor Stramignoni (2004, 184) thus calls us to "consider not only how law is everywhere in space but also, and somewhat more radically, how space is everywhere in law." Yet some legal geographers have criticized the discipline's failure to practice this core idea. David Delaney (2003, 71) observes that much legal geography scholarship privileges either law or geography by focusing on "law-in-space" or on "space-in-law." His solution to this conundrum is to introduce the concept of nomoscape, which he describes as "enormously complex and dynamic components of social- and life-worlds . . . condition[ing] the workings of nomic fields of power within which we are always positioned, through which we navigate" (Delaney 2010, 121–22).

I suggest that the rural nomoscape conditions how those in rural places move through the world by situating them farther—both physically and cognitively—from the state as a nomic field of power. Delaney (2010, 104) further explains that nomoscapes determine "how we are differentially positioned and repositioned with respect to nomic fields of power." In this regard, I posit that the rural nomoscape suggests different consequences for one's very presence in a rural place (i.e., creating suspicion that justifies legal intervention or justifying self-defense because of perceived threat). I use examples from case law to illustrate how courts use rural spatiality to draw lines regarding, for example, what law enforcement officers can and cannot do.

I deploy Delaney's concept of generic nomic setting (see the introduction to this volume) to frame my theorization of the mutual constitutivity of law and the rural. That is, I present the rural as generic nomic setting while referring to specific places and landscapes to illustrate some of the phenomena associated with that setting. I show how particular settings—specific places, specific landscapes (e.g., the "hollers" of Appalachia, Indian reservations in the West and Southwest, the timber woods of northern California), are more or less accessible or permeable to different and differently equipped legal actors and legal institutions.

Pitfalls are inherent in a reductivist practice such as designating the rural as generic nomic setting—"generalization destroys so much of what is of interest" (Halfacree 1993, 26)—and rural sociologists are fond of saying that if you've seen one rural place, you've seen *one* rural place. Speaking of the rural as a "broad category" in this way can "obfuscat[e], whether the aim is description or theoretical evaluation" (Hoggart 1990, 245), because differences among rural places may be enormous, and rural and urban share many similarities. At the same time, scholars have identified cultural similarities among rural communities (Albrecht and Albrecht 2004, 435; Willits, Bealer, and Crider 1982, 72). Further, some of these similarities persist across rural places, even in the face of advances in technology that better connect rural residents to the urban and cosmopolitan world (Tickamyer and Henderson 2003, 112–14). Generalization about places of similar population density and size and/or similar degrees of removal from a metropolitan area is thus reasonable for assessing the sociolegal consequences of material spatiality.

I begin by describing the rural sociospatial milieu, which lays the groundwork for theorizing how rural sociospatiality influences law and rural residents' relationship to it. I then discuss how law operates or performs in this generic nomic setting. If law is everywhere in space, how does rural sociospatiality mediate law's performance? If space is everywhere in law, where do we find rural spatiality expressed by or influencing legal actors? How do these expressions and performances in turn produce rural space?

Judges and legislators, like laypersons, make assumptions about rural sociospatiality (Pruitt 2006, 168–72). When formal legal actors manage their expectations of law's force in the context of the generic nomic rural setting, they recode those spaces, rendering them less "lawful." But this investigation looks beyond law on the books to consider law not only as it varies by judicial ruling but also as law in action (Pound 1910, 15), how "local practices influence the information and advice about the law transmitted by lawyers, court clerks, social workers, probation officers, friends, neighbors, employers, and others" (Kruse 2011–12, 660). To such "local practices" I add consideration of the availability—the very presence or absence—of law enforcement and other legal actors, as well as how rural sociospatiality shapes their performance.

I maintain that rural sociospatiality causes law to underperform in rural contexts, or at least to perform differently than in the presumptive urban norm. Rural spatiality disables or tames or limits law because it disables or tames or limits law's agents. Indeed, rural spatiality may be thought of as undermining law, even circumventing it. But rural spatiality also limits—we might say, manages—residents, judges, and other legal actors' expectations of what formal law can accomplish there. Nash writes of the tension between "wilderness" and "civilization," describing how in the ordinary (or at least modern) course of events civilization claims, tames, and/or colonizes wilderness and the natural environment. I posit a parallel tension between law as an ordering or "civilizing" force and rural or remote spatiality as an object of its efforts. Just as the pioneer sought to tame nature

(Cather [1913] 1993, 7), law seeks to tame rural spatiality, to make law's authority meaningful in that context. The struggle to do so is dynamic and ongoing, abetted by technology, yes, but requiring constant vigilance.

## RURALITY AS BOTH MATERIAL AND SOCIALLY CONSTRUCTED

Just as law and spatiality are mutually constitutive, so, too, are rural spatiality and rural culture. Like spatiality more generally, rural spatiality has both material and imagined components (Halfacree 2006, 51). Paul Cloke (2006, 24) asserts that "material, imaginative and practised ruralities" are "intrinsically and dynamically intertwined and embodied with 'flesh and blood' culture and with real life relationships." In *The Country and the City*, Raymond Williams (1973) explored rural and urban as imagined spaces. Similarly, scholars across disciplines increasingly acknowledge the existence of a rural imaginary or ideation apart from actual rural locales (Cloke 2006, 21; Halfacree 1993, 2006, 45). Linda Lobao (1996, 89) refers to this phenomenon as a "spatial loosening of elements once considered indicative of . . . rural and urban." Regarding rurality, I attend to both "the '*physicality*' of materiality, its '*thingness*,' and the '*imaginary*' aspect of materiality, that which conveys its social, cultural and historical meaning" (Dale 2005, 656). Halfacree (1993, 34) posits that material space gets recoded by the social representations of space, and I assert that the same is true of legal representations of space. Karen Dale (2005, 652) points out not only that materality "takes on social meanings, but that humans enact social agency through a materiality which simultaneously shapes the nature of that social agency." "Legal" can be substituted for *social* at each point in Dale's statement.

Certain geographers have assumed that individuals consider the enabling and disabling features of space in their decision making, even as their own actions modify spatial structures (Jones and Kodras 1990, 24–25). Marc Mormont (1990, 36) links this phenomenon to identity in rural contexts. He observes that "social identity exists primarily in *relation* to space . . . because it is by the practical apprehension of a structured space that the individual first becomes aware of the world and learns to define his or her position within it." In the sections that follow, I illustrate the influence of spatiality on the agency of both public and private actors in rural and remote places. Specifically, I show how rural residents' apprehension of space guides their perceived choices within it, as well as their relation to the state. I offer a parallel analysis with rural law enforcement as my subject. First, however, I take a deeper look at the material spatiality of the rural lawscape.

## THE MATERIAL SPATIALITY OF RURAL AND REMOTE PLACES

"Rural" and "urban" are inherently spatial constructs (Halfacree 2006, 44), just as they are inherently social. This is reflected in many nations' definitions of rural, which often reference population size and density, as well as proximity to an urban area (Australian Population and Migration Research Centre 2012; Pruitt 2011, 805; Vanegas and Pruitt 2012, 297–319). Thus, many nations, including the United States, define *rural* according to the physical space of material nature—the very vastness and relative "emptiness" of rural spaces and places. Many metaphors for the rural express this spatial character, as well as the apartness of these "empty" spaces: outback, middle of nowhere, up a holler, in the boonies, back of beyond, frontier, bush, countryside, wilderness, periphery, exurbia, open space (Halfacree 2006, 45; Pruitt 2006, 219).

This perceived lack of materiality, this relative absence of the type of substance associated with the built environment and with population density (Halfacree 1993, 24; Woods 2011, 1, 8–10), is the slate on which humans and their institutions—including legal ones—impose their will and write their story. But this relative absence of people and their stuff does not mean that rural and remote places are blank slates in the sense that power and knowledge are absent, that the spaces are uncontested or without sociospatial meaning or content (Halfacree 2006, 44). Rather, rural spatiality undoubtedly plays a role in producing power and knowledge, particularly as regards the relationship between individuals and the state.

Rurality itself is a "world-making" force (Delaney 2010, 20), but its character as such is associated with an apparent power vacuum of sorts. That is, sparsely populated space is arguably lacking in formal ordering because it is nearly always marked by an absence (at least relatively speaking) of state actors (e.g., law enforcement officers, regulators, safety inspectors, even public school educators and state services). Rural places may even lack road signs or official road names and be only partially mapped by the state.[5] Rural spaces are also typically farther from courts and from the ancillary institutions that could serve the needs and interests of both victims (e.g., social services, health care) and those accused of crimes (e.g., experts, investigators, criminal law specialist attorneys, juvenile detention, drug treatment facilities) (Pruitt 2008b, 360–62, 385; 2009a, 381; Pruitt and Colgan 2010, 242–43; Weisheit, Falcone, and Wells 2006, 7, 22).

Law cannot be everywhere at once because state and local legal actors cannot be everywhere at once.[6] In many rural places, especially in the US West, the presence of vast swaths of federal land aggravates the challenge.[7] Indeed, not only are law enforcement institutions challenged by the task of responding to rural crimes and assisting rural residents; they are challenged to find suspects who take rural cover. One way to avoid the state is to find seclusion, to find a space the state respects as private, or one that the state—as a practical matter—cannot easily surveil or reach. Rurality can provide this seclusion, undermining the reach of law enforcement, and thereby also the reach of law. For example, Ted Kaczynski, the notorious Unabomber, took refuge in rural Garfield County, Montana, which had only two law enforcement officials and fewer than half a dozen people per square mile (Egan 1996). Rural sociospatiality obscured Kaczynski even from private citizens: "virtually everybody in the hamlet near his one-room cabin knew him, but nobody asked who he really was" (Egan 1996, E1). Kaczynski eluded authorities for eighteen years, using mail bombs to kill three people and injure twenty-seven. A fundamentalist, polygamous Mormon group accused of arranging marriages for underage girls secluded itself at its Yearning for Zion Ranch, an isolated compound outside tiny Eldorado, Texas (McKinley 2009). Recall *Winter's Bone* and the hunt for Jessup—dead or alive—in the rural Missouri Ozarks (Granik 2010).

A 2011 story from nonmetropolitan Mendocino County, California, is also illustrative. Over the course of a couple of weeks, Aaron Bassler shot and killed two men, a conservationist and a county supervisor, in the timberland surrounding Fort Bragg, California (Hecht 2011). Bassler evaded law enforcement by taking refuge in those same woods. Officers expressed frustration, noting that Bassler's familiarity with the woods provided him impeccable cover: "He is still in the woods and knows them like the back of his hands.... It's his territory—and we're the interlopers'" (Hecht 2011, A1). Law enforcement officers eventually shot and killed Bassler in "his" woods, but rural spatiality thwarted their efforts for nearly two months.

A 2012 story, also from northern California, makes a similar point, while also illustrating how technological advances empower law enforcement to effectively "tame space"—that is, to govern and manage rural spatiality. Ranchers in nonmetropolitan Colusa, Butte, and Glenn counties complained about poachers for several months, but game wardens were unable to reach their outlying ranches in time to apprehend the suspects (Associated Press 2012). Law enforcement officers succeeded in arresting the poachers only after they put the area under aircraft surveillance and tracked some men who became suspects because of license plate numbers the ranchers reported. Spatiality—material distance—impeded law enforcement efforts, but technology ultimately helped overcome the challenge of distance in ways unavailable a century ago. Such uneven presence of law enforcement and other legal actors presumably fosters an ethos of self-reliance that influences attitudes about the role of law (Ellickson 1991; Engel 1984), as well as toward the state more generally. This sociospatial feedback loop between diminished state presence and enhanced self-reliance may explain the popular association of rural culture with gun culture (Bai 2008). Such self-reliance is both creature and feature of the rural lawscape.

The relative absence of the state that characterizes the generic nomic rural setting is suggested by the term *frontier justice*, which connotes a certain rough justice, perhaps even vigilante justice, a taking of the law into private hands, a fending for oneself (Gonzales-Day 2006, 10, 38, 42). Frontier justice is associated with an era gone by, when the American West in particular was wild and thus lawless (Nash 2001, 24; Ramsey 2006, 160–61). But such relative lawlessness persists in twenty-first-century rural places, where law enforcement agencies still struggle to execute their mandate—to fulfill the rule of law—in a meaningful way.

Just as material space—stretches of undeveloped, wild, or natural territory—separates rural people from legal actors, so it also separates them from one another. Private citizens, too, are legal actors of a sort (see Nicholas Blomley's discussion of habits in Chapter 3 of this volume), and their absence, like that of law enforcement, enhances both rural privacy and rural vulnerability. Courts sometimes exhibit a significant awareness of this sociospatial vulnerability. It is not unusual, for example, for a court to mention in a crime narrative the rural locale of the criminal event. Judges apparently do this to suggest that the rural setting enhanced the victim's vulnerability. For example, the US Supreme Court in *Stein v. New York* (1953, 160) described a murder as happening on "lonely country roads," and in the landmark death penalty case, *Furman v. Georgia* (1972, 253), Justice Douglas's concurring opinion described an intruder entering "the rural home of a 65-year-old widow" while she slept. The Eighth Circuit's narrative in *Lingar v. Bowersox* (1999) referred repeatedly to the rural, noting that the defendants picked up the victim on a "rural highway" in Missouri and then took him to a "rural area" where they ordered him to disrobe and masturbate before shooting him. The defendants then disposed of the weapon on a "country road in Kentucky" (*Lingar* 1999, 455–56). Courts sometimes observe that a defendant deliberately chose rural space to provide cover for nefarious activity. In *McElmurry v. State* (2002, 14), for example, an Oklahoma court described how the defendants approached the victim's rural house "through the woods, so they would not be seen." Here, as in the example noted earlier from Mendocino, California, the narrative suggests that the wild or natural character of rurality—the woods—did part of the concealment work, enhancing vulnerability, disabling law.

Courts factor this rural vulnerability into decisions about a range of issues, both civil and criminal, including those related to sentencing and damages. In *One v. State* (1979), the Alaska Supreme Court noted that police response times are longer in rural areas because of the lack of nearby law enforcement. This, the court reasoned, left residents of a rural fishing camp more threatened by an escaped criminal than those in a more developed area would be, thus justifying the maximum penalty for the defendant. The Maine Supreme Court in *State v. Brown* (1973) suggested that the rural setting caused the defendant both to feel and to actually be more vulnerable when two men approached him at midnight. Such vulnerability might justify defendant's use of a gun against the men, the court opined, even if the defendant knew the men were unarmed. The court wrote, "The manner in which the two men approached the Defendant, at midnight, in a rural area, must have appeared threatening" (325). Rural vulnerability is also occasionally acknowledged in civil cases. In *South Central Bell v. Epps* (1987), the Mississippi Supreme Court held that a phone company's wrongful termination of service justified greater compensatory damages because the plaintiff was an isolated elderly woman living in a rural area.

Courts also sometimes explicitly recognize the vulnerability of law enforcement officers in rural settings, naming that context to justify an officer's decision to arrest or search. In *State v. Klevgaard* (1981, 191–92), the North Dakota Supreme Court deferred to a law enforcement officer's decision to arrest the defendant, finding the officer's safety might have been at risk, especially because he was "alone in a rural community in the early morning hours" and confrontation with the suspects presented "a genuine possibility of danger." Similarly, a concurring opinion of the North Carolina Supreme Court in *State v. Peck* (1982, 644) explicitly highlighted the special danger faced by rural law enforcement, calling for a bright-line rule that would give officers discretion to search passengers at traffic stops because "in the more remote areas of our large and primarily rural state" when an officer is alone, "more often than not . . . no other law enforcement officers are close enough to . . . render assistance in any reasonable period of time."

Courts sometimes note the rural setting in warrantless search cases, signaling that it is a factor in their determination of the propriety of the search. For example, the US Supreme Court in *Michigan v. Long* (1983) upheld a warrantless search of an automobile pursuant to a lawful traffic stop because the late hour, a sighted knife on the floor of the defendant's car, defendant's behavior, and the rural setting supported the officers' reasonable belief that the defendant would pose a danger if he reentered his vehicle. In *State v. Bradford* (1992), a Utah court held that the defendant's speeding, the early hour, the presence of a rifle, and the remoteness of the area provided a reasonable basis for the warrantless search. Finally, in *United States v. Becker* (1993), a federal district court in New York listed various factors—a large knife in plain view, the rural area, and the time of night—when upholding a warrantless protective search.

In a similar vein, courts have recognized the vulnerability of citizens who interact with law enforcement in rural places. In *State v. Mirquet* (1992), the Utah Court of Appeals opined that a rural location—even one along an interstate highway—supported a finding that a man was in custody when a law enforcement officer pulled him over. The court reasoned that the man was "subject to a more police dominated setting than a citizen pulled over in an urban area where passing motorists are going slower and pedestrians are present" (999).

Legislative bodies, too, constitute the rural lawscape, as when they recognize the particular challenges facing rural law enforcement agencies and victims. The Crime Control Act of 1990, for example, provides rural states with special financial assistance for drug enforcement. Similarly, the Violence Against Women Act (VAWA) expressly recognizes rural women as an at-risk population. On that basis, the federal government awards grants to state and local government entities, Indian tribes, and nonprofit organizations that seek to improve responses and services to rural domestic violence victims. Seventy-five percent of the program's funding must go to eligible entities in rural states. Both the Crime Control Act and VAWA define a "rural state" by spatial measures: a state with a population density of 52 or fewer persons per square mile, or a state in which the largest county has fewer than 150,000 people.

At other times, legal actors are less sensitive—even oblivious—to the significance of spatial isolation to lived experiences, including the ways in which spatiality shapes agency. While VAWA seeks to ameliorate the sociospatial challenges facing rural women, courts do not consistently attribute legal significance to rural vulnerability when victims of domestic violence assert that it influenced their actions (Pruitt 2007, 444; 2008b, 360–66). Yet the vulnerability associated with rural isolation may be aggravated by features of physical geography in places like Appalachia, where the battered woman may "live up what is locally called a 'hollow' . . . with no public transportation and large distances between houses" (Websdale 1998, 5) or, as in *Hage v. State* (1999), be cut off from sources of assistance by a flooding river.

When courts, legislatures, and parties to litigation contest and articulate the meaning and contours of the rural lawscape, they shape and endow it with consequence, alternately denying its difference and articulating its parameters. So do the everyday assessments, priorities, resource allocations, and discretion of law enforcement, prosecutors, and citizens. Even overlooking rural context—ignoring space altogether—is a spatial act. We thus begin to see how "space is everywhere in law," even when legal actors look past that pervasiveness or deny the very salience of spatiality.

## THE SOCIOLEGAL CONSEQUENCES OF RURAL SPATIALITY

Rural spatiality is not only a material phenomenon; it is also entangled with and mutually constitutive of social phenomena. This is in part because the population sparseness associated with rurality results in a high density of acquaintanceship (Freudenberg 1996). Illustrating the mutually constitutive nature of rural space and rural society, sociologists link the "predominance of personal, face-to-face social relationships among similar people" (Willits, Bealer, and Crider 1982, 70) with stasis and reluctance to alter tradition, which are widely associated with rural culture. This stasis is, in turn, linked to "greater levels of consensus on important values and morals" (Albrecht and Albrecht 2004, 435). In contrast, urban settings, being larger and populated by a more diverse array of persons, are thought to "foster . . . the generation and acceptance of new ideas" (Willits, Bealer, and Crider 1982, 73; Mitchell 2003, 17), thus causing norms in metropolitan places to evolve more quickly because a critical mass of organizationally and occupationally diverse people innovate (Willits, Bealer, and Crider 1982, 73).

## LACK OF ANONYMITY AND SELF-RELIANCE

Another sociospatial consequence of the "high density of acquaintanceship" associated with rural places and small towns is a lack of anonymity, and therefore a diminution of privacy. Such diminished privacy may deter engagement with the state because law enforcement, prosecutors, and judicial officials are also neighbors, acquaintances, and even friends or family (Pruitt 2008b, 363). This begets a culture of self-reliance, which in turn is associated with distrust of government. This ethos may explain why rural residents are less likely to seek government assistance (Rank and Hirschl 1998, 191) or to report crime, even when the perpetrator is a stranger (Weisheit and Donnermeyer 2000, 329–30).

Courts in the United States have recognized the significance of lack of anonymity in some contexts, such as change of venue (moving a trial to a different courthouse, as to avoid local bias or local familiarity with the relevant events) and jury voir dire (the process of removing potentially biased individuals from a jury prior to trial) (Pruitt 2006, 230–31), as well as in cases that implicate a person's reputation (228–30). But reported cases rarely reveal express sensitivity, by judges or other state actors, to how this feature of the rural sociospatial milieu might influence whether and how rural residents engage law or other agencies of the state (Pruitt 2007, 478–79; Wallace and Pruitt 2012, 122–33).

A related issue is the consequent lack of anonymity between law enforcement and citizens. Although a great deal of scholarly literature focuses on racial profiling, the "usual suspects" phenomenon may be more significant in rural communities, where law enforcement officers are likely to be socially embedded with those whom they police (Pruitt 2009b, 162–63; Weisheit, Falcone, and Wells 2006, 130). While this aspect of rural lack of anonymity is rarely acknowledged in case law, it did influence a 2004 decision of the Connecticut Superior Court. In *Florence v. Town of Plainfield* the court upheld a woman's negligence suit against a municipality with a population of about fifteen thousand people when its police force failed to execute an arrest warrant to protect the victim from her boyfriend. This failure occurred in spite of the woman's repeated requests for assistance. The court suggested that officers in small towns are likely to know of ongoing domestic problems such as this one, thus rendering inexcusable police failure to act. This case is also unusual in that it seems to demand more—not less—of law enforcement in a smaller community.[8]

## THE PARADOX OF RURAL PRIVACY

I suggested in the prior section that the lack of anonymity that flows from material aspects of rurality (e.g., spatial isolation, low population density) effectively circumscribe autonomy, especially in the context of small towns. The paradox is that rural spatiality—the physical isolation from others that marks remote rural living—also serves to enhance privacy (Pruitt 2008b, 363). Material space itself—like the built environment—can be a shield from prying eyes, including those of the state. Not only does the built environment (e.g., physical walls, fences) create expectations of privacy, so do expanses of space that may be thought of as "empty" because they are undeveloped or underdeveloped (Mormont 1990, 28), dominated by nature. Recall Ted Kaczynski and the Yearning for Zion Ranch. Recall *Winter's Bone*.

Law enforcement officers and courts have recognized rural spatiality's concealing function in various contexts, and they have opined that those who break the law know of it, too. Several cases adjudicating the concept of probable cause are illustrative. A New Mexico court held in *State v. Walters* (1996) that an officer's knowledge and experience of rural criminality supported the officer's probable cause to stop a vehicle, partly because of the driver's decision to use a rural road. The court cited the officer's "knowledge, gained from police training and experience, that intoxicated drivers frequently take rural roads to avoid the police" (284). In *State v. Watkins* (1994), a North Carolina court held that the early morning hour and rural location of a parking lot where an officer spotted a car produced sufficient probable cause for an investigatory stop. A Kansas appellate court in *State v. Maxwell* (2003, 1) reasoned that the fact a man suspected of manufacture and sale of methamphetamine drove "into the country" supported probable cause because "80 percent of the methamphetamine labs the officers were familiar with had been discovered in rural areas."

Other courts similarly suggest an association between crime and rural locales, or that if a crime has occurred in a rural place, one's very presence there creates suspicion. Culprits are identified by a process of elimination—with few present to be eliminated. For example, the Supreme Court of Maine in *State v. Heald* (1973) upheld probable cause to arrest the defendant on the basis of officers' following tire tracks in newly fallen snow in a rural area, from the burglary site to the defendant's car. Somewhat similarly, the Fifth Circuit in *United States v. Maslanka* (1974, 215) held that officers properly stopped a truck in a remote location because the last car that had appeared there had yielded three men "covered with marijuana." In a sense, these cases sanction what might be thought of as rural profiling, though a federal district court in South Dakota resisted that practice in *United States v. Brandon in the Woods* (2005). That court suggested that a rural locale alone could not justify stopping or arresting a man near a crime scene; however, its decision may have been influenced by the sparsely populated nature of South Dakota, which is dominated by vast swaths of rural territory.

The links between concealment, enhanced privacy, and rurality are not only a function of material spatiality, of low population density and space's capacity to conceal. Rather, associations of rurality with privacy reflect long-standing social and cultural notions. Karl Marx famously made the link, albeit in opaque fashion, in his argument that the bourgeoisie, by creating cities, had "rescued a considerable part of the population from the idiocy of rural life," thereby making "the country dependent on the town" (Marx [1848] 1988, 56). Soja (1989, 235) interprets Marx's "the idiocy of rural life." Framing *idiocy* linguistically, Soja discusses the term's Greek provenance and links it to privacy in the sense of "relative political socialization and spatialization":

> To be urbanized still means to adhere, to be made an adherent, a believer in a specified collective ideology rooted in extensions of *polis* (politics, policy, polity, police) and *civitas* (civil, civic, citizen, civilian, civilization). In contrast, the population beyond the reach of the urban is comprised of *idiotes*, from the Greek root *idios*, meaning 'one's own, a private person,' unlearned in the ways of the polis. . . . Thus to speak of the 'idiocy' of rural life or the urbanity of its opposition is primarily a statement of relative political socialization and spatialization, of the degree of adherence/separation in the collective social order. (234–35)

Soja thus sees the "idiocy of rural life" as referring to a type of privacy, to rural sociospatial separation from the greater, norm-setting collective.[9] Law is one manifestation of that norm-setting enterprise, although it remains spatially and cognitively distant from the rural. (Recall that social norms evolve more slowly in rural places, where people value tradition). The "practical organization" (Delaney 2010, 104) of the rural or remote nomoscape situates its denizens differently to— at a greater distance from—the nomic power of the state. The rural lawscape thus keeps formal law at arm's length.

## PERFORMATIVITY IN THE RURAL LAWSCAPE

Delaney (2010, 18–19) suggests attending not only to the material but also to the performative in thinking about law and spatiality. Law performs by ordering and governing materiality (Cheah and Grosz 1996, 3), yet law does so unevenly, "differentially refracted through the social architecture of spatialities" (Delaney 2010, 46). I have already highlighted the materiality of rural spatiality's architecture. Here I illustrate how that materiality and associated sociospatial characteristics of rurality influence law's performance. I assert that rural spatiality mediates law's performance such that law is less likely to seep deeply into the nooks and crannies of rural space, into its hollows and forests, onto its plains.

Both material and social components of rural spatiality render law less effective at achieving its goals—at asserting its authority, flexing its muscle. Indeed, rural sociospatial characteristics thwart the power and legitimacy associated with the rule of law. This is largely because legal actors and institutions are not present—at least not consistently and meaningfully so—in rural places. A familiar adage queries, "If a tree falls in the forest and no one hears it, does it make a noise?" An analogous question regarding the operation of law in rural and remote places might ask, "If a law is broken but no legal actors are present to enforce it, does law exist? Is law present? Does law matter?" The rural lawscape's diminished permeability to the rule of law and to the efforts of legal actors gets reinforced by judicial pronouncements of rural difference that reference sociospatial characteristics such as vulnerability and privacy, as well as law's limits in the face of those characteristics. These judicial opinions create different expectations of formal or official law, marginalizing it, diminishing its potency, and further bolstering rural instincts toward self-reliance.

I have already discussed cases in which courts have recognized the heightened vulnerability associated with rural spatiality and the limits on what law can accomplish in rural contexts. A *New York Times* story from 2012 further illustrates how space mediates law's operation. "Higher Crime, Fewer Charges on Indian Land" discussed the increasing failure of US Attorneys to prosecute crimes in Indian Country—even the most serious crimes—over which the federal government has jurisdiction. Various reasons are offered for the failures, including lack of resources and jurisdictional complications. But spatiality, too, looms large. The story quotes a former chief judge of the Tonto Apaches in Arizona who observes—by way of explaining the inaction—that "federal prosecutors typically live, work and try cases hundreds of miles from Indian Country" (T. Williams 2012, A14). What the judge suggests is "out of sight, out of mind." This is also a contemporary manifestation of the long-standing association of Native Americans with the lawless wilderness (Nash 2001, xiii). Both the invisibility and the cultural association with lawlessness are aspects of the particular rural lawscape that is Indian Country, also which is additionally marked by a lack of federal will to take up violence against American Indians.

The delivery of indigent defense services in nonmetropolitan Apache County, Arizona, provides another illustration of how rural spatiality disables legal actors and undermines the delivery of justice. The county has insufficient funding to establish a public defender's office that would employ one or more full-time lawyers. Instead, the county hires lawyers on a contract basis to represent indigent defendants, and it requires those lawyers to appear in a different court of first impression several days each week to meet with new clients (Pruitt and Colgan 2010, 291). This means that the lawyers, most of whom live in the southern part of the county, must travel hundreds of miles a day, several times each week, just to cover the vast distances governed by Apache County, which spans nearly 12,000 square miles and stretches more than 250 miles between its southern and northern borders (US Census Bureau 2012b). This leaves the lawyers relatively little time to do the work of defending their clients, who often live in places distant from the defense lawyers' offices, places that may also be unreachable by telephone or Internet. Spatiality has implications, too, regarding the scale at which government services are funded. When trial courts, indigent defense, and law enforcement are locally funded, as at the county level, rural justice systems tend to be hamstrung by anemic tax bases and consequently shallow public coffers (Pruitt and Colgan 2010, 222–23).

Courts have lamented the practical limits of rural justice systems, but they have rarely shown sensitivity to equal protection arguments based on county-to-county variations of either funding levels or justice system amenities. In *North v. Russell* (1976), for example, the US Supreme Court found no constitutional infirmity when laypersons preside over courts of first impression in rural areas, even though judges in more populous places are trained lawyers. The Court saw no equal protection problem because "all people within a given city and within cities of the same size are treated equally" (338). By setting the scale of analysis at the municipality level rather than the state or national level—and by looking for parity only among cities "of the same size" (338)—the Court was able to justify a second-class justice system. Cases like *North* further diminish law's clout in rural places.[10]

These are just a few illustrations of how material space impedes law, or at least increases the difficulty and expense associated with law doing its business, the work of effecting the rule of law. If a body is hidden or a person is lost or hiding in a rural area, covering the territory represented by where the victim or perpetrator might be found is complicated by the very vastness of the territory, and perhaps also by the remoteness and terrain of the region. If the state intends to regulate or monitor or surveil a wide-open space, it is going to take "manpower" and technology—and it is going to cost money. Law's agents have to traverse territory to get to people, to crime scenes, to bodies, to contraband, to "situations" (Delaney 2010, 26, 40–42), even to clients and courthouses. It is a given that the challenges and costs of public safety increase with population size, but challenges and costs also rise with sheer volume of territory. This expense may lead formal law effectively to cede the rural and remote—as it once effectively ceded the frontier (Ramsey 2006, 160–61)—to private order or vigilante justice. Doing so sanctions—indeed, creates—a lawscape very different to the implicit urban norm.

## CONCLUSION

Law is not only everywhere in space, it is "enmeshed with space" (Martin, Scherr, and City 2010, 177). When law is enmeshed with rural space, that sociospatial milieu renders law less meaningfully or robustly present, less truly *everywhere*. This is because of the relative absence of official legal actors and legal institutions. It is also a consequence of the challenges formal legal actors face in transcending material space, whether to respond to a crime or to hold court in reasonable proximity to an incident or to litigants. In short, the state is functionally less capable of enforcing the rule of law in rural and remote places, a reality that may also beget the state's diminished vigilance in those places. Formal or official law thus matters less in everyday rural life because its performance is intermittent, occasional, or in name only. This vacuum invites informal order or frontier justice, with ancillary sociocultural consequences, such as self-reliance.

Rurality—as both imagined and lived—conditions the operation of the legal through the processes and the swarm of actors by which the state imposes its will, on both territory and the people present there. Such everyday legal processes, which effectively differentiate rural from urban, in turn shape the lived character of the rural. But rural spaces are marginalized not only spatially; they are marginalized cognitively and culturally, too. Law sometimes reinforces that marginalization by sanctioning inferior justice systems or otherwise ceding the rural to a relatively lawless fate.

The judicial opinions, legislation, and range of legal actors I have discussed illustrate how "the legal and the spatial, the discursive and the material are inextricable" (Delaney 2003, 71). We see that "the metaphors and spatial imaginings" regarding rural places "are not inert," but instead "work to justify 'on-the-ground' reconfigurations" (71). Just as social constructions can "operate with the full force of objective facts" (Harvey 1996, 211), so, too, do legal constructions. By articulating the rural as inaccessible, as enhancing vulnerability, and as self-reliant, legal actors and institutions constitute rurality as all of these things, endowing it with these characteristics as surely as material spatiality does the same work. Whether these legal actors and actions articulate the rural as different from the presumptive urban norm or deny that difference, whether a denial of difference is explicit or simply an oversight that stems from an urban-centric ignorance or myopia, these actors and processes constitute the rural lawscape.

These illustrations of how law differentiates along the rural-urban continuum teach us something about rurality, yes. But they also reveal lessons about the urban and about the very nature of law. That is, by setting the rural apart as dangerous, private, lawless, and self-reliant, law suggests—as did Marx and Soja—that the urban is more orderly, regulated, and lawful. Further, the practices I attend to (policing, judging, regulating, and so forth) recursively constitute the legal, underpinning and elaborating a legal differentiation that is spatial. This investigation into the rural lawscape thus reveals something about law and how it is constituted: a process of variegated or variable law that is otherwise obscured. Law is different here from there. By looking to the margins, we see something about the center because the process of differentiation depicts not only the rural but also the default urban norm. By investigating the rural—not merely as a foil for the urban but as a space worthy of critical study—we gain new understandings about the legal, the rural-urban continuum, and the mutual coproduction and codependency of rural and urban lawscapes.

## NOTES

1. Catharine MacKinnon (2005) uses this phrase to refer to law's proximity to, and relationship with, women's lives. I assert that it is also apt regarding law's proximity to rural people and places.

2. Even small towns have police departments and are more readily reached by other law enforcement (Weisheit, Falcone, and Wells 2006, 121). Also, houses in small towns are typically situated close enough to each other for neighbors to hear and assist one another if danger threatens.

3. A passage from Willa Cather's ([1913] 1993, 7) *O Pioneers!* captures this idea, describing a pioneer settler's efforts to cultivate his land on the Nebraska Divide: "In eleven long years John Bergson had made but little impression upon the wild land he had come to tame. It was still a wild thing that had its ugly moods." This reflects Nash's (2001, 30) depiction of the "pioneer's association of wilderness with hardship and danger in a variety of forms" and how "the rural, controlled state of nature was the object of his affection and goal of his labor."

Further, land claimed and tamed by "civilizing" forces can be reclaimed by wilderness if those forces are not vigilant. A recent example of this is presented by a 2012 *New York Times Magazine* cover story, "Jungleland." A promotional blurb for the story read: "In the years since Katrina, New Orleans' Lower Ninth Ward has undergone a reverse colonization: nature reclaiming civilization." The story went on to detail the array of wildlife now making their homes in the Lower Ninth, the untamed flora and fauna overtaking the urban space (Rich 2012).

4. By way of illustration of what I mean by wilderness, the US government has coined the phrase "wildland-urban interface," which it defines as places where homes and structures are positioned either adjacent to or among forests, brush, or other fire-influencing land-scape at densities as low as one structure per forty acres. Those living at this interface are at particular risk for wildfire damage. About 9.4 percent of the coterminous United States' land area is wildland-urban interface, and some 98.5 million people live there (Radeloff et al. 2005, 800–801). Scholars such as Cronon (1995) have complicated the concept of wilderness, revealing how its social construction idealizes by suggesting an absence of "civilization," a (relative) lack of human presence. My intent is not to evoke those associations. Rather, I use the word to describe a type of place for which I can find no more precise term. I nevertheless see idealized social constructions of "wilderness" as linked to idealized social constructions of other variations or forms of rurality, as discussed in this chapter.

5. This is recognized in cases like *Gatlin v. State* (1977), in which the court used rurality to justify the substitution of the owner's name for a description of the property to be searched "since houses in rural communities are commonly known by the name of the owner rather than by any technical legal description."

6. While technology increasingly does the state's surveillance work, such surveillance is costly, and constant monitoring of a sparsely populated area is not likely to be considered cost-efficient.

7. The presence of federal lands may raise, albeit only marginally, the law enforcement capacity associated with these places due to the presence of park rangers and game and fish officials (Congressional Research Service 2012).

8. Few courts show such sensitivity to rural difference. The South Carolina Supreme Court, in *Arthurs v. Aiken County* (2001), found the sheriff's department not liable for failure to protect a woman from her husband, who threatened her three times on the day he killed her. The court described the place where the murder occurred as "rural," but it did not suggest that the rural locale was relevant to the liability question.

9. Soja (1989, 234–35) asserts that the nodality of the urban core is critical to the collective social order. He explains that "the civic centre has always served as a key surveillant node of the state, supervising locales of production, consumption, and exchange" in order "to maintain adhesiveness."

10. In *State v. Hanger* (1985), for example, the Court of Appeals of Arizona expressed regret when nonmetropolitan Cochise County dropped a prosecution of a murder case

because the county could not afford the cost of indigent defense services. In *Wright v. Idaho* (1989), a dissenting judge noted in the context of a child molestation case that "many rural communities do not have the financial means to set up extensive videotape facilities to aid in the preparation of criminal cases," a deficit that may prejudice defendants.

## LIST OF CASES

*Arthurs v. Aiken County*, 551 S.E.2d 579 (S.C. 2001).
*Florence v. Town of Plainfield*, 849 A.2d 7 (Conn. Super. Ct. 2004).
*Furman v. Georgia*, 408 U.S. 238 (1972).
*Gatlin v. State*, 559 S.W.2d 12 (Ark. 1977).
*Hage v. State*, 595 N.W.2d 200 (Minn. 1999).
*Lingar v. Bowersox*, 176 F.3d 453 (8th Cir. 1999).
*McElmurry v. State*, 60 P.3d 4 (Okla. Crim. App. 2002).
*Michigan v. Long*, 463 U.S. 1032 (1983).
*North v. Russell*, 427 U.S. 328 (1976).
*One v. State*, 592 P.2d 1193 (Alaska 1979).
*South Central Bell v. Epps*, 509 So.2d 886 (Miss. 1987).
*State v. Bradford*, 839 P.2d 866 (Utah Ct. App. 1992).
*State v. Brown*, 302 A.2d 322 (Maine 1973).
*State v. Hanger*, 706 P.2d 1240 (Ariz. Ct. App. 1985).
*State v. Heald*, 314 A.2d 820 (Me. 1973).
*State v. Klevgaard*, 306 N.W.2d 185 (N.D. 1981).
*State v. Maxwell*, 77 P.3d 1008 (Kan. Ct. App. 2003).
*State v. Mirquet*, 844 P.2d 995 (Utah Ct. App. 1992).
*State v. Peck*, 291 S.E.2d 637 (N.C. 1982).
*State v. Walters*, 934 P.2d 282 (N.M. Ct. App. 1996).
*State v. Watkins*, 446 S.E.2d 67 (N.C. 1994).
*Stein v. New York*, 346 U.S. 156 (1953).
*United States v. Becker*, 823 F. Supp. 111 (W.D.N.Y. 1993).
*United States v. Brandon in the Woods*, 354 F. Supp. 2d 1087 (D.S.D. 2005).
*United States v. Maslanka*, 501 F.2d 208 (5th Cir. 1974).
*Wright v. Idaho*, 775 P.2d 1224 (Idaho 1989).

## REFERENCES

Albrecht, Don E., and Carol M. Albrecht. 2004. "Metro/Nonmetro Residence, Nonmarital Conception, and Conception Outcomes." *Rural Sociology* 69 (3): 430–52.
Associated Press. 2012. "3 Arrested in Suspected Northern California Poaching Ring." October 27.
Australian Population and Migration Research Centre. 2012. "ARIA (Accessibility/Remoteness Index of Australia)." http://www.adelaide.edu.au/apmrc/research/projects/category/about_aria.html.
Bai, Matt. 2008. "Working for the Working-Class Vote." *New York Times*, October 15.
Blainey, Geoffrey. 1966. *The Tyranny of Distance: How Distance Shaped Australia's History*. Melbourne: Macmillan.
Blomley, Nicholas K. 1994. *Law, Space, and the Geographies of Power*. New York: Guilford.

Blomley, Nicholas K., David Delaney, and Richard T. Ford. 2001. *The Legal Geographies Reader*. Oxford, UK: Blackwell.

Boso, Luke. 2013. "Urban Bias, Rural Sexual Minorities, and Courts' Role in Addressing Discrimination." *UCLA Law Review* 60 (3): 562–637.

Braverman, Irus. 2014. "Conservation Without Nature: The Trouble with *In Situ* Versus *Ex Situ* Conservation." *Geoforum* 51: 47–57.

Brenner, Neil. 2004. *New State Spaces: Urban Governance and the Rescaling of Statehood*. New York: Oxford University Press.

Cather, Willa. (1913) 1993. *O Pioneers!* New York: Dover.

Cheah, Pheng, and E. Grosz. 1996. "The Body of the Law: Notes Toward a Theory of Corporeal Justice." In *Thinking Through the Body of the Law*, edited by Pheng Cheah, David Fraser, and Judith Grbich, 3–25. New York: New York University Press.

Cloke, Paul J. 2006. "Conceptualizing Rurality." In *Handbook of Rural Studies*, edited by Paul J. Cloke, Terry Marsden, and Patrick Mooney, 18–28. London: Sage.

Cloke, Paul J., and Jo Little, eds. 1997. *Contested Countryside Cultures: Otherness, Marginalisation, and Rurality*. London: Routledge.

Cloke, Paul J., Terry Marsden, and Patrick Mooney, eds. 2006. *Handbook of Rural Studies*. London: Sage.

Congressional Research Service. 2012. *Federal Land Ownership: Overview and Data*. Document No. R42346. Washington, DC: Congressional Research Service.

Creed, Gerald W., and Barbara Ching. 1997. "Recognizing Rusticity: Identity and the Power of Place, Introduction." In *Knowing Your Place: Rural Identity and Cultural Hierarchy* edited by Barbara Ching and Gerald W. Creed, 1–38. New York: Routledge.

Crime Control Act of 1990. Pub. L. No. 101-647, 104 Stat. 4789 (1990) (codified as amended in scattered sections of 18 U.S.C.).

Cronon, William. 1995. "The Trouble with Wilderness; or, Getting Back to the Wrong Nature." In *Uncommon Ground: Rethinking the Human Place in Nature*, edited by William Cronon, 69–90. New York: W. W. Norton.

Dale, Karen. 2005. "Building a Social Materiality: Spatial and Embodied Politics in Organizational Control." *Organization* 12 (5): 649–78.

Delaney, David. 2003. "Beyond the Word: Law as a Thing of This World." In *Law and Geography: Current Legal Issues*, edited by Jane Holder and Carolyn Harrison, 5:67–84. New York: Oxford University Press.

———. 2010. *The Spatial, the Legal and the Pragmatics of World-Making*. New York: Routledge.

Egan, Timothy. 1996. "The Nation: Hiding Out Underneath the Big Sky." *New York Times*, April 7, E1.

Ellickson, Robert C. 1991. *Order Without Law: How Neighbors Settle Disputes*. Cambridge, MA: Harvard University Press.

Engel, David M. 1984. "The Oven Bird's Song: Insiders, Outsiders and Personal Injuries in an American Community." *Law and Society Review* 18 (4): 551–82.

Freudenberg, William R. 1996. "The Density of Acquaintanceship: An Overlooked Variable in Community Research." *American Journal of Sociology* 92 (1): 27–63.

Gonzales-Day, Ken. 2006. *Lynching in the West 1850–1935*. Durham, NC: Duke University Press.

Granik, Debra. 2010. *Winter's Bone*. Beverly Hills, CA: Roadside Attractions. DVD.

Halfacree, Keith H. 1993. "Locality and Social Representation: Space, Discourse and Alternative Definitions of the Rural." *Journal of Rural Studies* 9 (1): 23–37.

————. 2006. "Rural Space: Constructing a Three-Fold Architecture." In *Handbook of Rural Studies*, edited by Paul J. Cloke, Terry Marsden, and Patrick Mooney, 44–62. London: Sage.

Harvey, David. 1973. *Social Justice and the City*. Baltimore, MD: Johns Hopkins University Press.

————. 1996. *Justice, Nature and the Geography of Difference*. Oxford, UK: Blackwell.

Hecht, Peter. 2011. "Manhunt for Councilman's Killer Has Fort Bragg on the Edge." *Sacramento Bee*, September 16, A1.

Hoggart, Keith. 1990. "Let's Do Away with Rural." *Journal of Rural Studies* 6 (3): 245–57.

Jerke, Bud. 2011. "Queer Realism." *Harvard Journal of Law and Gender* 34 (1): 259–312.

Jones, John Paul, and Janet E. Kodras. 1990. "The State, Social Policy and Geography." In *Geographic Dimensions of United States Social Policy*, edited by Janet E. Kodras and John Paul Jones, 17–36. New York: Edward Arnold.

Kruse, Katherine. 2011–12. "Getting Real About Legal Realism, New Legal Realism, and Clinical Legal Education." *New York Law School Law Review* 56 (2): 659–84.

Lefebvre, Henri. 1996. *Writings on Cities*. Translated by Eleonore Kofman and Elizabeth Lebas. Cambridge, MA: Blackwell.

Little, Jo. 2006. "Gender and Sexuality in Rural Communities." In *Handbook of Rural Studies*, edited by Paul J. Cloke, Terry Marsden, and Patrick Mooney, 365–78. London: Sage.

Lobao, Linda. 1996. "A Sociology of the Periphery Versus a Peripheral Sociology: Rural Sociology and the Dimension of Space." *Rural Sociology* 61 (1): 77–102.

MacKinnon, Catharine A. 2005. *Women's Lives, Men's Laws*. Cambridge, MA: Belknap Press of Harvard University.

Martin, Deborah G., Alexander W. Scherr, and Christopher City. 2010. "Making Law, Making Place: Lawyers and the Production of Space." *Progress in Human Geography* 34 (2): 175–92.

Marx, Karl. (1848) 1988. *The Communist Manifesto: Annotated Text*. Edited by Frederic L. Bender. New York: W. W. Norton.

————. (1939) 1973. *Grundrisse: Foundations of the Critique of Political Economy (Rough Draft)*. Translated by Martin Nicolaus. New York: Penguin Putnam.

Massey, Doreen. 2007. *World City*. Cambridge, MA: Polity.

McDowell, Linda. 1994. "The Transformation of Cultural Geography." In *Human Geography: Society, Space and Social Science*, edited by Derek Gregory, Ron Martin, and Graham Smith, 146–73. Minneapolis, MN: Macmillan.

McKinley, James C. 2009. "Difficulties for Prosecutors in Trial of Sect Leader." *New York Times*, November 4.

Mitchell, Don. 2003. *The Right to the City: Social Justice and the Fight for Public Space*. New York: Guilford.

Mormont, Marc. 1990. "Who is Rural? Or, How to be Rural: Towards a Sociology of the Rural." In *Rural Restructuring: Global Processes and Their Responses*, edited by Terry Marsden, Sarah Whatmore, and Philip Lowe, 21–41. London: Fulton.

Nash, Roderick. 2001. *Wilderness and the American Mind*. 4th ed. New Haven, CT: Yale University Press.

Philippopoulos-Mihalopoulos, Andreas, and Sharron FitzGerald. 2008. "From Space Immaterial: The Invisibility of the Lawscape." *Griffith Law Review* 17 (2): 438–53.

Pound, Roscoe. 1910. "Law in Books, Law in Action." *American Law Review* 44 (1): 12–36.

Pruitt, Lisa R. 2006. "Rural Rhetoric." *Connecticut Law Review* 39 (1): 159–240.

———. 2007. "Toward a Feminist Theory of the Rural." *Utah Law Review* 2007 (2): 421–88.

———. 2008a. "Gender, Geography & Rural Justice." *Berkeley Journal of Gender, Law and Justice* 23 (2): 338–91.

———. 2008b. "Place Matters: Domestic Violence and Rural Difference." *Wisconsin Journal of Law, Gender and Society* 23 (2): 347–416.

———. 2009a. "The Forgotten Fifth: Rural Youth and Drug Abuse." *Stanford Law and Policy Review* 20 (2): 359–404.

———. 2009b. "Latina/os, Locality and Law in the Rural South." *Harvard Latino Law Review* 12: 135–69.

———. 2011. "Human Rights and Development for India's Rural Remnant: A Capabilities-Based Assessment." *UC Davis Law Review* 44 (3): 803–57.

Pruitt, Lisa R., and Beth A. Colgan. 2010. "Justice Deserts: Spatial Inequality and Local Funding of Indigent Defense." *Arizona Law Review* 52 (2): 219–316.

Radeloff, V. C., R. B. Hammer, S. I. Stewart, J. S. Fried, S. S. Holcomb, and J. F. McKeefry. 2005. "The Wildland-Urban Interface in the United States." *Ecological Applications* 15 (3): 799–805.

Ramsey, Carolyn B. 2006. "Intimate Homicide: Gender and Crime Control, 1880–1920." *University of Colorado Law Review* 77 (1): 101–91.

Rank, Mark R., and Thomas Hirschl. 1998. "A Rural-Urban Comparison of Welfare Exits: The Importance of Population Density." *Rural Sociology* 53 (2): 190–206.

Rich, Nathaniel. 2012. "Jungleland." *New York Times Magazine*, March 21, 32–37.

Smith, Neil. 1984. *Uneven Development*. Oxford, UK: Blackwell.

Soja, Edward W. 1985. "The Spatiality of Social Life: Towards a Transformative Retheorisation." In *Social Relations and Spatial Structures*, edited by Derek Gregory and John Urry, 90–127. London: Macmillan.

———. 1989. *Postmodern Geographies: The Reassertion of Space in Critical Social Theory*. Brooklyn, NY: Verso.

———. 2010. *Seeking Spatial Justice*. Minneapolis: University of Minnesota Press.

Stramignoni, Igor. 2004. "Francesco's Devilish Venus: Notations on the Matter of Legal Space." *California Western Law Review* 41 (1): 147–240.

Teather, Elizabeth. 1994. "Contesting Rurality: Country Women's Social and Political Networks." In *Gender and Rurality*, edited by Sarah Whatmore, Terry Marsden, and Phillip Lowe, 31–49. London: D. Fulton.

Thomas, Alexander R., Brian M. Lowe, Gregory M. Fulkerson, and Polly J. Smith. 2011. *Critical Rural Theory: Structure, Space and Culture*. Lanham, MD: Lexington.

Tickamyer, Ann R., and Debra A. Henderson. 2003. "Rural Women: New Roles for the New Century?" In *Challenges for Rural America in the Twenty-First Century*, edited by David L. Brown and Louis E. Swanson, 109–17. University Park: Pennsylvania State University Press.

US Census Bureau. 2012a. *2010 Census Urban and Rural Classification and Urban Area Criteria*. http://www.census.gov/geo/www/ua/2010urbanruralclass.html.

———. 2012b. *State and County Quickfacts: Apache County, Arizona*. http://quickfacts .census.gov/qfd/states/04/04001.html.

Vanegas, Marta R., and Lisa R. Pruitt. 2012. "CEDAW and Rural Development: Empowering Women with Law from the Top Down, Activism from the Bottom Up." *University of Baltimore Law Review* 41 (2): 263–320.

Violence Against Women Act. 1994. 42 U.S.C. § 13925 (21) (Supp. 2008).

Wallace, Janet L., and Lisa R. Pruitt. 2012. "Judging Parents, Judging Place: Poverty, Rurality and Termination of Parental Rights." *Missouri Law Review* 77 (1): 95–147.

Websdale, Neil. 1998. *Rural Woman Battering and the Justice System: An Ethnography.* Thousand Oaks, CA: Sage.

Weisheit, Ralph A., and Joseph Donnermeyer. 2000. "Change and Continuity in Crime in Rural America." In *Criminal Justice 2000: The Nature of Crime: Continuity and Change*, edited by Gary LaFree, 309–57. Washington, DC: National Institute on Justice.

Weisheit, Ralph A., David N. Falcone, and L. Edward Wells. 2006. *Crime and Policing in Rural and Small Town America.* Long Grove, IL: Waveland.

Wilkinson, Kenneth P. 1991. *The Community in Rural America.* Westport, CT: Greenwood.

Williams, Raymond. 1973. *The City and the Country.* New York: Oxford University Press.

Williams, Timothy. 2012. "Higher Crime and Fewer Charges on Indian Land." *New York Times*, February 20.

Willits, Fern K., R. C. Bealer, and D. M. Crider. 1982. "Persistence of Rural/Urban Differences." In *Rural Society in the US: Issues for the 1980s*, edited by Don A. Dillman and Daryl J. Hobbs, 69–76. Boulder, CO: Westview.

Woods, Michael. 2011. *Rural.* Abingdon, UK: Routledge.

# 9 RULES OF ENGAGEMENT

## *The Spatiality of Judicial Review*

*Melinda Harm Benson*

## OPEN SESAME!

In the story of Ali Baba and the Forty Thieves in *One Thousand and One Nights*, this magical phrase opens the mouth of a cave in which forty thieves have hidden treasure (Haupt 1926). Legal systems and processes have their own incantations that must be uttered, acts that must be performed, and conditions that must be present, before the doors of the courthouse open for prospective plaintiffs. Referred to here as the "rules of engagement," they are the operational tenets of litigation that create the space in which the various actors—plaintiffs, defendants, judges, juries, expert witnesses, and so on—perform within the highly formalized legal arena that is the courtroom. The rules of engagement established for occupying space within contemporary legal systems have implications for many, if not all, investigations into spaces of law.

Even when a given situation is seemingly "outside" of the formal legal system, the rules of engagement are there—often framing the way we perceive it. In Michael Smith's work (Chapter 6) on law and war, for example, we see the forces of jurisdictional boundaries that delineate where (if anywhere) the United States can be held accountable for war crimes. In Alexandre (Sandy) Kedar's (Chapter 4) comparative analysis of the legal ordering of conquest and settlement, there are underlying issues associated with the value of precedent and procedure that define the various contours of civil versus common law legal systems. And in David Delaney's (Chapter 10) investigation of "work," the felt experiences of the workplace are often conditioned by the extent to which workers may (or may not) enter legal spaces where claims against sexual and racial harassment, unsafe safety conditions, and other cases can be brought. The law's legitimating recognition of these claims is infused with formalized evidentiary burdens that exclude many workers from entering legal spaces that will uphold civil rights.

This chapter explores the idea that litigation is *itself* a space creating process that has, to date, commanded little attention from investigators of legal geographies.

Understanding the spatiality of legal processes highlights one of the many relational qualities of law. The rules of engagement are not essentialist edicts that define the courtroom setting. As the examination of one narrow subset of these rules will demonstrate, the rules of engagement are dynamic, unfolding processes that both expand and contract formal legal spaces. As such, they reflect corresponding cultural assumptions about privilege and authority. Understanding the rules of engagement and their productions can provide tools and resources for those seeking to understand the power formal legal processes play in determining how we perceive and understand virtually any investigation related to the spaces of law.

The rules of engagement examined in this chapter are those that dictate when citizens can bring federal court cases in the United States that challenge *government conduct*. These rules are often referred to as limits on "judicial review" or "justiciability." In theory, they are designed to keep the judicial branch from making decisions and enacting policies that should be left to the executive and legislative branches of government. As we will see, however, the judiciary also serves as a gatekeeper—judges are among the most privileged legal actors and hold an inordinate amount of power to construct and police the spaces they occupy.

More specifically, this chapter investigates the role of judicial review in challenging government actions related to natural resource and environmental management. Although the examples here involve environmental cases, it is important to acknowledge that these rules are also a key factor in many other realms in which government conduct is often challenged, including immigration and deportation (Marksity 2008), labor disputes (Estreicher 1982), and access to Social Security and other public benefit programs (Verkuil and Lubbers 2003). Often described as "procedural" as opposed to "substantive" aspects of the law, these legal requirements tend to operate under a veil of neutrality. In reality, the rules of engagement—which range from jurisdictional limitations to burdens of proof—reflect cultural values and consolidations of power worthy of examination.

There are a number of recent decisions made by the US Supreme Court that focus on the issue of when a case is appropriate and/or ready for judicial review. They include highly complex and interrelated questions regarding whether the dispute is "ripe" for review, whether the plaintiffs have the "standing" necessary to bring a case in court, and whether there is a "final agency action" that can be judged. This chapter explores three US Supreme Court cases with precedent-setting influence in the regard, *Ohio Forestry Association Inc. v. Sierra Club*, *Lujan v. Defenders of Wildlife*, and *Norton v. Southern Utah Wilderness Alliance*. Combined, an investigation into the pragmatics of these holdings provides an opportunity to conceptualize litigation as space. The chapter begins by situating itself within the current and evolving literature of legal geography. It then provides some necessary background on judicial review and how it produces legal spaces. An examination of the aforementioned cases then demonstrates the nature in which these seemingly "procedural" rules are playing an increasingly dispositive role in environmental litigation, policing the production of legal space and who gets to enter it. Finally, the chapter provides some suggestions regarding how to foster further investigations into these and other rules of engagement and their associated spatialities.

## RELATIONAL QUALITIES OF LAW AND SPACE

It is now widely acknowledged within the field of legal geography that the law is more than a forum for engaging in social disputes and adjudicating claims; it reflects a dynamic relationship between spatial forms and social discourses with corresponding productions of control, authority, and power. Those interested in understanding contemporary productions of space can use legal geography to critically examine these relationships and then consider how to tweak, shift, and change them. For the purposes of rethinking the legal geography project, it is important to note two observations related to the progression of this literature identified by Delaney (2010) in his book *The Spatial, the Legal and the Pragmatics of World-Making: Nomospheric Investigations*. First, he notes that much of this work can be aptly described as situating "the legal" within certain spatial contexts, or, conversely, locating "the spatial" aspects of legal rulings, controversies, and so on. Delaney argues that, while valuable, this work has resulted in a piece-meal, fragmented approach with no common ground on which to build theory. He explains: "the result is analogous to economists investigating 'the economic' one transaction at a time" (Delaney 2010, 12).

The second observation relates to the continued bifurcation of law and geography or law and space into two separate but overlapping realms. Delaney notes that much of the legal geography literature is still trapped in this binary. The law-geography binary is inherently limiting because it automatically restrains investigations within familiar disciplinary boundaries and, along with those boundaries, unnecessarily static lines of inquiry: "Thinking about space and law in these conventional ways promotes a conventional way of understanding their relationship as analogous to (or some version of) some of the ruling antimonies or dichotomies of modernist thought" (Delaney 2010, 13). He argues that there is a need to jump out of this "cognitive centrifugal force that impedes investigation of the richness of mutual constitutivity of the legal and the spatial" (13).

These and other factors contribute to the observation made by Delaney and others (see Blomley 1989; Philippopoulos-Mihalopoulos 2010) that the legal geography project has stalled. "While the quantity and sophistication of work in legal geography has increased significantly in the past 15 years, there is, at the moment, a palpable sense of impasse" (Delaney 2010, 12). In his book, Delaney attempts to address these problems by embracing "the nomosphere" as an investigative framework that provides a common language and approach—a possible pathway beyond the law and space bifurcation. Delaney's "nomosphere" refers to "the cultural-material environs that are constituted by the reciprocal materialization of 'the legal' and the legal signification of the 'sociospatial,' and the practical, performative engagements through which such constitutive moments happen and unfold" (25). Delaney proposes that "the concept 'nomosphere' is useful in so far as it successfully holds together the sociospatial and the sociolegal while foregrounding the dynamic interplay of forms of social meaning and materiality; these are implicated in the historical constitution of social-relational power and situated, embodied experience" (26–27). This new, nomospheric approach is put forward in hopes of at least loosening and perhaps even eliminating the troublesome law/geography binary. By instead investigating the mutual constitutivity of law and space, the emergence of law's world-making capacities begins to appear. World-making in the sense that sociolegal events, processes, and projects change the material world in both obvious and obscure ways.

Delaney describes the legal actors we call judges and lawyers as nomospheric technicians. They engage "legal moves" that advance or repudiate lines of argument in ways that have world-making consequences. Delaney (2010, 195) does not dwell on the courtroom, arguing that the "overwhelming amount of world-making happens elsewhere." Instead, he encourages nomospheric investigations of "everyday" situations—the supermarket, the school, the bedroom, and the like. I argue here that the rules of engagement are the legal realms' version of the "everyday." By providing the contextual framework for the production of legal space, these rules dictate who gets inside the realm of official legalities and can participate in the many and various world-making enterprises that take place in the courtroom. The procedural rules examined here provide just one of many potential examples of "everyday" aspects of litigation that are almost always assumed and rarely critically examined.

To date, few scholars have taken on litigation itself as space. Deborah Martin and her colleagues make this point in their review of the literature, noting that "legal geography can overlook the questions about the process of legalization itself" including how claims are made and by whom, and what processes shape the roles and capacities of various actors. In their work, they examine the role, in particular, of lawyers in the production of space, observing that "lawyers remain largely unseen in . . . accounts of legal interpretation and enactment" (Martin, Scherr, and

City 2012, 179). In his consideration of legal rulings related to boundary disputes involving rivers as lines of demarcation, Blomley (2008) studied the role of proof in boundary disputes. He notes the function of "experts" and the related position of science in legal disputes and identifies the sense in which "scientists and judges swim in different rivers" (183).

In Sandy Kedar's (2003, 425) examination of dispossession of native populations and the establishment settler states, he notes the crucial role the legal system itself plays in the transfer of lands in a way that simultaneously conceals and legitimates the new lands regime:

> Formalistic legal tools play a meaningful role in such legitimization. . . . Intricate legal tools and conventions serve as central instruments in defining and altering laws concerning natives' rights. These rules, embedded with a heavy dose of professional, technical and seemingly scientific language and methods, conceal the violent restructuring with an image of inevitability and neutrality. Procedural rules and obstacles such as time limits, and questions of jurisdiction and standing; rules of evidence such as admissibility and weight, presumptions and burdens of proof; the manipulation of past precedents and of legal categories, have the effect of dispossessing indigenous populations without even admitting the dispossession.

In rethinking the legal geography project, there is value in examining the dynamic interplay among the diverse roles of various nomospheric technicians and the conceptual rivers in which they take place. As we will see, these nomospheric technicians make legal meanings in ways that are mutually constitutive with the material world.

## JUDICIAL REVIEW AS A RULE OF ENGAGEMENT

The concept of judicial review arises from the basic institutional structure of the federal government in the United States. Often described as a "separation of powers," the government is divided into three branches—the judicial, the legislative, and the executive. In theory, each branch has its own role to play in the task of governing the nation: the legislative creates laws, the executive implements and enforces them, and the judiciary ensures that the other two branches are conducting themselves in accordance with statutory and constitutional provisions. In actual practice, of course, there is a much more complex, overlapping, and even contested suite of relationships involved with this system. Of interest here is the space the judiciary carved out for itself soon after the ratification of the nation's constitution. In the seminal Supreme Court case *Marbury v. Madison* the Court formed the basis for the exercise of judicial review under Article III of the US

Constitution. Chief Justice John Marshall officially declared that the judicial branch has the power to declare as unlawful any actions by the other two branches with regard to the constitutionality of government conduct.[1] Today, the judicial system still holds this ultimate "trump card" with regard not only to constitutional provisions but also to many laws passed by Congress, resulting from the fact that the legislative branch is increasingly incapable of passing new laws and amending others in response to unwelcome judicial interpretations of its enactments (Klyza and Sousa 2007). This later aspect of the judiciary's power will be revisited in an examination of its world-making capacities.

With regard to judicial review of actions taken by the executive branch, there are two main elements: the *standard* of review and its *scope*. The standard of review establishes the level of scrutiny the judiciary can bring to bear on actions taken by federal agencies, while the scope of judicial review relates the types of activities that are subject to scrutiny from the judicial branch. The main statutory provision outlining the general parameters of both of these constraints is the Administrative Procedures Act (APA). While subject to constitutional limitations, the APA generally determines the level of scrutiny brought to bear on state conduct, and it establishes a standard that is often deferential to agencies. Generally speaking, an agency's action is held unlawful only if it is deemed by the Court to be "arbitrary and capricious, an abuse of discretion, or otherwise not in accordance with the law."[2] Moreover, in *Chevron v. Natural Resources Defense Council*, the Supreme Court determined that if a statute being administered by an agency is ambiguous with respect to a specific issue or provision, the courts will defer to the agency's reasonable interpretation of the statute. This deference to agencies (as the primary agents of the executive branch) reflects the view that agencies have expertise resulting from their statutory duties and experience with implementation of the law (Glicksman and Levy 2010). With regard to scope of judicial review, federal court jurisdiction is confined in several ways. Under the APA, courts may review agency conduct under two circumstances: (1) where there is a "final agency action" that has been taken by the agency and (2) where it is necessary to compel an action that is "unlawfully withheld or unreasonably delayed."[3]

Because so much of environmental enforcement in the United States comes from legal actions against the government brought by nongovernmental environmental groups, environmental cases have played a large role in establishing precedent-setting cases that define the parameters of both the scope and the standard of review under the APA. The important gatekeeping role of this statute means that much of public interest environmental enforcement involves a sophisticated understanding and engagement of administrative law and its associated limitations and requirements.[4]

There are also various constitutional limitations on a court's ability to review agency actions. Article III limits the role of the federal judiciary by confining its jurisdiction to "cases or controversies." This limitation ensures that plaintiffs are seeking adjudication of an actual dispute, as opposed to attempting to engage the court in a legislative role. The Supreme Court has interpreted Article III to bar suits in federal courts seeking advisory opinions regarding hypothetical disputes (Mank 2010). As is examined in detail here, one element of the Article III limitation is the standing requirement. Prospective plaintiffs must establish standing by proving that they have been or will be injured by the challenged conduct in order to assure the Court that they have a sufficient stake in the outcome of an actual dispute. There are also limits on judicial review that are often at issue in environmental cases that are related to the temporal dimension of the government's conduct. They include doctrines related to whether the controversy is "ripe" (i.e., not ready for adjudication) or, conversely, "moot" (i.e., no longer an issue). Each of these rules of engagement can be thought of as forming a layer that shapes the functional contours of litigation—creating a dynamic and overlapping set of boundaries that vary over time in terms of their function, shape, and permeability.

In summary, judicial review can be seen as the mechanism that allows the judiciary to police the congressional and executive spaces of power and control, with the Court granting itself the discretion to condition its own incursions. And while the concept of judicial review is not new, it can be argued that it is being used by the judiciary in new ways. During the past two decades, legal moves have been made that are consolidating power in the executive branch and insulating government action from judicial review, particularly in the context of environmental cases.[5] The ripeness, standing, and final agency action requirements are now examined using the three main Supreme Court cases already noted to explore their corresponding spatialities.

## Ripeness

In recent years, the ripeness doctrine has gained great significance in the realm of environmental enforcement. The first main case that demarcates an era is *Ohio Forestry Association Inc. v. Sierra Club*. In *Ohio Forestry*, environmentalists challenged the US Forest Service's land resource management plan for the Wayne National Forest, arguing that it allowed too much logging—including significant amounts of clear-cutting—in violation of the National Forest Management Act's requirement to manage national forests for multiple use and sustained yield. The plan called for logging more than two-thirds of the area (approximately 126,000 acres, or 197 square miles) and authorized logging approximately 75 million board feet of lumber over ten years. The Forest Service estimated that the plan would lead to logging on about 8,000 acres (12.5 square miles.) over ten years, with about 5,000 acres (7.8 square miles) involving clear-cutting.

In *Ohio Forestry*, the Court began its analysis by referencing leading Supreme Court case regarding ripeness, *Abbott Laboratories v. Gardner*. In that seminal case, Judge Harlan described the rationale behind the ripeness doctrine:

> [I]ts basic rationale is to prevent the courts, through avoidance of premature adjudication, from entangling themselves in abstract disagreements over administrative policies, and also to protect the agencies from judicial interference until an administrative decision has been formalized and its effects felt in a concrete way by the challenging parties. The problem is best seen in a twofold aspect, requiring us to evaluate both the fitness of the issues for judicial decision and the hardship to the parties of withholding court consideration. (*Abbott Laboratories* 1967, 148–49)[6]

In nomospheric terms, the ripeness requirement plays a policing role; by ensuring that a case is ripe, the judiciary seeks to occupy its appropriate constitutional space and be certain that it has the necessary context to make a ruling.[7]

In the case of *Ohio Forestry*, environmental groups won their case on the merits both before the trial court and on appeal to the Sixth Circuit. Their victory, however, was short lived. A unanimous Supreme Court vacated on ripeness grounds. The Court first set forth its test for determining ripeness, which expanded the earlier *Abbott Laboratories* test:

> In deciding whether an agency's decision is, or is not, ripe for judicial review, the Court has examined both the "fitness of the issues for judicial decision" and the "hardship to the parties of withholding court consideration." To do so in this case, we must consider: (1) whether delayed review would cause hardship to the plaintiffs; (2) whether judicial intervention would inappropriately interfere with further administrative action; and (3) whether the courts would benefit from further factual development of the issues presented. (*Ohio Forestry* 1998, 733, citations omitted).

Using this framework, the Court determined that the case was not justiciable because "although the Plan sets logging goals, selects the areas of the forest that are suited to timber production and determines which probable methods of timber harvest are appropriate, the Plan itself did not authorize the cutting of any trees" (*Ohio Forestry* 1998, 729). Applying its three-part test, the Court determined that (1) the plan did not inflict significant practical harm upon Sierra Club's interests; (2) immediate judicial review directed at the lawfulness of logging and clear-cutting could hinder agency efforts to refine its policies; and (3) review of the Sierra Club's claims regarding logging and clear-cutting at the planning stage would require time-consuming judicial consideration of the details of an elaborate, technically based plan without benefit of the factual detail a particular logging proposal could provide.

In ruling that land use plans are in and of themselves not ripe for judicial review, the Court insulates the US Forest Service from scrutiny at a crucial decision-making stage—the point at which the agency determines the overarching management paradigm for its lands. Note the impracticality of this holding. From the perspective of administrative efficiency, use of the ripeness doctrine in this context is wasteful. The Sierra Club won its argument on the merits, but rather than allowing for course-correcting major legal errors at the initial stages in the government's implementation of the law, the Court requires delay and forces a piece-meal, fragmented approach to environmental enforcement.[8] The earlier rulings by the lower courts indicate not only that there was a sufficient factual basis for making a legal judgment but also that failure to adjudicate the case almost certainly leaves in place a forest plan that violates the law. By rendering land use plans unreviewable at the planning stage, the Court delays any meaningful judicial review of the agency's action prior to implementation (Stegmaier 1998).

As a result of *Ohio Forestry*, there was an increasing consolidation of power to the executive branch. It also highlights the role of temporality as an element of legal space. In the field of legal geography, there is a growing sense of the need to reintegrate the temporal and the spatial. "Temporality is an integral dimension of the work of jurisdiction, then. Future studies of the governance of governance will need to highlight and analyze the different 'whens' of governance—the temporal dimensions of the powers-knowledges that are arduously kept from clashing by the hard work of jurisdiction" (Valverde 2009, 155). As the Benda-Beckmanns emphasize in their description of the anthropological perspective on temporalities of space (Chapter 1), there is a need to explore the ways in which legal spaces appear and disappear, depending in part on the kind of legal system that constitutes the space.

## Standing

The next aspect of judicial review involves the constitutional requirement that the plaintiff has standing. As discussed already, Article III of the US Constitution limits the judiciary to hearing only "cases or controversies." The standing requirement ensures this by allowing plaintiffs to bring suit only when they can prove that the issue they seek to adjudicate is an actual dispute, the resolution of which will redress injuries suffered by the plaintiff as a result of the challenged conduct. It ensures that courts are not being called on to make a judicial ruling where no controversy between two parties actually exists and subsequently playing an inappropriately legislative role. It also ensures that the plaintiffs bringing the litigation are actually opposed to the government's action and will rigorously defend their position in court. There are three main elements to the standing requirement. First, the plaintiff must establish that he or she has suffered or will imminently suffer an injury. Second, the alleged injury must be fairly traceable to (i.e., caused by) the challenged conduct. Finally, there must be a likelihood that the injury can be redressed by a favorable court decision. These last two requirements can be viewed as part of a causal chain of events, with traceability focusing on the link between the challenged conduct and the plaintiff's injury and redress focusing on the connection between the alleged injury and judicial relief (Glicksman and Levy 2010, 1069). In other words, both require a particularized temporal and spatial nomospheric performance.

Early cases interpreting this requirement placed a relatively low burden on plaintiffs seeking to bring environmental actions. Two cases marking this era, *Sierra Club v. Morton* and *United States v. Students Challenging Regulatory Agency Procedures (SCRAPP)*. In these cases, the Court interpreted the scope of cognizable injuries broadly to include not only economic injury but also impairment of recreational and aesthetic enjoyment. In *Sierra Club v. Morton* (1972), environmentalists sought to challenge the US Forest Service's grant of a permit to Walt Disney Enterprises to develop a ski resort and summer vacation area in California's Mineral King Valley, located within Sequoia National Park. While Sierra Club was denied standing because it failed to allege that any of its members actually used or planned to use the area for recreational or other purposes, the Court's larger holding included recognition that impairment of recreational values, even if those values are widely shared, were injuries sufficient to establish standing.[9] In *SCRAPP*, a group of law students brought suit against the Interstate Trade Commission, claiming that the agency failed to conduct the necessary environmental impact review under the National Environmental Policy Act for its proposal to levy a 2.5 percent surcharge on railroad freight rates. The group argued that the subsequent increase in shipping costs would increase litter and discourage the use of recyclable materials, thereby adversely affecting their use and enjoyment of the parks and streams near the area of Washington DC, where they lived. The Court held that the group did have standing, even though its alleged recreational and aesthetic injuries were on the basis of "an attenuated line of causation" in relation to the challenged conduct (*SCRAPP* 1973, 688).

More recently, the Supreme Court has begun construing the standing space narrowly and thereby placing a higher burden on plaintiffs. Perhaps the main case in this regard is *Lujan v. Defenders of Wildlife*. It involved the scope of the Endangered Species Act's (ESA) "consultation" requirement. Under Section 7 of the Endangered Species Act, all federal agencies are required to consult with the appropriate federal wildlife agency to ensure that their actions are not likely to jeopardize the continued existence of a threatened or endangered species or result in destruction or adverse modification of its critical habitat. The consultation process applies to all federal actions, broadly interpreted by the courts to include not only direct construction projects but also the granting of licenses and contracts and the promulgation of regulations (Sullins 2001). In *Lujan*, environmentalists challenged the US Fish and Wildlife Service's regulations exempting US international projects from Section 7. The environmentalists provided as proof of standing the legal declarations of two of its members who alleged that they had traveled to Egypt and Sri Lanka to study ESA-listed species and that the federal activities undertaken in those countries would accelerate the decline of those species toward extinction. Writing for the majority, Justice Scalia concluded that the alleged injury was not sufficiently "actual and imminent" to meet the injury-in-fact requirement because, although the plaintiffs had visited the foreign countries at issue in the past and planned to do so again in the future, there was no evidence of any specific plans for future visits. The Court stated that such "some day intentions—without any description of concrete plans, or indeed even any specification of when the some day will be—do not support a finding of the 'actual or imminent' injury that our cases require" (*Lujan* 1992, 564). Without an established, prospective temporal link back to the contested legal space, the space necessary for bringing the court challenge did not exist.

The Court's holding that there was insufficient injury-in-fact formed the basis of its decision to deny standing. It is worth noting, however, a portion of Justice Scalia's opinion that did not command a majority.[10] Justice Scalia argued that the environmentalists failed to demonstrate the third element of standing—redressability—because there was no proof that requiring consultation on foreign projects would consequently affect the foreign project in a manner that would actually mitigate the harm to listed species:

> The most obvious problem in the present case is redressability. Since the agencies funding the projects were not parties to the case, the District Court could accord relief only against the Secretary: He could be ordered to revise his regulation to require consultation for foreign projects. But this would not remedy respondents' alleged injury unless the funding agencies were bound by the Secretary's

regulation, which is very much an open question. Whereas in other contexts the ESA is quite explicit as to the Secretary's controlling authority . . . with respect to consultation the initiative, and hence arguably the initial responsibility for determining statutory necessity, lies with the agencies. (*Lujan* 1992, 569)[11]

Although this reasoning did not command a majority opinion and therefore has no precedential value, Justice Scalia's approach here is significant for two reasons. First, it provides a window into one of his primary nomospheric projects that is discussed in more detail below—shielding the executive branch from judicial review. Second, it provides agencies with a map showing them how to insulate their actions from judicial review. Significantly in the case of *Lujan*, the agency had reversed its initial position regarding whether its regulations were binding on US governmental activities in international contexts.

Agencies are increasingly taking advantage of this reasoning. The subsequent case *Summers v. Earth Island Institute* provides insight into the legacy of the *Lujan* decision in this respect. The case involved a challenge to the Forest Service's decision to exempt from environmental review and administrative appeal a "salvage sale" of timber on 238 acres of federal land that was scheduled after a fire in the area. The decision to allow the sale without the standard environmental review and procedural safeguards was based on the agency's interpretation of Forest Service Decisionmaking and Appeals Reform Act.[12] Before the case was adjudicated, the Forest Service settled with environmentalists with regard to the specific timber sale in question, but the case moved forward challenging the agency's interpretation of the statute. As with *Ohio Forestry*, the plaintiffs won their legal challenge on the merits in the lower courts. The US District Court invalidated Forest Service's regulations and issued nationwide injunction against their application, and the Ninth Circuit confirmed that decision on appeal. The Supreme Court, however, overruled on the basis of lack of standing. Writing for a narrow majority, Justice Scalia held that the plaintiffs lacked standing to challenge the regulations still at issue absent a live dispute over a concrete application of those regulations. "We know of no precedent for the proposition that when a plaintiff has sued to challenge the lawfulness of certain action or threatened action but has settled that suit, he retains standing to challenge the basis for that action (here, the regulation in the abstract), apart from any concrete application that threatens imminent harm to his interests" (*Summers* 2009, 494). *Summer Earth Island Institute* allows agencies to game the system—it settled the case and consequently evaded review.[13]

The standing requirement can be thought of as a case within a case, with the necessary spatial and temporal nomospheric performances necessary to establish

standing playing a crucial role regarding the ability to challenge government conduct. The standing requirement itself demands of plaintiffs the production of a
specific type of nomospheric project—one that creates the power to challenge the
legitimacy of state action.[14]

## Compelling Agency Action

The final aspect of judicial review examined here relates to the issue of *compel-
ling* agency action (i.e., when plaintiffs can force agencies to perform their statutory duties). As noted earlier, the APA allows for judicial review not only of "final
agency actions" but also of "actions unlawfully withheld or unreasonably delayed."
In general, it is quite difficult to force an agency to act (Heckel 2004). Lack of funding and other limitations can be successfully used as excuses for failures to act. In
terms of environmental enforcement, the most recent and highly significant case
in this regard is *Norton v. Southern Utah Wilderness Alliance.*

*Norton* involved another legal challenge to a federal agency's resource management plan. This time, however, an attempt was made to compel the federal
agency to enforce some of the provisions contained within the plan. The federal
defendant, the Bureau of Land Management (BLM), is responsible for thirty-three
million acres of land in Utah. The agency created a land use plan in accordance
with the Federal Land Policy and Management Act. This law requires, among
other provisions, that the agency identify areas suitable for wilderness protection,
known as Wilderness Study Areas (WSAs). Because wilderness designations are
generally only appropriate when there are no roads or other evidence of significant human impact, the land use plan prohibited the use of motorized vehicles in
these areas. The land use plan also stated that the BLM would monitor off-road
vehicle use to protect the area. Environmental groups sued the BLM, arguing that
the agency had failed to engage in the monitoring of off-road vehicle use as outlined in the plan. They argued that, because the agency's own regulations stated
that "all future resource management authorizations and actions . . . and subsequent more detailed or specific planning, shall conform to the approved plan,"
the agency's failure to monitor was reviewable under the APA" (*Norton* 2004, 57).

Writing for the majority, Justice Scalia held that the land use plan did not create
a legally binding commitment to monitor and therefore the promised monitoring could not be compelled under the APA. He noted that, while the BLM could
not take actions *inconsistent* with the plan, it could not be *compelled* to take action
under the plan, which was essentially a statement of present and future uses and
priorities: "Quite unlike a specific statutory commitment . . . a land use plan is
generally a statement of priorities; it guides and constrains actions, but it does not

(at least in the usual case) prescribe them" (*Norton* 2004, 71). Again, we see a legal move that enhances agency discretion. By holding that the content of land use plans is generally unenforceable, the Court provides the executive branch with an enormous amount of discretion. Just as with the Court's ruling in *Ohio Forestry*, lack of legal accountability at the land use planning stage shifts the legal focus to site-specific projects. It also makes it more difficult to force agencies to meet their commitments, thus allowing the agency to strategically shift its actions and inter-pretations of its legal obligations as necessary, on a case-by-case basis.

Also of significance are the ways in which legal space is contingent upon a pro-cedural obstacle that bears little resemblance to the underlying substance or valid-ity of the plaintiffs' argument. The issue becomes not whether the state's action complies with its obligations but instead whether—on the basis of a combination of temporal and spatial factors—the plaintiffs' challenge is sufficiently timed (af-ter the planning stage) and spatially defined (confined to a specific project). So while the rules of engagement are procedural, they produce substantive and spa-tial outcomes. Without entry into legal space, the capacity to protect other spaces (e.g., endangered species habitats, public lands) becomes at best more difficult and at worst impossible.

## POLICING THE PRODUCTION OF LEGAL SPACE

As the cases discussed here illustrate, access to formalized legal space involves the successful negotiation of a number of obstacles that are encountered as (contin-gent) interpretive barriers, with court cases defining and redefining the boundar-ies of the spaces created by these barriers. While grounded in a range of statutory to constitutional requirements, they combine to provide a complex and dynamic set of circumstances and limitations with regard to the performative enactments necessary to invoke judicial review. As such, they police both the access to and the production of legal space. Using the language from Delaney's (2010) nomosphere, the requirements for judicial view can be seen as nomospheric *techniques*—stra-tegic moves by agencies, lawyers, and judges. Judges, as perhaps the most highly regarded and privileged agents of the legal system, use the nomospheric technique of reviewability to engage in world-making enterprises that are sanctioned by the state. Delaney (2010, 71) explains, "Part of the task of specialized interpre-tive practices engaged in by activists, lawyers and judges requires the ranking and privileging of one interpretation of a nomic setting (and associated power rela-tions) over alternatives such that the force of power is channeled one way rather than another."

The actions of nomospheric technicians are tactical. They seek to assert control and dictate outcomes within judicial settings as a means of advancing and consolidating their various agendas. Federal agency officials also deserve inclusion within the definition of nomospheric technicians in this respect. Charged with the responsibilities of implementing and enforcing laws, they play a critical role with regard to the world-making capacities of not only environmental but also all public welfare statutes. While always considerable, their role is becoming increasingly powerful for several reasons. First, as the cases examined here exemplify, the rules of engagement regarding judicial review are playing an increasingly dispositive role in public-interest environmental litigation (Birdsong 2006; Pierce 1999; Treangen 1991). By placing agency actions outside the space of judicial review, these nomospheric technicians can make decisions with impunity (Kedar 2003; Riles 2005).

A second and closely related factor is the advantage agency administrators as nomospheric technicians are taking of the Court's rulings. Increasingly, agencies are using plans, programmatic environmental assessments, internal memoranda, and informal agency guidance as primary vehicles for operationalizing their statutory duties (Fischman 2007). To date, court decisions regarding the enforceability of these types of management policies which take place outside of formal rule making are mixed. In general, the issue of whether an agency's position is subject to judicial review depends on a number of factors. They include the procedures taken, whether the policies prescribe substantive or interpretive rules, the agency's intent, and the congressional mandate involved (Fischman 2007). By using less formal types of action, the agencies avoid subjecting their statutory interpretations to the notice and comment opportunities afforded to the public as a result of the rule-making procedures under the APA. They also often shield the agency from judicial enforcement actions. The US Department of Interior's approach for implementing a new strategy referred to as "adaptive management" provides one example. Adaptive management is a new approach being taken by many federal agencies engaged in natural resource management that provides a more flexible and iterative approach to agency decision making. In 2007, the Secretary of the Interior issued an order requiring agency officials to use adaptive management whenever possible. That same year, the agency released a "technical guide" (revised in 2009) to "aid U.S. Department of the Interior managers and practitioners in determining when and how to apply adaptive management" (Williams, Szaro, and Shapiro 2009, v). The only formal regulatory provision related to adaptive management, however, is in the agency's regulations for its environmental impact assessment procedures under the National Environmental Policy Act, where it states that the agency "should use adaptive management, as appropriate, particularly in circumstances where long-term impacts may be uncertain and future monitoring will be needed to make adjustments in subsequent implementation decisions" (43 CFR § 46.145). This approach leaves the agency with a great deal of discretion regarding how and when adaptive management is "appropriate." At the same time, the agency's approach to adaptive management is becoming increasingly significant to its substantive decision making and management approaches (Ruhl and Fischman 2010). Yet the validity of the approach and the adequacy of the agency's actions with regard to adaptive management are not likely to be reviewable by the courts (Ruhl and Fischman 2010).

The Supreme Court's recent rulings indicate that it is becoming more difficult to hold agencies accountable for the positions they take relative to their statutory duties. Indeed, some agencies are actually including disclaimers of judicial reviewability when issuing agency guidance (Fischman 2007). By shielding the agency rationale upon which agency decisions are based, the Court has significantly undermined the capacity for citizen enforcement. In the absence of the ability to challenge agency plans, guidance, and so on, environmental plaintiffs are often left with the statutory language as a basis for enforcement. This language is—especially for cases involving environmental and other public welfare mandates—inevitably vague. In the case of *Ohio Forestry*, for example, the National Forest Management Act set forth a mandate to ensure a "supply of renewable resources from the Nation's public and private forests and rangelands, through analysis of environmental and economic impacts, coordination of multiple use and sustained yield opportunities" (16 U.S.C. 1602), and in the case of *Norton v. Southern Utah Wilderness Alliance*, the Federal Land Management and Policy Act's mandate for BLM lands is to manage them "in a manner that will protect the quality of scientific, scenic, historical, ecological, environmental, air and atmospheric, water resource, and archeological values; that, where appropriate, will preserve and protect certain public lands in their natural condition; that will provide food and habitat for fish and wildlife and domestic animals; and that will provide for outdoor recreation and human occupancy and use" (43 U.S.C. 1701). These mandates are sufficiently broad to allow for a number of management priorities and approaches.

The nomospheric strategies of agencies to insulate themselves from review have not escaped the notice of the lower courts. One observation along these lines was made in 2000 by the DC District Court in *Appalachian Power Company v. Environmental Protection Agency*. The case involved a legal challenge brought by industry plaintiffs regarding an Environmental Protection Agency (EPA) guidance document used by the agency in its regulation of stationary sources of air pollution under the Clean Air Act:

The phenomenon we see in this case is familiar. Congress passes a broadly worded statute. The agency follows with regulations containing broad language, open-ended phrases, ambiguous standards and the like. Then as years pass, the agency issues circulars or guidance or memoranda, explaining, interpreting, defining and often expanding the commands in the regulations. . . . Law is made, without notice and comment, without public participation, and without publication. . . . An agency operating in this way gains a large advantage. It can issue or amend its real rules, i.e., its interpretative rules and policy statements, quickly and inexpensively without following any statutorily prescribed procedures. The agency may also think there is another advantage-immunizing its lawmaking from judicial review. (*Appalachian Power* 2000, 1020)

In its pro-industry ruling, the DC Circuit held that the guidance document broadened the underlying the EPA's rule regarding stationary sources and that its promulgation was therefore improper absent compliance with formal rule-making procedures.

Note the date of this ruling. The case came after *Ohio Forestry* and *Lujan v. Defenders of Wildlife* but before *Norton v. Southern Utah Wilderness Alliance*. It is far from clear whether, at this point in the development of the Supreme Court's case law, it would agree with the DC Circuit's holding. In fact, Nichols (2003) notes that *Appalachian Power* is arguably inconsistent with prior cases and warns litigants not to rely on *Appalachian Power Company* alone when adjudicating the validity of agency documents. Regardless, the motives of these nomospheric technicians involved are clear—agencies are taking steps to actively modulate oversight by structuring their actions in ways that encourage courts to delay or deny review. Clark and Leiter (2011, 1731) argue that "courts should recognize this tactical activity for what it is: executive curtailment of judicial review and, possibly, encroachment on legislative and judicial prerogatives."

Citizen suit litigation is critical to the enforcement of environmental and other public welfare statutes. In his research involving citizen-suit litigation in natural resource management and conservation in the United States, Martin Nie (2008) argues that litigation, while an important environmental enforcement tool in and of itself, also plays a critical role in encouraging less adversarial conservation strategies. The threat of litigation is a nomospheric strategy that is frequently employed, and it is often sufficient motivation for agencies to make sure their actions are within the confines of their statutory mandates. But the current trend of rulings makes it much more difficult to encourage course corrections at the policy-making stage. Moreover, limitations on judicial review are of significant importance because of the current expansions and contractions of the various legal spaces occupied by the three branches of the federal government. While the framers originally intended that Congress would play the primary policy-making role, this branch is increasingly incapable of taking action. As a result, the spaces occupied by courts and agencies are expanding.

Like any nomospheric technician, agency officials seek to consolidate their power and control. The Supreme Court's recent rulings related to justiciability facilitate this. For his part, these actions by agencies in response to court rulings correspondingly advances Justice Scalia's well-documented nomospheric project of both insulating from review and expanding the authorities of the executive branch of government (Stabb 2006). He is the quintessential nomospheric technician, an ultimate expression of a "social actor who has a privileged and productive relationship with the nomosphere" (Delaney 2010, 157). As a result of his influence, the relative roles of the various legal actors are shifting, and there are profound world-making consequences. The policing of who gets to enter legal space can be thought of as a *cascading* world-making enterprise. It is cascading in the sense that access to one space (the courtroom) dictates outcomes in other spaces. In the cases outlined above, some of these spaces are what we call "public lands," that is, 30 percent of the nation's land, almost seven hundred million acres. They present a dramatic illustration in which an investigation into the rules of engagement is critical to understanding the relational qualities of space and law.

## OPPORTUNITIES AND SUGGESTIONS FOR FURTHER WORK REGARDING THE RULES OF ENGAGEMENT

Judicial review dictates both the creation of and access to formalized legal spaces. As such, it provides one example of the crucial role the rules of engagement play as they bound and operationalize this particular nomospheric setting. While this chapter provides a basic overview of a few of the elements of judicial review, there are many other aspects of justiciability equally worthy of consideration and that are similarly infused with cultural assumptions about not only the role of the various branches of government but also who has the right to makes claims in relationship to government action. Examples include judicial review limitations regarding "generalized grievances" and "political questions" (Miller 1990) and the requirement to prove "ongoing violations" of the law (Nauen 1987). This chapter limited itself to environmental cases, but it would be helpful to compare the way the Court constructs its rule of engagement in other contexts. And while environmental litigation often shapes the contours of the legal space referred to as administrative law, it would be interesting to see the gates and barriers to the space of legal litigation in regard to other issues, including civil rights, immigration, privacy, and so on, to map the influences of judicial review across substantive areas of law. Moving beyond issues of justiciability, there are many other rules of engagement that dictate the creation and maintenance of legal space, including questions relating to jurisdiction and choice of law. There are many constitutional, statutory and prudential elements at work.

David Delaney (2010, 7) notes that "how we understand the legal often depends on the, usually unacknowledged, assumptions about social space that we bring to the task." Further inquiry into the unacknowledged assumptions and relative outcomes of the rules of engagement has the potential to advance the legal geography project in new ways. To effectively examine of the spatialities of these various nomospheric techniques, it may prove fruitful for critical legal geographers to partner with law professors who are experts in various rules of engagement, including civil and criminal procedure, immigration law, and so on. These legal scholars have a depth of knowledge related to the development of case law that would be invaluable to someone without a legal background. Conversely, critical geographers can help legal scholars engage in critical investigations in ways that may assist law professors in placing their work within the larger nomospheric settings implicated. With notable exceptions, most legal scholarship (and virtually all legal training) is descriptive and normative. While there are an increasing number of scholars who possess educational backgrounds in both law and geography (see Carr 2012; Osofsky 2010; Ruhl 2005), bringing together experts who see the world via different disciplinary lenses might be particularly synergistic.

## CONCLUSION

The rules of engagement examined here determine not only when the government can be challenged in court but also the level of scrutiny brought to bear on state conduct. Used strategically, they can be used to insulate of agencies from review by judicial branch, and agencies are themselves becoming more sophisticated in crafting their work in ways that evade judicial review. These so-called procedural rules have substantive and correspondingly spatial consequences. Before the underlying concerns involved in environmental cases can be reached, plaintiffs must first gain access to judicial space. For these reasons, the rules of engagement are playing an increasingly dispositive role in public interest environmental litigation. The world-making capacities of these rules are thereby made visible. Lack of access to judicial review, especially when combined with the currently ineffectual nature of Congress, leaves a tremendous amount of power in the remaining branch of government: the executive. Agencies, as a primary vehicle for the actions and policies of the executive branch, are thereby provided a remarkable amount of power and control. Using this power to regulate and manage other spaces (e.g., national forests, critical species habitats) provides a noteworthy example of the mutually constitutive relationships between law and geography.

As an investigative approach, legal geography illuminates the ways in which legal processes and practices are implicated in the production of a host of social spaces and process of what Delaney invokes as world-making. As an institution, law has its own characteristic spaces that are constitutive of its operations. These more formalized and obvious legal spaces, which include not only courts but also legislative chambers, police stations, prisons, and government offices are central places in which law happens. Like others spaces, courtrooms are themselves analyzable in terms of conditions and consequences of access and exclusion. Among the ways in which they are distinctive are that they are putatively spaces for finding (legal) truth and rendering justice. Access implies the possibility of making claims, being heard, accomplishing redress. To that extent these are instrumental spaces.

Parties enter legal space to manifest legal realities that in turn order the world. In this way, these spaces of law are portals through which legal meanings are channeled out into the social world in ways that contours and configures the material world. When access is denied, the search for justice may be truncated and desired interventions blocked. In every adversarial contest only one party will prevail, ideally on substantive grounds. However, access is often restricted for procedural or technical reasons, seemingly without reference to substantive matters, before claims can be made. Legal restrictions and exclusions may be material (metal detectors), performative (armed guards) or even architectural. This chapter closely examines another sort of barrier. It considers courts as discursive or interpretive spaces within which law happens. As such, the barriers themselves can be seen as discursive products of interpretation that can (and should) be contested. Access to the space of law (and therefore the law itself) is policed through the validation of rival narratives that underpin the applicability (or not) of exclusionary doctrines such as ripeness, standing, and final agency action. Exclusion from these spaces may have numerous ramifications beyond the truncation of the search for justice. Moreover, these exclusions tend to build on and reinforce each other, as the availability of alternative interpretations becomes increasingly remote. By limiting the occasions for judicial review, state actions are shielded from scrutiny and insulated from citizen participation. For these reasons, litigation is itself a space worthy of further investigation.

## NOTES

1. Judge Marshall rejected the argument that the exceptions clause of Article III allows Congress to remove certain types of cases from the Supreme Court's jurisdiction, noting

that there would be in effect no separation of powers if Congress could remove the Court's original jurisdiction.

2. 467 U.S. 837 (1984); 5 U.S.C. § 706(a)(2). Note this is the standard for actions of broad and prospective applicability, known as "rules." When federal agencies take actions with regard to specific actions made on a case-by-case basis (e.g., in the determination of Social Security benefits), the standard of review for these adjudications requires the agency to support its decision with "substantial evidence."

3. 5 U.S.C. § 704. It is important to note that several environmental laws are self-enforcing in the sense that they contain statutory provisions allowing review of certain actions or failures to act. These "citizen suit" provisions are embedded in the Clean Air Act and Clean Water Act, and other laws and allow judicial review without invoking the APA. Other statutes, however, perhaps most notably the National Environmental Policy Act, rely heavily on the APA as the gateway to judicial review.

4. Prudential requirements are jurisdictional limits that the judiciary places *on itself* that are not specifically grounded in any specific constitutional or statutory framework (Glicksman and Levy 2010).

5. While not confined to environmental cases, many of the Supreme Court's rulings regarding judicial review come from this area of law, resulting from the sheer volume of case law in this area (Glicksman and Levy 2010).

6. In *Abbott Laboratories*, Abbott and thirty-six other drug companies sued the Food and Drug Administration, challenging the agency's decision to require all products to contain the name of the generic drug on their labels. The Court ruled that, because the rule was not yet in effect and none of the plaintiffs had been harmed the case was not ripe for review. In most cases, there are now statutory provisions that allow pre-enforcement review. For more information regarding the history of the ripeness requirement following *Abbott Laboratories*, see Floren (2001).

7. The ripeness doctrine involves both prudential and constitutional limits on judicial review.

8. This is particularly notable given that, in other contexts (e.g., constitutional challenges), the Court recognizes of the value of facial versus applied challenges. A facial challenge is one that does not provide specific facts but instead alleges that the law itself is unconstitutional, independent of what specific facts might be presented to the court. In *United States v. Salerno* the Court described this as a "no set of circumstances" test for facial challenges, meaning that regardless of application, the law itself is unconstitutional (Kreit 2010). The facts of *Ohio Forestry* do not present a "facial" challenge per se, but the reasoning is the same; there is no need to wait for government to act illegally, when challenging the government's position "on its face" would compel the necessary changes in planning in order to comply with the law.

9. In his famous dissent, Justice Douglas argued that the environment itself should be able to bring suit in order to ensure its own protection: "The critical question of 'standing' would be simplified and also put neatly in focus if we . . . allowed environmental issues to be litigated . . . in the name of the inanimate object about to be despoiled, defaced, or invaded by roads and bulldozers and where injury is the subject of public outrage. This suit would therefore be more properly labeled as Mineral King v. Morton" (*Morton* 1972, 742).

10. Supreme Court decisions include three types orientations with regard to the Court's opinion: majority opinions, concurrences, and dissents. The majority opinion is shared by

a majority of the judges and is therefore the official holding of the Court. It is enforceable and has precedential value. Concurrences often join in only part of the majority opinion and detail which portions are joined and why. Dissents are just that—they do not agree with the majority and judges use them to explain why they think the majority is wrong. In the case of *Lujan*, Justice Scalia authored the Court's opinion, but his argument on redressability (part III-B) was not joined by a majority. Justice Kennedy filed an opinion concurring in part and concurring in the judgment in which Justice Souter joined. Justice Stevens filed an opinion concurring in the judgment. Finally, Justice Blackmun dissented and filed an opinion in which Justice O'Connor joined. While it is not uncommon for members of the Court to have a variety of relationships to the final decision, it is important to emphasize that only the portions of the decision that command a majority become "law," and so Justice Kennedy, O'Connor and others who tend to author narrow concurrences are often considered the most influential (Lazarus 2005).

11. The agencies actually engaged in the dam project where not parties to the case because the focus of the environmentalists' challenges was on the US Fish and Wildlife Service's policy on consultation.

12. The statute provided exemptions for fire-rehabilitation activities on areas of less than 4,200 acres and salvage-timber sales of 250 acres or less.

13. This case is better known for the Court's rejection organizational standing based on the statistical probability that some members of a plaintiff organization will likely be harmed in the near future by the defendant's future actions (Mank 2010).

14. A detailed examination of the development of standing case law is beyond the scope of this chapter. It should be noted, however, that the Court continues to expand and contract standing space.

## LIST OF CASES

*Abbott Laboratories v. Gardner*, 387 U.S. 136 (1967).
*Appalachian Power Company v. Environmental Protection Agency*, 208 F.3d 1015 (2000).
*Chevron, Inc. v. Natural Resources Defense Council*, 467 U.S. 837 (1984).
*Friends of the Earth, Inc. v. Laidlaw Environmental Services, Inc.*, 528 U.S. 167 (2000).
*Lujan v. Defenders of Wildlife*, 504 U.S. 555 (1992).
*Ohio Forestry Association, Inc. v. Sierra Club*, 523 U.S. 726 (1998).
*Marbury v. Madison*, 5 U.S. (1 Cranch) 137 (1803).
*Monsanto Co. v. Geertson Seed Farms*, 130 S. Ct. 2743 (2010).
*Norton v. Southern Utah Wilderness Alliance*, 542 U.S. 55 (2004).
*Sierra Club v. Morton*, 405 U.S. 727 (1972).
*Summers v. Earth Island Institute*, 555 U.S. 488 (2009).
*United States v. Salerno*, 481 U.S. 739, 745 (1987).
*United States v. Students Challenging Regulatory Agency Procedures*, 412 U.S. 559 (1973).

## REFERENCES

Birdsong, Brett C. 2005. "Justice Scalia's Footprints on the Public Lands." *Denver University Law Review* 82 (2): 259–97.
Blomley, Nicholas K. 1989. "Text and Context: Rethinking the Law-Geography Nexus." *Progress in Human Geography* 13 (4): 512–34.

———. 2008. "Simplification Is Complicated: Property, Nature, and the Rivers of Law." *Environment and Planning A* 40 (8): 1825–42.

Carr, John. 2012. "Public Input/Elite Privilege: The Use of Participatory Planning to Reinforce Urban Geographies of Power in Seattle." *Urban Geography* 33 (3): 420–41.

Clark, Bryan, and Amanda C. Leiter. 2011. "Regulatory Hide and Seek: What Agencies Can (and Can't) Do to Limit Judicial Review." *Boston College Law Review* 5: 1682–1731.

Delaney, David. 2010. *The Spatial, the Legal and the Pragmatics of World-Making: Nomospheric Investigations.* New York: Routledge.

Estreicher, Samuel. 1982. "The Second Circuit and NRLB 1980-81: A Cases Study in Judicial Review of Agency." *Brooklyn Law Review* 48: 1063–94.

Fischman, Robert. L. 2007. "From Words to Action: The Impact and Legal Status of the 2006 National Refuge System Management Policies." *Stanford Environmental Law Journal* 26: 77–135.

Floren, David. 2001. "Pre-Enforcement Ripeness Doctrine: the Fitness of Hardship." *Oregon Law Review* 80: 1008–1136.

Glicksman, Robert L., and Richard E. Levy. 2010. *Administrative Law: Agency Action in Legal Context.* New York: Foundation Press.

Haupt, P. 1926. "Etymological and Critical Notes." *American Journal of Philology* 47: 305–18.

Heckel, Maria E. 2004. "Finding the Line Between Action and Inaction: *SUWA v. Norton* and Judicial Review of Statutory Land Management Standards." *Utah Law Review* 2004: 789–825.

Kedar, Sandy. 2003. "On the Legal Geography of Ethnocratic Settler States." In *Law and Geography: Current Legal Issues*, edited by Jane Hoder and Carolyn Harrison, 5:404–41. London: Oxford.

Klyza, Christopher, and David Sousa. 2007. *American Environmental Policy, 1990–2006: Beyond Gridlock.* Cambridge, MA: MIT Press.

Kreit, Alex. 2010. "Making Sense of Facial and As-Applied Challenges." *William and Mary Bill of Rights Journal* 18: 657–707.

Lazarus, Edward. 2005. *Closed Chambers: The Rise, Fall, and Future of the Modern Supreme Court.* New York: Penguin Books.

Mank, Bradford C. 2010. "*Summers v. Earth Island Institute*: Its Implications for Future Standing Decisions." *Environmental Law Reporter News and Analysis* 4: 10958–73.

Marksity, Drew. 2008. "Judicial Review of Agency Action: Federal Appellate Review of Board of Immigration Appeals Streamlining Procedure." *University of Cincinnati Law Review* 76: 645–79.

Martin, Deborah, Alexander Scherr, and Christopher City. 2010. "Making Law, Making Place: Lawyers and the Production of Space." *Progress in Human Geography* 34 (2): 175–92.

Miller, Michael B. 1990. "The Justiciability of Legislative Rules and the 'Political' Political Question Doctrine." *California Law Review* 78: 1341.

Nauen, Charles N. 1987. "Citizen Environmental Lawsuits after *Gwaltney*: The Thrill of Victory or the Agony of Defeat." *William Mitchell Law Review* 15: 327–51.

Nichols, Lindsay J. 2003. "D.C. Circuit Invalidates EPA Document as 'Binding on its Face.'" *Ecology Law Quarterly* 30: 793–97.

Nie, Martin. 2008. "The Underappreciated Role of Regulatory Enforcement in Natural Resource Conservation." *Policy Sciences* 41: 139–64.

Osofsky, Hari. 2010. "Multiscalar Governance and Climate Change: Reflections on the Role of States and Cities at Copenhagen." *Maryland Journal of International Law* 25: 64–85.

Philippopoulos-Mihalopoulos, Andreas. 2010. "Law's Spatial Turn: Geography, Justice and a Certain Fear of Space." *Law, Culture and the Humanities* 7 (2): 187–202.

Pierce, Paul R., Jr. 1999. "Is Standing Law or Politics?" *North Carolina Law Review* 77: 1741–89.

Riles, Annelise. 2005. "A New Agenda for the Cultural Study of Law: Taking on the Technicalities." *Buffalo Law Review* 53: 973–1033.

Ruhl, J. B. 2005. "Regulation by Adaptive Management—Is It Possible?" *Minnesota Journal of Law, Science and Technology* 7: 21–57.

Ruhl, J. B., and Robert L. Fischman. 2010. "Adaptive Management in the Courts." *Minnesota Law Review* 95 (2): 424–84.

Stabb, James B. 2006. *The Political Thought of Justice Antonin Scalia: A Hamiltonian on the Supreme Court.* New York: Rowman and Littlefield.

Stegmaier, Christian. 1998. "Trouble in the Forest: Citing Lack of Ripeness, the United States Supreme Court Vacates Sixth Circuit Decision in *Ohio Forestry Ass's v. Sierra Club.*" *South Carolina Environmental Law Journal* 7: 277–83.

Sullins, Tony. 2001. *ESA: Endangered Species Act.* Chicago: American Bar Association Section of Environment Energy and Resources Press.

Treangen, John. 1991. "Standing: Closing the Doors of Judicial Review—*Lujan v. National Wildlife Federation.*" *South Dakota Law Review* 36: 136–59.

Valverde, Mariana. 2009. "Jurisdiction and Scale: Using Law's Technicalities as Theoretical Resources." *Social and Legal Studies* 18: 139–57.

Verkuil, Paul R., and Jeffery S. Lubbers. 2003. "Alternative Approaches to Judicial Review of Social Security Disability Cases." *Administrative Law Review* 55: 731–55.

Williams, Byron K., Robert Carl Szaro, and C. D. Shapiro. 2009. *Adaptive Management: The U.S. Department of the Interior Technical Guide.* Washington, DC: US Department of the Interior.

# 10    AT WORK IN THE NOMOSPHERE

## *The Spatiolegal Production of Emotions at Work*

### David Delaney

The starting point for much of human geography, legal geography, and critical scholarship more generally is the recognition that what the world is like strongly conditions what it's like to be and live in the world. Social spatializations are a fundamental feature of any world, and *how* the social is spatialized (what kinds of spaces are produced, how they are arranged, how they are rendered meaningful, how they are invested with power, and so on) is fundamental to what social being is like—indeed, what it *feels* like to be.

This project considers it axiomatic that *to be* is to suffer—at least to some extent. But it also assumes that the character of *social* suffering (Charlesworth 2005; Frost and Hoggett 2008; Renault 2010) is contingent and, at least to some extent, revisable, and that social worlds can be spatialized in ways that affect the social distribution of forms of suffering, the intensity of suffering, the means (or hope) of ameliorating or mitigating suffering, and the capacity to recognize and respond to the suffering of others. These are contingent. We can imagine worlds that seem to be precisely designed to produce excessive suffering or to affect a maldistribution of suffering. We know that prisons—cells, holes, special housing units, camps, torture chambers—are intentionally produced and specifically designed with suffering in mind. Likewise, sanctuaries and hospices are social spaces that are fabricated toward the end of alleviating suffering. We can imagine revising lifeworlds with the aim of reducing suffering or correcting such maldistributions. Such projects would be responding to calls to justice. For our immediate purposes these issues address one of the "so what?" questions of legal geography.

My primary operating assumption in this chapter is that the insights of legal geography are immensely valuable for the task of redescribing the contingencies of social spatializations as they affect the production and distribution of forms of social suffering. I suggest that some of what we do may render more visible and thinkable what is often obscure or unthinkable. We may incite the imagination of a more just socio-spatial-legal order. As I understand it, the "legal" is not simply poured into preexisting "spaces" but, rather, is constitutive of spatialities, spatial relationships, spatial performances, and experiences, as these, in turn, condition the lived character of the legal.

The assignment of the workshop that resulted in the chapters to this volume was to imagine what legal geography could be—now that it is well beyond the initial "bridge-building" phase and into its third generation. One way of responding to this is to ask how it might be brought into conversation with discourses or lines of inquiry that have been neglected. To this point, twenty or so years on, legal geography has illuminated a plethora of topics. Some studies focus on world-making projects, institutions, practices, and ideologies; some are more attentive to otherwise obscure aspects of "being-in-the-world." Among the key thematics that have given legal geography its distinctive flavor are a concern with how power operates and generates effects through the mutual constitution of the (socio)legal and the (socio)spatial and attention to the pragmatics of how distinctively legal meanings are made, unmade, remade, and contested.

As a still rather small enterprise, legal geography has been characterized by uneven coverage of the kinds of events that we examine and by incomplete connections with other strands of scholarship. It has stronger affinities with political geography, for example, than with cultural geography (Delaney 2013); it is generally more likely to be aligned with post–critical legal studies tendencies than, say, law and economics. This is not, in itself, a problem. Nonetheless, the development of new lines of connection could be useful, if only as provocation. My project here aims to engage a thicker, more complex conception of personhood—of subjects and the social processes of intersubjectification—than is usually the case in legal geography.

So, part of my project is to *enliven* legal geography a bit. To that end this chapter makes two primary contributions. First, I undertake an investigation of the legal workplace-as-*place* and as generic nomic setting (Delaney 2010b).[1] In the larger project of which this chapter is a first pass this will facilitate linking legal geography more closely to the concerns of political economy, labor studies, and critical analyses of neoliberalism. I will not be able to pursue these issues here. Second, I begin to take into account dimensions of personhood and relationality that I have neglected in my own work. I draw on and seek to contribute to work in geography and emotions, psychoanalytic geography, law and emotions, and critical organizational studies—and especially scholarship on the psychodynamics of work. Again, the aspiration is to enliven legal geography, to "people" it with characters who are more recognizably like us. The aim here is also to extend the reach of legal geography so as to engage questions relating to the social processes of intersubjectification, to ask to what extent who we are or who we feel ourselves to be can be illuminated by the kind of socio-spatio-legal analysis offered here. This is pursued more in the spirit of curiosity than of commitment. My question is, basically, what would legal geography look like if it worked with a thicker, more problematic conception of the subjects who live (and work) in the nomosphere?[2]

This chapter is divided into two parts. The first part has three sections. First, I introduce the topics of work, working and working-*for*, that is, the employment relation. Important to establish here are the ins and outs of working-for, the pains of being without work, out of a job, and the boundary conditions of hiring and dismissal. Then I offer a sketch of key elements of the spatiality of working-for. The focus here is on the generic nomic setting (Delaney 2010b) of "the work-place." It is important to note that this study is restricted to contemporary American workplaces. In light of Kedar's advocacy of a comparative legal geography (Chapter 4), the legal constitution of the workplace is an excellent candidate for comparative analysis. Certainly, the ways in which these settings are produced through distinctively legal means varies considerably even among broadly similar legal regimes—indeed, even state by state within the United States. A comparative study would reveal a range of contingencies and potentials that the present study is unable to provide.

The second part of the chapter has two main sections. In the first I return to the notion of workplace-as-place and relational space. Here I begin to enliven or animate relationality through a discussion of emotions at work. More important, I discuss elements of governing emotions and of governing *through* emotions; governing and ruling the denizens of the workplace through the (nomic) management of emotions and governing space through the emotions. My primary focus here is on the social production of humiliation, fear, and anxiety and their implication in the fabrication of the workplace-as-place and lived, embodied space. Some instances of the extremes of this are legally cognizable as "hostile environments." For the purposes of this chapter, the focal point of discussion is the social generation of a common spatiolegal (nomospheric) predicament shaped by the twin fears of entrapment and banishment: can't stay and can't not.

The second section then forges connections between legal geography and psychoanalytic geography, law, and psychoanalysis and critical organizational studies to suggestively capture some of the social processes and mechanisms of the production of social suffering under the spatiolegal (nomospheric) conditions presented to this point. Emotions are both targets and instruments of private government. Governing and governing *through* emotions implicate processes of intersubjectification, commonly under conditions of domination and exploitation. The chapter posits that "becoming an employee" frequently involves a confrontation between "organizational structures" and "psychic structures" (Allcorn

2004) that, under conditions of radical power asymmetries, is conducive to the social production of anxieties and fears, which, in turn, calls forth defensive reactions in the denizens of many workplaces. These affects are themselves "ingredients" of workplaces-as-places, as lifeworlds. Moreover, the normalization of workplace-generated forms of social suffering facilitates its social invisibilization and, thereby, its depoliticization (Deranty 2008). After summarizing some of the main points for the collective endeavor of reimagining legal geography or what this chapter might contribute to, I briefly gesture toward a set of "transformative nomospheric projects" (Delaney 2010b) aimed at lessening the intensity of social suffering and ameliorating its maldistribution by way of legal reconstitutions of the workplace. These ways of reimagining the workplace-as-place address the spatio-legal-existential suffering associated with the entrapment-banishment predicament. The presupposition here is that social actors are capable of engaging the means of legal production in order to resignify social space.

## WHAT WORK IS

Let's stipulate that what we call work in the widest sense is about effortful, goal-oriented activities. Of course, there is an enormous variety of tasks, conditions, and motivations that make up the social regime of work and working (Castillo 2002; Ciulla 2000; Drew, Mills, and Gassaway 2007; Méda 1996). Among the key distinctions through which the division of labor is understood are those of paid and unpaid work, manual and symbolic work, skilled and unskilled work, relatively secure and precarious work, intrinsically rewarding and stultifying work, and working independently and working for, that is under the control of, others. The focus of this chapter is on work in the narrower, conventional sense of employment: working *for* others, in exchange for "compensation," work that is structured and governed by employment relations law. As a (set of) formal legal relationships that of employer-employee is both like and unlike other formal relationships (e.g., the marriage relation, the parent-child relation, the landlord-tenant relation). It is similar in that the contours or parameters of the relationship (say, what acts constitute formation or dissolution of the relationship, how rights and duties are distributed between the parties) are structured by formal legal enactments which condition the felt terms of the practices (what is done and how), but they leave participants a large degree of "liberty" to structure most of what happens in the relationship within these parameters. Needless to say, such "liberties" tend to be unevenly distributed in many relationships.

This chapter assumes the centrality of work to one's life, sense of well-being, identity, and so on, and also the centrality of work and the work regime to social life more generally (Dejours 2006; Dejours and Deranty 2010). For most people the centrality of work entails the fundamental importance of the employment relationship and of the workplace as, at the very least, central to one's social (well-) being. Indeed, for many, the workplace may be more existentially significant than is the home (Delaney 2010a; Rosenbury 2011). The home, of course, is a primary site of unremunerated work, but consider too the unpaid work of *looking for* work, and the lived, social difference between being employed and being unemployed (of having or not having work, a job, a boss). One can, indeed work very hard to find work. One may fail to find it, or one may find work that is easier to do than the work of having had to find it. The point, especially under present conditions of a "jobless recovery," is that it is no mean feat to find a (work)place. Practically speaking, there is an inside and an outside of the regime of paid work. The anxieties associated with the inability to get inside, the trauma of being involuntarily outside, may, for some, be a form of social death; for others, for example, those for whom joblessness induces homelessness, it may impair biological life as well.

As both the history and the anthropology of work demonstrate, a social work regime can be organized in any number of ways. That is, while work may be a human universal, how it is socially organized is highly variable and contingent. How we organize it under present conditions of US or Western liberal capitalism differs both from conditions elsewhere and from previous generations. It is widely recognized that the contemporary work regime (its institutions, practices, ideologies, spaces) is characterized by increasing precariousness and degradation (Beck 2000; Dubet 2009; Fraser 2001; Shulman 2003). At the same time, many are working on instituting a new work regime. Among the instruments required to fabricate these new places are those associated with law: rights, rules, duties, sanctions (Befort 2001–2, 2003; Geoghegan 2005; Stone 2009). Needless to say, these would also presuppose a change in "legal consciousness."

## THE SPATIALITY OF WORK

The number and diversity of kinds of jobs, careers, tasks that make up the division of labor is enormous: any one of us can make a list of ten, one hundred, or one thousand "occupations": stock analyst, sex worker, prison guard, dock worker, nurse, day laborer, psychotherapist, scavenger, clerical temp, judge (Terkel 1985). The practical, effective doings associated with these livelihoods imply an equally wide array of sociospatial arrangements. Most work takes place in fixed locations generally referred to as the workplace. For some, though, the workplace is more fluid, shifting from location to location, ephemeral or literally moving, or in between other workplaces—the trucker, the day laborer, the domestic, the carnival worker, the mercenary.

For the purposes of this investigation my focus is on the former. Still, some fixed workplaces are large, some small; some outside, some inside; in public or not. Regardless of these differences, the work regime can be thought of as being made out of social spaces: factories, offices, stores, hotels, cubicles, sets, classrooms, hospital wards, other people's homes, and so on. These spaces are also *places*. They are occupied, inhabited, meaningful, lived in. As a practical matter, given the centrality of work, a primary accomplishment of most adult human beings (and many children) is to gain admittance to such a space by becoming "employed." That is, forming an employment relationship, becoming someone's "employee." When one accepts a "position," one becomes inserted into a relational world in which the organizing principle of the relationship is an exchange: work (the performance of assigned tasks) and time (segments of a finite life, portions of days, weeks) in exchange for remuneration—typically money (with which one may . . .) and other "benefits." Of course, we know that work is necessarily much more than this exchange. But this does seem to be the overt principle of organization with reference to which spatialities are configured.

Work as activity, and working *for* and *with* others as central aspects of social relationality are characterized by complex, dynamic social spatialities. One may investigate these at the level of the global division of labor, at the level of intracorporeality and many scales of analysis in between. These two extremes (the global and the intracorporeal) may be linked through the workplace. For the purposes of the present investigation I want to draw attention to three spatial dimensions of the workplace: (1) the inside-outside boundary conditions; (2) elements of authoritarian territoriality that give form and structure to the insides; and (3) aspects of relational or affective space, or how the workplace-as-place is generated. Again, think of what has become known (and legally cognizable) as a "hostile environment."[3]

As I already mentioned, a central, life-sustaining task for most people is the necessity of finding an employer and a workplace. For most, being hired, becoming an employee, occupying a subordinate position in an employment relation, entails giving over to another control over basic corporeal aspects of being: location, bodily position, movements; from simple presence in space to extreme immobilization and Taylorized repetitions. No less than homes, the conditions of workplaces vary enormously. Some are enriching, supportive, comfortable; some are hellholes; many are mixed or in between. Conditions "on the inside" may be felt by some, though not all, as oppressive, exploitative, alienating, stressful. But so long as those conditions are experienced as preferable to banishment, the specter of unemployment and the cascade of catastrophes that would likely ensue, general compliance can be expected. (Though in the new casualized work world, some workplaces have 100 percent turnover in a year. This may mean that there is no incentive for management to maintain safe or humane working conditions.) Nearly every command issued and received is done so in the shadow of the employer's right to dismiss, terminate, or expel an employee. At the same time, a host of "rights" pertaining to privacy, association, expression, and more are left outside in the parking lot (Barry 2007; Koster 2007).

Among the conditions that count as "working conditions" many are directly related to the spatialization of workplaces (Baldry 1997; Halford 2005). Again, there is enormous variation: separations by task, rank, gender; differential mobility; managed proxemics; modes of surveillance and supervision. Most employees, when hired or transferred, are inserted into preexisting spatial arrangements. At their orientation they are told, "Here is your work station, here is the break room, here is the loading dock, the mail room. These areas are 'off limits,'" and so on. Some of this positioning is directly related to the flow of tasks. But, arguably, some elements of spatial management are more immediately a function of workplace governance as such: the relative ease of supervision, institutionalized isolations, other forms of psychosocial management of "human resources." I refer to this aspect of spatialization as authoritarian territorialism.

Workplaces as *places* are also constituted by other sociospatialities, for example, relational spaces (Jones 2010; Malpas 2012). Human beings are relational beings (Nedelsky 2011). That is, much of who we are is constituted by and through our lived or imagined relationships with others: intimates, familiars, strangers. Workplaces are "sites" of many social, psychological, and affective *lived* relationships—relationships with coworkers, superiors, subordinates, clients, colleagues in other organizations. As Christophe Dejours (2006, 56) argues:

> Ordinary work situations cannot be described as the juxtaposition of individual experiences and intelligences, for, as a rule, we work for someone—a boss, a foreman or immediate supervisor, subordinates or colleagues, a client, and so on. Work is not just an activity but also a social relationship; in other words, it takes place in a human world characterized by its relationships of inequality, power and domination. Working means involving one's subjectivity in a world that is hierarchical, ordered, constrained, and rife with struggles for domination. . . . The reality of work is not only the reality of the objective world but also of the social world.

That is to say, workplaces are lifeworlds.

But workplaces are more than simply sites or containers of relationships. It is useful to consider that workplaces-as-places are also *constituted* through the specificities of relationships and the lived dynamics that characterize them. And those relationships are generative of distinctive spatialities formed in terms of co-presences, being-with, being without. For many, the relational characteristics of a (work)place may have existential priority over the actual work that is performed. That is, for many the workplace is a genuine lifeworld and a primary one at that. In "Psychotherapy of the Lived Space: A Phenomenological and Ecological Concept" Thomas Fuchs (2007, 425) writes:

> "World," of course, does not mean something outside of as opposed to inside, the external world against the internal or mental world. It is rather the totality of life in the sense of an all-embracing framework of meaning in which a person's experience, thinking and acting are embedded.

So it is that even relatively boring tasks can be satisfying in the company of conge-nial others or in the context of satisfying relationships while otherwise engaging work that takes place in a "hostile environment" can be extremely deleterious to one's sense of well-being. Again, many workplaces are felt to be humane; some are decidedly not.

## WORKPLACE AS LEGALLY CONSTITUTED PLACE

Workplaces-as-*places* are also legally constituted spaces. "The workplace" is a ge-neric nomic setting (see note 1). Any workplace is the loci or referent of countless legal directives: statutes, rules, regulations. It is a complexly governed space, like, but distinct from, other generic and specific settings such as home, public space, prison, the border. The central formal legal relationship at or with reference to the legal constitution of the workplace is the employer-employee relationship. But in any workplace this abstract relationship manifests differently in each instantia-tion. Like all formal legal relationships it is lived in its particularities. In the United States, elements of federal, state, and municipal public governance give form and structure to the terms of the lived relationships. In unionized workplaces the re-lationships are also governed by elements of labor law (as distinct from employ-ment law) and by contract law. In addition, traces of insurance law, building codes, environmental regulations, constitutional law, tort, and so on, structure events and relational dynamics in the workplace. Here I will mention three core elements of the legal constitution of the workplace as they pertain to the present project: (1) formal deference to private governance, (2) property doctrines, and (3) the legal ideology of at-will-ism.

While obviously very important, both formally and practically, traces of what I refer to here as the public law of the workplace typically affect only the parameters

or margins of what unfolds in the governed relationships. Generally, of more immediate salience are the legal traces that manifest modes of *private* governance,
even in putatively "public" workplaces.' In her analysis of the notion of legal pluralism Sally Merry discusses Stuart Macaulay's conception of private government
"as that governing done by groups not part of state and federal constitutions but
which may mimic symbols and structures of the public legal system." Macaulay's
"private government perspective," she says, "recognizes private associations that
affect governing and also treats distinctions between public and private as problematic" (Merry 1988, 877). This certainly characterizes the workplace. Most pertinent for present purposes, Macaulay (1986, 1) argues that "while it may be . . .
necessary to draw a sharp line between public and private government even to
think about law, actually there is no such line but situations of interpenetration,
overlapping jurisdictions and opportunities for harmony and conflict." The conditions of interpenetration and overlap in the workplace are aspects or processes
of spatiality which problematize the ins and outs of law.

Most workplaces are owned as property. With or without contract the legal
foundation of workplace governance is property. The employer-employee relationship is, after all, at base a property relation genealogically derived from the
law of master-servant (Tomlins 1992). As with all property relationships a fundamental element of this is the owner's "right to exclude" and so, the owner's right
to dismiss, discharge, terminate or banish. *Ruling a workplace entails ruling over
people.* As property rights, the right to exclude and the right to expel are both con-
ferred and enforced (and, in some cases, limited) by the state. The enforcement
may entail the use of physical violence if necessary. The owner's (or the principal's
agent; e.g., management, supervisor, foreman) right to rule can be enormously
capacious and vary widely from workplace to workplace, even within the same
organization—say, the research laboratory versus the cafeteria. These elements of
governance are typically much more salient in the lives of the denizens of a workplace than are the parametric formal traces associated with "public law."

The interface of these two legal regimes invokes a version of the public-private
distinction. The workplace, like "the home," as a socially, legally, politically produced space and as a historically shifting space, is a spatialization of this conceptual artifact. Many workplace struggles (understood as place-making, world-
making projects and counterprojects) take place at, about, or in the shadow of
"the boundary" between what is taken for the public and what is taken as the
private. The terms of entry and exit (e.g., fair hiring practices, unlawful discharge,
Americans with Disabilities Act accommodations, sexual harassment) are set with
reference to understandings of the appropriate limits of regulation (sovereignty)
and ownership. Regulation is commonly metaphorized by opponents in spatial

terms such as infringement, invasion, intrusion. Among current boundary issues some are work, that is, task, related: disputes over hours, mandatory overtime, break time, unionization. But many more are only indirectly, if at all, task related: those concerning protections against transgender discrimination, breast-feeding, rights of religious expression, language use, immigrant screening, privacy, political activities, appearance and grooming, fraternization, romance and sexual activity, smoking, off-premises "lifestyles." That is, what is at stake in these disputes are the terms of private governing *as such*. Of course, most "issues" don't even get close to the boundary (Weiler 1990). They are regarded as unquestionably within the un-contested "zone of the owner's discretion" or jurisdiction.

While an owner's right to exclude may be exercised against "all the world," it also underpins a fundamental aspect of the normal American employer-employee relationship. Not simply addressed to "strangers to the land" but operative in the context of ongoing, often long-standing relationships, the right to exclude is un-derpinned by the at-will doctrine and the (spatiolegal) ideology of at-will-ism. As Philip Selznick (1969, 134–35) describes its premises:

> If the contract is at will, no legal limits are set on the authority of the employer, especially on the key issue of dismissal. The employer is free to hire and fire unrestrained by the legal requirement that he has just cause for rescinding a contract not yet expired. . . . Since there is no definite duration, the terms of the contract are not binding for the future. The employer is free to modify them at any time, without notice.

That is, there is no "contract," and so, no contractual rights or obligations. In Hol-ger's (1985, 28) words, "The employment at will principle established the employ-er's legal power to dictate all terms and conditions of employment in the workplace and to discharge with impunity any employee who failed to satisfy those condi-tions." For our present purposes this (official, formal, "public") doctrine-ideology is profoundly important not only to how the (private) workplace is governed but also for how working-for is lived. Not surprisingly, at-will-ism has been the subject of scathing criticism by pro-labor legal scholars. Clyde Summers (2000–2001, 65) has written that the at-will doctrine (and associated jurisprudence)

> endow[s] employers with divine rights over their employees. This doctrine has been, and still is, a basic premise undergirding American labor law. . . .
> [A]t its roots [it] is a fundamental assumption regarding the relation between an employer and its employees. The assumption is that the employee is only a supplier of labor who has no legal interest or stake in the enterprise other than the right to be paid for labor performed. The employer, as owner of the enterprise,

is legally endowed with the sole right to determine matters concerning the operation of the enterprise. This includes the work performed and the continued employment of its employees. The law, by giving total dominance to the employer, endows the employer with the divine right to rule the working lives of its subject employees.

This is illustrative of the legal constitution of social relations generally and the terms of private government more specifically. As Summers (2000–2001, 78) also explains, these relationships of private rule are ideologically grounded in and legitimized by common-sense conceptions of property.

> Employment at will draws its strength from the deeply rooted conception of the employment relation as a dominant subservient relation rather than one of mutual rights and obligations. The employer, as owner of the enterprise, [for present purposes, owner of the space and place] is viewed as owning the job with the property right to control the job and the worker who fills it. That property right gives the employer the right to impose any requirement on the employee, give any order and insist on obedience, change any term of employment, and discard the employee at any time. The employer is sovereign over his or her employee.

My focus of attention here are the legalities that are constitutive of the workplace-as-place and as a kind of social space. However, it should be clear that these produced spatialities are also, at the same time, constitutive of the legal as such and that they strongly condition the ways in which the legal is worlded. The ambiguous and unstable differentiation and relationship of public law and private law; the imagined terms of their interpenetration, insulation, relative privileging; the complex spatiality of legal plurality; the spatial constitution of illiberal liberalism; the spatial contingency of rights, duties, forms of legal consciousness—these are not simply incidental to what law is or to how it is lived. Without at least tacit understanding of how space is supposed to work none of what happens "at work" makes any sense at all.

## FEELING AT WORK AND THE WORK OF FEELING

For the purposes of this project (as an intervention into legal geography) some conventional understandings of the workplace need to be provisionally set aside to more clearly focus on the task at hand. The first is that what takes place in the workplace is only or primarily about work and working. Of course the tasks matter, but it there is also much more than that going on. For this or that denizen of the workplace the actual work may be decidedly of secondary significance. For some, work may be a context or even pretext for other forms of human engagement and interaction. In "Working Relationships," legal scholar Laura Rosenbury (2011, 19) writes, "Many adults spend half or more of their waking hours at work, in the process forming relationships with supervisors, co-workers, subordinates, customers, and other third parties . . . Workplaces are thus often sites of both intimacy and production, much like the home is a site of both intimacy and production." That is, again, workplaces are *places*, segments and components of lifeworlds. We live there.

A second conventional understanding that should also, then, be suspended is that the actual, lived human relationships at work are accurately or adequately captured by the categories of employment law, the employer-employee relation, or the fellow servant rule. That said, reducing the lived realities of the workplace-as-place to these terms—as is commonly done in legal settings—while false, is also extremely consequential.

The workplace, or better yet, actual workplaces, are inhabited as fully or as shallowly as the case may be, by human beings. All sorts of human beings may be "thrown together" by the vagaries of hiring practices and assignments as they unfold over, perhaps, a number of years. People find themselves as significant *to* others, as fellow subjects and, indeed, as psychic objects (Allcorn 2002; Diamond 1993). Versions of who we are occupy the imaginations, perhaps fantasies, of those with whom we work. Human beings interact through work and working with one another, but again, there may be more. As lived in by nonatomistic relational beings—beings who are *who* we are, to a large extent, *in consequence of* our various relationships with others—workplaces can be thought of as dynamic fields of relational interconnections. Some of these interconnections may be relatively "thin," ephemeral, perhaps little more than instrumental, some much thicker and enduring over long time spans; some simple, some complex, some characterized by low affect, some more intense. That is to say, workplaces-as-places may be intensely affective fields of experience (Orbach 2008).

There are a number of strands of inquiry concerning emotions in the workplace. I'll mention and draw on three. First, there is the recognition that much work is in itself "emotional labor." Amy Wharton (1999, 60) defines this as "the effort involved in displaying organizationally sanctioned emotions by those whose jobs require interactions with clients or customers and for whom these interactions are an important component of their work." That is, emotion or affect (genuine or feigned) may be inseparable from the explicit tasks and performance. One may be hired, assigned, supervised, rewarded, promoted or dismissed on the basis of how competently one performs emotions at work or on the assessment of the alignment of emotions with organizational or management objectives. As Astrid Kersten (2001, 454) says, the "performance of emotion and its proper management is a key element in many jobs today, service jobs in particular, thereby expanding the bureaucratic reach from external behavior to the internal life world of the employee." Emotional labor tends to be nearly as strongly gendered as is the division of labor itself: receptionists, nurses, teachers do some kinds of emotional work but cops, guards and other paid purveyors of fear or professional displayers of anger also participate.

Second, at the same time, emotions at work are the *focus of and objects of governance* (Ashkanasy, Härtel, and Zerbe 2000; Fineman 2003; Raz 2002; Spicer 2011). They are policed, regulated, deemed inappropriate, and sanctioned. The emotional lives of employees are often the business of organizations, managers, and other "human resources" specialists. In contrast to "emotional labor" these emotions are not intrinsic to the task—and, indeed, they may be assessed to be at odds with the tasks—they are, however, internal to organizational relations and the affective constitution of place. Some negative emotions (or their expression toward others) such as anger or disgust may be considered disruptive or counterproductive; some, such as love or desire, may be considered detrimental to workplace cohesion or other organizational goals. They also may be understood as exposing management to liability. Much management effort has gone into producing a "sanitized workplace" (Schultz 2003) or the workplace as an affect-free zone. As Schultz (2003, 2069) argues, the sanitized workplace is not so different from "the old Taylorist dream of the workplace as a sterile zone in which workers suspend all their human attributes while they train their energies solely on production." Other strategies of emotional management may be oriented toward the generation of loyalty or "team building" (Sinclair 1992).

A third dimension of emotional governance in the workplace is often intrinsic to the employment relationship under conditions of domination and subordination—and under the prevailing wider social conditions of increasing insecurity and precariousness of work. For example, a very significant cluster of affects is that associated with humiliation (Miller 1993). In "Humiliation at Work" (an important contribution to the literature in law and the emotions [see Abrams and Keren 2009–10]), Catherine Fisk (2001–2, 81) writes, "The workplace is an especially likely site for humiliation and . . . systematic humiliation of some workers is uniquely destructive to the psyche of the victims and to their full participation at work." I will examine shortly other accounts as to why and how this may be the case. "People," she says, "experience humiliation when others treat them as objects or as having worth not equal to that of the humiliator or witness. Humiliation . . . occur[s] when one is trying to relate to the other as a subject but feels objectified. . . . Part of [humiliation's] destructiveness is in the pervasive power-lessness that the victim experiences" (Fisk 2001–2, 89).

As the growing literature on workplace bullying demonstrates, in some work-places "insecurity" may be fostered and promoted as a governing policy of con-trol (Yamada 2010–11). Kersten (2001, 452) reminds us that "many of us live and work in dysfunctional, neurotic, psychotic or otherwise disturbed organizations where conflict, contradictions, and recurring problematic behaviors are the norm rather than the exception." In these places the management *objective* is deliberately to induce anxiety and fear in employees to solidify compliance and intensify the terms of domination and exploitation. Fear, of course, is an emotion focused on possible, undesirable futures. In the workplace, fear may be focused on the *space of tomorrow*: fear of expulsion, banishment, and the associated cascade of possible catastrophes—material, social, psychological. For some employees this may in-duce an intolerable predicament whereby "going to work" is felt as nearly intoler-able, but being banished from this place is imagined as even worse. "As employees are [fired or] laid off," writes Rosenbury (2011, 117), "they lose not just paychecks and job security but also the daily support of co-workers. Employees left behind also lose that support while coping with anxiety over the possibility of additional layoffs and new workplace social dynamics." Refocusing on the spatiality of the workplace, this may induce an existential crisis of entrapment analogous to that associated with domestic abuse (Price 2002). Moreover, regarded as a social phe-nomenon and not only of biographical significance, the workplace-as-place and as governed space becomes *the instrument for the production* of social suffering at the service of organizational objectives (and/or career objectives of managers).

As part of a reimagining of legal geography the discussion to this point has suggested that sociospatialities and legalities may be combined in distinctive ways with various forms of power to produce "the workplace" and *through* "the workplace" to generate particular kinds of lived, human relationships with their particular affective dynamics. Living here *feels* like something and the feeling-like is, in part, attributable to how legalities and spatialities are combined. These af-fective dynamics are not irrelevant, not incidental, not residual, and not simply outcomes. Rather, at least in some cases, they are integral to how power works through the heart and psyche. They are integral to how legalities work at work and to how *work* works. The relationships at issue are affective *and* "legal." The legal structure of the employer-employee or manager-worker relations positions some human beings as "having the right" to command, control, and condition, and correlatively, the right to threaten, sanction, or reward, and most especially, to expel or banish. It positions other human beings as "having the duty" to obey, to comply, to recognize the superior's right to induce fear and anxiety, indeed, in many cases, to terrorize—this is both the root and the function of authoritarian territorialism. These place-based and place-constituting relational dynamics are contingent on how one becomes the kind of subject called "the boss." How this human being forms a conditional subjecthood and intersubjective relationality with others. It's as if one were to say, "I can intersubjectively relate to you this way *because* I'm the boss. I can say this, I can do that, I can, if I will, treat you as a disposable object or an object of desire because I have been legally constituted as 'your boss' and we are positioned 'at work.'"

But, of course, one does not have to say this, because rights and the legal constitution of work say this for him or her. The other must negotiate, accommodate, or contemplate resistance to this relational dynamic because he or she has been legally subjectified as "an employee." What it means to have rights and duties is that, if desired, agents of the state will validate and enforce them. Ultimately, the situated, experiential dimension of such workplace-based dynamics is underpinned by ideologies of property, ownership and the right to exclude, and the prevalence of at-will-ism. Again the public and the private provide ideological structure to a range of border skirmishes. Can the boss forbid breast-milk pumping, speaking Spanish, praying? Can he mandate skirt length or makeup? "How far" can management or employees go? How and when does one "cross the line" into "actionable behavior"? How intense, pervasive, or humiliating must the interaction be before the ideas of constructive discharge[4] and hostile environment (see note 3) become appropriate?

## THE WORK OF THE MIND AND THE MIND AT WORK

For my original task it would be sufficient if I left it at this: the identification of the complex recursive dynamics of spatiolegal co-construction, the social relational dynamics of emotion and affect as these flow into and out of the co-conditioning of this nomic setting. Attending to such themes may enliven and animate legal geography: what "space" is like and why, what the world is like, what it feels like, how "feelings" are constitutive of place and place making (Pile 2010). However, I'd also like to avail myself of other lines of inquiry and suggest here that critical legal geography might go "beyond" emotions. I'd like to suggest that we fold other novel resources into our collective interpretive tool kit to account for socio-spatial-legal (or nomospheric) episodes and situations. These other strands are critical organizational studies and the literature on the psychodynamics of work. A couple of caveats before I sketch this out. First, again, as with emotions, my recourse to psychodynamics and psychoanalysis is not individualist (although it is concerned with questions of subject formation and intersubjectification). My concern is thoroughly social and political. My interest is in politics and ethics *of* the social production of kinds of selves. It is also thoroughly relational. Again, even if the primary effects of psychodynamic processes are registered most immediately "in the psyche" of "the person," my project is one of social critique (the social production and social distribution of social suffering) not of the diagnosis of individual psychopathologies. Second, at this level of suggestiveness psychodynamics and psychoanalysis are not taken as truths. Rather, I deploy them heuristically as rather well-developed vocabularies for thinking about what happens between people; as conceptual frames that highlight social relationality (and therefore the dynamics of relational space) and the dynamic unfolding of situational processes. At this most general level of suggestion useful orientations are Freudian, Lacanian, object relations, relational, and feminist psychology. The differences and disagreements among them, though often profound, don't matter to the task at hand. The central aims here are, first, to connect social relational dynamics to the social production of emotions (and therefore, bodily states, actions, lived social relations, the world); and second, to provisionally suspend the assumption of inner-outer; self-other; self-organization; self-world. This also means that the legal is not an "outside" to the psyche's "inside" (indeed, it may be productive to posit the workings of the legal unconscious) and that the domain of psyche is as much *of the world* as of the singular self.

What I aim to do is, depending on your perspective, enrich or impoverish our understanding of what emotions are, how they work, how they arise and are experienced as a manifestation of social relationality, and how they are implicated in social processes of intersubjectification. The suggestion is this: if this sketch remains connected to what I've said so far about law, space, place, power, and emotions, I will have opened a possible connection between legal geography and theories of the subject. We might see that the contingencies of law-space or nomosphericity may be generative of particular (contingent) *kinds* of subjects or modes of subjectification. Perhaps they are generative of a distinctively neoliberal subject forged and reproduced in the (neoliberal) workplace. All I can do here is suggestively sketch a model of the psychodynamic processes that others have claimed may be operative in these settings. These are processes which have a tendency to generate particularly intense, largely negative, painful emotions; emotions that are gathered under the heading or are indicative of "social suffering." The suggestion here is that legal geography may be useful in helping us to discern "the workplace" as a site of production, yes, but more precisely, as a site of production and distribution of forms of social suffering.

Analytically we can begin with the arrival or insertion of a subject into a preexisting organizational "environment," "structure," or culture. In "The Psyche at

Work" Seth Allcorn (2004, 88) describes this process as entailing "the confrontation of organizational structure with psychic structure (soul or spirit)." This confrontation is, of course, most often highly asymmetric, and, as I've suggested to this point, the asymmetries are closely connected to the constitution of the workplace as a nomic setting. Allcorn (2004, 90) asks, "In what way are the structures of our minds (or brains) externalized to create the structure of organizations that we work within? Conversely, how does the workplace with its many attributes serve to structure our minds and who we are?"

These questions comport with a phenomenologically informed suspension of a radical self-world distinction. It expresses a richer, dynamic sense of place and of being-in-the-world than is commonly the case in legal and social scientific scholarship. Allcorn quotes organizational psychoanalyst W. Czander (1993, 12) on the point that

> the structure assumes regulatory authority over the subordinate only when
> the subordinate assumes a submissive position. . . . [T]he regulatory authority
> is external; it is embedded in the structure and is, under certain conditions,
> incorporated by employees over time through participation in organizational
> activities, rituals, myths, ceremonies and tasks.

For our immediate purposes references to processes such as "externalization," "incorporation," or "internalization" can be understood as (psychosocial) *spatial* processes or flows constitutive of the formation of dynamic, intersubjective relational spaces. That is, effective legality (or nomicity; Delaney 2010b) is both embedded in the structure of an organizational workplace and becomes incorporated into relational embodied subjectivities:

> Our experience of organization and the workplace unavoidably and out of
> awareness influences (bounds) what we think, feel and do. Much of the behavior
> observed in the workplace is an outcome of organizational artifacts such as work
> design, hierarchical structure, rules, positions, ideals, values, and culture that
> possess an autistic nature that shapes member experience. (Allcorn 2004, 97)

And, of course, except for genuinely cooperative workplaces such designs, structures, rules, and so on, are the prerogative of management, often under the guidance of "human resource" specialists.

The psychodynamic expression of this confrontation or collision and the dynamics of organizational enculturation and "incorporation" may generate a range of feelings or psychosomatic experiences—some positive perhaps, some not, some low intensity, some high:

The workplace may then be understood to be composed of 'stuff' that evokes anxiety and psychological defensiveness that, when acted on, creates a rich milieu where organization members transform themselves and the organization in pursuit of psychic safety [where] these two worlds collide within the context of one's workplace experience. (Allcorn 2004, 94)

It is easy to imagine that *governing through the emotions* would tend to foster such collisions and anxiety-inducing defenses insofar as our very subjecthood as experienced is the object and instrument of ruling-over and, again, as the possibility of banishment is always present. In "Emotion Work and Emotion Space: Using a Spatial Perspective to Explore the Challenging of Masculine Emotion Management Practices" Patricia Lewis uses a spatial metaphor (if indeed it is metaphorical) to capture some of the dynamics intrinsic in being ruled-by for the benefit of an alien force. She refers to a similar process as "a colonization of workers' affects and subjectivities through a range of new work practices and culture management programmes" (Lewis 2008, S132). Organizational scholars have offered heuristic typologies of the "personalities" of organizations that new employees may confront. Especially significant is how some workplaces seem to take on the personality characteristics of their primary makers, again, those positioned as being "in charge." Such pathological places are where employees live. One may or may not successfully accommodate him- or herself. So, for example, Kersten (2001, 459) discusses

the compulsive organization [as having] control as a major fantasy. . . . There are extensive and elaborate policies, rules and procedures extending not merely to the programming of production procedures, but to dress code, frequent sales meetings, and a corporate credo that includes suggested employee attitudes. Since all relationships are perceived in terms of dominance and submission, the organizational structure is hierarchical, positioned based, centralized, controlling and formalized. The compulsive executive relies on formal controls . . . resulting in feelings of suspicion [and] manipulation.

Working and having one's life unfold in such a lifeworld is conducive to the generation of fear. Jean-Philippe Deranty (2008, 446) speaks of "the fear of tomorrow, the most basic uncertainty, felt in one's bones and making one's existence miserable." And again, the temporality of fear of tomorrow has a spatial aspect: exile, banishment, finding oneself "without." He continues:

The affect that arises at work and from work, to subsequently vitiate all social bonds, is fear: the fear of losing one's job; the fear arising from systematically organized competition with other workers both inside and outside the workplace;

the fear of not being able to achieve ever increasing productivity targets; the fear
of not coping when the productivity targets and the work organization are in
contradiction; the fear of being caught at fault by the surveillance of management
(when using shortcuts is the only way to achieve targets): the fear of not being
able to adapt in the face of systematic compulsion to introduce rapid and constant
changes, and so on. . . . [T]hose different types of fear all ask of the subjects
the same terrible question: will you be able to cope, and for how long? . . .
[T]he impossibility of coping, an impossibility of doing anything with one's finite
array of skills, strengths and capacities because they will have been too massively
undermined or overwhelmed by physical or psychical attacks. (Deranty 2008, 456)

Again, it is not simply that "feelings" are being generated. Rather, Deranty is describing a microsocial *process* that is putatively connected to macrosocial and
political economic processes. Something is *happening*, being shaped, perhaps de-
stroyed, to achieve a desired "fit" that may not be possible, or, if possible, only at
significant existential cost. Under these conditions something's got to give. Allcorn
(2004, 88) writes, "This confrontation leads to psychological defensiveness and the
restructuring of either the workplace or ourselves to alleviate the anxiety." That
is, some workplaces—the hostile environment, the compulsive organization—are
claimed to produce anxieties, which, in turn, call forth typical "defenses" that, in
their turn, condition the production of other deleterious emotions, discursive
thoughts, behaviors, and performances. These, then, feed back into the setting *for
others* to continuously condition the character of relational space:

Individuals must defend themselves from the at times hostile, threatening and
inappropriate thoughts, feelings and actions of their superiors as well as peers
and subordinates. Anxieties are readily evoked as a result of losses of individual
autonomy that accompany entry into and submission to their organization.
(Allcorn 2004, 93).

Refocusing on workplace itself, Allcorn (2004, 94) claims:

In the process of embracing and otherwise incorporating elements of this culture-
based reality filter, we are changed. . . . Organizational members must not only
take up the culture, they must manage to feel less anxious by extinguishing those
parts of themselves that conflict with the basic assumptions of the culture.

One last point. Lest we misunderstand what is being posited here as primarily concerned with individual pathological conditions (that may be remedied by
individualized therapeutic responses: pharmacological treatments, neurological
interventions or inhibitors), the central focus of this work is on discerning the

*social* conditions for the *social* production of *social* suffering. Deranty (2008, 458, 459) also calls attention to "the massive invisibilization of suffering. . . . The structural impossibility for suffering occurring in contemporary workplaces to express itself reverberates throughout society," and how "the experience of suffering becomes unsayable, and for the subject, a forbidden thought." Workplace suffering is so deeply normalized that, for many, the very word *work* is associated with drudgery, and not the necessarily humanizing practice of "labor" (Méda 1996). It is nearly impossible for many to imagine that "work" could be otherwise! Deranty (2008, 460) argues that this has wider social ramifications:

> The inability to say the suffering, even to one's self, contributes directly to the emergence and increase in pathologies. . . .
>     . . . [S]uffering becomes an acceptable reality of present society, or even a reality for which some good justification can be found. Basically, the conditions of the contemporary economic world require that everyone be ready to accept to suffer through their work, to witness the suffering of others, and as the case may be, to make others suffer.

He notes that one of the consequences of "the acceptance of fear as a necessary affect of the new social conditions" is "the silencing of moral sense [which] . . . makes individuals incapable of feeling compassion for the other's suffering" (460). Emotions such as fear, humiliation, shame, resentment, and so on, are less significant as discrete intersubjective feelings than as manifestations of forms of *social* suffering. Astrid Kersten (2001, 461) is more specific still with respect to the social conditions of the social production of social suffering through the new workplace:

> Within capitalism, it is the social context in particular that not only creates but also necessitates compulsive and other neurotic cultures to maintain the inequities of the status quo. Put simply, unequal relationships create dynamics of dominance, submission, resistance and control. The more systemic the inequality, the greater the need for a neurotic culture that emotionally interprets and justifies these inequalities. . . . And employees have learned to doubt their own sanity rather than critique the sanity of their companies.

Or, we might say, the sanity of the world.

## CONCLUDING REMARKS

One does not have to "believe" in psychodynamics to find value in these interpretive resources. For the purposes of this project this is offered simply as an available vocabulary, a way of thinking, that may be useful for interpretation. If we accept that the legal spatialization of work is conducive to particular kinds of relational dynamics, and that these, in turn, are particularly conducive to the production (intensification, distribution, irremediableness) of social suffering, then we might want to investigate how this works at work. These suggestive interpretations of the psychodynamic "mechanisms" implicated in the process of intersubjectification at work point toward the contingent conditions of the social production of emotions, especially fear, anxiety, humiliation, shame, and so on, and so, of suffering. This perspective opens up new questions *for legal geographers* about the contingent spatiolegal or nomospheric conditions of the social production of suffering such that many workplaces might reasonably be described as socially and politically produced spatiolegal devices for the production, distribution, and dissemination of forms of suffering. In some cases these psychosocial events register in the sociospatial experiential predicament of entrapment and banishment. As I stressed, among the central legal traces that constitute "the workplace" as a nomic setting are presumptive deference to private governing and employer prerogatives to govern through the emotions; the fundamental incidents of property (the right to exclude, expel, avail oneself of enforcement power of the state); and the normative prevalence of at-will conceptions of the employer-employee relation. If this captures, even partially, the nomospheric conditions of working-*for*; and if these conditions are contingent and therefore revisable, then another part of this work is to examine a range of counterprojects that are currently proposed by labor law academics and activists. These include abolition of at-will-ism (Stone 2009), enhanced job security, the institutionalization and normalization of workplace democracy, robust promotion of unionization, the right to a job or a guaranteed income (Quigley 2003), and a host of "dignitarian" reforms (Hodson 2011; Yamada 2008–9).

Tracing these connections one way, we might imagine how new legalities might induce or incite changes in relations of power, changes in the spatiality and relationality of workplaces, and so what it might feel like to be in the world. Tracing them another way might focus attention on the politics of the re-spatialization of "the legal" as such. In either case looking more closely at the social production of emotions, psychodynamic defenses—and hence, contingent, revisable political forms of social suffering might raise new questions about what legal geography might be good for.

## NOTES

1. "Nomic settings" are discussed more fully in *Nomospheric Investigations* (Delaney 2010b). For present purposes they are "determinable segments of the material world that

are socially fabricated by way of the inscription or assignment of traces of legal meanings. They are invested with significance and they, in turn, signify. They confer significance onto actions, events, relationships, and situations" (59).

2. The "nomosphere" is discussed more fully in *Nomospheric Investigations* (Delaney 2010b). For present purposes it can be thought of as "the cultural–material environs that are constituted by the reciprocal materialization of 'the legal,' and the legal signification of the 'socio-spatial,' and the practical, performative engagements through which such constitutive moments happen and unfold" (Delaney 2010b, 25).

3. The Supreme Court has defined a hostile work environment as a "workplace permeated with discriminatory intimidation, ridicule, and insult that is sufficiently severe or pervasive to alter the conditions of the victim's employment and create an abusive working environment." See *Harris v. Forklift Systems, Inc.*, 510 U.S. 17 (1993) at 21.

4. "A 'constructive' action is one that acquires its meaning 'in consequence of the way in which it is regarded by a rule or policy of law' (*Black's Law Dictionary* 313, 6th ed. 1990). Hence, although resigning is clearly not the same as being fired, if one resigns under conditions regarded by the law as intolerable, the resignation is construed as being equivalent to a termination, and a 'constructive discharge' has occurred" (Shuck 2002, 402–3).

## REFERENCES

Abrams, Kathryn, and Hila Keren. 2009–10. "Who's Afraid of Law and the Emotions?" *Minnesota Law Review* 94: 1997–2074.

Allcorn, Seth. 2002. *Death of the Spirit in the American Workplace*. Westport, CT: Greenwood.

———. 2004. "The Psyche at Work." *Consulting Psychology Journal: Practice and Research* 56: 88–103.

Ashkanasy, Neal M., Charmine E. J. Härtel, and Wilfred J. Zerbe, eds. 2000. *Emotions in the Workplace: Research, Theory, and Practice*. Westport, CT: Quorum Books.

Baldry, Christopher. 1997. "The Social Construction of Office Space." *International Labour Review* 136: 365–78.

Barry, Bruce. 2007. *Speechless: The Erosion of Free Expression in the American Workplace*. San Francisco: Berrett-Koehler.

Beck, Ulrich. 2000. *The Brave New World of Work*. Cambridge, UK: Polity Press.

Befort, Stephen. 2001–2. "Labor and Employment Law at the Millennium: A Historical Review and Critical Assessment." *Boston College Law Review* 43: 351–462.

———. 2003. "Revisiting the Black Hole of Workplace Regulation: A Historical and Comparative Perspective of Contingent Work." *Berkeley Journal of Employment and Labor Law* 24: 153–78.

Castillo, J. J. 2002. "The Sociology of Work Today: Looking Forward to the Future." In *Worlds of Work: Building an International Sociology of Work*, edited by D. B. Cornfield and R. Hodson, 347–59. New York: Kluwer Academic/Plenum Publishers.

Charlesworth, S. J. 2005 "Understanding Social Suffering: A Phenomenological Investigation of the Experience of Inequality." *Journal of Community and Applied Social Psychology* 15: 296–312.

Ciulla, Joanne B. 2000. *The Working Life: The Promise and Betrayal of Modern Work*. New York: Three Rivers Press.

Czander, William. 1993. *The Psychodynamics of Work and Organization*. New York: Guilford Press.

Dejours, Christophe. 2006. "Subjectivity, Work, and Action." *Critical Horizons* 7: 45–62.

Dejours, Christophe, and Jean-Philippe Deranty. 2010. "The Centrality of Work." *Critical Horizons* 11: 167–80.

Delaney, David. 2010a. "Home as Nomic Setting: Seeing How the Legal Happens." *English Language Notes* 48: 63–70.

———. 2010b. *The Spatial, the Legal and the Pragmatics of World-Making: Nomospheric Investigations.* London: Routledge.

———. 2013. "Seeing Seeing Seeing the Legal Landscape." In *Wiley-Blackwell Companion to Cultural Geography*, edited by Nuala Johnson, Richard Schein, and Jamie Winders, 238–55. Oxford, UK: Blackwell.

Deranty, Jean-Philippe. 2008. "Work and the Precarisation of Existence." *European Journal of Social Theory* 11: 443–63.

Diamond, Michael. 1993. *The Unconscious Life of Organizations.* Westport, CT: Quorum Books.

Drew, Shirley, Melanie Mills, and Bob Gassaway, eds. 2007. *Dirty Work: The Social Construction of Taint.* Waco, TX: Baylor University Press.

Dubet, François. 2009. *Injustice at Work.* Boulder, CO: Paradigm Publishers.

Fineman, Stephen. 2003. *Understanding Emotion at Work.* Thousand Oaks, CA: Sage Publications.

Fisk, Catherine. 2001–2. "Humiliation at Work." *William and Mary Journal of Women and Law* 8: 73–95.

Fuchs, Thomas. 2007. "Psychotherapy of the Lived Space: A Phenomenological and Ecological Concept." *American Journal of Psychotherapy* 61: 423–39.

Fraser, Jill Andresky. 2001. *White-Collar Sweatshop: The Deterioration of Work and Its Rewards in Corporate America.* New York: Norton.

Frost, Liz, and Paul Hoggett. 2008. "Human Agency and Social Suffering." *Critical Social Policy* 28: 438–60.

Geoghegan, Thomas. 2005. *The Law in Shambles.* Chicago: Prickly Paradigm.

Halford, Susan. 2005. "Hybrid Workspace: Re-spatializations of Work, Organization and Management." *New Technologies, Work and Employment* 20: 19–33.

Hodson, Randy. 2001. *Dignity at Work.* Cambridge: Cambridge University Press.

Holger, Raymond. 1985. "Employment at Will and Scientific Management: The Ideology of Workplace Control." *Hofstra Labor Journal* 3: 27–58.

Jones, Martin. 2010. "Limits to 'Thinking Space Relationally.'" *International Journal of Law in Context* 6: 243–355.

Kersten, Astrid. 2001. "Organizing for Powerlessness: A Critical Perspective on Psychodynamics and Dysfunctionality." *Journal of Organizational Change Management* 14: 452–67.

Koster, Paul. 2007. "Workplace Searches by Public Employers and the Fourth Amendment." *Urban Lawyer* 39: 75–84.

Lewis, Patricia. 2008. "Emotion Work and Emotion Space: Using a Spatial Perspective to Explore the Challenging of Masculine Emotion Management Practices." *British Journal of Management* 19: S130–S140.

Macaulay, Stuart. 1986. "Private Government." In *Law and the Social Sciences*, edited by Leon Lipson and Stanton Wheeler, 445–518. New York: Russell Sage Foundation.

Malpas, Jeff. 2012. "Putting Space in Place: Philosophical Topography and Relational Geography." *Environment and Planning D: Society and Space* 30: 226–42.

Méda, Dominique. 1996. "New Perspectives on Work as Value." *International Labour Review* 135: 633–44.

Merry, Sally Engle. 1988. "Legal Pluralism." *Law and Society Review* 22: 869–96.

Miller, William Ian. 1993. *Humiliation: And Other Essays on Honor, Social Discomfort, and Violence.* Ithaca, NY: Cornell University Press.

Nedelsky, Jennifer. 2011. *Law's Relations: a Relational Theory of Self, Autonomy and Law.* Oxford: Oxford University Press.

Orbach, Susie. 2008. "Work Is Where We Live: Emotional Literacy and the Psychological Dimensions of the Various Relations There." *Emotions Space and Society* 1: 14–17.

Pile, Steve. 2010. "Emotions and Affect in Recent Human Geography." *Transactions of the Institute of British Geographers* 35: 5–20.

Price, Joshua. 2002. "The Apotheosis of Home and the Maintenance of Spaces of Violence." *Hypatia* 17: 39–70.

Quigley, William. 2003. *Ending Poverty as We Know It: Guaranteeing a Right to a Job at a Living Wage.* Philadelphia: Temple University Press.

Raz, Aviad E. 2002. *Emotions at Work: Normative Control, Organizations, and Culture in Japan and America.* Cambridge, MA: Harvard University Asia Center.

Renault, Emmanuel. 2010. "A Critical Theory of Social Suffering." *Critical Horizons* 1: 221–41.

Rosenbury, Laura. 2011. "Working Relationships." *Journal of Law and Policy* 35: 117–50.

Schultz, Vicki. 2003. "The Sanitized Workplace." *Yale Law Journal* 112: 2061–2193.

Selznick, Philip. 1969. *Law, Society and Industrial Justice.* New York: Russell Sage Foundation.

Shuck, Cathy. 2002. "That's It, I Quit: Returning to First Principles in Constructive Discharge Doctrine." *Berkeley Journal of Employment and Labor Law* 23: 401–48.

Shulman, Beth. 2003. *The Betrayal of Work: How Low-Wage Jobs Fail 30 Million Americans and Their Families.* New York: New Press.

Sinclair, Amanda. 1992. "The Tyranny of a Team Ideology." *Organization Studies* 13: 611–26.

Spicer, André. 2011. "Guilty Lives: The Authenticity Trap at Work." *Ephemera* 11: 46–62.

Stone, Katherine. 2009. "Dismissal Law in the United States: The Past and Present of At-Will Employment." Law and Economic Research Paper Series, Research Paper 09-03. UCLA School of Law, Los Angeles.

Summers, Clyde. 2000–2001. "Employment at Will in the United States: The Divine Right of Employers." *University of Pennsylvania Labor and Employment Law Journal* 3: 65–86.

Terkel, Studs. 1985. *Working: People Talk About What They Do All Day and How They Feel About What They Do.* New York: Ballantine Books.

Tomlins, Christopher. 1992. "Law and Power in the Employment Relationship." In *Labor Law in America: Historical and Critical Essays*, edited by Christopher Tomlins and Andrew J. King, 71–98. Baltimore: Johns Hopkins University Press.

Weiler, Paul. 1990. *Governing the Workplace: The Future of Labor and Employment Law.* Cambridge, MA: Harvard University Press.

Wharton, Ann. 1999. "The Psychosocial Consequences of Emotional Labor." *Annals of the American Academy of Political and Social Sciences* 561: 158–76.

Yamada, David. 2008–9. "Human Dignity and American Employment Law." *University of Richmond Law Review* 43: 523–70.

———. 2010–11. "Workplace Bullying and American Employment Law: A Ten-Year Progress Report and Assessment" *Comparative Labor Law and Policy Journal* 32: 251–84.

# INDEX